Teaching and Learning at a Distance

Foundations of Distance

SECOND EDITION

Michael Simonson
Nova Southeastern University

Sharon Smaldino
University of Northern Iowa

Michael Albright
California State University, Monterey Bay

Susan Zvacek
University of Kansas

Merrill
Prentice Hall

Upper Saddle River, New Jersey
Columbus, Ohio

Library of Congress Cataloging-in-Publication Data

Teaching and learning at a distance : foundations of distance education / Michael
Simonson . . . [et al.].—2nd ed.
   p.cm.
Includes bibliographical references and index.
ISBN 0-13-094629-X (pbk.)
   1. Distance education. I. Simonson, Michael R.
LC5800 .T43 2003
371.3'5—dc21

2002016509

Vice President and Publisher: Jeffery W. Johnston
Executive Editor: Debra A. Stollenwerk
Editorial Assistant: Mary Morrill
Production Editor: Kimberly J. Lundy
Production Coordination: Emily Hatteberg, Carlisle Publishers Services
Design Coordinator: Diane C. Lorenzo
Photo Coordinator: Kathleen Kirtland
Cover Designer: Melissa J. Cullen
Cover Image: Corbis Stock Market
Production Manager: Pamela D. Bennett
Director of Marketing: Ann Castel Davis
Marketing Manager: Krista Groshong
Marketing Coordinator: Tyra Cooper

This book was set in Minion by Carlisle Communications, Ltd. It was printed and bound by Phoenix Color Corp.
The cover was printed by Phoenix Color Corp.

Photo Credits: Property of AT&T Archives, reprinted with permission of AT&T, p. 3; Audio-Technica, p. 105 *(lower right);*
Canon U.S.A., Inc., p. 111 *(upper left);* POLYCOM, pp. 100 *(upper left),* 103; TANDBERG, pp. 98, 112; VTEL Corporation,
pp. 5, 7, 13, 20–22, 27, 61, 85, 100 *(upper right),* 104, 105 *(lower left),* 106–107, 110, 111 *(upper right),* 117, 143, 165, 167, 170,
189, 192, 196, 209, 231, 237, 242, 263, 277, 285; Zigy Kaluzny/Getty Images Inc., pp. 17, 19.

Pearson Education Ltd.
Pearson Education Australia Pty. Limited
Pearson Education Singapore Pte. Ltd.
Pearson Education North Asia Ltd.
Pearson Education Canada, Ltd.
Pearson Educación de Mexico, S.A. de C.V.
Pearson Education—Japan
Pearson Education Malaysia Pte. Ltd.
Pearson Education, *Upper Saddle River, New Jersey*

10 9 8 7 6 5 4 3
ISBN 0-13-094629-X

PREFACE

Everett Rogers, in his landmark book *Diffusion of Innovations,* defined an innovation as "an idea, practice, or object that is perceived as new by an individual. . .". Certainly, distance education is new to most of us. This text attempts to link what teachers and trainers know and understand about the learning and teaching process to what is new—the idea of learners in different locations and times. The authors of *Teaching and Learning at a Distance* believe that once educators become familiar with the innovation called distance education, they will find out how important and how much fun it really is.

Teaching and Learning at a Distance is written for use in an introductory distance education course for preservice or in-service teachers, and for those in training programs who wish to teach at a distance or manage distance education systems. It provides readers with the basic information they need in order to be knowledgeable distance educators.

The teacher or trainer who uses this book will be able to distinguish between appropriate uses of distance education and those uses best met by other techniques. In this text we take the following philosophical positions:

- Students prefer not to learn at a distance, but are demanding to be permitted to learn at a distance. This tension between personal preferences and the realities of jobs and geography challenges the distance educator. Certainly, the convenience of distance education often outweighs other considerations, but if given a choice, almost everyone prefers to sit in a classroom, laboratory, or conference room with other learners and the instructor.
- Equivalent learning experiences are critical to the success of distance education. Some advocate providing equal learning experiences for learners no matter their location. This is impossible. Rather, designers of instruction for distant learners should provide alternatives that are equivalent and that provide a variety of ways to learn.
- It is well documented that students do not learn any better at a distance, nor do they learn any less. Considerations other than distance have a greater impact on learning. Many feel that as technologies mature and develop, the concept of distance will become relatively unimportant.
- Distance education is a dramatic idea. It may change—even restructure—education, but only if it is possible to make the experience of the distance learner as complete, satisfying, and acceptable as that of the local learner. If distance education is to be a successful and mainstream approach, then distance education

systems should be based on the belief that the more equivalent the learning experience of the distant student is to that of the local student, the more equivalent will be the outcomes of the learning experience.

- Educators should not promote distance education as the next great technological solution to education's problems or make grand claims about the impact of telecommunications. Rather, educators should strive to use technology and technological approaches to make the experiences of distant and local learners positive and equivalent.

Organization of the Text

Teaching and Learning at a Distance has two types of chapters—foundation chapters and application chapters. Chapters 1 through 4 are designed to provide a conceptual, theoretical, and research-based foundation for the rest of the text. Chapters 5 through 12 are designed to provide educators with the practical skills and information they need to function immediately in a distance learning environment.

Chapter 1 discusses the status of distance education for the educator who may not be familiar with this idea. Chapter 1 also explains what distance education is and its impact on education. The chapter concludes with a vision for schools and learning that is possible because of distance education.

Chapter 2 reviews definitions of distance education that have been and still are used. Since distance education is a field with a long history, that background is discussed. Beginning with correspondence study, the chapter reviews the field up to the current period. Finally, theories related to the practice of distance education are presented, including a proposed American theory of distance education—equivalency theory.

Chapter 3 reviews the extensive research on distance education, including specific areas of practice as well as more general and comprehensive summaries of what the research says. *Teaching and Learning at a Distance* is a research-based textbook based on a thorough study of the empirical information about distance. This research-based approach is found in all chapters, but is emphasized in Chapter 3.

Chapter 4 presents comprehensive information about the technologies used in distance education systems. Technology is broadly defined, and this chapter includes discussions, explanations, and many visuals to provide the reader with a working knowledge of how information is communicated and how distance education systems operate.

Chapter 5, the first of the application chapters, deals with the rules, regulations, and procedures of copyright that the distance educator needs to understand. Distance educators transmit information, much of which may be copyrighted.

Chapter 6 presents the basic intellectual technique of the technology-using educator—instructional design. Instructional design is the systematic process followed by educators using technology. This chapter presents the procedures to be followed when courses or components of courses are designed for distance delivery.

Chapters 7 and 8 explain the unique responsibilities of the learner and instructor involved in distance education. The authors of *Teaching and Learning at a Distance* believe that learning and teaching at a distance are not that different from traditional education. However, there are some special responsibilities and expectations of those involved in distance education.

Chapter 9 may be the most important chapter of the book. Handouts, study guides, and visuals are important tools and techniques of the effective educator, generally, and the distance educator, specifically. The interactive study guide with its word pictures, visual analogies, and visualization is a significant tool used in distance education systems of all kinds.

Chapter 10 provides an in-depth coverage of the Internet and the World Wide Web as delivery mechanisms. The Internet and Web are explained, discussed, and evaluated. Finally, procedures for designing Internet/web-based courseware are discussed.

The final two chapters discuss two very important and closely related topics: (1) assessment of learning and learners and (2) evaluation of teaching and systems. Assessment and evaluation are closely related, but their importance is special to the distance educator. These chapters discuss procedures for assessment and evaluation and give specific examples of procedures to follow.

Features

Each chapter has goals and objectives to provide an organizational plan for the student. Chapters usually have from three to seven subsections that structure the information of the chapter for each study. Visuals are used liberally in an attempt to *show* the reader in addition to *telling*. Each chapter has self-test questions and answers that review key ideas. Most self-test questions are divided into two sections. The first part of the question concerns a fact, idea, or concept that is important. The second part of each question requires an analysis that may not have a specific answer and is best answered by participating in a group discussion with classmates or with the instructor. Finally, each chapter has a comprehensive list of references and additional readings. In some instances, nonprint resources, especially World Wide Web locations, are provided.

New to This Edition

As distance education has matured and become more widespread, the importance of online, World Wide Web-based instruction has grown. This edition has added considerable information in all chapters about how online instruction can be designed, delivered, and evaluated. Online instruction will not replace other forms of distance education, but will become a primary method for reaching the distant learner. Dozens of new visuals have been added to clarify ideas and explain procedures. Updated references and resources have been added to each section and every chapter in order to make this book as current and relevant as possible.

Additional Resources

Four categories of additional resources are available to support the user of *Teaching and Learning at a Distance:*

1. A web site
2. A series of 11 videos
3. A collection of interactive study guides
4. A series of PowerPoint presentations

Web Site. A comprehensive site at www.prenhall.com/simonson has been designed to support this text and courses that use it. This site includes audio introductions from the authors, PowerPoint presentations and student interactive study guides to support each chapter, chapter resources, including self-testing examinations, graphics, and visuals that relate to the contents of each chapter, and short video clips that explain key ideas.

Videos. The following 11 videos are available for use during class and outside of class. They were developed to support courses such as this one. These videos are available from the Association for Educational Communications and Technology, 1800 N. Stonelake Dr., Suite 2, Bloomington, IN 47404 (877-677-2328).

Introductory Video Title: *A Room with a View*
Description: Distance education offers significant new opportunities to learners of all
    ages. With construction of the Iowa Communications Network, linking more
    than 100 educational sites, Iowa has demonstrated its commitment to a high-
    quality, innovative educational system. This video discusses the opportunities
    offered by this new technology and presents vignettes from actual distance
    education classrooms. *(15 min.)*

Foundations and Applications of Distance Education

Foundations

Definitions and Background	The historical development of distance education and the definition of distance education. *(12 min.)*
Research and Theory	The implications of research for distance education practice. *(13 min.)*
Technologies and Terminology	An explanation of telecommunications technologies. *(14 min.)*
The Classroom	The hardware of a typical two-way interactive distance education classroom. *(14 min.)*
Distance Education Costs	The costs involved in constructing a distance education system, including distance education classrooms. *(12 min.)*

Applications

The Teacher	The skills needed for successful distance teaching. *(18 min.)*
The Student	The skills needed for successful distance education. *(7 min.)*
The Curriculum	How distance education can support and enrich the curriculum. *(11 min.)*
ICN	The purpose, structure, and capabilities of Iowa's 3,000-mile fiber-optic network. *(12 min.)*

Three Statewide Approaches   How distance education is practiced in three states—Kentucky, Mississippi, and Iowa. *(18 min.)*

Interactive Study Guides and PowerPoint Presentations.   These materials are designed to be used together during classroom presentations. The masters for the PowerPoint presentations and interactive study guides are available on the web site. The titles include

1. Copyright
2. Definitions, Theories, and Research
3. Distance Education and the World Wide Web
4. World Wide Web—Course Design
5. Preparing Faculty for Distance Education
6. Telelaw
7. Telepharmacy
8. Managing the Mandate—Distance Education and Teacher Education
9. Equivalency and Distance Education
10. Assessment of the Distant Learner
11. Distance Education Systems
12. Handouts and Study Guides
13. Instructional Design
14. Interaction
15. Internet and the World Wide Web
16. Teaching Techniques

ACKNOWLEDGMENTS

While this text has four authors, a number of others participated in the development of many of the ideas presented. In particular, Dan Hanson, Nancy Maushak, Charles Schlosser, and Mary Anderson of the Technology Research and Evaluation Group at Iowa State University contributed a great deal to the development of *Teaching and Learning at a Distance*. We would also like to thank the reviewers for their comments and suggestions: Francis Harvey, Drexel University; Nancy Nelson Knupfer, Kansas State University; Kay Persichitte, University of Northern Colorado; and Jennifer Summerville, Emporia State University.

Distance education is a new concept to many. It is possible that distance education as an idea may provide educators in rural, isolated, or economically disadvantaged areas the opportunity to overcome the problems inherent in their situations. *Teaching and Learning at a Distance* gives teachers and trainers the background and skills needed to function effectively and critically in the educational environment of the 21st century. Remember, make no little plans; they have no magic to stir the blood.

Michael Simonson, Sharon Smaldino, Michael Albright, and Susan Zvacek

Discover the Companion Website Accompanying This Book

The Prentice Hall Companion Website: A Virtual Learning Environment

Technology is a constantly growing and changing aspect of our field that is creating a need for content and resources. To address this emerging need, Prentice Hall has developed an online learning environment for students and professors alike—Companion Websites—to support our textbooks.

In creating a Companion Website, our goal is to build on and enhance what the textbook already offers. For this reason, the content for each user-friendly website is organized by chapter and provides the professor and student with a variety of meaningful resources.

For the Professor

Every Companion Website integrates **Syllabus Manager™,** an online syllabus creation and management utility.

- **Syllabus Manager™** provides you, the instructor, with an easy, step-by-step process to create and revise syllabi, with direct links into Companion Website and other online content without having to learn HTML.
- Students may logon to your syllabus during any study session. All they need to know is the web address for the Companion Website and the password you've assigned to your syllabus.
- After you have created a syllabus using **Syllabus Manager™,** students may enter the syllabus for their course section from any point in the Companion Website.
- Clicking on a date, the student is shown the list of activities for the assignment. The activities for each assignment are linked directly to actual content, saving time for students.
- Adding assignments consists of clicking on the desired due date, then filling in the details of the assignment—name of the assignment, instructions, and whether it is a one-time or repeating assignment.

- In addition, links to other activities can be created easily. If the activity is online, a URL can be entered in the space provided, and it will be linked automatically in the final syllabus.
- Your completed syllabus is hosted on our servers, allowing convenient updates from any computer on the Internet. Changes you make to your syllabus are immediately available to your students at their next logon.

For the Student

Common Companion Website features for students include:

- **Chapter Objectives**—outline key concepts from the text
- **Interactive Self-quizzes**—complete with hints and automatic grading that provide immediate feedback for students

    After students submit their answers for the interactive self-quizzes, the Companion Website **Results Reporter** computes a percentage grade, provides a graphic representation of how many questions were answered correctly and incorrectly, and gives a question-by-question analysis of the quiz. Students are given the option to send their quiz to up to four email addresses (professor, teaching assistant, study partner, etc.).

- **Web Destinations**—links to www sites that relate to chapter content
- **Learning Network**—the Pearson Learning Network offers a wealth of additional resources to aid in their understanding and application of content
- **Message Board**—serves as a virtual bulletin board to post—or respond to—questions or comments to/from a national audience
- **Chat**—real-time chat with anyone who is using the text anywhere in the country—ideal for discussion and study groups, class projects, etc.

To take advantage of the many available resources, please visit the Companion Website that accompanies *Teaching and Learning at a Distance: Foundations of Distance Education,* Second Edition, at

www.prenhall.com/simonson

CONTENTS

PART I ■ FOUNDATIONS   **1**

Chapter 1   FOUNDATIONS OF DISTANCE EDUCATION   3
     Chemistry at a Distance? A True Story   4
     Distance Education Today and Tomorrow   5
     What Is Distance Education?   8
       Facts About Distance Education   8
     Media in Education: Earlier Debates   9
     Status of Distance Education   11
       Worldwide Examples   11
       United States   13
     Characteristics of Distance Education: A Vision   19
     Summary   22
     Self-Test Questions   23
     Answers to Self-Test Questions   23
     References   24
     Additional Readings   25

Chapter 2   DEFINITIONS, HISTORY, AND THEORIES OF DISTANCE EDUCATION   27
     Defining Distance Education   28
     Emerging Definitions   31
     A Brief History of Distance Education   32
       Correspondence Study   32
       Electronic Communications   34
       Distance Teaching Universities   35
     Theory and Distance Education   36
       The Need for Theory   36
       Theory of Independent Study—Charles Wedemeyer   38

Theory of Independent Study—Michael Moore   39
Theory of Industrialization of Teaching—Otto Peters   40
Theory of Interaction and Communication—Börje Holmberg   42
Andragogy—Malcolm Knowles   44
A Synthesis of Existing Theories—Hilary Perraton   45
Equivalency Theory: An Emerging American Theory of Distance Education   46
A Theoretical Framework for Distance Education—Desmond Keegan   47
Fordism, Neo-Fordism, Post-Fordism: A Theoretical Debate   49
Summary   52
Self-Test Questions   54
Answers to Self-Test Questions   55
References   56
Additional Readings   58

Chapter   3   RESEARCH AND DISTANCE EDUCATION   61
The Focus of Distance Education Research   62
Learning Outcomes   62
Learner Perceptions   64
Learner Attributes   67
Interaction   71
Barriers to Distance Education   74
Distance Education Technology   75
Myths Regarding Distance Education Research   77
Summary   79
Self-Test Questions   80
Answers to Self-Test Questions   80
References   81
Additional Readings   84

Chapter   4   DISTANCE EDUCATION TECHNOLOGIES   85
A True Story   86
A Model of Communication   86
The Cone of Experience   88
A Taxonomy of Distance Education Technologies   90
Correspondence Study   90
Prerecorded Media   92
Two-Way Audio   92

Two-Way Audio With Graphics   93

One-Way Live Video   94

Two-Way Audio, One-Way Video   95

Two-Way Audio/Video   96

An Example: Two-Way Audio/Video in Iowa   99

Desktop Two-Way Audio/Video   101

Distance Education Classrooms   104

Two-Way Video/Audio Classrooms   104

Classroom Technologies for Online Instruction   107

Summary   113

Self-Test Questions   113

Answers to Self-Test Questions   114

References   114

Additional Readings   114

URL for Information About Distance Education Classrooms   115

PART II ■ APPLICATIONS   117

Chapter   5   COPYRIGHT AND DISTANCE EDUCATION   119

Copyright Myths   120

Copyright Essentials   121

Exclusive Rights of Copyright Holders   122

Fair Use   123

Public Performance and Display   124

Duration of Copyright   124

Public Domain   125

Guidelines   126

Recent Copyright-Related Legislation   127

Digital Millennium Copyright Act   127

Uniform Computer Information Transactions Act (UCITA)   130

Copyright Applications in Distance Education   131

Printed Materials   131

Audiovisual Materials   132

Computer-Based Distance Education   134

Obtaining Permission   135

Intellectual Property Rights   137

Summary   138

Self-Test Questions   138

Answers to Self-Test Questions   139
References   139
Additional Readings   140
Sources of Information   140

Chapter 6   INSTRUCTIONAL DESIGN FOR DISTANCE EDUCATION   143
"Signal Fires"?   144
Why Plan for Teaching at a Distance?   144
Principles of Instructional Design Systems   145
Systematic Process   145
Planning for Instruction at a Distance   146
Issues to Address in the Planning Process   147
Who Are the Learners?   147
What Is the Essential Content?   150
What Teaching Strategies and Media Should Be Used?   151
What Is the Learning Environment?   154
Planning to Teach on the World Wide Web   155
How Do You Determine the Quality of the Instruction?   156
Other Issues to Be Considered   157
Student Handouts   157
Distribution of Materials   157
Site Coordinators and Facilitators   158
Models for Designing World Wide Web Courses   158
Summary   163
Self-Test Questions   163
Answers to Self-Test Questions   163
References   164

Chapter 7   THE DISTANCE EDUCATION STUDENT   165
An Emphasis on the Student   166
Attitude   167
Experience   168
Cognition   168
Learning Styles   168
Learner Responsibilities   169
Microphones and Other Equipment   170
Attendance and Class Participation   171

Tone of Responses   172
Time for Class   172
Equipment Requirements   173
Technical Know-How   173
Technical Difficulties   173
Assignments   173
Sixty Frequently Asked Student Questions About Distance Education   173
Summary   186
Self-Test Questions   186
Answers to Self-Test Questions   186
References   187

Chapter 8   TEACHING AT A DISTANCE   189
Aspects of Distance Education   190
Role of the Teacher   190
Lesson Organization   190
Instructional Methods   191
Teaching at a Distance   191
Policy Issues Related to Distance Education   198
Importance of Policy   198
Policy Categories   199
Summary   204
Self-Test Questions   205
Answers to Self-Test Questions   206
References   206
Additional Readings   208

Chapter 9   HANDOUTS, STUDY GUIDES, AND VISUALS   209
Printed Media   210
Distance Education Syllabus   210
The Interactive Study Guide   211
Graphic Design Principles   214
Elements of Design   216
Principles of Design   217
Word Pictures   221
Visual Analogies   224
Summary   227

Self-Test Questions   227
Answers to Self-Test Questions   228
References   230
Additional Readings   230

Chapter 10   DISTANCE EDUCATION, THE WORLD WIDE WEB, AND THE INTERNET   231
The Implications of the Internet for Education and Training   232
The Internet and K–12 Education   232
Higher Education   233
Training and Development   234
What Is the Internet?   236
Internet Management   236
Evolution of the Internet and Its Services   237
Structure of the Internet   239
Further Internet Discussion   240
Overview of Web/Internet-Based Distance Education   240
Clarification of Terminology   241
Advantages of Internet-Based Courses   243
Limitations of Internet-Based Courses   244
Components of Web/Internet-Based Courses   244
Internet Communication Tools   248
Computer Conferencing (Non-Web)   248
Computer Conferencing (Web)   251
Teaching With the World Wide Web   251
The Web as a Learning Resource   251
The Web as a Course Delivery Vehicle   253
Summary: Thoughts on the Future of Online Learning   257
Self-Test Questions   257
Answers to Self-Test Questions   258
References   259
Sources of Information About the Internet   261

Chapter 11   ASSESSMENT FOR DISTANCE EDUCATION   263
Assessing Learning Gains   264
What Is Assessment?   264
Assessment and Evaluation   265
Assessment and Instructional Design   266

Characteristics of Good Assessments   266

Norm-Referenced and Criterion-Referenced Scoring   268

Traditional Assessment Tools   268

Using Traditional Assessments in Nontraditional Environments   271

Alternative Assessment   272

Advantages and Disadvantages of Alternative Assessment   275

Assessment and Distance Education   277

Cheating and Plagiarism   280

Summary   281

Self-Test Questions   282

Answers to Self-Test Questions   283

References   283

Chapter 12   **EVALUATING TEACHING AND LEARNING AT A DISTANCE**   285

Research and Evaluation   286

Evaluation and the Open University   286

The AEIOU Approach   288

Program Evaluation: Examples   292

South Dakota   292

Iowa   293

Summary   295

Self-Test Questions   295

Answers to Self-Test Questions   296

References   296

Additional Readings   297

INDEX   **299**

NOTE: Every effort has been made to provide accurate and current Internet information in this book. However, the Internet and information posted on it are constantly changing, so it is inevitable that some of the Internet addresses listed in this textbook will change.

PART

FOUNDATIONS

Chapter 1

FOUNDATIONS OF DISTANCE EDUCATION

Chapter 2

DEFINITIONS, HISTORY, AND THEORIES
OF DISTANCE EDUCATION

Chapter 3

RESEARCH AND DISTANCE EDUCATION

Chapter 4

DISTANCE EDUCATION TECHNOLOGIES

1

FOUNDATIONS OF DISTANCE EDUCATION

CHAPTER GOAL

The purpose of this chapter is to discuss the importance of distance education and the impact that distance education has on the improvement of education.

CHAPTER OBJECTIVES

After reading and reviewing this chapter, you should be able to

1. Explain the reason why students demand to learn at a distance even though they prefer to learn in the classroom with the teacher and their classmates.
2. Define *distance education.*
3. Explain Coldeway's quadrants.
4. Discuss Richard Clark's "mere vehicles" quote as it relates to distance education.
5. Explain how Jim Finn might compare stirrups with distance education.
6. Give examples of how distance education is being used in several locations of the world and in the United States.
7. Discuss telemedicine and relate the topic to distance education. Explain a vision for education and schooling in the future.

CHEMISTRY AT A DISTANCE? A TRUE STORY

Chemistry is a hands-on, laboratory-based course that many consider one of the most rigorous in the average high school curriculum. Many students dread taking chemistry, and in many small communities there is only one chemistry teacher in the school.

Recently, four high school chemistry teachers decided that they could improve their basic chemistry course if they collaborated and team-taught. The only problem was that their schools were about 60 miles from each other.

This did not stop them, however, because their schools were connected with a fiber-optic network that permitted full-motion video signals to be sent between the four schools. The network also carried a high-speed Internet connection that allowed easy access to the World Wide Web.

Not only did the four teachers want to collaborate, but more important, they wanted their students to collaborate. To accomplish this, they decided on some basic objectives and then planned the curriculum.

The teachers decided that they would teach concepts cooperatively, act as laboratory supervisors for each other's students, and serve as partners with student collaborators. They also decided upon another important goal: to have their students cooperate across schools.

Finally, they decided that the chemistry projects should be authentic and deal with local, real-world issues.

Next, the four teachers met to plan their curriculum. They identified eight modules that could be shared among the four schools. These modules were taught by one or two of the four chemistry teachers, and required collaboration by the students from the four schools. The modules included live television instruction presented by one of the teachers, collaborative work by students who communicated with each other by television and the Internet, and class assignments that dealt with various aspects of the same chemistry concept, such as the local ecology. Students investigated their portion of the problem and then shared results with their distant classmates. Each module ended with a live, interactive discussion, presentation, and sharing of information over the fiber-optic television network.

For all practical purposes, the students in the four schools became one large class, with subgroups of students who worked with classmates from their own school and also with distant friends. The teachers served as presenters some of the time, but most often as tutors who worked with subgroups of students. The Internet and e-mail were used to keep everyone communicating outside of class, and even outside of school.

By any measure, the course was a huge success. Students learned chemistry; test scores showed that. They also discovered how to collaborate as real scientists with colleagues at distant locations, and they discovered the power of distance education to open up their school to resources available elsewhere.

Telecommunications technology made this possible. Their chemistry classroom became a "room with a view," connected to other chemistry classrooms and to the resources of the world available through the Internet. The course became more like real chemistry—chemistry practiced to solve actual problems outside the school involving experts from a number of areas brought together because of their expertise, without regard for geography or time.

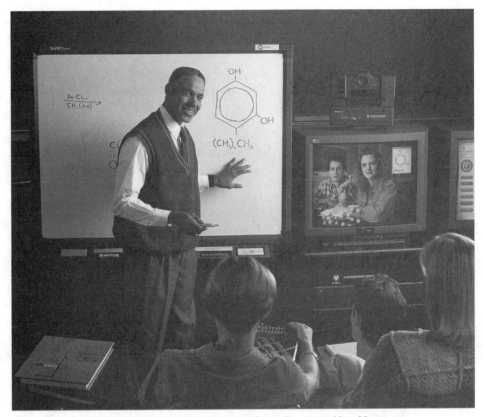

Increasingly, courses like chemistry are being taught to distant and local learners simultaneously.

Distance education is one of the most dramatic of the recent technology-based innovations influencing education. The scenario above is just one of thousands of examples of how distance education is changing learning and teaching.

DISTANCE EDUCATION TODAY AND TOMORROW

In the last few years, distance education has become a major topic in education. In the last year, over 60 conferences dealt with some aspect of distance education, and almost every professional organization's publications and conferences have shown a huge increase in the number of distance education–related articles and papers.

Many educators are making grand claims about how distance education is likely to change education and training. Certainly, the concept of distance education is exciting, and recent hardware and software innovations are making telecommunications distance education systems more available, easier to use, and less costly. Distance education has begun to enter the mainstream.

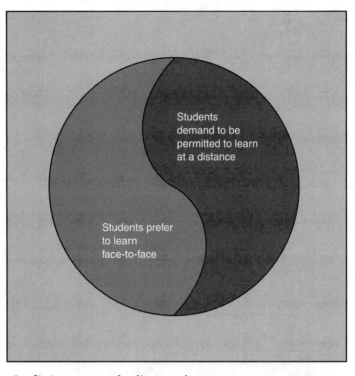

FIGURE 1–1   Conflicting pressures for distance educators.

However, two conflicting pressures confront distance educators (Figure 1–1). First, *students say they do not really want to learn at a distance*. When asked, they say they prefer meeting with the learning group and the instructor in the classroom, the lecture hall, the seminar room, or the laboratory. Students report that they value the presence of a learning group, and that the informal interactions that occur before and after, and sometimes during, a formal class are valuable components of the total learning experience. Second, and conversely, evidence suggests that *students are increasingly demanding to be allowed to learn at a distance*. They want to be able to supplement, and even replace, conventional learning experiences with distance education experiences. Learners say this is because many other considerations besides personal preferences motivate them, especially considerations about where and when they learn.

These opposing preferences pose a dilemma for the educational community. Should resources be dedicated to improving the traditional educational infrastructure of buildings, classrooms, laboratories, and offices, and should students be transported to these facilities? Or should money be used to develop modern and sophisticated telecommunications systems? The trend seems to be toward telecommunications. Because of advances in technology, effective educational experiences can be provided for learners, no matter where they are located. In other words, technologies are now available to develop cost-effective distance learning systems.

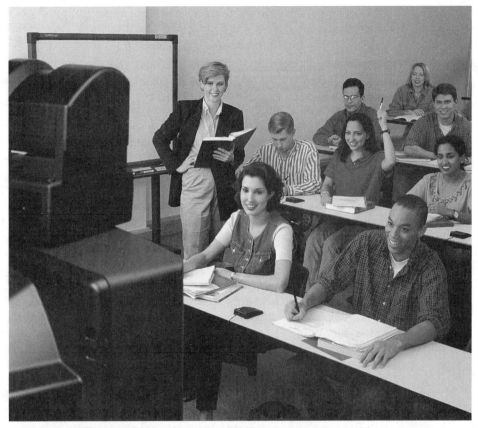

Compressed video systems that use regular telephone lines make it possible to originate or receive distance education courses from virtually anywhere.

Virtual schools are becoming important in many locations. The Florida High School, established in the late 1990s, offers a wide selection of courses and has plans to offer a diploma. Universities are also offering virtual schools. A recent article in the *Chronicle of Higher Education* (Carr, 1999) talked about Indiana University High School and the University of Missouri's Columbia High School. The North Central Association of Colleges and Schools has accredited both schools. The Indiana and Missouri schools are financially independent of their universities. Students pay tuition for courses that are developed and taught by certified teachers. A large number of other states are following the lead of Florida, Indiana, and Missouri.

Concepts such as the virtual school have caused the practice of distance education to dramatically change in the last decade. Traditional approaches to distance education based on the delivery of print and broadcast media technologies are no longer as relevant to the field as it is practiced in the United States as they once were.

As a matter of fact, a redefinition of distance education has occurred. Distance education is now often defined as: institution-based, formal education where the learning group is separated, and where interactive telecommunications systems are used to connect learners, resources, and instructors.

WHAT IS DISTANCE EDUCATION?

It is the nature of questions that they are easier to ask than to answer. This is true of the question "What is distance education?" for at least several reasons. First, *distance* has multiple meanings. Distance can mean geographical distance, time distance, and possibly even intellectual distance.

Second, the term *distance education* has been applied to a tremendous variety of programs serving numerous audiences via a wide variety of media. Some use print, some use telecommunications, and many use both. Finally, rapid changes in technology challenge the traditional ways in which distance education is defined.

Dan Coldeway, of South Dakota's Dakota State University, provided a framework useful in helping to define four ways in which education can be practiced. This framework, which considers the two variables of time and place, gives insight into different approaches to the practice of education and distance education. Combinations of time and place result in four approaches to education. The four are same-time, same-place education (ST-SP); different-time, same-place education (DT-SP); same-time, different-place education (ST-DP); and different-time, different-place education (DT-DP).

Traditional education takes place at the same time in the same place. This is typically the regular self-contained classroom that most often is teacher-centered. Different-time, same-place education means that individual learning occurs in a learning center, or that multiple sections of the same classes are offered so students can attend the class in the same place at a time they chose. This is education that is available at different times to students but in the same place, such as the media center or computer laboratory.

The last two categories focus on education occurring in different places. Instruction can take place in different places at the same time when telecommunications systems are used. Often, television is used to connect the local classroom with the teacher and students to learners at a distance. Satellite, compressed video, and fiber-optic systems are increasingly used for same-time, different-place education. This approach is also called *synchronous* distance learning. Students can also learn at different times and in different places. Coldeway has said that the purest form of distance education occurs at different times and in different places. In other words, learners choose when and where to learn and when and where to access instructional materials. Recently, World Wide Web courses have been offered to learners anywhere they have access and whenever they choose. This approach is called *asynchronous* distance learning.

Facts About Distance Education

- Last year, 1,680 institutions offered over 54,000 online courses.
- The eminent historian Frederick Jackson Turner ran the correspondence program of the University of Wisconsin in the late 1800s.

- The state of Iowa has a state-owned, 2,800-mile fiber-optic network, called the Iowa Communications Network, with over 700 high-tech classrooms for the purpose of offering distance instruction throughout the state.
- "Telemedicine" refers to medicine at a distance, and "telelaw" refers to law at a distance.
- Research on the effectiveness of distance education clearly shows that students who learn at a distance do not learn any worse, or any better, than traditional students.
- The United States Distance Learning Association is a professional organization of those involved in distance education.
- Universities such as the University of Chicago, the University of Wisconsin, and the University of Iowa championed correspondence education in the later years of the 19th century and early in the 20th century.
- Satellites used for distance education orbit approximately 23,000 miles about the equator at an orbiting speed that matches the rotation of the earth. This geosynchronous orbit makes these satellites appear to be stationary on the surface of the earth. The location where the satellites orbit is called the Clarke Belt, after science fiction writer Arthur C. Clarke who wrote about communication satellites in geosynchronous orbit in a story published in the 1940s.
- The foundations of the Internet were begun by the Department of Defense and by a number of research universities as a way to share scientific and technical information between scientists.
- *IP* stands for Internet Protocol, the rules used to send information over the Internet.
- The Internet is a Packet-Switched network meaning that messages are divided into packets that are disassembled and then sent to the distant site where the packets are reassembled into the complete message.
- Star Schools is the name of a program of the U.S. Department of Education that funds the implementation of distance education in schools and colleges in the United States. The term was coined by Senator Ted Kennedy who was opposed to the use of satellites for "star wars," so he advocated the use of satellites for education and proposed the Star Schools program.

MEDIA IN EDUCATION: EARLIER DEBATES

The discussion about distance education is somewhat reminiscent of a recent debate in the educational technology field that began when Richard Clark, a researcher and theorist, published a classic article containing his now famous "mere vehicles" analogy. Clark summarized over six decades of educational media research. It was obvious to him that many researchers were reporting about flawed studies involving media. Clark believed that many educators did not understand the last 60 years of research about media and learning.

Even more alarming was that many practitioners were making unrealistic claims about the impact of technology on learning. According to Clark, a large segment of the educational community felt that mediated instruction was inherently better than teaching when media were not used.

In 1983, Clark wrote in volume 53 of the *Review of Educational Research* that

> the best current evidence is that media are *mere vehicles* that deliver instruction but do not influence student achievement any more than the truck that delivers our groceries causes changes in nutrition . . . only the content of the vehicle can influence achievement. (p. 445)

Clark's article went on to convincingly claim that instructional media were excellent for storing educational messages and for delivering them almost anywhere. However, media were not responsible for a learning effect. Learning was not enhanced because instruction was media-based. Rather, the content of the instruction, the method used to promote learning, and the involvement of the learner in the instructional experience were what, in part, influenced learning. Although many did not, and still do not, agree with Clark, his article caused a reassessment of how educators looked at the impact of media. Clark continued to implore the education community to "give up your enthusiasm for media effects on learning," which was the theme of an additional publication on this topic (Clark, 1994). "Give up your enthusiasm" has become the new rallying cry for those who do not believe there is a media effect.

Certainly, some distance educators claim that distance education is the best way to learn because it allows students to acquire knowledge when it is most relevant to them. However, most who have studied distance learning make few claims about the approach being better. Rather, they say it is a viable and important approach to learning and teaching that should be one option of many available.

A second analogy by another great technology pioneer also has relevance to distance education. In the 1960s, Jim Finn from the University of Southern California talked about the stirrup as a technological innovation that changed society. He often told a story that went like this:

> The Anglo-Saxons, a dominating enemy of Charles Martel's Franks, had the stirrup but did not truly understand its implications for warfare. The stirrup made possible the emergence of a warrior called the knight who understood that the stirrup enabled the rider not only to keep his seat, but also to deliver a blow with a lance having the combined weight of the rider and charging horse. This simple concept permitted the Franks to conquer the Anglo-Saxons and change the face of western civilization. Martel had a vision to seize the idea and to use it. He did not invent the stirrup, but knew how to use it purposefully. (Finn, 1964, p. 24)

Finn (1964) summarized the implications of this story as follows:

> The acceptance or rejection of an invention, or the extent to which its implications are realized if it is accepted, depends quite as much upon the condition of society, and upon the imagination of its leadership, as upon the nature of the technological item itself. . . . The Anglo-Saxons used the stirrup, but did not comprehend it; and for this they paid a fearful price. . . . It was the Franks alone—presumably led by Charles Martel's genius—who fully grasped the

possibilities inherent in the stirrup and created in terms of it a new type of warfare supported by a novel structure of a society that we call feudalism. . . . For a thousand years feudal institutions bore the marks of their birth from the new military technologies of the eighth century. (p. 24)

What Clark strongly proposed with his "mere vehicles" and "give up your enthusiasm" arguments was that media and technology did not directly affect learning. He forcefully argued that educators should not claim that technology-based learning, such as modern distance education systems, had any inherent advantage (or disadvantage for that matter) over other methods of learning. Like Finn, Clark proposed that technologies might provide ways of accomplishing tasks that are new and not readily obvious.

Finn advocated that practitioners should attempt to identify unique approaches for change by using new technologies in new ways. Finn's story explained that the stirrup not only made getting on and off a horse easier, but also made possible a new, previously unheard-of consequence—the emergence of the knight—and it was the knight who caused significant and long-lasting changes in society. Perhaps the correct application of distance education will significantly change and restructure learning and teaching on par with the societal change called feudalism needed to support the knight.

The implication of the arguments of these two educators is that when new technologies emerge, they often allow users to be more efficient. However, it is not technologies themselves that cause changes; rather changes occur because of new ways of doing things that are enabled by technologies. The stirrup made riding horses easier and more efficient, but it was the knight who changed medieval society.

STATUS OF DISTANCE EDUCATION

Worldwide Examples

Distance education has a major and varied impact worldwide. Whereas politics and economics influence how distance education is employed, a strong demand exists in the world for distance education opportunities. The five examples that follow illustrate some of the factors that influence distance education and show the demand for distance learning opportunities.

1. Anadolu University in Turkey reaches over 500,000 distance education students, which makes it the largest university on earth, according to the world bank (Macwilliams, 2000). The university was created in 1981 during a sweeping reorganization of Turkey's higher education system. Its mission is to provide distance instruction to the citizens of Turkey. In 1983, it had almost 30,000 students in business administration and economics, making the university an immediate success. As of 2000, approximately 34% of the students that enrolled in the 2-year degree programs graduated in 2 years, and about 23% of those enrolled in 4-year programs graduated in 4 years. The vast majority of the students enrolled at Anadolu University were working adults with full- or part-time jobs. Distance education offered by Anadolu University has made post-secondary education a possibility to many in Turkey who would not have access to higher education.

2. The Open University of Hong Kong opened in 1989 to serve residents of that huge metropolitan area. Recently, the university has begun to market itself to learners in China, and it has over 1,000 students from the mainland (Cohen, 2000). Unlike Hong Kong's eight conventional universities, the Open University accepts all applicants. It has had over 100,000 students, of which approximately 10% have graduated. Administrators from the Open University of Hong Kong plan to offer distance education throughout China and Southeast Asia.

3. In Sub-Saharan Africa, political instability and economic depression have caused a decline in educational standards in some countries. As the population increased in these countries, a tremendous classroom shortage emerged, and both the number of qualified teachers and the availability of instructional materials became inadequate.

Distance education is seen as having the potential to contribute to national reconstruction by providing economically feasible educational opportunities to many people. Collaboration with a variety of international distance education organizations has provided expertise and support for the practice of distance education. As a result, distance education at a basic level, as it is practiced in many regions of Africa, has expanded quite sharply. However, although growth in distance education in Sub-Saharan African countries is evident, it does not yet have a wide impact. Lack of funding prevents distance education institutions from reaching many potential students.

4. China developed a national higher distance education program in the late 1970s and early 1980s in response to a growth in population and a high cost per capita for the craftlike approach to regular higher education in the country. Because China could not afford to meet the higher education needs of the expanding population, a national radio and TV university system was developed. By 1985, China had over 30,000 TV classes throughout the country and employed almost 25,000 academics. One in five students studying in higher education was enrolled in a radio and TV university. This national system incorporated a centralized approach to course development, delivery, and examinations. However, despite an increase in offerings, student numbers have significantly decreased. Recently, only 1 in every 13 students in higher education was enrolled in a radio and TV university.

Socioeconomic factors have caused changes in the mass market for higher education in China. The centralized approach to course development and delivery no longer meets the diverse needs of learners and does not adapt itself quickly to the new conditions. In response, China's radio and TV universities have changed from a central system of course development and delivery to a regionally responsive system that provides a wide variety of both diploma and nondiploma courses (Ding, 1994, 1995).

5. Distance education has had a long history in European countries. The continuation of this tradition is evident in the vast array of programs offered by European Union countries. In some countries, open distance teaching universities offer the majority of the country's distance education programming. Spain's Universidad Nacional de Educacion a Distancia is Europe's largest distance teaching university, with a current enrollment of about 130,000 students. In other countries, traditional universities deliver the majority of the courses. France, for example, has no national distance teaching university, but offers higher distance education through 22 offices within traditional universities. Recently, 34,000 students were enrolled in these programs. In some cases, governments provide substantial distance education training opportunities that do not lead to a university degree. France is a leader in this area, providing over 350,000 students a year with opportunities at a range of levels: elementary school, high school, technical and professional qualifications, teacher training, and university-level and postgraduate courses. In addition, 250,000 students are served by proprietary distance training providers in France (Keegan, 1994). Distance instruction in the European Union uses a wide variety of media to deliver courses. These range from traditional correspondence delivery, to computer conferencing, to two-way audio and video virtual classrooms (Holmberg, 1995; Keegan, 1995). Using these technologies, the established distance education and training organizations of Europe will continue to play a significant role in education in and beyond the European Union.

United States

In the United States, the emergence of new technologies has brought on increased interest in distance education and learning.

> Electronic mail, electronic bulletin boards, facsimiles, and interactive computer networks now augment or replace mail carriers in delivering curricular materials, textbooks, and examinations to distance learners. New transmission media capable of providing two-way, full-motion, real-time (live) interaction between the student and teacher replace non-interactive, one-way systems. (Tompkins, 1993, pp. 265–266)

American distance education often focuses on students in primary and secondary schools.

The U.S. Department of Education has found that the number of distance education programs in higher education had increased 72% between 1995 and 1998 (Carnevale, 2000). Additionally, the Internet was the medium of choice for most institutions providing distance education. The use of interactive video remained about the same during this period, indicating that most of the growth in distance education involved use of the Internet. Tuition for online and traditional courses was the same at 77%, and most institutions did not charge an additional fee for distance education courses. According to the U.S. Department of Education, distance education was being considered by almost 90% of higher education institutions larger than 10,000 students.

At the university level, it is reported that distance education enrollments are in the high six figures nationally. This includes enrollment in courses offered by traditional universities and those offered by distance learning universities. The U.S. military is heavily involved in distance education technology because distance education is viewed as a cost-efficient way to deliver technical training to a large number of soldiers. The development of new weapons systems and other technologies increases the demand for this type of training. The army's Interactive Teletraining Network, the navy's Video Teletraining Network, and the air force's Teleteach Expanded Delivery System all provide distance training opportunities for personnel across the United States and around the world.

A focus on education in the primary and secondary schools separates American distance education from traditional European distance education. This emphasis on kindergarten through Grade 12 (K–12) students is demonstrated in the federally funded Star Schools projects. The U.S. Department of Education began the Star Schools program "to encourage improved instruction in mathematics, science, foreign languages, literacy skills, and vocational education for underserved populations through the use of telecommunications networks" (Simonson, 1995, pp. 3–4). Although these projects are not limited to K–12 programming, their primary emphasis is on K–12 students and teachers. A variety of network technologies including satellite, cable, telephone networks, fiber-optics, microcomputer-based laboratories, multimedia, and electronic networking technologies have been used to deliver instructional programming to over 6,000 schools nationwide through the Star Schools project (U.S. Department of Education, 1995).

Typically the Star Schools project has funded programs that provide satellite delivery of instruction to a large number of students in many states. One of the largest is the Connections 2000 Star Schools Project of Los Angeles County Office of Education, which is a consortium of education and public television agencies in over 10 states. The consortium provides math, science, social science, language arts, and technology programming to over 1,300 school sites and 125,000 students in Grades 4 through 7. In addition, the project provides professional development opportunities for over 4,000 teachers. The Star Schools project funds a number of similar satellite-based projects.

The Star Schools project has sponsored several special statewide projects that fund the development of statewide infrastructures, allowing for synchronous interaction between students and instructors. The most comprehensive is in Iowa. Currently, Iowa's 3,000-mile statewide fiber-optic network connects more than 700 educational sites, with over 300 more sites to be added in the next few years. Hundreds of thousands of hours of K–12 programming are provided each year, in addition to teacher professional development and

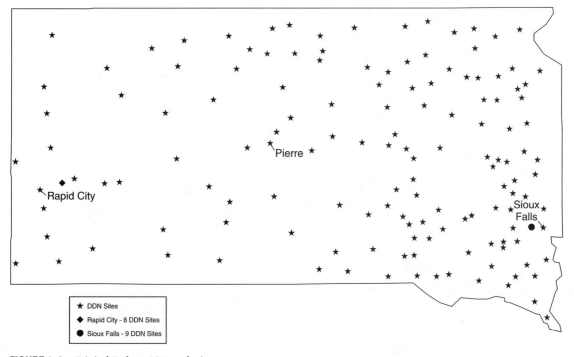

FIGURE 1–2   Digital Dakota Network sites.

higher education course opportunities. Kentucky and Mississippi have joined Iowa in developing statewide systems that promote personalized interactive instruction and learning.

South Dakota is another state that has significantly committed to distance education for K–12 students. In South Dakota, the Digital Dakota Network links every school building to a compressed video network. Over 300 sites are located throughout the state (Figure 1–2). Teachers have been trained in special month-long Distance Teaching and Learning Academies, and teachers and university faculties have designed curriculum materials, including entire courses. South Dakota educators have also conducted major research and evaluation activities to document the impact of distance education in the state (Bauck, 2001). As the examples show, distance education has a major impact worldwide. In addition to economics and politics, the growth and impact of distance education is directly linked to the availability of new technologies. "As technology links distant sites in an electronic web of information and new communication channels, people around the globe are pulled together" (Thach & Murphy, 1994, p. 5). This type of communication has contributed to globalization. Globalization implies that people are connected more or less contemporaneously with distant events. The new computer-mediated communications and telecommunications technologies contribute to globalization. Distance educators will be challenged both by globalization and by the emerging technologies. How they take advantage of these opportunities will give new meaning to the practice of distance education.

Accreditation.   Many in traditional education worry about the quality of distance education programs. Some have called distance education institutions diploma mills, especially those that are profit-generating. A diploma mill has the following characteristics: no classrooms, untrained or nonexistent faculties, and unqualified administrators with profit as their primary motivation (Noble, Schneiderman, Herman, Agre, & Denning, 1998).

Legitimate institutions have expended considerable effort to demonstrate the quality of their distance education programs. One of the most important activities involves accreditation. Probably the most important form of accreditation, which involves in-depth scrutiny of a school or college's entire program by outside evaluators, comes from regional accrediting agencies, such as the North Central Association (NCA) and the Southern Association of Colleges and Schools (SACS). NCA and SACS are examples of regional agencies that accredit institutions in their geographic areas. Generally, the same standards are applied to traditional and distance education programs. National accreditation agencies also accredit colleges.

Telemedicine.   **Tele** means "at a distance," so in its simplest form, **telemedicine** is defined as *medicine at a distance*. The Institute of Medicine defines telemedicine as *the use of electronic information and communications technologies to provide and support health care when distance separates the participants* (Grigsby & Sanders, 1998). Grigsby and Sanders (1998) define telemedicine as the use of telecommunications and information technology to provide health care services to persons at a distance from the provider. Actually, there exist in the literature dozens of definitions of telemedicine, but all contain these components:

1. Separation or distance between individuals and/or resources
2. Use of telecommunications technologies
3. Interaction between individuals and/or resources
4. Medical or health care.

Also, it is implied in most definitions that telemedicine refers to health care offered by recognized, formally accredited medical organizations. Organizational affiliation differentiates telemedicine from self-diagnosis, unsanctioned medical treatment, or quackery.

Background.   The term *telemedicine* has become common in the medical literature during the last decade. However, most give credit for originating the term to Kenneth Byrd, who with several other physicians formed a video microwave network in 1968 from Massachusetts General Hospital to Boston's Logan Airport. There were a number of other projects at about the same time, but this effort is considered the modern launching of the concept of telemedicine.

Telemedicine is a growing field within the profession of medicine. It has journals, such as the *Journal of Telemedicine* and *Telemedicine Today,* has a professional association (the American Telemedicine Association; http://www.atmeda.org/), and holds an annual professional meeting.

Articles dealing with various aspects of telemedicine can be found in the journals of the various subdisciplines of medicine, and scientific research is being conducted and re-

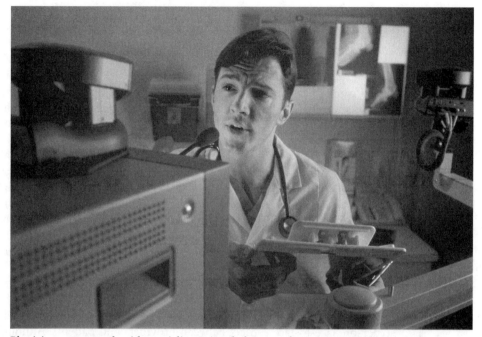

Physicians can consult with specialists using desktop conferencing systems.

ported with increasing frequency in prestigious journals of the profession. Finally, federal and state governments and private organizations are funding telemedicine projects totaling tens to hundreds of millions of dollars. The communications revolution is having an impact on medicine just as it is on education, training, government, business, and law.

Applications.   Kvedar, Menn, and Loughlin (1998) list four major applications for telemedicine: remote consultation, remote monitoring, remote education, and telementoring.

Remote consultation is the most common telemedicine application and what most refer to when they use the term telemedicine. This application implies one health care provider seeking the advice of a professional colleague or subspecialist to resolve a patient's problem.

Remote monitoring is a longstanding application where the most common use is to access a patient's vital signs at a distance using telecommunications technologies.

Remote education is increasingly important as the geographically concentrated expertise of a medical unit is redistributed to isolated practicing professionals, and professionals in training.

Telementoring involves the development of techniques to share the output of surgical tools such as endoscopes and laparoscopes to distant locations.

The Institute of Medicine (Grigsby & Sanders, 1998) organizes applications of telemedicine differently and identifies five areas of emphasis: patient care, professional education, patient education, research, and health care administration.

Impediments to Telemedicine.   The Institute of Medicine identifies five concerns that prevent and slow the growth of telemedicine. The five issue areas are professional licensure; malpractice liability; privacy, confidentiality, and security; payment policies; and regulation of medical devices.

Professional licensure issues stem from the traditional view of professional practice as involving a face-to-face encounter between clinician and patient. Telemedicine breaks the physical link and may complicate where a telemedicine practitioner should be licensed if the professional and the patient are in different states. Currently, multiple state licenses are required.

Malpractice liability is usually described as a deviation from the accepted medical standard of care. For telemedicine practitioners, the subject of malpractice presents potentially complicated legal issues, since state law generally governs liability.

Privacy, confidentiality, and security issues relate to serious questions that have been raised about current legal protections for medical privacy and confidentiality. The Hippocratic oath requires that physicians keep silent about what they learn from people, "counting such things to be as sacred secrets." Information and telecommunications links present new opportunities for privacy infringements.

Payment policies for telemedicine are a major barrier to the growth of telemedicine. Until 1999, telemedicine did not meet the requirements of the Health Care Financing Administration (now known as the Centers for Medicare and Medicaid Services) for in-person, face-to-face contact between providers and patients. Although most medical consultations using telemedicine have been ineligible for payment in the past, guidelines for reimbursement are still evolving. Currently, Medicare covers interactive video systems (Grigsby & Sanders, 1998), and for this reason most health care organizations are using two-way videoconferencing for their initial telemedicine initiatives.

Regulation of medical devices is of concern because the federal Food and Drug Administration (FDA), through its center, regulates some of the devices used in telemedicine.

In summary, the issues that have slowed the growth of telemedicine are important and should be addressed. However, they are not necessarily unique within the medical profession. Rather, they are issues that are resolved continuously as the health care field adopts new technologies, medical and informational.

Limited research is reported on the medical effectiveness and cost-effectiveness of telemedicine. Current research seems to support the conclusion that telemedicine is effective when practiced correctly, but that additional evaluation and assessment activities need to be conducted (Grigsby & Sanders, 1998).

Telemedicine will continue to be a dynamic influence within the profession of medicine. The benefits of this innovation will be in two primary areas: medical benefits and cost benefits. First, telemedicine is a logical extension of the growth of the technical and technological aspects of health care. The medical benefits of an active telemedicine program are related to how professionals use the technology. A modification of a famous analogy used in educational research when applied to telemedicine summarizes the medical impact of telemedicine. Telemedicine and information technologies are *mere vehicles* that permit the delivery of health services, but they have no greater impact on health care than the truck that delivers our groceries has on nutrition. It is the content of the vehicle that permits effective health care, not the vehicle

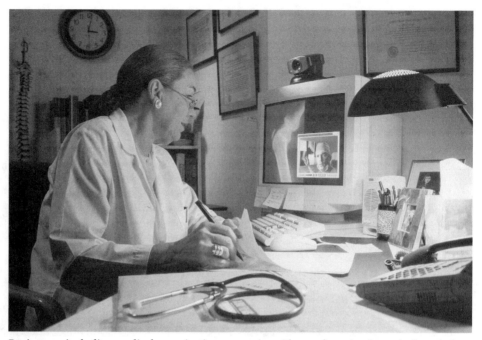

Businesses, including medical organizations, are using videoconferencing instead of expensive traveling.

itself (Clark, 1983). Second, cost-effectiveness is likely to be the most significant outcome of telemedicine. The significant costs of medical care and the increased requirements for services that are projected for the next several decades forecast a cost advantage for the organizations that understand and utilize technologies effectively. Certainly, telemedicine is only one category of technology, but it may soon be the "ears and eyes" of the health care organization.

In summary, telemedicine is a recognized subcategory of the health services profession. As a technique and tool in the modern medical center it has the potential to expand and accelerate the services offered and the impact made. Other professions, such as law, are moving cautiously to adopt distance education concepts. Nova Southeastern University's law school was recently recognized as the "nation's most wired law school." Telecommunications technologies will have increasing impact on most fields of endeavor, not just education, as they improve and become more widely available.

CHARACTERISTICS OF DISTANCE EDUCATION: A VISION

Recently, a number of advances have been made in the study of learning and teaching that are providing educators with strategies for improving the educational experience. Often, these advances are considered to be in opposition to the common practices of distance education because of the misconception that teachers lecture to distant learners.

Training of staff located at remote sites is facilitated and made cost-effective by using teleconferencing systems.

This is changing dramatically, however, as distance education systems attempt to provide a learning site that is a *room with a view*.

This emerging approach relies strongly on distance education and suggests a scenario for the school and classroom of the future similar to the following scenario, which implies that classrooms of the future will be technology-rich and will continue to have teachers who are responsible for the learning events that occur:

> In every community and neighborhood there are schools surrounded by playgrounds and sports fields with trees and grass. The schools themselves look modern but very familiar. The schools are open 24 hours per day, every day, all year. Each is a part of a locally controlled and supported district that is one of several hundred that make up a technology-rich statewide educational system. Classrooms are considered rooms with a view. Every learner and teacher possesses a high-powered multimedia computer that is connected to a worldwide network containing virtually unlimited educational resources. The network connects the learner to multisensory multimedia resources that are accessible from school, home, and business. Education is learner- and learning-centered and technology-supported. Schools are small, with about 600 to 800 students, and classes never exceed 25. In the evenings the classrooms are converted to learning laboratories that are used by the entire community. Each classroom has full-motion video links to state and national

Students can interact with students from other schools.

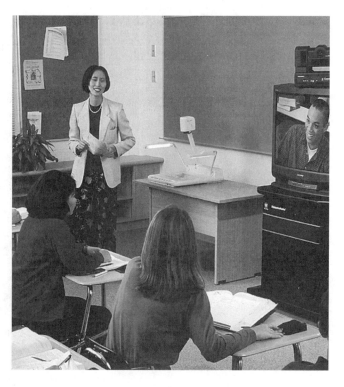

networks that permit true interactive learning. Students have desktop video access through their computers, also. The educational philosophy of this school is to promote authentic, student-centered learning activities that are cognitively situated whenever possible in real-world events. The school and its classrooms are a community resource.

This scenario could be considered a dream rather than a vision. However, it is based on the following widely available and general accepted techniques and technologies.

First, instruction is learner-centered. The networked computer permits the learner to access events of instruction that can be tailored to meet individual needs. Second, multimedia instruction is routine, especially when networked computer and video systems are used. Interactive instruction is possible because telecommunications technologies permit the learner to contact databases, information sources, instructional experts, and other students in real-time and interactive ways. For example, individual students can use their computers to contact other students or individuals who have information they need. Also, the entire class can participate in interactive video sessions with teachers from remote sites or with groups of students from other schools. Instruction is authentic because it is not teacher-centered; rather it is content- and learner-centered. The teacher orchestrates the individual learning activities of students who collaborate with classmates, with distant learners, with the teacher, and with multimedia technology available locally or from the World Wide Web. Finally, the learning

Distance education is used on the plant floor anytime outside expertise is needed.

environment of the future encourages collaboration without the limitations inherent in the self-contained classroom.

Much of this is possible because of the concept of distance education, which is the bringing of learners and the content of instruction together no matter where each is located. Interactive, real-time, on-demand, learner-centered, authentic, and learner-constructed events will characterize the educational environment of the future. Ultimately, the concept of distance will disappear as insignificant, and the idea of interaction will replace it.

SUMMARY

Separation of the student and the teacher is a fundamental characteristic of distance education. Increasingly, educators are using technology to increase the access of the distant learner to the local classroom, to improve access of all learners to resources, and to make the experience of the remote student comparable to the experience of the local learner.

Distance education is a dramatic idea. It may change, even restructure, education, but only if it is possible to make the experience of the distant learner as complete, satisfying, and acceptable as the experience of the local learner. If distance education is to be a successful and mainstream approach, then it is imperative that distance education systems be designed to permit equivalent learning experiences for distant and local students. Distance education using telecommunications technologies is an exciting emerging field. However, practitioners should not promote distance education as the next great technological solution to education's problems, nor make grand claims about the impact of telecommunications systems. Rather, distance education specialists should strive to understand technology and technological approaches that make the experiences of distant and local learners positive and equivalent, at least until someone's genius identifies an approach to learning using telecommunications systems to change education, just as Charles Martel's use of the stirrup changed society.

SELF-TEST QUESTIONS

1. What are Coldeway's quadrants, and which quadrant did Coldeway consider the purest form of distance education? What are the pros and cons of dividing educational events into one of Coldeway's four categories?
2. What is the fundamental characteristic of distance education? Discuss what this means. What are the various kinds of distance?
3. True/False. Learners prefer not to learn at a distance. Explain your answer.
4. Richard Clark says media are "mere vehicles that deliver instruction but do not influence student achievement." Discuss Clark's analogy and decide if it is accurate. Are media vehicles? What does the word *mere* imply?
5. What do stirrups and distance education have in common? Discuss the concept of innovations and how they are used or not used. Has the computer changed teaching and learning?
6. Write a vision for a school 10 years from today.
7. Define *telemedicine.*

Answers to Self-Test Questions

1. Coldeway's quadrants for education are ST-SP (same time, same place), ST-DP (same time, different place), DT-SP (different time, same place), and DT-DP (different time, different place). Coldeway considered DT-DP as the purest form of distance education. In many new applications of distance education in the United States, telecommunications technologies are being used for ST-DP teaching and learning.
2. Separation (of the learner and the teacher) is the fundamental characteristic of distance education.
3. True. However, learners often demand to be allowed to learn at a distance because of other constraints such as availability, time, or cost.
4. Clark made this claim in 1983 when he published a review of a number of decades of media research. Others have attacked Clark's position.
5. Stirrups, according to Finn, were an invention that permitted a person to ride a horse easier. However, Charles Martel took this simple idea and created something new and unique—the knight, who used the stirrup in a way that no one had ever thought of before. Distance education permits learners to take

classes and courses at a distance, but it may prove to significantly change education, even if right now no one is quite sure how.

6. A vision should be a dream for how education will look and what it will do. The vision should create a mental image in the reader's mind.

7. Telemedicine is medicine at a distance. The Institute of Medicine defines telemedicine as *the use of electronic information and communications technologies to provide and support health care when distance separates the participants.*

For additional information and activities, visit the Prentice Hall Companion Website at http://www.prenhall.com/simonson

REFERENCES

Bauck, T. (2001). Distance education in South Dakota. *Tech Trends, 23*(2), 22–25.

Carnevale, E. (2000). Survey finds 72% rise in number of distance education programs. *Chronicle of Higher Education,* January 7, A57.

Carr, S. (1999). Two more universities start diploma-granting virtual high schools. *Chronicle of Higher Education,* December 10, A49.

Clark, R. (1983). Reconsidering research on learning from media. *Review of Educational Research, 53*(4), 445–459.

Clark, R. (1994). Media will never influence learning. *Educational Technology Research and Development, 42*(2), 21–29.

Cohen, D. (2000). Hong Kong's boom in distance education may be a sign of what's to come in Asia. *Chronicle of Higher Education,* July 14, A50.

Ding, X. (1994). China's higher distance education—Its four systems and their structural characteristics at three levels. *Distance Education, 15*(2), 327–346.

Ding, X. (1995). From Fordism to new-Fordism: Industrialisation theory and distance education—a Chinese perspective. *Distance Education, 16*(2), 217–240.

Finn, J. (1964). The Franks had the right idea. *NEA Journal, 53*(4), 24–27.

Grigsby, J., & Sanders, J. (1998). Telemedicine: Where it is and where it is going. *Annals of Internal Medicine, 129*(2), 123–127.

Holmberg, B. (1995). The evolution of the character and practice of distance education. *Open Learning, 10*(2), 47–53.

Keegan, D. (1994). *Distance training in the European Union* (ZIFF Papiere). Hagen, Germany: Institute for Research into Distance Education, Fern Universitat. (ERIC Document Reproduction Service No. ED381684)

Keegan, D. (1995). *Distance education technology for the new millennium: Compressed video teaching.* (ERIC Document Reproduction Service No. ED 389931)

Kvedar, J., Menn, E., & Loughlin, K. (1998). Telemedicine: Present applications and future prospects. *Urologic Clinics of North America, 25*(1), 137–149.

Macwilliams, B. (2000). Turkey's old-fashioned distance education draws the largest student body on earth. *Chronicle of Higher Education,* September 22, A41–42.

Noble, D., Schneiderman, G., Herman, R., Agre, P., & Denning, P. (1998). Technology in education: The fight for the future. *Educom Review, 33*(3), 22–30, 32–34.

Simonson, M. (1995). Overview of the Teacher Education Alliance, Iowa Distance Education Alliance research plan. In C. Sorensen, C. Schlosser, M. Anderson, & M. Simonson (Eds.), *Encyclopedia of distance education research in Iowa* (pp. 3–6). Ames, IA: Teacher Education Alliance.

Simonson, M., Schlosser, C., & Hanson, D. (1999). Theory and distance education: A new discussion. *The American Journal of Distance Education, 13*(1), 60–75.

Thach, L., & Murphy, L. (1994). Collaboration in distance education: From local to international perspectives. *The American Journal of Distance Education, 8*(3), 5–21.

Tompkins, L. S. (1993). A new light on distance learning—fiber optics. *Journal of Educational Technology Systems, 21*(3), 265–275.

U.S. Department of Education. (1995). *The Star Schools program.* (Available from Star Schools, U.S. Department of Education, 555 New Jersey Avenue NW, Washington, DC 20208-5644).

ADDITIONAL READINGS

Hanna, D. (1995). *Mainstreaming distance education.* Conference of the National Association of State University and Land Grant Colleges, Madison, WI.

Jurasek, K. (1993). *Distance education via compressed video.* Unpublished master's thesis, Iowa State University, Ames.

Kozma, R. (1994). Will media influence learning: Reframing the debate. *Educational Technology Research and Development, 42*(2), 7–19.

Schlosser, C., & Anderson, M. (1994). *Distance education: Review of the literature.* Washington, DC: Association for Educational Communications and Technology.

Simonson, M. (1996). *Reinventing distance education.* Paper presented at the 1996 Annual Convention of the U.S. Distance Learning Association, Washington, DC.

Simonson, M., & Schlosser, C. (1995). More than fiber: Distance education in Iowa. *Tech Trends, 40*(3), 13–15.

Willis, B. (1994). *Distance education: Strategies and tools.* Englewood Cliffs, NJ: Educational Technology Publications.

chapter **2**

DEFINITIONS, HISTORY, AND THEORIES OF DISTANCE EDUCATION

CHAPTER GOAL

The purpose of this chapter is to review the definitions, history, and theories of distance education.

CHAPTER OBJECTIVES

After reading and reviewing this chapter, you should be able to

1. Discuss the reason for different definitions of distance education.
2. Describe the various definitions of distance education that have been offered.
3. List and explain the five main elements of the various definitions of distance education given by Keegan.
4. Give the emerging definition of distance education that is appropriate for the United States.
5. Outline the general history of distance education, explaining how it began with correspondence study and evolved into the use of electronic communications media.
6. Discuss the emergence of distance teaching universities.
7. Explain the various theoretical approaches to distance education, including theories of independence, industrialization, and interaction and communication.
8. Synthesize the various theories of distance education.
9. Describe the emerging theory of distance education that relates to equivalence of learning experiences.
10. Explain Fordism, neo-Fordism, and post-Fordism.

DEFINING DISTANCE EDUCATION

Distance education was defined in Chapter 1 as institution-based, formal education where the learning group is separated, and where interactive telecommunications systems are used to connect learners, resources, and instructors.

Four main components comprise this definition (Figure 2–1). First is the concept that distance education is institutionally based. This is what differentiates distance education from self-study. Whereas the institution referred to in this definition could be a traditional educational school or college, increasingly there are emerging nontraditional institutions that offer education to students at a distance. Businesses, companies, and corporations are offering instruction at a distance. Many educators and trainers are advocating the accreditation of institutions that offer distance education to add credibility, improve quality, and eliminate diploma mills.

The second component of the definition of distance education is the concept of separation of the teacher and student. Most often, separation is thought of in geographic terms—teachers are in one location and students in another. Also implied by the definition is the separation of teachers and students in time. Asynchronous distance education means that instruction is offered and students access it at separate times, or anytime it is convenient to them. Finally, intellectual separation of teachers and learners

FIGURE 2–1   Components of distance education.

is important. Obviously, teachers have an understanding of the concepts presented in a course that students do not possess. In this case, the reduction of separation is a goal of the distance education system.

Interactive telecommunications is the third component of the definition of distance education. Interaction can be synchronous or asynchronous—at the same time, or at different times. Interaction is critical, but not at the expense of content. In other words, it is important that learners be able to interact with each other, with resources of instruction, and with their teacher. However, interaction should not be the primary characteristic of instruction but should be available, commonplace, and relevant.

The words "telecommunications systems" implies electronic media, such as television, telephone, and the Internet, but this term need not be limited to only electronic media. *Telecommunications* is defined as "communicating at a distance." This definition includes communication with the postal system, as in correspondence study, and other nonelectronic methods for communication. Obviously, as electronic telecommunications systems improve and become more pervasive, they likely will be the mainstay of modern distance education systems. However, older, less sophisticated systems of telecommunication will continue to be important.

Finally, we examine the concept of connecting learners, resources, and instructors. This means that there are instructors who interact with learners and that resources are available that permit learning to occur. Resources should be subjected to instructional design procedures that organize them into learning experiences that promote learning, including resources that can be observed, felt, heard, or completed.

The definition of distance education includes these four components. If one or more are missing, then the event is something different, if only slightly, than distance education.

This definition is not the only one and certainly is not the first offered for distance education. As a matter of fact, distance education has been defined from a number of perspectives over the years. For example, Rudolf Manfred Delling stated in general that distance education is a planned and systematic activity that comprises the choice, didactic preparation and presentation of teaching materials as well as the supervision and support of student learning and which is achieved by bridging the physical distance between student and teacher by means of at least one appropriate technical medium.

For Hilary Perraton (1988), distance education is an educational process in which a significant proportion of the teaching is conducted by someone removed in space and/or time from the learner.

The U.S. Department of Education's Office of Educational Research and Improvement defines distance education as "the application of telecommunications and electronic devices which enable students and learners to receive instruction that originates from some distant location." Typically, the learner may interact with the instructor or program directly, and may meet with the instructor on a periodic basis.

Grenville Rumble (1989) offered a definition of distance education. He noted that, in any distance education process, there must be: a teacher; one or more students; a course or curriculum that the teacher is capable of teaching and the student is trying to learn; and a contract, implicit or explicit, between the student and the teacher or the institution employing the teacher, which acknowledges their respective teaching-learning roles.

- Distance education is a method of education in which the learner is physically separate from the teacher. It may be used on its own, or in conjunction with other forms of education, including face-to-face. In distance education, learners are physically separated from the institution that sponsors the instruction.
- The teaching/learning contract requires that the student be taught, assessed, given guidance and, where appropriate, prepared for examinations that may or may not be conducted by the institution. This must be accomplished by two-way communication. Learning may be undertaken individually or in groups; in either case, it is accomplished in the physical absence of the teacher.

For Desmond Keegan (1986), the following four definitions were central to an attempt to identify the elements of a single, unifying definition of distance education:

- The French government, as part of a law passed in 1971, defined distance education as education which either does not imply the physical presence of the teacher appointed to dispense it in the place where it is received or in which the teacher is present only on occasion or for selected tasks.
- According to Börje Holmberg, distance education covers the various forms of study at all levels which are not under the continuous, immediate supervision of tutors present with their students in lecture rooms or on the same premises but which, nevertheless, benefit from the planning, guidance and teaching of a supporting organization.
- Otto Peters emphasized the role of technology, saying that distance teaching/education (*Fernunterricht*) is a method of imparting knowledge, skills and attitudes. It is rationalized by the application of division of labor and organizational principles as well as by the extensive use of technical media, especially for the purpose of reproducing high quality teaching material which makes it possible to instruct great numbers of students at the same time wherever they live. It is an industrialized form of teaching and learning.
- For Michael Moore, the related concept of "distance teaching" was defined as the family of instructional methods in which the teaching behaviors are executed apart from the learning behaviors, including those that in a contiguous situation would be performed in the learner's presence, so that communication between the teacher and the learner must be facilitated by print, electronic, mechanical or other devices.

Keegan identified five main elements of these definitions, using them to compose a comprehensive definition of distance education.

- The quasi-permanent separation of teacher and learner throughout the length of the learning process (this distinguishes it from conventional face-to-face education).
- The influence of an educational organization both in the planning and preparation of learning materials and in the provision of student support services (this distinguishes it from private study and teach-yourself programs).

- The use of technical media—print, audio, video or computer—to unite teacher and learner and carry the content of the course.
- The provision of two-way communication so that the student may benefit from or even initiate dialogue (this distinguishes it from other uses of technology in education).
- The quasi-permanent absence of the learning group throughout the length of the learning process so that people are usually taught as individuals and not in groups, with the possibility of occasional meetings for both didactic and socialization purposes.

Garrison and Shale (1987) argued that, in light of advances in distance education delivery technologies, Keegan's definition was too narrow and did not correspond to the existing reality to future possibilities. Although declining to offer a definition of distance education, Garrison and Shale offered the following three criteria they regarded as essential for characterizing the distance education process:

- Distance education implies that the majority of educational communication between (among) teacher and student(s) occurs noncontiguously.
- Distance education must involve two-way communication between (among) teacher and student(s) for the purpose of facilitating and supporting the educational process.
- Distance education uses technology to mediate the necessary two-way communication.

Keegan's definition and the definitions preceding it define the traditional view of distance education. Rapid changes in society and technology are challenging these traditional definitions.

EMERGING DEFINITIONS

The contemporary period is often characterized as one of unpredictable change. Globalization, brought on by supersonic air travel, satellite television, computer communications, and societal changes, has inspired new ways of looking at distance education. Edwards (1995) uses the term *open learning* to describe a new way of looking at education in a quickly changing and diverse world. He indicates that distance education and open learning are two distinct approaches to education. Although he does not define the two, he states that distance education provides distance learning opportunities using mass-produced courseware to a mass market. In contrast, open learning places greater emphasis on the current specific needs and/or markets available by recognizing local requirements and differences instead of delivering an established curriculum. Open learning shifts from mass production and mass consumption to a focus on local and individual needs and requirements. Edwards states that this can occur outside of the traditional organization of education. This is a major difference between his description of open learning and the previous definitions of distance education.

A BRIEF HISTORY OF DISTANCE EDUCATION

Distance education seems a new idea to most educators of today. However, the concepts that form the basis of distance education are more than a century old. Certainly, distance education has experienced growth and change recently, but the long traditions of the field continue to give it direction for the future. This section offers a brief history of distance education, from correspondence study, to electronic communications, to distance teaching universities.

Correspondence Study

The roots of distance education are at least 160 years old. An advertisement in a Swedish newspaper in 1833 touted the opportunity to study "Composition through the medium of the Post." In 1840, England's newly established penny post allowed Isaac Pitman to offer shorthand instruction via correspondence. Three years later, instruction was formalized with the founding of the Phonographic Correspondence Society, precursor of Sir Isaac Pitman's Correspondence Colleges. Distance education, in the form of correspondence study, was established in Germany by Charles Toussaint and Gustav Langenscheidt, who taught language in Berlin. Correspondence study crossed the Atlantic in 1873 when Anna Eliot Ticknor founded a Boston-based society to encourage study at home. The Society to Encourage Studies at Home attracted more than 10,000 students in 24 years. Students of the classical curriculum (mostly women) corresponded monthly with teachers, who offered guided readings and frequent tests.

From 1883 to 1891, academic degrees were authorized by the state of New York through the Chautauqua College of Liberal Arts to students who completed the required summer institutes and correspondence courses. William Rainey Harper, the Yale professor who headed the program, was effusive in his support of correspondence study, and confident in the future viability of the new educational form: The student who has prepared a certain number of lessons in the correspondence school knows more of the subject treated in those lessons, and knows it better, than the student who has covered the same ground in the classroom.

The day is coming when the work done by correspondence will be greater in amount than that done in the classrooms of our academies and colleges; when the students who shall recite by correspondence will far outnumber those who make oral recitations.

In 1891, Thomas J. Foster, editor of the *Mining Herald,* a daily newspaper in eastern Pennsylvania, began offering a correspondence course in mining and the prevention of mine accidents. His business developed into the International Correspondence Schools, a commercial school whose enrollment exploded in the first two decades of the 20th century, from 225,000 in 1900 to more than 2 million in 1920. In 1886, H. S. Hermod, of Sweden, began teaching English by correspondence. In 1898, he founded Hermod's, which would become one of the world's largest and most influential distance teaching organizations.

Correspondence study continued to develop in Britain with the founding of a number of correspondence institutions, such as Skerry's College in Edinburgh in 1878 and

University Correspondence College in London in 1887. At the same time, the university extension movement in the United States and England promoted the correspondence method. Among the pioneers in the field were Illinois Wesleyan in 1877 and the University Extension Department of the University of Chicago in 1892. Illinois Wesleyan offered bachelor's, master's, and doctoral degrees as part of a program modeled on the Oxford, Cambridge, and London model. Between 1881 and 1890, 750 students were enrolled; and in 1900, nearly 500 students were seeking degrees. However, concerns about the quality of the program prompted a recommendation that it be terminated by 1906.

Correspondence study was integral to the University of Chicago. The school, founded in 1890, created a university extension as one of its five divisions, the first such division in an American university. The extension division was divided into five departments: lecture study, class study, correspondence teaching, library, and training.

The correspondence study department of the University of Chicago was successful, at least in terms of numbers. Each year, 125 instructors taught 3,000 students enrolled in 350 courses. Nevertheless, enthusiasm within the university for the program waned, partly for financial reasons.

At the University of Wisconsin, the development of the "short course" and farmers' institutes in 1885 formed the foundation for university extension. Six years later, the university announced a program of correspondence study led by the eminent historian, Frederick Jackson Turner. However, as at the University of Chicago, faculty interest waned. Further, public response was minimal, and the correspondence study program was discontinued in 1899. Correspondence study would have to wait another 7 years to be reborn under a new, stronger, correspondence study department within the school's university extension division.

Moody Bible Institute, founded in 1886, formed a correspondence department in 1901 that continues today with a record of over 1 million enrollments from all over the world. Correspondence study/distance education has had a significant impact on religious education that emphasizes the social context within which a student lives.

Distance education began to enrich the secondary school curriculum in the 1920s. Students in Benton Harbor, Michigan, were offered vocational courses in 1923, and 6 years later, the University of Nebraska began experimenting with correspondence courses in high schools.

In France, the Ministry of Education set up a government correspondence college in response to the impending Second World War. Although the Centre National d'Enseignement par Correspondences was established for the education of children, it has since become a huge distance teaching organization for adult education.

The original target groups of distance education efforts were adults with occupational, social, and family commitments. This remains the primary target group today. Distance education provided the opportunity to widen intellectual horizons, as well as the chance to improve and update professional knowledge. Further, it stressed individuality of learning and flexibility in both the time and place of study.

Two philosophies of distance education became identifiable. The full liberalism of programs offered by Hermod's, in Sweden, emphasized the free pacing of progress through the program by the student. Other programs, such as those offered by the University of Chicago, offered a more rigid schedule of weekly lessons.

Electronic Communications

Europe experienced a steady expansion of distance education, without radical changes in structure, but with gradually more sophisticated methods and media employed. Audio recordings were used in instruction for the blind and in language teaching for all students. Laboratory kits were used in such subjects as electronics and radio engineering. Virtually all large-scale distance teaching organizations were private correspondence schools.

In the United States, advances in electronic communications technology helped determine the dominant medium of distance education. In the 1920s, at least 176 radio stations were constructed at educational institutions, although most were gone by the end of the decade. The surviving stations were mostly at land grant colleges.

In the early 1930s, experimental television teaching programs were produced at the University of Iowa, Purdue University, and Kansas State College. However, it was not until the 1950s that college credit courses were offered via broadcast television: Western Reserve University was the first to offer a continuous series of such courses, beginning in 1951. Sunrise Semester was a well-known televised series of college courses offered by New York University on CBS from 1957 to 1982.

Satellite technology, developed in the 1960s and made cost-effective in the 1980s, enabled the rapid spread of instructional television. Federally funded experiments in the United States and Canada, such as the Appalachian Education Satellite Project (1974–1975), demonstrated the feasibility of satellite-delivered instruction. However, these early experiments were loudly criticized for being poorly planned. More recent attempts at satellite-delivered distance education have been more successful. The first state educational satellite system, Learn/Alaska, was created in 1980. It offered 6 hours of instructional television daily to 100 villages, some of them accessible only by air. The privately operated TI-IN Network, of San Antonio, Texas, has delivered a wide variety of courses via satellite to high schools across the United States since 1985.

In the late 1980s and early 1990s, the development of fiber-optic communication systems allowed for the expansion of live, two-way, high-quality audio and video systems in education. Whereas the initial cost of fiber-optic systems may be high, the long-term savings and benefits of the technology outweigh the initial costs. Many now consider fiber-optic delivery systems as the least expensive option for the high-quality, two-way audio and video required for live two-way interactive distance education. Iowa has the largest statewide fiber-optic system. Currently the Iowa Communications Network (ICN) provides full-motion, two-way interactive video, data (Internet), and voice services to over 600 Iowa classrooms. In the near future, all school districts, area education agencies, and public libraries in Iowa will have classrooms connected to the fiber-optics of the ICN. The ICN also serves as the backbone for computer telecommunications, and asynchronous, Internet-based programs are being offered to distant learners. Over 100,000 hours of formal educational opportunities were offered during the first 18 months of the network's service. Recently, 100,000 hours were being offered every month.

Distance education opportunities are quickly growing through the use of computer-mediated communications. Tens of thousands of networks are connected to the Internet, with millions of people using the Internet worldwide (Ackermann, 1995). Both credit and noncredit courses have been offered over computer networks since the mid-1980s. In most cases, a teacher organizes the course materials, readings, and assignments. The students read the material, complete assignments, and participate in online discussions with other classmates. The advent of computer conferencing capabilities has had an impact on the traditional approach to the design of distance education instruction. Computer conferencing increases the potential for interaction and collaborative work among the students. This type of collaboration among students was difficult with previous forms of distance education.

In addition, computer networks are a convenient way to distribute course materials to students around the world. Many faculty members now use the convenient user interface of the World Wide Web to make course materials available to their students. The British Open University, Fern Universität of Germany, and the University of Twente in the Netherlands are some of the leading providers of online courses in Europe. In the United States, the American Open University, Nova Southeastern University, and the University of Phoenix have been traditional leaders in providing distance education. They, along with many other universities, now offer hundreds of courses online.

Distance Teaching Universities

The 1962 decision that the University of South Africa would become a distance teaching university brought about a fundamental change in the way distance education was practiced in much of the world. Another landmark was the founding, in 1971, of the Open University of the United Kingdom, a degree-giving distance teaching university offering full degree programs, sophisticated courses, and the innovative use of media (Holmberg, 1986). The Open University brought heightened prestige to distance education and spurred the establishment of similar institutions in industrial nations such as West Germany, Japan, and Canada, as well as in such lesser-developed nations as Sri Lanka and Pakistan.

Although the distance teaching universities shared numerous similarities, they were not identical in their mission or practice. Two of the largest and most influential, the Open University of the United Kingdom and the German Fern Universität, differ widely. The British school favors employed, part-time students of above-normal study age, and allows them to enroll without formal entrance qualifications. By 1984, some 69,000 of its students had completed work for the bachelor of arts degree.

The German Fern Universität, founded in 1975, offers a more rigorous program than its British counterpart. Despite strict, formal entrance requirements, it had 28,000 students in 1985. However, the dropout rate is very high, and in its first decade, only 500 students completed the full curricula for a university degree.

Holmberg (1986) offers numerous political, economic, and educational reasons for the founding of distance teaching universities, including:

- The need felt in many countries to increase the offerings of university education generally
- A realization that adults with jobs, family responsibilities, and social commitments form a large group of prospective part-time university students

- A wish to serve both individuals and society by offering study opportunities to adults, among them disadvantaged groups
- The need found in many professions for further training at an advanced level
- A wish to support educational innovation
- A belief in the feasibility of an economical use of educational resources by mediated teaching

THEORY AND DISTANCE EDUCATION

Most students, and many teachers, cringe at the thought of a discussion of theory. This need not be the case. This section is designed not to intimidate or to bore, but to inform. Theory is important to the study of distance education because it directly impacts the practice of the field.

Traditionally, theories of distance education have come from sources external to America. Recently, the field in the United States has matured to the point where indigenous definitions and theories have begun to emerge.

The Need for Theory

Although forms of distance education have existed since the 1840s and attempts at theoretical explanations of distance education had been undertaken by leading scholars in the field, the need for a theory base of distance education was still largely unfulfilled in the 1970s. Holmberg (1985) stated that further theoretical considerations would contribute results that will give distance educators a firmly based theory, a touchstone against which decisions can be made with confidence. In 1986, Holmberg continued to recognize the need for theoretical considerations.

> One consequence of such understanding and explanation will be that hypotheses can be developed and submitted to falsification attempts. This will lead to insights telling us what in distance education is to be expected under what conditions and circumstances, thus paving the way for corroborated practical methodological application. (p. 3)

Moore (1994) was concerned that the progress of distance education would be hindered by the lack of attention to what he called the "macro factors." He indicated that in this area of education there was a need to describe and define the field, to discriminate between the various components of the field, and to identify the critical elements of the various forms of learning and teaching.

Keegan (1988) implied the continued need for a theory of distance education when he lamented the lack of it.

> Lack of accepted theory has weakened distance education: there has been a lack of identity, a sense of belonging to the periphery and the lack of a touchstone against which decisions on methods, on media, on financing, on student support, when they have to be made, can be made with confidence. (p. 63)

More recently, Keegan stated his ideas about what the theory should encompass. According to Keegan, a firmly based theory of distance education will be one which can provide the touchstone against which decisions—political, financial, educational, social—when they have to be made can be made with confidence. This would replace the ad hoc response to a set of conditions that arises in some "crisis" situation of problem solving, which normally characterizes this field of education.

In a general sense, theory is taken to mean a set of hypotheses logically related to one another in explaining and predicting occurrences. Holmberg (1985) stated the following:

> the aim of the theoretician is to find explanatory theories; that is to say, the theories that describe certain structural properties of the world, and which permit us to deduce, with the help of initial conditions, the effects to be explained. . . . Theoretical, to bring explanation, on the other hand practical, to provide for application or technology. (p. 5)

Keegan added (1995):

> A theory is something that eventually can be reduced to a phrase, a sentence or a paragraph and which, while subsuming all the practical research, gives the foundation on which the structures of need, purpose and administration can be erected. (p. 20)

In 1995 Holmberg gave a more specific definition of the concept of theory. He stated that a theory means:

> a systematic ordering of ideas about the phenomenon of our field of inquiry and an overarching logical structure of reasoned suppositions which can generate intersubjectively testable hypotheses. (p. 4)

Holmberg suggested that distance education has been characterized by a trial-and-error approach with little consideration being given to a theoretical basis for decision making. He suggested that the theoretical underpinnings of distance education are fragile. Most efforts in this field have been practical or mechanical and have concentrated on the logistics of the enterprise.

To some, distance education represents a deviation from conventional education. Holmberg claimed it was a distinct form of education. Keegan (1986) concluded that distance education is a distinct field of education, parallel to and a complement of conventional education. Shale (1988) countered that all of what constitutes the process of education when teacher and student are able to meet face-to-face also constitutes the process of education when the teacher and student are physically separated.

Cropley and Kahl (1983) compared and contrasted distance education and face-to-face education in terms of psychological dimensions and claimed neither set of principles emerged in a pure form. Peters (1988) strongly stated that:

> Anyone professionally involved in education is compelled to presume the existence of two forms of instruction which are strictly separable: traditional face-to-face teaching based on interpersonal communication and industrialized teaching, which is based on objectivized, rationalized technologically-produced interaction. (p. 20)

In his landmark work, *The Foundations of Distance Education,* Keegan (1986) classified theories of distance education into three groups:

- Theories of independence and autonomy
- Theories of industrialization of teaching
- Theories of interaction and communication

A fourth category seeks to explain distance education in a synthesis of existing theories of communication and diffusion, as well as philosophies of education.

Theory of Independent Study—Charles Wedemeyer

For Wedemeyer (1981), the essence of distance education was the independence of the student. This was reflected in his preference for the term *independent study* for distance education at the college or university level. Wedemeyer was critical of contemporary patterns of higher education. He believed that outdated concepts of learning and teaching were being employed, and that they failed to utilize modern technologies in ways that could alter the institution.

Wedemeyer set forth a system with 10 characteristics emphasizing learner independence and adoption of technology as a way to implement that independence. According to Wedemeyer, the system should do the following:

- Be capable of operation anyplace where there are students—or even only one student—whether or not there are teachers at the same place at the same time
- Place greater responsibility for learning on the student
- Free faculty members from custodial-type duties so that more time can be given to truly educational tasks
- Offer students and adults wider choices (more opportunities) in courses, formats, and methodologies
- Use, as appropriate, all the teaching media and methods that have been proved effective
- Mix media and methods so that each subject or unit within a subject is taught in the best way known
- Cause the redesign and development of courses to fit into an "articulated media program"
- Preserve and enhance opportunities for adaptation to individual differences
- Evaluate student achievement simply, not by raising barriers concerned with the place, rate, method, or sequence of student study
- Permit students to start, stop, and learn at their own pace

Wedemeyer proposed separating teaching from learning as a way of breaking education's "space-time barriers." He suggested six characteristics of independent study systems:

- The student and teacher are separated.
- The normal processes of teaching and learning are carried out in writing or through some other medium.

- Teaching is individualized.
- Learning takes place through the student's activity.
- Learning is made convenient for the student in his or her own environment.
- The learner takes responsibility for the pace of his or her own progress, with freedom to start and stop at any time.

Wedemeyer noted four elements of every teaching-learning situation: a teacher, a learner or learners, a communications system or mode, and something to be taught or learned. He proposed a reorganization of these elements that would accommodate physical space and allow greater learner freedom. Key to the success of distance education, Wedemeyer believed, was the development of the relationship between student and teacher.

Theory of Independent Study—Michael Moore

Formulated in the early 1970s, Moore's theory of distance education, which he calls "independent study," is a classification method for distance education programs. Shaped in part by Moore's adult education and university extension experience, it examines two variables in educational programs: the amount of learner autonomy and the distance between teacher and learner.

For Moore, distance is composed of two elements, each of which can be measured. First is the provision for two-way communication (dialog). Some systems or programs offer greater amounts of two-way communication than others. Second is the extent to which a program is responsive to the needs of the individual learner (structure). Some programs are very structured, while others are very responsive to the needs and goals of the individual student.

In the second part of his theory, Moore addresses learner autonomy. He notes that in traditional school settings, learners are very dependent on teachers for guidance, and that in most programs, conventional and distance, the teacher is active, while the student is passive. In distance education, there is a gap between teacher and student, so the student must accept a high degree of responsibility for the conduct of the learning program. The autonomous learner needs little help from the teacher, who may be more of a respondent than a director. Some adult learners, however, require help formulating their learning objectives, identifying sources of information and measuring objectives.

Moore classifies distance education programs as "autonomous" (learner-determined) or "nonautonomous" (teacher-determined), and gauges the degree of autonomy accorded the learner by answers to the following three questions:

- Is the selection of learning objectives in the program the responsibility of the learner or of the teacher (autonomy in setting of objectives)?
- Is the selection and use of resource persons, of bodies and other media, the decision of the teacher or the learner (autonomy in methods of study)?
- Are the decisions about the method of evaluation and criteria to be used made by the learner or the teacher (autonomy in evaluation)?

Theory of Industrialization of Teaching—Otto Peters

In a major treatise on education, Otto Peters of Germany developed a view of distance education as an industrialized form of teaching and learning. He examined a research base that included an extensive analysis of the distance teaching organizations of the 1960s. This led him to propose that distance education could be analyzed by comparing it with the industrial production of goods. He stated that from many points of view, conventional, oral, group-based education was a preindustrial form of education. His statement implied that distance teaching could not have existed before the industrial era. Using economic and industrial theory, Peters proposed the following new categories (terminology) for the analysis of distance education:

- **Rationalization.** The use of methodical measures to reduce the required amount of input of power, time, and money. In distance education, ways of thinking, attitudes, and procedures can be found, which only established themselves in the wake of an increased rationalization in the industrialization of production processes.
- **Division of labor.** The division of a task into simpler components or subtasks. In distance education, the tasks of conveying information, counseling, assessment, and recording performance are performed by separate individuals. To Peters, the division of labor is the main prerequisite for the advantages of distance education to become effective.
- **Mechanization.** The use of machines in a work process. Distance education, Peters noted, would be impossible without machines. Duplicating machines and transport systems are prerequisites, and later forms of distance teaching have the additional facilities of modern means of communication and electronic data processing installations.
- **Assembly line.** Commonly, a method of work in which workers remain stationary, while objects they are working on move past them. In traditional distance education programs, materials for both teacher and student are not the product of an individual. Rather, instructional materials are designed, printed, stored, distributed, and graded by specialists.
- **Mass production.** The production of goods in large quantities. Peters noted that because demand outstrips supply at colleges and universities, there has been a trend toward large-scale operations not entirely consistent with traditional forms of academic teaching. Mass production of distance education courses, however, can enhance quality. Peters believed that the large number of courses produced forced distance teaching organizations to analyze the requirements of potential distance learners far more carefully than in conventional teaching and to improve the quality of the courses.
- **Preparatory work.** Determining how workers, machines, and materials can usefully relate to each other during each phase of the production process. Peters believed that the success of distance education depended decisively on a preparatory phase. The preparatory phase concerns the development of the distance study course involving experts in the various specialist fields with qualifications often higher than those of other teachers involved in distance study.

- **Planning.** The system of decisions which determines an operation prior to it being carried out. Peters noted that planning was important in the development phase of distance education, as the contents of correspondence units, from the first to the last, must be determined in detail, adjusted in relation to each other, and represented in a predetermined number of correspondence units. The importance of planning is even greater when residential study is a component of a distance education program.
- **Organization.** Creating general or permanent arrangements for purpose-oriented activity. Peters noted the relationship between rational organization and effectiveness of the teaching method. Organization makes it possible for students to receive exactly predetermined documents at appointed times, for an appropriate university teacher to be immediately available for each assignment sent in, and for consultations to take place at fixed locations at fixed times. Organization, Peters pointed out, was optimized in large distance education programs.
- **Scientific control methods.** The methods by which work processes are analyzed systematically, particularly by time studies, and in accordance with the results obtained from measurements and empirical data. The work processes are tested and controlled in their elementary details in a planned way, in order to increase productivity, all the time making the best possible use of working time and the staff available. In distance education, some institutions hire experts to apply techniques of scientific analysis to the evaluation of courses.
- **Formalization.** The predetermination of the phases of the manufacturing process. In distance education, all the points in the cycle, from student, to distance teaching establishment, to the academics allocated, must be determined exactly.
- **Standardization.** The limitations of manufacture to a restricted number of types of one product, in order to make these more suitable for their purpose, cheaper to produce, and easier to replace. In distance education, not only is the format of correspondence units standardized, so are the stationery for written communication between student and lecturer, the organizational support, and also the academic content.
- **Change of function.** The change of the role or job of the worker in the production process. In distance education, change of function is evident in the role of the lecturer. The original role of provider of knowledge in the form of the lecturer is split into that of study unit author and that of marker; the role of counselor is allocated to a particular person or position. Frequently, the original role of lecturer is reduced to that of a consultant whose involvement in distance teaching manifests itself in periodically recurrent contributions.
- **Objectification.** The loss, in the production process, of the subjective element that was used to determine work to a considerable degree. In distance education, most teaching functions are objectified as they are determined by the distance study course as well as technical means. Only in written communication with the distance learner or possibly in a consultation or the brief additional face-to-face events on campus has the teacher some individual scope left for subjectively determined variants in teaching method.

- **Concentration and centralization.** Because of the large amounts of capital required for mass production and the division of labor, there has been a trend to large industrial concerns with a concentration of capital, a centralized administration, and a market that is monopolized. Peters noted the trend toward distance education institutions serving very large numbers of students. The Open University of the United Kingdom, for instance, recently had more than 70,000 students. It is more economical to establish a small number of such institutions serving a national population, rather than a larger number of institutions serving regional populations.

Peters concluded that for distance teaching to become effective, the principle of the division of labor is a constituent element of distance teaching. The teaching process in his theory of industrialization is gradually restructured through increasing mechanization and automation. He noted that:

- The development of distance study courses is just as important as the preparatory work—taking place prior to the production process.
- The effectiveness of the teaching process particularly depends on planning and organization.
- Courses must be formalized and expectations from students standardized.
- The teaching process is largely objectified.
- The function of academics teaching at a distance has changed considerably vis-à-vis university teachers in conventional teaching.
- Distance study can only be economical with a concentration of the available resources and a centralized administration.

According to Peters, within the complex overall distance teaching activity, one area has been exposed to investigation that had been regularly omitted from traditional analysis. New concepts were used to describe new facts that merit attention. He did not deny a theory of the industrialization of teaching had disadvantages, but in any exploration of teaching, the industrial structures characteristic of distance teaching need to be taken into account in decision making.

Theory of Interaction and Communication— Börje Holmberg

Holmberg's theory of distance education, what he calls guided didactic conversation, falls into the general category of communication theory. Holmberg noted that his theory had explanatory value in relating teaching effectiveness to the impact of feelings of belonging and cooperation as well as to the actual exchange of questions, answers, and arguments in mediated communication.

Holmberg offers seven background assumptions for his theory:

- The core of teaching is interaction between the teaching and learning parties; it is assumed that simulated interaction through subject matter presentation in preproduced courses can take over part of the interaction by causing students to consider different views, approaches, and solutions and generally interact with a course.

- Emotional involvement in the study and feelings of personal relation between the teaching and learning parties are likely to contribute to learning pleasure.
- Learning pleasure supports student motivation.
- Participation in decision making concerning the study is favorable to student motivation.
- Strong student motivation facilitates learning.
- A friendly, personal tone and easy access to the subject matter contribute to learning pleasure, support student motivation, and thus facilitate learning from the presentations of preproduced courses, i.e., from teaching in the form of one-way traffic simulating interaction, as well as from didactic communication in the form of two-way traffic between the teaching and learning parties.
- The effectiveness of teaching is demonstrated by students' learning of what has been taught.

These assumptions, Holmberg (1986) believes, are the basis of the essential teaching principles of distance education. From these assumptions he formed his theory that distance teaching will support student motivation, promote learning pleasure and make the study relevant to the individual learner and his or her needs, creating feelings of rapport between the learner and the distance-education institution (its tutors, counselors, etc.), facilitating access to course content, engaging the learner in activities, discussions and decisions and generally catering for helpful real and simulated communication to and from the learner.

Holmberg himself notes that this is admittedly a leaky theory. However, he adds, it is not devoid of explanatory power: it does, in fact, indicate essential characteristics of effective distance education.

In 1995, Holmberg significantly broadened his theory of distance education. His new comprehensive theory of distance education is divided into eight parts. This expanded theory encompasses the theory just stated above, plus these additions:

- Distance education serves individual learners who cannot or do not want to make use of face-to-face teaching. These learners are very heterogeneous.

Distance education means learners no longer have to be bound by decisions made by others about place of study, division of the year into study terms and vacations, timetables, and entry requirements. Distance education thus promotes students' freedom of choice and independence.

- Society benefits from distance education, on the one hand, from the liberal study opportunities it affords individual learners, and, on the other hand, from the professional/occupational training it provides.

Distance education is an instrument for recurrent and lifelong learning and for free access to learning opportunities and equity.

- All learning concerned with the acquisition of cognitive knowledge and cognitive skills as well as affective learning and some psychomotor learning are effectively provided for by distance education. Distance education may inspire metacognitive approaches.

- Distance education is based on deep learning as an individual activity. Learning is guided and supported by noncontiguous means. Teaching and learning rely on mediated communication, usually based on preproduced courses.
- Distance education is open to behaviorist, cognitive, constructivist, and other modes of learning. It has an element of industrialization with division of labor, use of mechanical devices, electronic data processing, and mass communication, usually based on preproduced courses.
- Personal relations, study pleasure, and empathy between students and those supporting them (tutors, counselors, etc.) are central to learning in distance education. Feelings of empathy and belonging promote students' motivation to learn and influence the learning favorably. Such feelings are conveyed by students being engaged in decision making; by lucid, problem-oriented conversation-like presentations of learning matter that may be anchored in existing knowledge; by friendly, noncontiguous interaction between students and tutors, counselors, and others supporting them; and by liberal organizational-administrative structures and processes.
- While it is an effective mode of training, distance education runs the risk of leading to mere fact learning and reproduction of accepted "truths." However, it can be organized and carried out in such a way that students are encouraged to search, criticize, and identify positions of their own. It thus serves conceptual learning, problem learning, and genuinely academic ends.
- In sum, the above represents, on the one hand, a description of distance education and, on the other hand, a theory from which hypotheses are generated and which has explanatory power in that it identifies a general approach favorable to learning and to the teaching efforts conducive to learning.

Andragogy—Malcolm Knowles

Most do now consider Knowles's work to be a theory of distance education; it is relevant because most often adults are involved in distance education, and andragogy deals with frameworks for programs designed for the adult learner. At its core is the idea that "the attainment of adulthood is concomitant on adults' coming to perceive themselves as self-directing individuals" (Brookfield, 1986).

Knowles spent a career formulating a theory of adult learning based on research and experience related to the characteristics of the adult learner (Knowles, 1990). The andragogical process consists of seven elements:

- The establishment of a climate conducive to adult learning, that includes a physical environment which is conducive to the physical well being of the adult learner, and a psychological environment that provides for a feeling of mutual respect, collaborativeness, trust, openness, and authenticity.
- The creation of an organizational structure for participatory learning that includes planning groups where learners provide input about what is to be learned, and options regarding learning activities.

- The diagnosis of needs for learning that includes differentiating between felt needs and ascribed needs.
- The formulation of directions for learning that includes objectives with terminal behaviors to be achieved and directions for improvement of abilities.
- The development of a design for activities that clarifies resources and strategies to accomplish objectives.
- The development of a plan that provides evidence when objectives are accomplished.
- The use of quantitative and qualitative evaluation that provides a rediagnosis of needs for learning.

Knowles's andragogy suggests a number of characteristics needed in distance education systems designed for adults. For example:

- The physical environment of a television classroom used by adults should be able to see what is occurring, not just hear it.
- The physiological environment should be one that promotes respect and dignity for the adult learner.
- Adult learners must feel supported, and when criticism is a part of discussions or presentations made by adults, it is important that clear ground rules be established so comments are not directed toward a person, but concentrate on content and ideas.
- A starting point for a course, or module of a course, should be the needs and interest of the adult learner.
- Course plans should include clear course descriptions, learning objectives, resources, and timelines for events.
- General to specific patterns of content presentation work best for adult learners.
- Active participation should be encouraged, such as by the use of work groups, or study teams.

A Synthesis of Existing Theories—Hilary Perraton

Perraton's theory of distance education is composed of elements from existing theories of communication and diffusion, as well as philosophies of education. It is expressed in the form of 14 statements, or hypotheses. The first 5 of these statements listed below concern the way distance teaching can be used to maximize education:

- You can use any medium to teach anything.
- Distance teaching can break the integuments of fixed staffing ratios that limited the expansion of education when teacher and student had to be in the same place at the same time.
- There are circumstances under which distance teaching can be cheaper than orthodox education, whether measured in terms of audience reached or of learning.
- The economies achievable by distance education are functions of the level of education, size of audience, choice of media, and sophistication of production.

- Distance teaching can reach audiences who would not be reached by ordinary means.

The following 4 statements address the need to increase dialog:

- It is possible to organize distance teaching in such a way that there is dialog.
- Where a tutor meets distance students face-to-face, the tutor's role is changed from that of a communicator of information to that of a facilitator of learning.
- Group discussion is an effective method of learning when distance teaching is used to bring relevant information to the group.
- In most communities, resources are available that can be used to support distance learning to its educational and economic advantage.

The final 5 statements deal with method:

- A multimedia program is likely to be more effective than one that relies on a single medium.
- A systems approach is helpful in planning distance education.
- Feedback is a necessary part of a distance learning system.
- To be effective, distance teaching materials should ensure that students undertake frequent and regular activities over and above reading, watching, or listening.
- In choosing between media, the key decision on which the rest depend concerns the use of face-to-face learning.

Equivalency Theory: An Emerging American Theory of Distance Education

The impact of new technologies on distance education is far-ranging. Desmond Keegan (1995) suggests that electronically linking instructor and students at various locations creates a virtual classroom. Keegan goes on to state:

> The theoretical analyses of virtual education, however, have not yet been addressed by the literature: Is it a subset of distance education or to be regarded as a separate field of educational endeavor? What are its didactic structures? What is the relationship of its cost effectiveness and of its educational effectiveness to distance education and to conventional education? (p. 21)

It is in this environment of virtual education that the equivalency theory of distance education has emerged. Some advocates of distance education have mistakenly tried to provide identical instructional situations for all students, no matter when or where they learn. Since it is more difficult to control the situations of distant learners, some have decided that all learners should participate as distant learners. This is based on the belief that learners should have identical opportunities to learn. This is a mistake. Simonson theorizes that for distance education to be successful in the United States its appropriate application should be based on the belief that the more equivalent the learning experiences of distant students are to that of local students, the more equivalent will be the outcomes of the learning experience. In other words, each learner might use different instructional strategies, varying instructional resources, or individually prescribed activities. If the distance education course is effectively designed and equivalent experiences are available, then potential learners will reach the course's instructional objectives.

This theory is based on the emerging definition of distance education as formal, institutionally based education that takes place using interactive telecommunication systems. Simonson and Schlosser (1995) in elaborating on this theory state:

> It should not be necessary for any group of learners to compensate for different, possibly lesser, instructional experiences. Thus, those developing distance educational systems should strive to make equivalent the learning experiences of all students no matter how they are linked to the resources or instruction they require. (pp. 71–72)

One key to this theoretical approach is the concept of equivalency. Local and distant learners have fundamentally different environments in which they learn. It is the responsibility of the distance educator to design learning events that provide experiences with equal value for learners. Just as a triangle and a square may have the same area and be considered equivalent even though they are quite different geometrical shapes, the experiences of the local learner and the distant learner should have equivalent value even though these experiences might be quite different.

Another key to this approach is the concept of the learning experience. A learning experience is anything that promotes learning, including what is observed, felt, heard, or done. It is likely that different students in various locations, learning at different times, may require a different mix of learning experiences. Some will need a greater amount of observing, and others a larger dosage of doing. The goal of instructional planning is to make the sum of experiences for each learner equivalent. Instructional design procedures should attempt to anticipate and provide the collection of experiences that will be most suitable for each student or group of students.

This approach is supported by Shale (1988), who argued that distance education is not a distinct field of education. He states that the process of education when students and teacher are face-to-face is the same as when students and teachers are at a distance.

A Theoretical Framework for Distance Education—Desmond Keegan

Keegan (1986) suggested that the theoretician had to answer three questions before developing a theory of distance education:

- *Is distance education an educational activity?* Keegan's answer was that, although distance education institutions possess some of the characteristics of businesses, rather than of traditional schools, their educational activities are dominant. Distance education is a more industrialized form of education. The theoretical bases for distance education, Keegan pointed out, were within general education theory.
- *Is distance education a form of conventional education?* Keegan believed that, because distance education was not based on interpersonal communication and is

characterized by a privatization of institutionalized learning (as is conventional education), it is a distinct form of education. Therefore, while the theoretical basis for distance education could be found within general education theory, it could not be found within the theoretical structures of oral, group-based education.

However, Keegan considered virtual systems based on teaching face-to-face at a distance a new cognate field of study to distance education. He believed that a theoretical analysis of virtual education still needed to be addressed.

- *Is distance education possible, or is it a contradiction in terms?* Keegan pointed out that if education requires intersubjectivity—a shared experience in which teacher and learner are united by a common zeal—then distance education is a contradiction in terms. Distance instruction is possible, but distance education is not.

Again, the advent of virtual systems used in distance education challenges the traditional answer to this question.

Central to Keegan's concept of distance education is the separation of the teaching acts in time and place from the learning acts. Successful distance education, he believes, requires the reintegration of the two acts:

> The intersubjectivity of teacher and learner, in which learning from teaching occurs, has to be artificially recreated. Over space and time, a distance system seeks to reconstruct the moment in which the teaching-learning interaction occurs. The linking of learning materials to learning is central to this process. (pp. 43–45)

Reintegration of the act of teaching at a distance is attempted in two ways. First, learning materials, both print and nonprint, are designed to achieve as many of the characteristics of interpersonal communication as possible. Second, when courses are presented, reintegration of the teaching act is attempted by a variety of techniques, including communication by correspondence, telephone tutorial, online computer communication, comments on assignments by tutors or computers, and teleconferences.

The process of reintegrating the act of teaching in distance education, Keegan suggests, results in at least five changes to the normal structure of oral, group-based education:

- The industrialization of teaching
- The privatization of institutional learning
- Change of administrative structure
- Different plant and buildings
- Change of costing structures

Keegan offers three hypotheses drawn from his theoretical framework:

- Distance students have a tendency to drop out of those institutions in which structures for the reintegration of the teaching acts are not satisfactorily achieved.
- Distance students have difficulty achieving quality of learning in those institutions in which structures for the reintegration of the teaching acts are not satisfactorily achieved.
- The status of learning at a distance may be questioned in those institutions in which the reintegration of the teaching acts is not satisfactorily achieved.

FORDISM, NEO-FORDISM, POST-FORDISM: A THEORETICAL DEBATE

Recently, Peters's view of distance education has received renewed attention. His theory of industrialized education is a point of departure and is extended and revised based on contemporary industrial transformation in a debate on the future of distance education. *Fordism* and *post-Fordism* are the terms borrowed from industrial sociology to classify the opposing views of the debate. This debate deals with changes in the practice of distance education and represents wider debates about the nature of change in the contemporary period (Edwards, 1995). While not all would agree that the Fordist framework applies to distance education (Rumble, 1995a, 1995b, 1995c), it has become the mainstream theory of distance education in international literature and provides a useful analogy in debating the practice of distance education.

The term *Fordism* is derived from Henry Ford's approach to the mass production for mass consumption of automobiles early in the 20th century. *Fordism, neo-Fordism,* and *post-Fordism* are terms that represent three ways to conceptualize the production of distance education. Each of these ideal-type models suggests very different social, political, and educational outcomes. Badham and Mathews (1989) provide a clear model for understanding the three categories of distance education production.

They proposed that a firm's production process and its production strategy can be defined in terms of these three variables—product variety, process innovation, and labor responsibility—and they suggested that a production paradigm represents an exemplary model of efficient production, which guides organizational strategy.

In looking at these three variables, Fordism would be described as having low product innovation, low process variability, and low labor responsibility. Neo-Fordism would have high product innovation and high process variability, but would maintain the low labor responsibility of the Fordism definition. High product innovation, high process variability, and high labor responsibility would typify the post-Fordism model. Campion (1995) illustrated how these three different production processes relate to distance education:

- *The Fordist strategy* for distance education suggested a fully centralized, single-mode, national distance education provider, gaining greater economies of scale by offering courses to a mass market, thereby justifying a greater investment in more expensive course materials. Rationalization of this kind allows for increased administrative control and a more extreme division of labor as the production process is fragmented in an increasing number of component tasks.
- *The neo-Fordist strategy* extends the Fordist system by allowing much higher levels of flexibility and diversity, and by combining low volumes with high levels of product and process innovation. However, neo-Fordist production retains a highly centralized Fordist approach to labor organization and control. A neo-Fordist expression of distance education might well be represented by a centrally controlled, perhaps multinational, yet locally administered model of distance education. By also using self-instructional course materials for teaching on-campus students, it has the potential to massively reduce costs across the whole student population. However, and most important, a neo-Fordist manifestation

of distance education bears a strong relationship to that of the Fordist route inasmuch as it has an overall despoiling effect on academic staff.

■ *High levels of all three variables characterize the post-Fordist strategy:* product innovation, process variability, and labor responsibility. It is opposed to neo-Fordism and to Fordism, dispensing with a division of labor and rigid managerial control and deliberately fostering a skilled and responsible workforce. A post-Fordist model of distance education would be decentralized and retain integration between the study modes. Academic staff would, however, retain autonomous control of their administered courses, and in so doing, would be able rapidly to adjust course curriculum and delivery to the changing needs of students.

In general, Fordist distance education involves mass production for mass consumption. It encompasses centralized control, a division of work tasks associated with distance education, and the creation of management for the division of the work tasks. Courses are developed by a small core of skilled workers and delivered centrally with a de-skilling effect on the teacher. In a neo-Fordist system course development, delivery and administration are mixed between a centralized office and regional or local offices. This allows for more flexibility in course development and delivery. In the neo-Fordist model, the teacher is still given little responsibility beyond delivering the developed materials. The post-Fordist approach to distance education would focus on the consumer rather than the product. Administration would be decentralized, democratic, and participatory, and the division of labor would be informal and flexible. Teachers would have a high responsibility to develop curriculum and respond to the learning needs of their students. Much of education as it developed over the past century fits the Fordist paradigm. Renner (1995) states that education became a formalized system of production that could be monitored, maintained, and controlled in the same way as the factory. The practice of distance education has also been greatly influenced by the Fordist paradigm. It has been argued that Fordism is still the dominant international paradigm in distance education.

Distance education has been influenced by the Fordist paradigm because it is the model that has been most successful in business throughout this century. Evans (1995) states that distance education can be seen as both a product and a process of modernity. Its administrative systems, distribution networks, and print production processes are characteristic of modern societies with developed mass production, consumption, and management. The Fordist approach to distance education provides cost-efficiencies and quality production of materials unachievable outside of the Fordist model. In addition, global competition in distance education will favor the marketing power of large educational providers. The Fordist approach to the practice of distance education provides obvious advantages.

However, major concerns about the continuation of the Fordist paradigm in distance education have been expressed. These concerns revolve around the following themes:

1. Mass markets for delivered instruction have changed, reducing the demand for centrally produced instruction for mass delivery.

2. The Fordism model is unable to adapt to the needs of a fast-changing society.
3. The focus on instructional production and the systematic use of preprogrammed curricula are incompatible with higher levels of educational quality.

With heightened competition, diversification of demand, and rapid developments in communication and information technology, the Fordist rationale, which presumes a uniform mass market to support mass production, is inappropriate. As a result, the cost-effectiveness and cost-efficiency of centrally developed and delivered instruction has declined. Ding (1995), in reporting on China's distance education system, indicates that the market for many of the traditional disciplines is close to saturation, while there are many demands for specific disciplines and specialties. However, Ding states that a relatively small demand exists in each specialty, such as English for foreign trade, tourist economics, manufacture of household appliances, and so on. In addition, different regions of the country report differing needs. Renner concludes that open education markets are becoming more fragmented, competitive, and specialized. A search for more efficient and flexible forms of organizational structure is an inescapable outcome.

The Fordist structure is not well suited to easily adapt to the changing needs in society. If we combine an increasingly differentiated consumer market with the power and speed of contemporary interactive computer communications technologies and add to this a more highly educated workforce, then the bureaucratic practices of the past would seem far from sustainable. This new environment requires a flexible structure in which ideas are readily tried and shared. In China, Ding found that the Fordist structure could not adapt itself to the new conditions of the market immediately and quickly. He stated that the Fordist structure could not adapt curricula to the regional needs of the country or alter the structure and content of the course to the needs of the students. The answer, according to Renner, is to place an emphasis on labor flexibility that would allow individual academics to produce and deliver quality curriculum more readily customized to student needs. It is felt that post-Fordist systems of distance education would be able to rapidly respond to the needs of society.

Renner's statement that the systematic use of preprogrammed curricula is incompatible with higher levels of educational quality suggests a controversy that goes beyond the debate on Fordism. Preprogrammed curricula used in the Fordist approach to distance education are products of instructional design based on behaviorism.

Post-Fordism is directly linked to constructivism. Renner states that the relationship between constructivism and post-Fordism is intimate. The constructivist believes that the individual gives meaning to the world through experience. Ideally, it is a process of personal and cooperative experimentation, questioning, and problem solving through which meaning can be constructed. This approach to learning is viewed as incompatible with mass production of instructional curricula developed with instructional design methods based in behaviorism that assume a more passive approach to learning. For constructivist learning to occur, teaching must remain flexible and sensitive to learner needs, from intellectual, cognitive, and psychological perspectives. Centrally devised educational courseware that dictates teaching sequences to students and de-skilled tutor-grade staff discourage the customization and construction of knowledge.

For the advocates of post-Fordism, neo-Fordism is no more acceptable than Fordism. Although there is higher product innovation and process variability, labor responsibility is still low. This view of the role of labor divides the new-Fordist approach from the post-Fordist approach. The neo-Fordism division of labor leaves the teacher and the academic staff divorced from research, curriculum development, and scholarly inquiry. They simply deliver the curriculum prepared for them. Proponents of the post-Fordist paradigm have two disagreements with this approach. First, this approach again assumes a behavioral-based instructional design method for curricula development. The preceding paragraph outlined the post-Fordist's concerns about this method. Second, post-Fordists would see this approach as exploiting the worker. High product innovation and high process variability put additional demands on the worker without additional compensation. The neo-Fordism and post-Fordism approaches to distance education are fundamentally different.

The debate about Fordism is intricate, heated, and tied in with differing political, economic, aesthetic, ethical, and educational perspectives. The issues raised in this debate are important because policymakers introduce regulations, generate institutional structures, and effectively organize workplace practices on the basis of such paradigms. How students learn, and frequently what they learn, is a product of these decisions. As the role of distance education is defined in a changing society, these issues need to be given careful consideration.

There is little involvement in the Fordism/post-Fordism debate by American distance educators. In the United States, local control, small classes, rapport between teachers and students, and highly personalized instruction are hailed as important characteristics of its highly respected educational system (Simonson, 1995). This approach to education is diametrically opposed to the mass production, centralized control advocated by a Fordist approach to distance education. While Thach and Murphy (1994) suggest that there is a need for national coordination of higher distance education and that local and state control of education inhibit opportunities for collaboration at a distance among institutions, the United States' traditional approach to education is prevalent. This focus on student needs, personalized instruction, and interaction is evident in the following statement by Michael Moore (1994):

> In a typical United States course that uses teleconferencing technologies to link, let us say, six sites, the curriculum problem is how to integrate the local interests and needs, as well as the local knowledge that lies at each site, into the content to be taught. (p. 5)

SUMMARY

In the rapidly changing and diverse environment in which distance education is practiced, many questions remain unanswered. In this environment it is difficult to arrive at one definition or agree on a theory of how to practice and do research in the field of distance education. New technologies, globalization, and new ideas about student learning challenge the traditional approaches to the practice of distance education. This theme of change is evident in the discussions of distance education and its definition, history, status, and theory.

Numerous definitions of distance education have been proposed. Most include the separation of teacher and learner, the influence of an educational organization, the use of media to unite teacher and learner, the opportunity for two-way communication, and the practice of individualized instruction. The traditional definitions describe distance education as taking place at a different time and in a different place, whereas recent definitions, enabled by new interactive technologies, stress education that takes place at the same time but in a different place. The role of educational organizations in the distance education process has also been challenged. For example, open learning is a form of distance education that occurs without the influence of an educational organization. These issues will continue to be debated as distance educators seek definitions that fit a changing world.

Investigating the relatively brief history of distance education reveals both diversity and an ongoing change in its practice. Historically, diverse practices of distance education have been developed according to the resources and philosophies of the organizations providing instruction. The history also shows that advances in technology have promoted key changes in distance education. These changes have been most evident in the rapid development of electronic communications in recent decades. How the future of distance education will be shaped by the integration of its history and these new technologies is yet to be seen.

Changes in society, politics, economics, and technology are impacting the status of distance education around the world. In some cases, distance education is seen as an answer to inadequate educational opportunities caused by political and/or economic instability. In other situations, established distance education providers are being required by a changing society to convert from mass instruction to a more decentralized approach to meet the diverse needs of their students. In many countries, the need for continuing education or training and access to degree programs is accelerated by the demands of a changing society. Students in rural or isolated parts of the world look to distance education for opportunities to "keep up" with the outside world. Again, technology advances are a major influence for change in distance education worldwide. The globalization of the world enabled by these new technologies will challenge distance educators to rethink the practice of distance education to take advantage of these new opportunities.

The changing and diverse environment in which distance education is practiced has inhibited the development of a single theory upon which to base practice and research. A variety of theories have been proposed to describe traditional distance education. They include theories that emphasize independence and autonomy of the learner, industrialization of teaching, and interaction and communication. These traditional theories emphasize that distance education is a fundamentally different form of education. Recent emerging theories, based on the capabilities of new interactive audio and video systems, state that distance education is not a distinct field of education. Both utilization of existing educational theory and the creation of like experiences for both the distant and local learner are emphasized. Traditional distance education theorists will need to address the changes to distance education facilitated by new technologies. Advocates of the new theories will need to consider their impact on the traditional strengths of distance education. Specifically, the focus of the new theories on face-to-face instruction eliminates the advantage of time-independent learning that traditional theories of distance education value. The debate on these theoretical issues will only increase in the face of continued change. One indication of the impact of change in distance education theory is the Fordist/post-Fordist/neo-Fordist debate. Fordist distance education is administered centrally and involves mass production of curricula for mass consumption. Rapid changes in society have resulted in diverse market needs. The Fordist paradigm is unable to respond quickly to these needs. The post-Fordist paradigm implements a decentralized, democratic administration that focuses on the consumer. In this paradigm, teachers have a high responsibility to respond to individual needs of students. Central to the debate between Fordists and post-Fordists are changing views about how learning occurs. The Fordist approach is based in behaviorism learning theory in which knowledge is delivered to the learner. The constructivist approach to learning in which individuals give meaning to the world through experience underlies the post-Fordist position. The debate on these differences will continue as distance education adapts to meet the needs of a changing society.

An environment in which technology, society, economics, politics, and theories of learning are all in transition suggests that definitions, theories, and the practice of distance education will continue to be contested. This theme of change will both challenge and motivate distance educators and researchers as they strive to understand and develop effective ways to meet the needs of learners around the world.

SELF-TEST QUESTIONS

1. Why are there different definitions of distance education? Discuss and develop the definition that you feel is most appropriate.
2. List Desmond Keegan's five main elements of the various definitions of distance education. Write a paragraph explaining which of the elements is most critical and which is least critical.
3. True/False. Many believe that in the near future the concept of distance will become relatively unimportant. What do you think this means?
4. True/False. Correspondence study is a relatively recent form of distance education that developed during World War II. Is correspondence study still important today?
5. Give at least two reasons for the founding of special distance teaching universities. Why is there no national distance learning university in the United States?
6. True/False. Distance education has a long history in European countries. Why is distance learning considered more commonplace in Europe than in the United States?
7. True/False. Keegan believes that the lack of an accepted theory of distance education has weakened the field. Discuss the importance of theory and how theory helps the practitioner of distance education.

8. List at least two of Wedemeyer's six characteristics of independent study systems. Why would Wedemeyer's perspective be important to American educators?

9. Explain the concept of the assembly line as it relates to the industrialization of teaching. Will industrialized education ever be important in American education? Explain.

10. Give Simonson's emerging theory of distance education. List learning experiences that are different for local and distant learners.

Answers to Self-Test Questions

1. Distance education has evolved as technological media have been developed. Newer technologies make possible different ways to allow students to learn at a distance, and this promotes the development of new definitions of distance education. The practice of a profession determines the definition of the profession.

2. Keegan identified five main elements of these definitions, using them to compose a comprehensive definition of distance education:

   • The quasi-permanent separation of teacher and learner throughout the length of the learning process (this distinguishes it from conventional face-to-face education)

   • The influence of an educational organization both in the planning and preparation of learning materials and in the provision of student support services (this distinguishes it from private study and teach-yourself programs)

   • The use of technical media—print, audio, video, or computer—to unite teacher and learner and carry the content of the course

   • The provision of two-way communication so that the student may benefit from or even initiate dialogue (this distinguishes it from other uses of technology in education)

   • The quasi-permanent absence of the learning group throughout the length of the learning process so that people are usually taught as individuals and not in groups, with the possibility of occasional meetings for both didactic and socialization purposes

3. True.

4. False.

5. Holmberg (1986) cites numerous reasons for the founding of distance teaching universities, including:

   • The need felt in many countries to increase the offerings of university education generally

   • A realization that adults with jobs, family responsibilities, and social commitments form a large group of prospective part-time university students

   • A wish to serve both individuals and society by offering study opportunities to adults, among them disadvantaged groups

   • The need found in many professions for further training at an advanced level

   • A wish to support educational innovation

   • A belief in the feasibility of an economical use of educational resources by mediated teaching

6. True.
7. True.
8. Wedemeyer proposed the separation of teaching from learning as a way of breaking education's "space-time barriers." He suggested six characteristics of independent study systems:
   - The student and teacher are separated.
   - The normal processes of teaching and learning are carried out in writing or through some other medium.
   - Teaching is individualized.
   - Learning takes place through the student's activity.
   - Learning is made convenient for the student in his or her own environment.
   - The learner takes responsibility for the pace of his or her own progress, with freedom to start and stop at any time.
9. Commonly, the assembly line is a method of work in which workers remain stationary, while objects they are working on move past them. In traditional distance education programs, materials for both teacher and student are not the product of an individual. Rather, instructional materials are designed, printed, stored, distributed, and graded by specialists.
10. For distance education to be successful, its appropriate application should be based on the belief that the more similar the learning experience of the distant student is to that of the local student, the more similar will be the outcomes of the learning experience.

For additional information and activities, visit the Prentice Hall Companion Website at http://www.prenhall.com/simonson

REFERENCES

Ackermann, E. (1995). *Learning to use the Internet.* Wilsonville, OR: Franklin, Beedle and Associates Inc.

Badham, R., & Mathews, J. (1989). The new production systems debate. *Labour and Industry, 2*(2), 194–246.

Brookfield, S. (1986). *Understanding and facilitating adult learning.* San Francisco, CA: Jossey-Bass Publishers.

Campion, M. (1995). The supposed demise of bureaucracy: Implications for distance education and open learning—More on the post-Fordism debate. *Distance Education, 16*(2), 192–216.

Cropley, A. J., & Kahl, T. N. (1983). Distance education and distance learning: Some psychological considerations. *Distance Education, 4*(1), 27–39.

Ding, X. (1995). From Fordism to new-Fordism: Industrialisation theory and distance education—a Chinese perspective. *Distance Education, 16*(2), 217–240.

Edwards, R. (1995). Different discourses, discourses of difference: Globalisation, distance education, and open learning. *Distance Education, 16*(2), 241–255.

Evans, T. (1995). Globalisation, post-Fordism and open and distance education. *Distance Education, 16*(2), 256–269.

Garrison, D. R., & Shale, D. (1987). Mapping the boundaries of distance education: Problems in defining the field. *The American Journal of Distance Education, 1*(1), 7–13.

Holmberg, B. (1985). *The feasibility of a theory of teaching for distance education and a proposed theory* (ZIFF Papiere 60). Hagen, (West Germany: Fern Universität, Zentrales Institute fur Fernstudienforschung Arbeitsbereich. (ERIC Document Reproduction Service No. ED290013)

Holmberg, B. (1986). *Growth and structure of distance education.* London: Croom Helm.

Holmberg, B. (1995). *The sphere of distance-education theory revisited.* (ERIC Document Reproduction Service No. ED386578)

Keegan, D. (1986). *The foundations of distance education.* London: Croom Helm.

Keegan, D. (1988). Theories of distance education: Introduction. In D. Sewart, D. Keegan, & B. Holmberg (Eds.), *Distance education: International perspectives* (pp. 63–67). New York: Routledge.

Keegan, D. (1995). *Distance education technology for the new millennium: Compressed video teaching.* (ERIC Document Reproduction Service No. ED389931)

Knowles, M. (1990). *The adult learner: A neglected species* (4th ed.). Houston, TX: Gulf Publishing Co.

Moore, M. (1994). Autonomy and interdependence. *The American Journal of Distance Education, 8*(2), 1–5.

Perraton, H. (1988). A theory for distance education. In D. Sewart, D. Keegan, & B. Holmberg (Eds.), *Distance education: International perspectives* (pp. 34–45). New York: Routledge.

Peters, O. (1988). Distance teaching and industrial production: A comparative interpretation in outline. In D. Sewart, D. Keegan, & B. Holmberg (Eds.), *Distance education: International perspectives* (pp. 95–113). New York: Routledge.

Renner, W. (1995). Post-Fordist visions and technological solutions: Education technology and the labour process. *Distance Education, 16*(2), 285–301.

Rumble, G. (1989). On defining distance education. *The American Journal of Distance Education, 3*(2), 8–21.

Rumble, G. (1995a). Labour market theories and distance education I: Industrialisation and distance education. *Open Learning, 10*(1), 10–21.

Rumble, G. (1995b). Labour market theories and distance education II: How Fordist is distance education? *Open Learning, 10*(2), 12–28.

Rumble G. (1995c). Labour market theories and distance education III: Post-Fordism the way forward? *Open Learning, 10*(3), 47–52.

Shale, D. (1988). Toward a reconceptualization of distance education. *The American Journal of Distance Education, 2*(3), 25–35.

Simonson, M. (1995). Overview of the Teacher Education Alliance, Iowa Distance Education Alliance research plan. In C. Sorensen, C. Schlosser, M. Anderson, & M. Simonson (Eds.), *Encyclopedia of distance education research in Iowa* (pp. 3–6). Ames, IA: Teacher Education Alliance.

Simonson, M., & Schlosser, C. (1995). More than fiber: Distance education in Iowa. *Tech Trends, 40*(3), 13–15.

Thach, L., & Murphy, L. (1994). Collaboration in distance education: From local to international perspectives. *The American Journal of Distance Education, 8*(3), 5–21.

Wedemeyer, C. (1981). *Learning at the backdoor.* Madison, WI: University of Wisconsin Press.

ADDITIONAL READINGS

Albright, M. (1988). *A conceptual framework for the design and the delivery of a university-level credit course by communications satellite.* Unpublished doctoral dissertation, Iowa State University, Ames.

Barry, M., & Runyan, G. B. (1995). A review of distance-learning studies in the U.S. military. *The American Journal of Distance Education, 9*(3), 37–47.

Bruder, I. (1989). Distance learning: What's holding back this boundless delivery system? *Electronic Learning, 8*(6), 30–35.

Buckland, M., & Dye, C. M. (1991). *The development of electronic distance education delivery systems in the United States. Recurring and emerging themes in history and philosophy of education.* (ERIC Document Reproduction Service No. ED345713)

Holmberg, B. (1989). *Theory and practice of distance education.* London: Routledge.

Johnson, J. K. (1988). *Attitudes of high school students in small rural schools toward interactive satellite instruction.* Unpublished master's thesis, Iowa State University, Ames.

Keegan, D. (1988). On defining distance education. In D. Sewart, D. Keegan, & B. Holmberg (Eds.), *Distance education: International perspectives* (pp. 6–33). New York: Routledge.

Lintz, M., & Tognotti, S. (1996). Distance education on the WWW [World Wide Web]. Available: http://tecfa.unige.ch/edu-ws94/contrib/peraya.fm.html.

Magnus, J. (1996). Distance education in Sub-Saharan Africa: The next five years. *Innovations in Education and Training International, 33*(1), 50–56.

Riel, M., & Harasim, L. (1994). Research perspectives on network learning. *Machine-Mediated Learning, 4* (2–3), 91–113.

Rose, S. N. (1991). Collegiate-based noncredit courses. In B. B. Watkins & S. J. Wright (Eds.), *The foundations of American distance education* (pp. 67–92). Dubuque, IA: Kendall/Hunt.

Simonson, M. (1995). Distance education revisited: An introduction to the issue. *Tech Trends, 40*(30), 2.

Simonson, M. (1995). Does anyone really want to learn at a distance? *Tech Trends, 40*(3), 2.

Sorensen, C., Maushak, N., & Lozada, M. (1996). *Iowa Distance Education Alliance preliminary evaluation report.* Ames: Iowa State University, Research Institute for Studies in Education.

Tompkins, L. S. (1993). A new light on distance learning—Fiber optics. *Journal of Educational Technology Systems, 21*(3), 265–275.

U.S. Department of Education. (1995). *The Star Schools program.* (Available from Star Schools, U.S. Department of Education, 555 New Jersey Avenue NW, Washington, DC 20208-5644)

Watkins, B. L. (1991). A quite radical idea: The invention and elaboration of collegiate correspondence study. In B. L. Watkins, & S. J. Wright (Eds.), *The Foundations of American Distance Education* (pp. 1–35). Dubuque, IA: Kendall/Hunt.

Young, J. R. (1995). Classes on the Web. *Chronicle of Higher Education,* November 3, A27, A32–A33.

chapter 3

RESEARCH AND DISTANCE EDUCATION

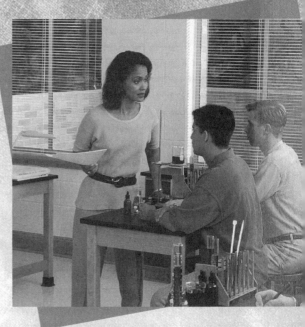

CHAPTER GOAL
The purpose of this chapter is to summarize the research on distance education.

CHAPTER OBJECTIVES
After reading and reviewing this chapter, you should be able to

1. Explain research dealing with learning outcomes in distance education environments.
2. Explain research on learner perceptions concerning distance education.
3. Explain research on learner attributes and other variables in distance education situations.
4. Describe research related to interaction in distance education.
5. Summarize research on distance education.

THE FOCUS OF DISTANCE EDUCATION RESEARCH

Emerging technologies have forced a redefinition of distance education. At the same time, the distance education research agenda has also evolved. The focus has shifted to a more learner-centered approach. Researchers are not merely looking at achievement but are examining learner attributes and perceptions, as well as interaction patterns and how these contribute to the overall learning environment. Although there is continued interest in the technology, the focus is not on which medium is best, but on what attributes of the medium can contribute to a positive, equivalent learning experience. This chapter will provide a review of distance education research literature. In his 1987 article, "The Development of Distance Education Research," Börje Holmberg, a leading distance education theorist and researcher, suggested that the structure of distance education research include:

- Philosophy and theory of distance education
- Distance students and their milieu, conditions, and study motivations
- Subject matter presentation
- Communication and interaction between students and their supporting organization (tutors, counselors, administrators, other students)
- Administration and organization
- Economics
- Systems (comparative distance education, typologies, evaluation, etc.)
- History of distance education

Leading researchers attending the Third Distance Education Research Symposium-Conference organized discussions around four areas: course design, instruction, policy and administration, and learners and learning. In the area of course design, the need for evaluation of learner affective reactions, learning, transfer of knowledge to other settings, and impact on the organization was stressed. Research to support the intuitive sense that interaction is important and necessary is needed under research on instruction.

LEARNING OUTCOMES

> It is likely that when different media treatments of the same informational content to the same students yield similar learning results, the cause of the results can be found in a method which the two treatments share in common . . . *give up your enthusiasm* for the belief that media attributes cause learning. (Clark, 1994, p. 28)

Hundreds of media comparison studies indicate, unequivocally, that no inherent significant difference exists in the achievement effectiveness of media (Clark, 1983). These results support Clark's position summarized in the above quote. The specific medium does not matter. That being the case, the focus of future research should be on instruction itself since it is the truly critical factor in determining student achievement (Whittington, 1987).

Unfortunately, much of the research in distance education is still of the media comparison type. This is to be expected given the rapid development of distance education technology, especially in the area of two-way interactive television systems. With each technological advance, the temptation is to conduct media comparison research on the off chance that the new technology might truly bring about higher student achievement.

A typical study reported by Cheng, Lehman, and Armstrong (1991) compared performance of graduate-level students enrolled in traditional and computer conferencing classrooms. The on-campus class had 25 graduate students, and the off-campus group included 28 in-service teachers. The groups differed significantly only in age; the average age of the off-campus students was older. A pretest/posttest format was used measuring attitude and knowledge. Results indicated no significant difference in overall course performance or in attitudes.

Bruning, Landis, Hoffman, and Grosskopf (1993) compared learning outcomes of an interactive telecourse in introductory high school Japanese with those of a traditional class. The telecourse originated in Nebraska and was transmitted to 170 schools (911 students) the first year, 255 schools (1,157 students) the second year, and 259 schools (1,330 students) the third year. The achievement test had two parts and measured listening and writing.

An evaluation of the first year showed that the achievement of students in the telecourse schools was significantly higher than that of students in the comparison schools for both listening and writing. The results for the second year were similar. The researchers observed that the older students in the distant class were highly motivated, and this had a significant impact on their achievement, much more than the fact that they learned at a distance.

Additional data were collected in the third year to investigate possible effects of motivation (measured by self-efficacy rating) and differences in student characteristics of self-reported grades in school and prior language learning experience. The mean achievement test scores for the telecourse students continued to be significantly higher than those of students in the comparison schools even when the variables of self-efficacy, self-reported ability, and prior language experience were controlled. This indicates that the achievement differences between the telecourse students and the comparison group were not related to motivational, self-reported ability, or prior experience factors.

A study by Martin and Rainey (1993) compared the effectiveness of interactive satellite delivery with that of traditional instruction. There was no important difference between the two groups on the pretest. However, the average posttest score for the experimental group, the students who participated in the course by satellite, was significantly higher than that of the control group.

Bramble and Martin (1995) investigated the effectiveness of teletraining in the military. Participants were 275 individuals enrolled in five different teletraining project courses. Standard multiple-proficiency, criterion-based tests were used where available, and achievement tests were developed for the other courses. In all but one course, both pretests and posttests were administered.

Students were allowed a second chance at taking the proficiency tests, and when these retakes were taken into account, all students reached acceptable performance levels. No comparison data were available from schools offering these courses in traditional settings, but knowledgeable training personnel indicated that this performance is as high as or higher than one would normally expect. In all courses where precourse and postcourse performances were measured, the gain was statistically significant.

Students in all five courses were asked if they felt the teletraining was as effective as live instruction. In all but one of the courses, 75% or more responded in the affirmative.

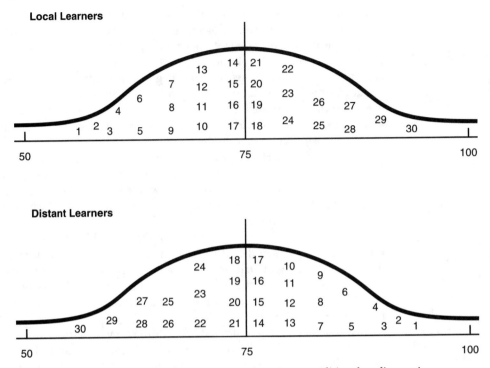

FIGURE 3–1   Example: Achievement of students learning at traditional or distant sites.

The course that had only a 54% affirmative rate was the first course offered, and adjustments may have been made prior to delivery of the other courses. This pattern was repeated when students were asked if they felt that the instructor was in the same room. For the first class only 78% responded yes, while for subsequent classes 84% or more responded in the affirmative.

Although comparative research studies on achievement tend to show no significant difference between different delivery systems and between distance education and traditional education, several recent studies indicate a significant higher achievement level for those learning at a distance (Figure 3–1). The accepted position is that the delivery system affects no inherent difference on achievement (Clark, 1994), therefore future research needs to examine what factors do, indeed, contribute to this difference in achievement. In general, a safe conclusion is that distant and local learners will achieve at the same level, and that distance education is an effective method for delivering instruction that works. In other words, distance is not a predictor of learning.

LEARNER PERCEPTIONS

Ross, Morrison, Smith, and Cleveland (1991) evaluated two programs for tutoring at-risk elementary school children at a distance: One used a local electronic bulletin board system, and the other used Applelink, a national network system featuring both electronic mail and teleconferencing. For both studies, both tutor and tutee attitudes were assessed.

In the first program, student reactions ranged from mixed to negative. More than half of the students did not understand corrections made by their tutors, received little help with their writing skills, did not have enough time with their tutors, found the assignments difficult, and said they did not learn much from their tutors. On the positive side, slightly more than half the students felt they had enough online time to complete messages.

Most tutors felt they possessed the computer skills and content knowledge to do the work. They also felt they related well to their tutees and had the materials necessary. A need for more intensive training was expressed, and a majority (67%) said they would have liked more personal contact with their students.

More positive results were found in the second study. Tutees felt they had a positive relationship with their tutors and preferred talking to their tutors instead of their friends. They regretted the limited amount of time for online communication.

The tutors, similar to those in the first study, felt they possessed the necessary skills. They cited communication problems as a negative aspect. Many (60%) expressed indecision on whether they had found the experience enjoyable or not.

Distant learner satisfaction is an important dimension in understanding the success of interactive telecourses. Biner, Dean, and Mellinger (1994) conducted two studies to identify the major dimensions of learner satisfaction. In the first study, the telecourse evaluation questionnaire (TEQ), developed by Biner, was administered to 201 students enrolled in live, interactive televised courses at the beginning of the last class meeting. Using factor analysis, the researchers identified seven factors, including satisfaction with:

- Instructor/instruction
- Technology
- Course management
- At-site personnel
- Promptness of material delivery
- Support services
- Out-of-class communication with the instructor

The second study, conducted the following year, confirmed the results of the preliminary study. The researchers concluded by emphasizing the importance of assessment of learner satisfaction to the overall success of a distance education program.

Jegede and Kirkwood (1994) investigated the anxiety level of distance education students and the factors contributing to anxiety. Two instruments, an anxiety checklist and an opinionnaire on factors that affect learning at a distance, were administered at the beginning of the semester and at the end of the semester. Complete results were obtained from 222 distance education students enrolled at the University of Southern Queensland.

Analysis of data from the anxiety checklist indicated that participants had a high anxiety level and were generally more anxious about their studies at the end of the semester than at the beginning. Results showed a statistically significant difference between the presemester means and the postsemester means.

A factor analysis of the opinionnaire identified seven factors affecting learning at a distance: content, environment, finances, readiness, time, employment, and family support. A comparison of presemester and postsemester opinions showed five factors were significantly different at the end of the class than at the beginning. Students' concerns related to content, finance, and readiness were higher at the beginning of the class than at the end, while concerns related to time and employment increased toward the end of the class (Jegede & Kirkwood, 1994).

The results of this study indicated that anxiety felt by distance education learners played a higher role in attrition than previously considered. The researchers suggested future research on the role of anxiety probably comparing on-campus with off-campus students, along with the introduction of other variables like achievement outcomes and a longer period of study.

As part of a larger study, Sorensen (1995) identified the most important predictors of student satisfaction. Surveys were returned by 210 community college students enrolled in two-way interactive televised courses. In general, the students were satisfied with their distance learning experience.

Fast (1995) investigated multisite instruction of students enrolled in foreign language courses delivered by fiber-optics that allowed interactive instruction. Nineteen students participated in the study, 11 at the origination site and 8 at the remote site. Post-instruction questionnaires administered to all students provided data on three variables: student motivation, perceived learning, and involvement. Remote students had a significantly more favorable attitude toward interactive TV than the origination-site students. Responses to open-ended questions requesting the likes and dislikes of interactive TV classes help clarify this difference.

Students at both locations cited two reasons for liking the multisite instruction: human interest and facilitation of learning. Students at the remote site felt the delivery system provided opportunities for learning that would not be available otherwise.

The two groups differed strongly on their list of dislikes. A high number (over 40%) of the dislikes identified by the origination-site students were organizational issues. Of special concern was the loss of class time because of the need to transport students to the technology classroom. This was not an issue for the remote-site students.

The majority of criticisms (60%) from the remote-site students focused on problems with interaction. They disliked the lack of opportunity to interact one-on-one with the instructor. Discussions were difficult because everyone talked at once, and posing questions necessitated interrupting class. Origination-site students also identified the loss of interaction with the instructor as a problem. These results suggested that remote-site students tended to experience difficulty in being accepted as part of the discourse, whereas origination-site students found it more difficult to share their teacher with the remote-site group. Analysis of questions related to perceived learning showed no important differences between remote-site students and on-site students.

A similar situation was found when data about perceptions of interaction were analyzed. Although there were no important differences between sites, there was a major difference between learning group levels. Higher level students at the remote site indicated that having the teacher at a distance hindered learning.

Research related to learners' perceptions has focused on identifying factors related to satisfaction, attitudes, and perceived learning and interaction. Factors affecting satisfaction are often considered to be organizational and involve the environment, management, and support services. In other words, there are identifiable factors that relate to distant learners' perceptions about the effectiveness of their instructional experiences, and these factors are similar to those of local, traditional learners.

LEARNER ATTRIBUTES

Coggins (1988), in a study of students associated with the University of Wisconsin System External Degree Program, examined the relationship between personal variables (learning style and demographic data) and program completion rate. She found that completers and noncompleters did not differ significantly on variables related to gender, occupation, marital status, presence or absence of children, distance from campus, or age of entry into the baccalaureate program. However, significant differences existed between the two groups for a number of other variables. Completers had entered the program with higher levels of education, and they had greater expectations of earning higher grades as well as greater expectations of earning a degree. The two groups of students differed in their preference for course content. Noncompleters tended to be more concrete learners, preferring a content that allowed them to work with things instead of people. Completers preferred a content that involved interviewing and counseling of people.

The relationship between gender and success in distance education courses was the subject of a study by Ross and Powell (1990). Data from Athabasca University, in Alberta, Canada, indicated that a greater percentage of women passed distance education courses. Further, this higher completion trend was visible irrespective of the student's general study area, the specific course selection, the course level, the mode of course delivery, the student's program status, or the number of courses the student had previously taken. An exploratory analysis assessing demographic, motivational, support, and learning style variables indicated some possible reasons for the gender differences in academic achievement. These include differences in marital status, employment, and use of institutional support between the two groups. An important difference was noted in the motivational variable. Women felt gaining a university credential was critical and the impact of failing was serious.

Dille and Mezack (1991) studied locus of control and learning style as predictors of risk among college distance education students. In their study, 151 students enrolled in telecourses completed the assessment instruments, which included demographic information, the internal-external locus of control scale (IELC), and the learning style inventory (LSI).

The locus of control measure was a significant predictor of two variables: success, defined as receiving a grade of C or above, and actual letter grade. Students with a more internal locus of control were more likely to be successful and to obtain a higher grade. Students with an external locus of control were less likely to persevere when faced with the perceived tougher challenge of a telecourse.

An analysis of the data from the learning style inventory indicated that students who were more successful had a lower LSI average score measuring concrete experience. On the abstract conceptualization/concrete experience scale where a lower score indicated a more concrete learner, successful students had a significantly higher score than non-successful students. These findings support the idea that the less concrete one's learning style, the better suited one is to learn in the telecourse format. Although examining the abstract/concrete scale was helpful in predicting success in a distance learning environment, individual learning style was not found to be a significant predictor of success.

Based on Dille and Mezack's (1991) study, the profile of a high-risk telecourse student would be:

- 25 years or older
- Divorced
- Less than 30 college credit hours completed
- GPA less than 3.0–2.9
- external locus of control
- Lower than average AC-CE score, indicating an abstract learner

Laube (1992) examined the relationship between academic and social integration variables and the persistence of students in a secondary distance education program. Students were divided into two groups based on persistence. Completer/persisters were those who completed or still persisted in coursework 1 year after enrollment, whereas dropout/nonstarters had dropped out during the same time.

Out of 351 surveys mailed, 181 surveys were returned, 124 in the completer/persister group and 57 in the dropout/nonstarter group. Interestingly, in the non-returned surveys there were 44 completer/persisters and 126 dropout/nonstarters.

Two variables showed important differences between the groups. Completer/persisters were more likely than dropout/nonstarters (1) to have higher educational goals and (2) to study more than 10 hours a week.

Three variables related to social integration were studied: self-initiated contact with the school, student attitudes toward their tutors, and student attitudes toward missing peer socialization. The two groups differed significantly only in their attitudes toward their tutors, with completer/persisters indicating a more positive attitude. Both groups indicated a positive attitude toward their tutors, but a large percentage of dropout/nonstarters selected "undecided" as a response, which contributed to the significant results obtained. Stone (1992) examined the relationship of contact with a tutor and locus of control to course completion rates for students enrolled in print-based, distance training courses. One group received weekly phone calls from the training staff, whereas the second group received only minimal feedback. Results did not show any important difference between the two groups in course completion rates. However, Stone did find that students with relatively external loci of control completed their coursework at significantly faster rates when exposed to regular telephone cues from their tutors.

How study practices and attitudes of students in a distance learning program relate to academic success was examined by Bernt and Bugbee (1993). This study examined approximately 300 students. The most important result reported was that students who were considered high passers were likely to have advanced degrees.

Two types of study strategies with distance education students were also examined. The researchers concluded that those who passed differed significantly from failers in their test strategies, concentration, and time management skills, but they were not significantly different in active processing of information, diligence, and positive attitude.

The researchers also found that students with varying education levels differed in their study strategies, notably time management, concentration, and testing strategies. This, they concluded, suggested that distance learning students who have not completed college are "at risk" primarily because they lack metacognitive or executive skills for approaching coursework and taking examinations. Distance education instructors need to be aware that, similar to traditional education students, learners are different and some need more direction and structure than others.

Garland (1993) used ethnographic procedures to identify barriers to persistence in distance education. Building on the framework of Rubenson (1986), Garland classified barriers into four categories: situational, institutional, dispositional, and epistemological. Face-to-face interviews were conducted with 47 students enrolled in primarily print-based introductory academic courses. Participants in the study included 17 students who did not complete the final exam and 30 persisting students, students who took the final exam regardless of outcome.

Barriers to persistence in all four categories were encountered by both withdrawal students and persisting students. Situational barriers included poor learning environment and lack of time. Students indicated that a lack of support from both family and peers contributed to poor learning environments. They also identified resource availability and a quiet place to study as important. Students felt the course took more time than anticipated, especially as many were juggling the demands of work, home, and school.

Cost, institutional procedures, and course scheduling/pacing were reported as institutional barriers. In this study, students said that tuition was not a problem, but add-on costs of texts and labs were seen as barriers to persistence. Students who felt the university did not try to meet their needs identified both institutional procedures and course scheduling/pacing as problems. Limited office hours made reaching staff for assistance difficult.

The largest number of barriers to persistence related to the psychological and sociological nature of the student. These barriers included: (1) uncertainty of an educational or professional goal, (2) stress of multiple roles (school, work, home), (3) time management problems, (4) problems associated with learning style differences, and (5) adult pride indicated by overachievement and/or fear of failure. The study pointed to the individualness of learning, whether at a distance or in a traditional setting. Regardless of the setting, the focus needs to be on creating optimal learning conditions for each individual.

Pugliese (1994) investigated psychological variables as predictors of persistence in telecourses. Variables studied included loneliness, communication apprehension, communication competence, and locus of control. Of those urban commuter students enrolled in telecourses, 306 (a 39% response rate) responded to Pugliese's telephone survey.

The study's results were interesting. In a traditional classroom, it would be expected that the students possessing greater social interaction skills would be more likely to persist and complete the course. Results appeared to indicate that telecourses were the social equalizer. Telecourses apparently minimize the impact of social skills.

Fjortoft (1995) similarly investigated predictors of persistence in distance learning programs. Fjortoft developed a model, based on the literature of adult education, that related adult learners to persistence. The variables studied included age, gender, grade point average at the time of college graduation, satisfaction with the college experience, intrinsic job satisfaction, ease of learning on one's own, intrinsic benefits of degree completion, and extrinsic benefits of degree completion. Persistence was defined by active enrollment status.

The 395 students surveyed included those actively enrolled in a distance learning program in pharmacy and those who had been admitted but had withdrawn before completion. The response rate was 50%, with a sample size of 198.

Three variables were significant in predicting persistence in distance learning programs. Results indicated a positive relationship between perceived intrinsic benefits and continued enrollment, whereas a negative relationship between both age and ease of learning on their own and persistence was indicated. An internal desire for more satisfaction and challenge in one's career more than desires for enhanced salary and career mobility motivated adults to continue their education. The respondents ranged in age from the upper 20s to just over 60. Results indicated it was more difficult for the older students to persist in the distance learning program than it was for younger students.

Fjortoft concluded that only individuals who recognized that they possessed the skills necessary to learn on their own elected to enter a distance learning program. Alternatively, adults might not be able to realistically assess their individual learning styles.

Biner, Bink, Huffman, and Dean (1995) investigated the role of personality characteristics in predicting achievement in televised courses. The Sixteen Personality Factor Questionnaire was administered to both traditional-course and televised-course students to determine how the two groups differed and also to identify personality factors predictive of success in televised courses.

The personality profiles of the two groups differed. Telecourse students tended to be more intelligent, emotionally stable, trusting, compulsive, passive, and conforming than traditional students.

Results indicated that several personality characteristics correlated significantly with course achievement. The group-oriented/self-sufficient student was more likely to have high performance, indicating successful telecourse students tended to be self-sufficient. A negative relationship was found between the introvert/extrovert dimension and course performance. This indicated that the more introverted a student was, the better the student performed in a distance education setting.

Higher levels of expedience were associated with higher grades in the telecourse group. This was in contrast to higher levels of conscientiousness associated with higher grades in the traditional course group. Telecourse students tended to be older and were juggling responsibilities of job and home.

A review of the above studies indicates that several learner characteristics have some effect on the success of the learner in a distance education environment. Although studies on the effects of gender indicated mixed results, students who were younger and had a higher level of education were more likely to complete a distance education course.

Motivation is important. Intrinsically motivated learners and those with high expectations for grades and completion of a degree tended to have higher success rates. A positive attitude toward the instructor would also be a factor contributing to the success of distant learners.

Dille and Mezack (1991) and Stone (1992) both found locus of control to be a significant factor. More abstract learners with internal locus of control and skills in learning alone tended to be more successful. Providing students possessing external locus of control with regular contact with the instructor increased their chances of success. Individual learning style was not a significant predictor of success. Distance education systems proved to be adept in providing for the learning needs of students with a variety of learning styles. Once again, the distant learner and the local learner are not generally different from each other.

INTERACTION

Beare (1989) compared the effectiveness of six instructional formats that allowed differing levels of interaction: (1) lecture, (2) lecture with videotape backup, (3) telelecture, (4) audio-assisted independent study, (5) video-assisted independent study, and (6) video on campus. Study participants consisted of 175 nontraditional teacher education students.

Not surprisingly, given the history of media comparison research, individual instructional formats had little effect on student achievement. The amount of interaction also appeared to have had no impact on student achievement.

Course evaluations yielded some interesting results, however. Analysis showed that distant learners found the course just as stimulating, were equally interested in the subject matter, and judged the instructor equally as skilled as did those receiving face-to-face instruction. The on-site students in the telecourse strongly disliked the medium. It was reported that one night, when the electronic equipment failed temporarily, the class spontaneously cheered. Bauer and Rezabek (1992) compared verbal interaction under three conditions: (1) two-way audio and video, (2) two-way audio, and (3) traditional instruction. The study included 172 students pursuing teacher certification randomly assigned to one of the three treatment groups.

No significant difference existed in total number of interactions between the audio/video group and the audio group. However, a statistically significant difference occurred between the audio/video group and the traditional group as well as between the audio group and the traditional group. Results seem to indicate that merely the addition of video in the distance education format does not increase interaction. This could be a result of the conditioned passive response of individuals to viewing television. Simply measuring interaction may not be the answer in discovering variables contributing to increased interaction.

Souder (1993) investigated interaction and achievement of students in traditional delivery courses compared with students in a distance delivery course. Three groups of students in the same course participated in the study. One group was in a traditional classroom; the second group was on-site with the instructor while the class was broadcast to the third group at a distance. The instructor, the course content, and the course evaluation requirements were the same for each group.

There was no significant difference between the two traditional-delivered courses for evaluation questionnaire items addressing face-to-face interaction. However, the responses of the distance group were significantly different from both the on-site group and the traditional group. The students at a distance defended their distance learning experiences. They did not agree that face-to-face instruction with a live instructor was vital, nor did they believe that real-time interactions with other students were vital. The students in traditional settings disagreed and did not feel that a distance class would be of the same quality as the more traditional approach to instruction.

The results seemed to indicate that students at a distance tended to bond more with their fellow classmates and the instructor. They appeared supportive of each other and, in general, felt they performed better than the other two groups. In fact, the overall achievement of the distance group was significantly higher than that of the on-site group.

Souder (1993) concluded that:

> the distance learners in this study were observed to gain much more than a traditional education from their experiences. They gained a broadened network of valuable colleagues, skills in working with others and collaborating across distances, and many social skills beyond those offered by traditional settings. (p. 50)

Using semistructured personal interviews, May (1993) investigated the contribution of interaction to women's learning experiences in women's studies courses delivered using distance education. Nine women of varied backgrounds and experiences were interviewed. Course delivery was mostly one-way technology, and content focused on the dissemination of knowledge. There was very little interaction.

Students did not appear to miss the interaction or to recognize its potential benefits. The general feeling was that increasing student interaction required arranging face-to-face meetings. Making time for these meetings was not desirable. Distant learners questioned the value and desirability of increased collaboration.

The women in this study did not believe that isolation among distance learners necessitated a negative learning experience. The researcher concluded that increased learner interaction was not an inherently or self-evidently positive educational goal or strategy.

Fulford and Zhang (1993) examined the relationship of perceived interaction and satisfaction in an in-service training course delivered by the Hawaiian Interactive Television System (HITS). In their study, 123 students completed surveys at the beginning, midpoint, and end of a 10-week course. Participants responded to questions about three variables: personal interaction, overall interaction, and satisfaction with the value and quality of instruction.

Level of personal interaction was considered only a moderate predictor of satisfaction. Perceived level of overall interaction was almost three times more important.

Learner satisfaction was considered to be attributed more to perceived overall interactivity than to individual participation. Probably instructors using interactive television should focus more on building group interaction rather than individual participation.

This study also examined the variable of time. Learners' perceptions of interaction and satisfaction decreased over the length of the course; however, overall interaction was a more stable predictor of satisfaction as learners became more experienced with the technology. In a follow-up study, Zhang and Fulford (1994) investigated the variable of time. Participants were 260 students enrolled in a course delivered by HITS. Although this study also looked at perceived interaction and satisfaction, variables were expanded to include attitude toward interaction and actual interaction time determined by analyzing videotapes of each session.

The correlation between perceived interaction and actual interaction time was nonsignificant. Reserving a considerable portion of TV time for interaction, a common strategy among TV instructors, did not seem to be quite as important as some suggest. This seems to support the work of May (1993), which indicated that more interaction was not necessarily better.

Although the correlation between actual interaction time and attitude was clear, the relationship between perceived interaction and attitude was near perfect. Similar relationships were found when correlating actual interaction and perceived interaction with satisfaction. Increasing interaction time merely for more time's sake is not necessary.

Communication and teaching patterns that contributed to student participation were examined in a study by Schoenfelder (1995). Schoenfelder studied 44 students and 11 teachers participating in interactive television courses. A questionnaire was used to measure teachers' and students' perceptions of ways to increase interaction and involvement.

Both teachers and students thought that an enthusiastic teacher with a sense of humor was an important factor in enhancing involvement. They also felt that addressing students by name and providing timely feedback were factors that made a positive contribution to interaction. Specific teaching habits were found to help increase student involvement. These included varying the learning activities and using a variety of visual materials.

Using observations, interviews, and videotapes, Baker (1995) examined the interactive television teaching behaviors of five faculty members teaching courses using distance education technology. Seven broad categories of teaching behaviors were identified:

- Nonverbal "immediacy" behaviors
- Verbal "immediacy" behaviors
- Behaviors that personalize the class
- Technology management strategies
- Methods for acquiring student feedback
- Methods used to manage student participation
- Active learning strategies

Nonverbal behaviors that conveyed a feeling of approachability and warmth increased involvement of students at the remote site. Specific behaviors included making eye contact with the camera, using gestures, and using camera angles and shots that allowed students to see facial expressions. Verbal "immediacy" behaviors that were found to contribute to student involvement included the use of humor, frequent positive encouragement, and the frequent sharing of personal examples. Teachers used a variety of methods for acquiring student feedback that improved student involvement. Most of the teachers relied, at least partially, on the nonverbal cues of the students at the origination site. Some used a variety of questioning techniques, while others used more formal, written formative evaluations.

Research regarding interaction and distance education technologies indicates that different technologies allow differing degrees of interaction. However, similar to comparison studies examining achievement, research comparing differing amounts of interaction showed that interaction had little effect on achievement (Beare, 1989; Souder, 1993). Those students who had little or no interaction as part of a course did not seem to miss it (May, 1993).

BARRIERS TO DISTANCE EDUCATION

Berge and Muilenburg (2000) recently reviewed the literature and identified 64 potential barriers to the implementation of distance education. They surveyed several thousand persons involved in distance education, instructional technology, and training. Of those responding, 1,150 were teachers or trainers, 648 were managers, 167 were administrators in higher education, and the remaining responders were researchers and students.

When the data were analyzed, the strongest barriers to distance education were identified. Their rank order is:

1. Increased time commitment
2. Lack of money to implement distance education programs
3. Organizational resistance to change
4. Lack of shared vision for distance education in the organization
5. Lack of support staff to help course development
6. Lack of strategic planning for distance education
7. Slow pace of implementation
8. Faculty compensation/incentives
9. Difficulty keeping up with technological changes
10. Lack of technology-enhanced classrooms, labs, or infrastructure

Additionally, Berge and Muilenburg identified the least important barriers to implementation. They were:

54. Competition with on-campus courses
55. Lack of personal technological expertise
56. Lack of acceptable use policy
57. Lack of transferability of credits
58. Problems with vast distances and time zones
59. Technology fee

60. Tuition rate
61. Local, state, or federal regulations
62. Ethical issues
63. Existing union contracts
64. Lack of parental involvement

Berge and Muilenburg concluded by identifying the need for cultural change within organizations involved or contemplating involvement with distance education. Five of the top barriers related directly to organizational culture include:

- Organizational resistance to change
- Lack of shared vision for distance education in the organization
- Lack of strategic planning for distance education
- Slow pace of implementation
- Difficulty keeping up with technological change

In South Dakota (Simonson, 2001), a recent series of focus groups of teachers revealed the following reasons why they were reluctant to be involved in distance education:

- Fear
- Training
- Time
- Changes needed

These same groups indicated the following impediments to implementing distance education in schools were

- Need for training
- Need for and lack of support
- Time needed
- Fear of the process
- Scheduling problems
- Technical problems

DISTANCE EDUCATION TECHNOLOGY

Numerous studies have described or examined the efficacy of individual forms of distance education, whereas others have examined aspects or components of those forms. Garrison (1990) used a description of audio teleconferencing to argue for an appropriate concentration on the role of the teacher and the importance of two-way communication in the education process. Along the way, he argued for the appropriate, conservative use of interactive communication technologies.

The core of Garrison's argument was the following:

education, whether it be at a distance or not, is dependent upon two-way communication. There is an increasing realization in the educational community that simply accessing information is not sufficient. In an educational experience information must be shared, critically analyzed, and applied in order to become knowledge. (p. 13)

A goal of some distance education programs is to make education more student-centered through the prepackaging of instructional materials that students may use when convenient. However, Garrison argued that this approach ignores the essential nature of an educational learning experience. Garrison reported that this simply risked making learning more private and therefore less likely to transform the views and perspectives of the learner in a positive developmental manner.

Garrison argued that the quality and the integrity of the educational process depend upon sustained, two-way communication. Such communication, between student and teacher, and between student and student, is the prime benefit of teleconferencing. When this technology is applied to distance education, the result is that distance education is no longer necessarily an independent and isolated form of learning but, instead, begins to approach the interactive ideal of an educational experience.

Garrison supports audio teleconferencing, which he regards as a distinct generation of distance education capable of providing unique and varied teaching and learning possibilities. Independent and isolated study is no longer the hallmark of distance education. Egan, Welch, Page, and Sebastian (1992) examined graduate students' perceptions of three instructional delivery systems: (1) conventional delivery, (2) closed-circuit microwave system (EDNET), and (3) videotape recordings (Professor Plus). Near the conclusion of the course, 514 students evaluated the delivery systems using the Media Evaluation Survey. This instrument allows individuals the opportunity to evaluate instructional media on 10 elements:

> 1) amount of material covered, 2) level of difficulty, 3) degree to which the course content was well organized, 4) clarity of the content, 5) degree to which the various programs and instructional activities were relevant to the course objectives, 6) excellence or lack of excellence of the presenter's delivery, 7) extent to which text and weekly assignments were integrated with each week's class, 8) value of slides, films, and other visual materials, 9) value of text screens to support the presenter's delivery, and 10) degree to which the course held the student's interest. (p. 50)

Results showed 6 of the 10 variables to be different for distant learners. The conventional delivery group gave higher ratings to organization, clarity, relevance, integration, value of visuals, and value of text screens. A comparison of conventional delivery to Professor Plus yielded similar results, with significant differences shown on the two additional variables of adequacy of presenter's delivery and student interest, which were rated higher by the conventional delivery group.

A comparison of the two television delivery systems, EDNET and Professor Plus, showed a significant difference for distant learners for only one variable. The average of the EDNET group's ratings on the value of visuals variable was higher than the mean of the Professor Plus group's ratings.

An analysis of the educational attributes of two forms of communication technology was reported by Tuckey (1993). The electronic white board, a form of synchronous audioconferencing, and asynchronous computer conferencing were reviewed. It was not the intent of the analysis to identify one form of communication as better than the other.

Face-to-face interaction was available in the uses of the electronic white board reviewed. Students met in small groups with the aural presence of the instructor. This element provides opportunities for social interaction, for mutual support, and for collaborative learning, and provides more possibilities for group work than does audioconferencing.

Computer conferencing permitted only text-based communication. Several negative aspects, including limits in display capabilities, contributed to difficulties in collaboration. Group work is also difficult due to the asynchronous nature of this technology. Tuckey concluded that each form of communication has its advantages. There is a need to review the attributes of the technology used for distance education. Visual channels may be more important in subject areas such as mathematics and the sciences, whereas computer conferencing may be more suitable in areas requiring extensive discourse.

Ahern and Repman (1994) examined two different delivery technologies and their relationship to interaction. They found that interaction was sometimes inhibited in distance education systems. The attributes of specific delivery technologies may contribute to both the quantity and the quality of teacher-student and student-student interactions. In the first study, the researchers analyzed videotapes of a class delivered using two-way audio/two-way video technology. Levels of teacher-student interaction were identified. Teachers talked 62% of the time, with students talking 38% of the time. The percent of questions asked was divided almost equally between students and teachers.

In the second study, Ahern and Repman (1994) evaluated computer-mediated communication systems and the impact on interaction. Two versions of software were developed for this study. The first used a graphic-based discussion map; the second was a more traditional text version. Students in the graphic interface produced significantly more messages than students using the textual interface. The students using the graphic version spent approximately 25% more time per visit.

As with any medium used for instruction, it is important to examine attributes and their contribution to the learning outcome. The studies above suggest that different distance education technologies meet different needs. Two-way communication is an essential component of the learning environment. Collaboration with other students and with the instructor is more possible and easier today than previously because of advancements in technology. Continued research needs to examine the setting and context as well as the media attributes to determine variables contributing to learner outcomes.

MYTHS REGARDING DISTANCE EDUCATION RESEARCH

A myth is an invented story, and it does not always begin with "Once upon a time." In any field, including distance education, ideas and approaches quickly emerge that seem to gain a life of their own, even though there is little, if any, factual support for them. The myth of the media effect has been discussed for decades, making the rounds every time a new instructional technology is introduced. It implies that merely using media for instruction somehow has an impact on learning. This myth has been widely discussed and soundly rebuked (Clark, 1983). Three more myths about distance education deserve the same fate.

Myth 1: For video-based distance education, the higher the frames per second (fps) the better.   At the heart of this myth is the belief that full-motion video that shows 30 images or frames per second (fps) is always the best. Television produces an image that the brain perceives as motion because 30 separate screens are displayed each second (actually there are 60 half-frames which when combined produce 30 complete images). Because of the phenomenon of persistence of vision, the eye cannot distinguish between images received at that speed so they blend together and the brain perceives motion.

This is where the 30 fps myth originates; emulating broadcast television is thought somehow to be good. It is easy to debunk this myth. First, the 30 fps rate is for National Television System Committee (NTSC) video, the "American" standard. In Europe and most of the rest of the world where 50-cycle alternating current is the norm, the standard for full-motion video is 25 fps. Second, the eye can only distinguish up to about 15 or 20 fps, so the 30 (or 25) fps rate is more than what is needed. Finally, unless considerable change occurs in the image being transmitted there is no need to display high-frame rates. Fully, 90% of teleconferences and video-based distance education involves transmission of still, or nearly non-moving images, such as instructor's faces, still pictures, or PowerPoint slides, so a rate as low as 15 fps or even 10 fps is quite adequate.

The literature is quite clear; a video image broadcast rate of 15 fps is adequate 90% of the time. Specifically, compressed video systems that have a normal maximum rate of 15 fps cost much less than top-of-the-line systems with high-speed connections (at 30 fps). Economically if the more expensive systems provide unneeded quality, they are not worth it. From a learning standpoint, the higher fps rates and more costly systems are not needed. Effective instruction and necessary learning have little if anything to do with the rate at which images are transmitted between instructional sites.

Myth 2: The more interaction there is in a distance education class, the better.   This myth is also easy to trace to its roots. Early research on distance education demonstrated clearly that the *provision* for interaction was critical. In other words, some early forms of distance education were one way, or had interaction that was so delayed that students had little if any feeling of involvement with their instructors. Students need to be able to interact with their teacher, at least to ask questions.

Interaction is *needed and should be available*. However, interaction is not "end all and be all" of learning. It is only necessary to look at a few research studies, such as Fulford and Zhang (1995) to discover that interaction is not a magic potion that miraculously improves distance learning. Interaction is important, and the potential for all involved in teaching and training to be able to confer is essential. However, the forcing of interaction can be as strong a detriment to effective learning as is its absence.

Myth 3: Instructor training is required for anyone planning to teach at a distance.
Naturally, the more training a person has, the more likely it is that he or she will learn,

assuming education works. However, training in how to teach distant learners is only one of a collection of interrelated competencies needed by an effective teacher.

By far the most important competency of any teacher is content knowledge. Understanding a subject and the ability to break down the topic into meaningful and manageable concepts is fundamental for any effective teacher. In some distance education systems, the course delivery specialist may not need to know much about content, notably the industrialized systems of Europe where an assembly-line approach and division of labor are typical, and where different people prepare courses and course content. If there is only one person, the teacher, who is responsible for the entire process—from course design and course delivery, to course evaluation—then knowledge of content is essential.

SUMMARY

Although it is always perilous to summarize research in a few sentences, it is also the obligation of those who have studied the literature extensively to provide others with their best estimates of what has been reported.

The distance education literature has several characteristics that make summarization difficult. The largely anecdotal nature of distance education literature, reporting results of a specific project, makes it difficult to generalize. Widely criticized comparison studies continue to be popular. Comparing the achievements of distance learners with those of traditional learners or between distance learners using different technologies continues to show "no significant difference." Subjects tend to be highly motivated, with adult learners providing little help in generalizing to other populations.

In spite of these limitations, it is possible to draw the following tentative conclusions from the research literature. Although these summary statements should be interpreted skeptically, they are supported by the literature.

- Distance education is just as effective as traditional education in regard to learner outcomes.
- Distance education learners generally have a more favorable attitude toward distance education than do traditional learners, and distance learners feel they learn as well as if they were in a regular classroom.
- Successful distance education learners tend traditionally to be abstract learners who are intrinsically motivated and possess internal locus of control.
- Although interaction seems intuitively important to the learning experience, interaction should not be added without real purpose.
- Focusing on building collaboration and group interaction may be more important than focusing on individual participation.
- Each form of distance education technology has it own advantages and disadvantages in contributing to the overall quality of the learning experience.

The research clearly shows that distance education is an effective method for teaching and learning. Future research needs to focus on different populations, particularly

K–12 students; psychological and social attributes of the learner; the impact of distance education on the organization; and the contributions of different media attributes to learning outcomes.

SELF-TEST QUESTIONS

1. True/False. Many distance education researchers are now concentrating on learner-centered approaches in distance education environments. What are educators saying about the need for learner-centered approaches in regular education?
2. List at least three of Holmberg's categories for how research on distance education should be structured. Discuss whether the research presented in this chapter relates to Holmberg's categories.
3. Why did Richard Clark say "*give up your enthusiasm* for the belief that media attributes cause learning"? Discuss your opinions about this statement.
4. True/False. Generally speaking, distant learners do not achieve as well as do local, traditional learners. What predicts a distant learner's achievement?
5. True/False. Generally, distant learners feel they learn as much as local, traditional learners. Why might this finding be suspect?
6. Give at least three conclusions from the research literature about distance education. Why do these conclusions have impact on the practice of distance education?
7. List areas where additional distance education research is needed. Why?

Answers to Self-Test Questions

1. True.
2. Börje Holmberg, a leading distance education theorist and researcher, suggested that the structure of distance education research include:
   • Philosophy and theory of distance education
   • Distance students and their milieu, conditions, and study motivations
   • Subject matter presentation
   • Communication and interaction between students and their supporting organization (tutors, counselors, administrators, other students)
   • Administration and organization
   • Economics
   • Systems (comparative distance education, typologies, evaluation, etc.)
   • History of distance education
3. Clark was attempting to advocate that there is no inherent significant difference in the educational effectiveness of various media. It is not the medium that influences learner outcomes. Rather, it is the instructional message or the learning event that has a direct impact on outcomes.
4. False. Generally, local and distant learners tend to learn at about the same level.
5. True.

6. Although these summary statements should be interpreted skeptically, they are supported by the literature.
   - Distance education is just as effective as traditional education in regard to learner outcomes.
   - Distance education learners generally have a more favorable attitude toward distance education than do traditional learners, and distance learners feel they learn as well as if they were in a regular classroom.
   - Successful distance education learners tend to be abstract learners who are intrinsically motivated and possess internal locus of control.
   - Whereas interaction seems intuitively important to the learning experience, interaction should not be added without real purpose.
   - Focusing on building collaboration and group interaction may be more important than focusing on individual participation.
   - Each form of distance education technology has it own advantages and disadvantages in contributing to the overall quality of the learning experience.
7. Future research needs to focus on different populations, particularly K–12 students; psychological and social attributes of the learner; the impact of distance education on the organization; and the contributions of different media attributes to learning outcomes.

For additional information and activities, visit the Prentice Hall Companion Website at http://www.prenhall.com/simonson

REFERENCES

Ahern, T. C., & Repman, J. (1994). The effects of technology on online education. *Journal of Research on Computing in Education, 26*(4), 537–546.

Baker, M. H. (1995). Distance teaching with interactive television: Strategies that promote interaction with remote-site students. In C. Sorensen, C. Schlosser, M. Anderson, & M. Simonson (Eds.), *Encyclopedia of distance education research in Iowa* (pp. 107–115). Ames, IA: Teacher Education Alliance.

Bauer, J. W., & Rezabek, L. L. (1992). *The effects of two-way visual contact on student verbal interactions during teleconferenced instruction.* (ERIC Document Reproduction Service No. ED347972)

Beare, P. L. (1989). The comparative effectiveness of videotape, audiotape, and telelecture in delivering continuing teacher education. *The American Journal of Distance Education, 3*(2), 57–66.

Berge, Z., & Muilenburg, L. (2000). Barriers to distance education as perceived by managers and administrators: Results of a survey. In M. Clay (Ed.), *Distance learning administration annual 2000.* Baltimore, MD: University of Maryland–Baltimore.

Bernt, F. L., & Bugbee, A. C. (1993). Study practices and attitudes related to academic success in a distance learning programme. *Distance Education, 14*(1), 97–112.

Biner, P. M., Bink, M. L., Huffman, M. L., & Dean, R. S. (1995). Personality characteristics differentiating and predicting the achievement of televised-course students and traditional-course students. *The American Journal of Distance Education, 9*(2), 46–60.

Biner, P. M., Dean, R. S., & Mellinger, A. E. (1994). Factors underlying distance learner satisfaction with televised college-level courses. *The American Journal of Distance Education, 8*(1), 60–71.

Bramble, W. J., & Martin, B. L. (1995). The Florida teletraining project: Military training via two-way compressed video. *The American Journal of Distance Education, 9*(1), 6–26.

Bruning, R., Landis, M., Hoffman, E., & Grosskopf, K. (1993). Perspectives on an interactive satellite-based Japanese language course. *The American Journal of Distance Education, 7*(3), 22–38.

Cheng, H. C., Lehman, J., & Armstrong, P. (1991). Comparison of performance and attitude in traditional and computer conferencing classes. *The American Journal of Distance Education, 5*(3), 51–64.

Clark, R. E. (1983). Reconsidering research on learning from media. *Review of Educational Research, 53*(4), 445–459.

Clark, R. E. (1994). Media will never influence learning. *Educational Technology Research and Development, 42*(2), 21–29.

Coggins, C. C. (1988). Preferred learning styles and their impact on completion of external degree programs. *The American Journal of Distance Education, 2*(1), 25–37.

Dille, B., & Mezack, M. (1991). Identifying predictors of high risk among community college telecourse students. *The American Journal of Distance Education, 5*(1), 24–35.

Egan, M. W., Welch, M., Page, B., & Sebastian, J. (1992). Learners' perceptions of instructional delivery systems: Conventional and television. *The American Journal of Distance Education, 6*(2), 47–55.

Fast, M. (1995, April). Interaction in technology: Mediated, multisite, foreign language instruction. Paper presented at the Annual Meeting of the American Educational Research Association, San Francisco, CA.

Fjortoft, N. F. (1995). *Predicting persistence in distance learning programs.* (ERIC Document Reproduction Service No. ED387620)

Fulford, C. P., & Zhang, S. (1993). Perceptions of interaction: The critical predictor in distance education. *The American Journal of Distance Education, 7*(3), 8–21.

Fulford, C. & Zhang, S. (1995). Interactivity in distance education television: A constructed reality. *Distance Education Symposium 3.* The Pennsylvania State University.

Garland, M. R. (1993). Student perceptions of the situational, institutional, dispositional, and epistemological barriers to persistence. *Distance Education, 14*(2), 181–198.

Garrison, D. R. (1990). An analysis and evaluation of audio teleconferencing to facilitate education at a distance. *The American Journal of Distance Education, 4*(3), 13–24.

Holmberg, B. (1987). The development of distance education research. *The American Journal of Distance Education, 1*(3), 16–23.

Jegede, O. J., & Kirkwood, J. (1994). Students' anxiety in learning through distance education. *The American Journal of Distance Education, 15*(2), 279–290.

Laube, M. R. (1992). Academic and social integration variables and secondary student persistence in distance education. *Research in Distance Education, 4*(1), 2–5.

Martin, E. E., & Rainey, L. (1993). Student achievement and attitude in a satellite-delivered high school science course. *The American Journal of Distance Education, 7*(1), 54–61.

May, S. (1993). Collaborative learning: More is not necessarily better. *The American Journal of Distance Education, 7*(3), 39–50.

Pugliese, R. R. (1994). Telecourse persistence and psychological variables. *The American Journal of Distance Education, 8*(3), 22–39.

Ross, L. R., & Powell, R. (1990). Relationships between gender and success in distance education courses: A preliminary investigation. *Research in Distance Education, 2*(2), 10–11.

Ross, S. M., Morrison, G. R., Smith, L. J., & Cleveland, E. (1991). *An evaluation of alternative distance tutoring models for at-risk elementary school children.* (ERIC Document Reproduction Service No. ED335009)

Rubenson, K. (1986). Distance education for adults: Old and new barriers for participation. In G. van Enckevorrt, K. Harry, P. Morin, and H. G. Schutze (Eds.), *Distance higher education and the adult learner: Innovations in distance education* (Vol. 1), pp. 39–55. Heelern, the Netherlands: Dutch Open University.

Schoenfelder, K. R. (1995). Student involvement in the distance education classroom: Teacher and student perceptions of effective instructional methods. In C. Sorensen, C. Schlosser, M. Anderson, & M. Simonson (Eds.), *Encyclopedia of distance education research in Iowa* (pp. 79–85). Ames, IA: Teacher Education Alliance.

Simonson, M. (2001). Connecting the schools: Final evaluation report. North Miami Beach, FL: Nova Southeastern University. Available: http://www.tresystems.com/projects/sdakota.cfm.

Sorensen, C. K. (1995). Attitudes of community college students toward interactive television instruction. In C. Sorensen, C. Schlosser, M. Anderson, & M. Simonson (Eds.), *Encyclopedia of distance education research in Iowa* (pp. 131–148). Ames, IA: Teacher Education Alliance.

Souder, W. E. (1993). The effectiveness of traditional vs. satellite delivery in three management of technology master's degree programs. *The American Journal of Distance Education, 7*(1), 37–53.

Stone, T. E. (1992). A new look at the role of locus of control in completion rates in distance education. *Research in Distance Education, 4*(2), 6–9.

Tuckey, C. J. (1993). Computer conferencing and the electronic white board in the United Kingdom: A comparative analysis. *The American Journal of Distance Education, 7*(2), 58–72.

Whittington, N. (1987). Is instructional television educationally effective? A research review. *The American Journal of Distance Education, 1*(1), 47–57.

Zhang, S., & Fulford, C. P. (1994). Are interaction time and psychological interactivity the same thing in the distance learning television classroom? *Educational Technology, 34*(6), 58–64.

ADDITIONAL READINGS

American Journal of Distance Education. University Park, PA: The Pennsylvania State University.

Journal of Distance Education. Ottawa, ON: Canadian Association for Distance Education.

Moore, M. G. (1995). The 1995 distance education research symposium: A research agenda. *The American Journal of Distance Education, 9*(2), 1–6.

Quarterly Review of Distance Education. Greenwich, CT: Information Age Publishing.

chapter 4

DISTANCE EDUCATION TECHNOLOGIES

CHAPTER GOAL

The purpose of this chapter is to discuss the
technologies used for distance education systems and
distance education classrooms.

CHAPTER OBJECTIVES

After reading and reviewing this chapter, you should be able to

1. Describe systems for categorizing media used for
   distance education.
2. Explain the technologies used to connect teachers and
   learners for distance education, including
   correspondence, audio, video, and desktop systems.
3. Explain the configuration of a modern distance
   education classroom.

A TRUE STORY

In the 1980s, the southeast African nation of Zimbabwe was founded from the British Commonwealth country of Rhodesia after a long and painful process. Before the founding of Zimbabwe the educational system of Rhodesia enrolled less than 500,000 learners, and most were located in the major cities and towns of the country. One of the first acts of the new government was to offer free and universal education to the nation's children, no matter where they were located. This meant that the enrollment in the country's schools increased tenfold overnight.

The teacher education faculty at the University of Zimbabwe in Harare and at other institutions of teacher training had to face the immediate problem of preparing the thousands of teachers needed by the many new and enlarged schools of the country. The approach selected was part ingenious and part necessity-based.

It was decided that teachers in training should attend one of the institutions of higher education for their first year of preparation. For their second and third years these teacher education students were assigned to a school where they taught classes of students.

College students functioned as regular educators with two exceptions. First, they were under the guidance of a more experienced colleague, and second they continued their teacher education and higher education coursework at a distance. In other words, they enrolled in a full curriculum of coursework while they also functioned as novice teachers. Their coursework was delivered to them from a distant, higher education institution. For their fourth year they returned to the university or college and completed their degrees.

In Zimbabwe, distance education became the primary technique for preparing the thousands of teachers needed to staff the new country's schools. Interestingly, the technology used to connect professors, such as those of the faculty of education at the University of Zimbabwe, and students located in the many cities, towns, and villages of the country was the postal system. Students received written assignments and printed resources from the university. They used, studied, and interacted with these materials to complete assignments, which then were returned to the faculty of education for evaluation. Follow-up assignments and materials were then posted back to students. This process continued until the second and third years of the bachelor's degree were completed. Periodic visits to the campus occurred, but the majority of the learning events and activities took place at a distance.

This system, born of the necessity of educating millions of students, used the most appropriate technology available—the postal system. Certainly, a major social, political, and ultimately educational problem was solved, even though the approach was not high-tech. However, it was efficient and effective. Whatever technology is used, the purpose is to promote communication.

A MODEL OF COMMUNICATION

Communication occurs when two or more individuals wish to share ideas. Communication in a distance education environment happens when learners interact with one another and with their instructor. Communication, including communication for dis-

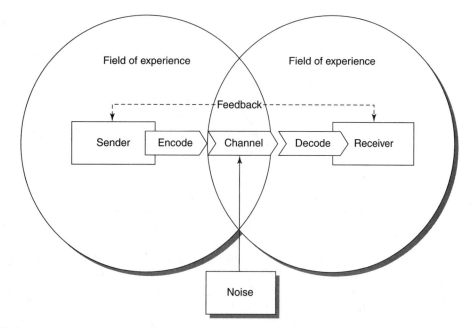

FIGURE 4–1   A model of communication.

tance education, is possible because individuals have overlapping fields of experience. In other words, they have things in common, such as language and culture (Figure 4–1).

Communication must be based on what the senders of messages—distance educators—have in common with the receivers of messages—distant learners. Effective instructional messages are designed according to the situation, experiences, and competencies of learners.

In order to communicate, instructional ideas are encoded into some transmittable form, such as spoken words, pictures, or writing. The instructional message is then sent to the learner over a channel. If the receiver of the message is nearby, such as in the same classroom, the sender—the teacher—may speak or show pictures in order to communicate. If the learner is at a distance, then the instructional message will need to be sent over a wire (e.g., the telephone), hand-delivered (e.g., the mail), or broadcast through the air (e.g., television). In other words, media are used to communicate to distant learners. In fact, media extend the senses, so instructional messages can be sent over long distances, or stored for learning at different times.

When the distant learner receives the message it must be decoded. This means the words spoken must be heard and defined, or the pictures shown must be seen and understood. If communication is successful, the receiver—the learner—will have the same idea or understanding as the sender—the teacher.

Effective communication requires an active audience. The response of the learners who receive messages is called *feedback*. Feedback allows the sender and receiver, the teacher and learner, to determine if the message was understood correctly. Feedback in distance education systems is often referred to as *interaction*. Feedback permits those involved in communication in a distance education system to evaluate the process.

Noise is also part of the communication process. Any disturbance that interferes with or distorts the transmission of a message is called *noise*. Audible static is one form of noise. Classroom distractions are noise, as is ambiguous or unfamiliar information.

The model of communication has been widely used to describe the interaction between message designers and audiences—teachers and learners. It is also quite relevant for distance education. Specifically, instruction must be designed in a way to capitalize on what learners already know and what they have already experienced—their fields of experience. Then messages should be encoded so they can be effectively transmitted to distant learners.

Channels of communication, the media that connect the teacher and the distant learner, should be appropriate for the learner and the instruction. In other words, the media used to connect the learner, teacher, and learning resources must be capable of conveying all necessary information.

When instruction is designed and when feedback and interaction are planned, efforts should be made to minimize anything that might interfere with the communication process (e.g., noise). One way this can be accomplished is by sending information through multiple channels.

Models of communication provide a general orientation to the process of distance education. The model described in Figure 4–1 contains the elements to be considered when instructional messages are communicated.

THE CONE OF EXPERIENCE

One long-standing method of categorizing the ability of media to convey information is the cone of experience, introduced by Edgar Dale (1946). Dale's "cone of experience" helps organize the media used in distance education systems (Figure 4–2).

Children respond to direct, purposeful experiences, not only because they are young, but also because they are learning many new things for the first time. Real experiences have the greatest impact on them because they have fewer previous experiences to look back on and refer to than do older learners. Real experiences provide the foundation for learning.

As learners grow older and have more experiences, it is possible for them to understand events that are less realistic and more abstract. Dale first stated this basic idea when he introduced his cone of experience. Dale proposed that for students to function and learn from experiences presented abstractly (those at the higher levels of the cone), it was necessary for them to have sufficient and related experiences that were more realistic (those at the lower levels). Learners need to have direct, purposeful experiences to draw upon in order to successfully learn from more abstract events. For example, if children are to look at pictures of flowers and know what they are, they must have first seen, smelled, and touched real flowers.

Media permit the educator to bring sights and sounds of the real world into the learning environment—the classroom. However, when *new* information is presented, it

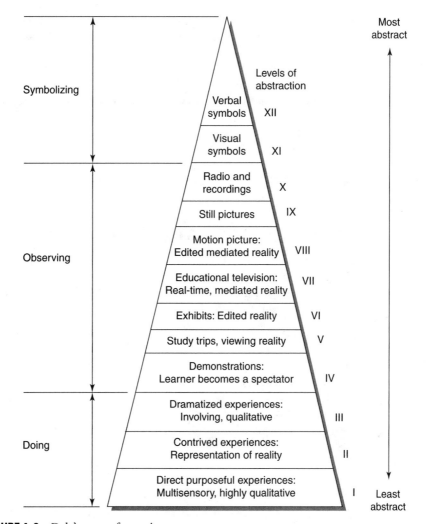

FIGURE 4–2   Dale's cone of experience.

is important that it be as realistic as possible. Similarly, when younger learners are involved, more realistic instruction is needed.

Still, one misunderstanding about the cone of experience is the belief that "more realistic" is always better. This is definitely not true. More realistic forms of learning are considerably less efficient in terms of uses of resources, and they are often less effective because of the many distractions of realistic instruction.

The critical job of the educator, especially the designer of distance education materials, is to be only as realistic as needed in order for learning to effectively occur. If instruction is too realistic, it can be inefficient. It may cost too much, it may have too much irrelevant information, or it may be difficult to use. Similarly, learning experiences that are too abstract may be inexpensive, but may not contain enough relevant information and may not be understood. To clarify the conflict between realistic and abstract experiences, Dale told a story about the life of a Greek sponge fisherman. The most realistic way to learn about the fisherman's life was to go to Greece and work on a sponge boat. This approach to learning would be very realistic, effective, and authentic. It would also take a long time and cost a great deal, both in money and in learning time. An abstract way to learn about the life of a sponge fisherman would be to read about it in a book. This would take only a few hours and would cost little, even though the experience would not be overly authentic. Today, most would opt for something that is in the middle of Dale's cone, such as a 28-minute video on cable television's Discovery Channel titled "A Day in the Life of a Greek Sponge Fisherman."

A TAXONOMY OF DISTANCE EDUCATION TECHNOLOGIES

In distance education, it is imperative that educators think about how communication will occur and how to apply experiences that will promote effective and efficient learning. Most likely, a variety of techniques will be needed to provide equivalent learning experiences for all students (Figure 4–3):

Correspondence
Prerecorded media
Two-way audio
Two-way audio with graphics
One-way live video
Two-way audio, one-way video
Two-way audio/video
Desktop two-way audio/video

Correspondence Study

The simplest and longest-lived form of distance education is generally considered to be correspondence study. This approach to distance education uses some kind of mail system, such as regular post office mail or electronic mail, to connect the teacher and the learner asynchronously (Figure 4–4). Usually, lessons, readings, and assignments are sent to the student, who then completes the lessons, studies the readings, and works on the assignments, which are mailed to the instructor for grading. For a college-level course worth three credits there are often 10 to 12 units to be completed. Each is finished in turn, and when all are completed satisfactorily, the student receives a grade.

Sophisticated forms of correspondence study have used techniques of programmed instruction to deliver information. Linear-programmed instruction is most common, but for a period of time a number of correspondence study organizations attempted to develop print-based branched programmed instruction. Programmed instruction normally has a block of content, followed by questions to be answered. Depending on the answers students give, they move to the next block of text (linear

FIGURE 4–3 Distance education technologies.

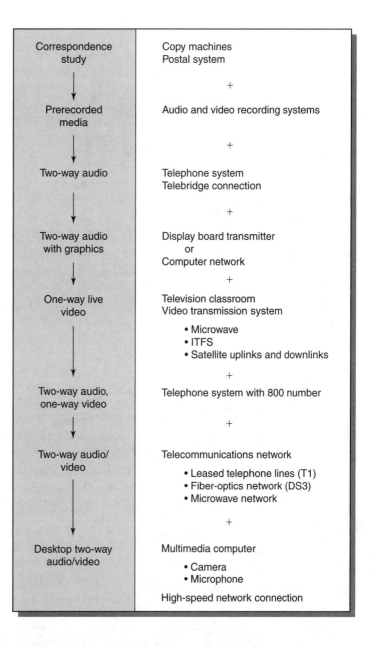

Correspondence study	Copy machines Postal system
↓	+
Prerecorded media	Audio and video recording systems
↓	+
Two-way audio	Telephone system Telebridge connection
↓	+
Two-way audio with graphics	Display board transmitter or Computer network
↓	+
One-way live video	Television classroom Video transmission system • Microwave • ITFS • Satellite uplinks and downlinks
↓	+
Two-way audio, one-way video	Telephone system with 800 number
↓	+
Two-way audio/ video	Telecommunications network • Leased telephone lines (T1) • Fiber-optics network (DS3) • Microwave network
↓	+
Desktop two-way audio/video	Multimedia computer • Camera • Microphone High-speed network connection

programmed instruction) or to another section of the programmed text (branched programmed instruction). Sometimes remedial loops of instruction would be provided to help students through difficult content, or content that supposedly had been covered in previous courses or blocks of instruction. Advanced students do not need to study remedial loops. In this manner, the rate and route of instruction are varied for students of correspondence courses. Correspondence study is relatively inexpensive, can be

Instructor

Letter
carriers

Copy
machine

Post
office
box

Mailboxes

FIGURE 4–4   Correspondence study utilizing the post office to connect the teacher and the learners.

completed almost anywhere, and has been shown to be effective. Correspondence study has been used by millions of learners of all ages since the 19th century.

Prerecorded Media

The next logical step in the development of distance education technologies, both historically and conceptually, was the incorporation of media other than print media into correspondence study systems. First, pictures and other graphics were added to correspondence study texts. Then, audiotapes and finally videotapes were added to the collection of materials sent to distant learners. Usually, the correspondence study guide would direct the learner to look at, listen to, or view various media, in addition to assigning more traditional readings.

One interesting approach used by distance educators was borrowed from advocates of individualized instruction. This approach used audiotapes to guide the distant learner through a series of learning events, very similar to how a tutor would direct learning. This *audio-tutorial approach* was quite popular for a number of years, and it is still used by commercial organizations that present self-help materials for individual study.

Two-Way Audio

Correspondence study filled a terrific void for those who wanted to learn when they could and wherever they were located. However, many wanted direct, live communication with the teacher, especially for those in precollege schools.

The first widely used live, synchronous form of distance education employed two-way audio, with either a telephone hookup, a radio broadcast with telephone call-in, or short-wave radio transmissions (Figure 4–5). In all cases, the distant learner and the instructor are interacting with some form of live, two-way audio connection. Teachers lecture, ask questions, and lead discussions. Learners listen, answer, and participate. Often, print and nonprint materials are sent to distant learners, similar to correspondence study.

FIGURE 4–5   Two-way audio—audioconferencing.

The key to this approach is the participation of the teacher and learners in a class session at a regularly scheduled time, or a set period of time, over a predetermined number of weeks or months, such as a semester. For example, a high school class in French might be offered by telephone, radio station broadcast, or short-wave signal every weekday from 10:00 A.M. until 10:50 for 9 weeks. Students would tune in at home, assignments would be made and activities completed. In other words, this form of distance education models the traditional classroom—except the teacher and learners can only hear one another, they cannot see each other.

Two-Way Audio With Graphics

Recently, an embellishment of the two-way audio form of distance education has incorporated electronic methods of sending graphics information synchronously to distant learners. Two general approaches are used. The first incorporates a special display board that looks like a chalkboard but that actually transmits whatever is drawn on it to a similar display board at a distant site. Since the electronic boards are connected to one another, whatever the students at the distant site draw is also seen by the instructor. The main disadvantage of this approach is the limited visual capability of the system and the difficulty in connecting more than two locations. A modification of this approach uses personal computers that are connected to one another, either through a central bridge computer or by using special software. For these systems, the instructor sends graphics, visuals, pictures, and even short video clips to desktop computers located at distant sites. Members of the class are connected by telephone or some other two-way audio system, so they can discuss the visual information being sent via the computer.

This approach is relatively inexpensive and permits the visualization of the teleclass. The major problem is the availability of powerful, networked computers at distant learning sites.

One-Way Live Video

This approach is often referred to as broadcast distance education, popularized in the 1950s by programs such as *Sunrise Semester,* which was broadcast over commercial television stations. Presently, most broadcast television approaches to distance education are offered by public television stations or are broadcast in the early morning hours by commercial stations (Figure 4–6).

Programs are broadcast in installments over a 12- to 15-week period. Often, each program is about 60 minutes in length and is accompanied by packets of printed materials and readings. Sometimes, instructors are available for telephone office hours, but most commonly students watch the programs on television and respond to assignments that are described in the course packet. Completion of the assignments depends on viewing each television program, which is often broadcast several times. For those students who miss a broadcast, videotape versions are available, or students can tape the program with their own videocassette recorder.

One advantage of this approach is the relatively high quality of the video broadcasts. Public television stations offer excellent productions of important historical, political, and social events. Educational institutions use these broadcasts as the basis for high school and college courses related to the topics of the television shows. The Civil War series and the Lewis and Clark series are examples of public television programming that was modified into distance education courses.

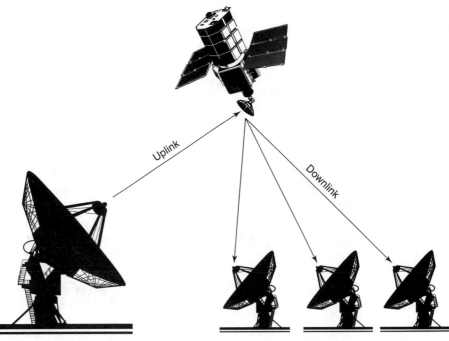

FIGURE 4–6   Satellite transmission—one-way audio, one-way video.

Two-Way Audio, One-Way Video

In the last few decades, a number of organizations have begun to use live television to broadcast high school and college courses. Initially, this approach used microwave transmission systems, instructional television fixed service (ITFS), or community cable television networks (Figures 4–7 and 4–8).

Recently, satellite communications systems have become widely available (Figure 4–9). In these systems, the courses are offered synchronously (e.g., live) to students in as few as two to as many as hundreds of locations. Students are given a toll-free telephone number to call to ask questions of the instructor both during class and after class. Normally, students have a packet of instructional materials, including interactive study guides, that they use and complete during the class presentation. Interaction between instructor and students is stressed in these kinds of courses, even ones where hundreds of students are enrolled.

In the last decade as satellite uplinks and downlinks have become more prevalent, the concept of the teleconference has become popular. Teleconferences are short courses on specialty topics such as copyright, classroom discipline, sexual harassment, due process, or funding strategies that are offered by an organization to individuals or small groups spread

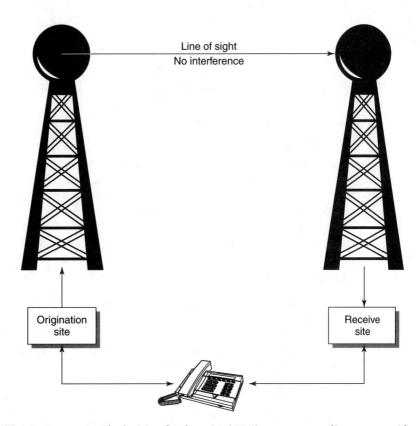

FIGURE 4–7   Instructional television fixed service (ITFS)—two-way audio, one-way video.

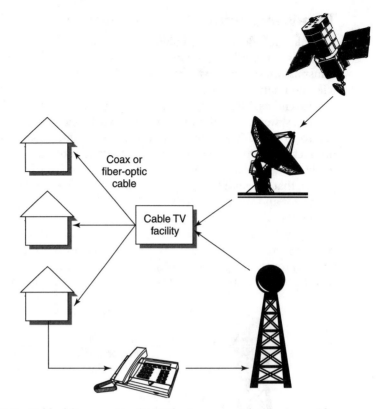

FIGURE 4–8   Cable delivery system (CATV)—two-way audio, one-way video.

throughout a wide geographic area. Since one satellite in geosynchronous orbit in the Clarke Belt above the equator can transmit a video signal to nearly one-third of the earth's surface, it is possible to offer satellite programming to literally thousands of learners.

A number of educational organizations have used satellite broadcast coursework to offer entire high school and college curricula. The TI-IN Network from San Antonio, Texas, offers an entire high school curriculum and has since the mid-1980s.

Two-Way Audio/Video

Recently, especially in the United States, distance education is being widely practiced using live, synchronous television employing one of several technologies. The prevalent technology is called *compressed video* (Figure 4–10). This approach, commonly applied in corporate training, uses regular telephone lines to send and receive audio and video signals. The approach is called compressed video because fewer than the normal number of 30 video fps are transmitted between the sites. In the compressed video form, usually 15 video fps are transmitted using what is called a T1 connection. This level of quality is acceptable for most instruction, except when some kind of rapid motion or movement is part of instruction.

FIGURE 4–9 Satellite transmission—two-way audio, one-way video.

FIGURE 4–10 Two-way audio/video—compressed videoconferencing system.

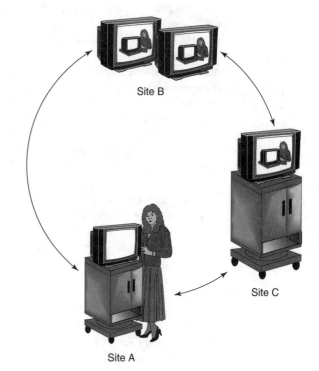

Tandberg single-monitor roll-around compressed
video system.

Compressed video systems are often used in teleconferences for corporate training.
Increasingly, schools and colleges are installing compressed video networks. For this approach, a special classroom is needed that has video and audio equipment to capture
the sights and sounds of instruction. The video and audio signals are manipulated by a
device called a CODEC (coder/decoder) that removes redundant information for
transmission to the distant site. At the receive site another CODEC converts the compressed information back into video and audio signals. Camera control information is
also transmitted between sites, so it is possible for the instructor to pan, tilt, and zoom
cameras.

One major advantage of compressed video systems is their portability. Many systems are installed in movable carts that can be set up in almost any classroom or
training site where there is a telephone connection. Recently, the size of the classroom
systems has been reduced significantly. The best-selling systems are called "set-top"
systems because they can be set on top of a television monitor. Set-top systems contain a camera, microphone, and the electronics necessary to compress and decompress outgoing and incoming transmissions. Set-top systems cost less than 25% of
traditional compressed video systems, yet are of similar quality. The Digital Dakota
Network (DDN) in South Dakota is a compressed video network that links over 200
educational sites for live two-way video and audio instruction (Figure 4–11). The
DDN uses traditional "roll-around" and "set-top" systems.

A second, more technically sophisticated approach to two-way audio/video instruction uses fiber-optic cable to connect sites. Fiber-optic cable is the telecommuni-

FIGURE 4–11   Digital Dakota Network layout.

cations medium of choice for new and updated telephone, video, and computer net-working. Fiber's cost inhibits its installation in all situations, but fiber's high capacity makes it possible for one fiber (sometimes called a DS-3 connection) to carry full-motion video signals, in addition to high-quality audio signals and almost unlimited amounts of other voice and data information. One exemplary use of fiber-optics for distance education is Iowa's publicly owned Iowa Communications Network.

An Example: Two-Way Audio/Video in Iowa

In Iowa, distance education is being redefined on a statewide basis. Iowa's approach to distance education is based on the belief that live, two-way interaction is fundamental to effective learning. The Iowa Communications Network (ICN) makes high-quality

Special "distance learning" carts are sometimes used. These carts can be wheeled into any classroom or office.

Polycom set-top videoconferencing unit.

interaction possible in the state. The ICN is a statewide, two-way, full-motion interactive fiber-optic telecommunications network with hundreds of connected classrooms. It is designed to be used by teachers and students in learning situations where they can and expect to see and hear each other. Distant and local students function together and learn from and with one another.

A key to Iowa's successful distance education system is the concept of sharing. Iowa's vision for distance education is being built around the development of partnerships of schools that share courses and activities. For example, a physics class originating in Jefferson, a small town in west central Iowa, may have students in Sac City and Rockwell City, schools in two other counties. French students in Sac City have distant classmates in Jefferson and Rockwell City, and a calculus class that originates in Rockwell City is shared with students in Sac City and Jefferson. All three schools provide courses to partner schools and receive instruction from neighbors. Classes are small, with enrollments of 30 to 35 or less, and are taught by teachers prepared in the skills needed by distance educators.

The use of fiber-optic technology, because of its extensive capacities and flexibility of use, provides unique opportunities for augmenting the instructional process beyond what is possible with other distance delivery technologies. The Iowa approach demonstrates the use of a system that emphasizes:

- Local control of the distance education curriculum
- Active involvement by educators from local school districts
- Interactive instruction
- Statewide alliances and regional partnerships
- Preservice, in-service, and staff development activities to support teachers
- Implementation using existing organizations and expertise
- Research-based instructional decision making

The Iowa Communications Network.   Central to distance education in Iowa is the Iowa Communications Network. The ICN is a statewide, two-way, full-motion interactive fiber-optic telecommunications network with at least one point of presence in each of Iowa's 99 counties. The ICN links colleges, universities, and secondary schools throughout the state and was constructed entirely with state and local funds. Part 1 of the Iowa Communications Network connected Iowa Public Television, Iowa's 3 public universities, and Iowa's 15 community colleges to the network. Part 2 connected at least one site in each of Iowa's 99 counties. Most Part 2 sites were high schools. Part 3 of the system is still under construction and is being expanded constantly. Currently it connects an additional 700 schools, libraries, armories, area education agencies, and hospitals.

The plan for the ICN was completed and adopted by the Iowa legislature in 1987. Construction of Parts 1 and 2 of the network was completed during 1993. In addition to the capability of transmitting up to 48 simultaneous video channels, the ICN carries data and voice traffic; as demand increases, the system can be easily expanded without the need for "opening the trench" to lay more fiber.

In Iowa and South Dakota, and in many other states and regions, traditional education works. Educators in these two states adopted distance education, but wanted to preserve their beliefs about effective education. The fiber-optics–based Iowa Communications Network and the compressed video Digital Dakota Network permit this since both are live, two-way audio/video networks.

Desktop Two-Way Audio/Video

One disadvantage of the video telecommunications systems described in this chapter is their cost and their cumbersomeness. In order to provide video-based distance education, special electronic devices are needed, satellite or telephone network time must be reserved, and equipped classrooms are required. Desktop systems often reduce the need for special high-cost equipment or special networking. Desktop systems use personal computers and the Internet to connect local and distant learners (Figure 4–12). Increasingly, the Internet and Internet II have the capacity to connect personal computers for the sharing of video and audio information. Inexpensive servers that function as reflector sites for connecting multiple sites are also available.

Early systems used CU/SeeMe technology that was free and used very inexpensive video cameras. These systems permitted two sites to connect and to share video and audio. Multiple sites could be connected if a reflector computer was available. The CU/SeeMe approach was relatively low quality and was used mostly for conferencing and meetings. However, it pioneered the use of desktop systems. Now higher quality

FIGURE 4–12   Computer conferencing—desktop two-way audio/video.

cameras and even complete classrooms can be connected to a personal computer for transmission of instruction to distant learners. Certainly the desktop personal computer will be the telecommunications tool of the future.

There are four categories of desktop audio/video systems: analog, high speed, medium speed, and low speed. These systems permit sharing of audio and video from the instructor's computer to a student's computer.

Analog systems use existing telephone wiring in buildings, commonly called twisted-pair wires. The major advantage of this approach is the high quality of the audio and video. Since existing wiring is used, connections are limited to relatively short distances—several thousand feet. Analog systems are limited to a campus, or a building, which significantly reduces this application in distance education.

High-speed videoconferencing sends video at millions of bits per second. Even at this high rate, the video signal is compressed using a compression protocol such as MPEG or motion JPEG. The H.310 protocol is used for high-speed desktop videoconferencing. Currently, high-speed videoconferencing is used primarily with dedicated networks within individual schools or businesses.

Medium-speed desktop videoconferencing is currently the primary approach used today. This type of desktop video transmits at speeds of 128,000 or 256,000 bits per second. The video signal is compressed so it can be transmitted over the Internet (H.323 protocol). There are both hardware and software methods to compress and decompress the video signal. Since the Internet is used, medium-speed systems have considerable promise for distance education.

Low-speed desktop video includes all systems that transmit at speeds lower than 56,000 bits per second (56 kbps). This category permits conferencing using the

An inexpensive desktop video camera system.

Internet and modems at speeds of 28.8 kbps. A V32 model modem with v.80 extension is generally what is needed for low-speed desktop video. Once again H.323 protocols are used, and software and hardware compression systems are available. Very inexpensive systems are currently in use. However, the quality is quite poor and the video signal is usually limited to a small window on the computer screen. Low-speed systems are widely used for limited types of instructor/student conferencing, rather than for course delivery.

When the Internet is used, rather than a special or dedicated network, the H.323 standard is used. The primary problem with desktop videoconferencing using the Internet is the poor quality of the video and the limited capacity of the Internet to carry video signals. Since the Internet is a "packet-switched" network, a video signal is broken into packets that are disassembled and then sent to the distant site where the packets are reassembled into a signal. Obviously, this approach is a limiting factor when live, interactive video is sent. Video streaming is a growing subset of this category of distance education. Video streaming is usually defined as the progressive downloading of a video file (Mallory, 2001). A storage space (buffer) that is much smaller than the video file is identified on the computer's hard drive. The video file begins to download into the file location and the file begins to display on the computer screen. The file continues to download from the origination site somewhere on the Internet to the buffer and onto the local computer screen. Often the video file is a prerecorded event, but live video can be streamed, also.

The three most popular video file types are Apple QuickTime (.mov files), Microsoft Windows Media Player (.avi files), and RealNetworks RealPlayer (.rm files). QuickTime's .mov files are very popular for standard movie downloads, but are not used as much for streamed video and audio. The most widely used format is the RealPlayer .rm file format (Mallory, 2001). A commonly used strategy is to store video segments on a CD or DVD and ship them to the distant learner to use as part of a course or lesson. CDs can store approximately 650 megabytes (approximately 1 hour of video), and DVDs can store about 1.6 gigabytes or about 2 hours of video.

A computer board is just about all that is necessary to convert a computer into a desktop teleconferencing system.

Desktop videoconferencing is a critical area for growth in distance education. Increasingly, the Internet will be used to connect learners for sharing of video, in addition to data (text and graphics). Before this happens, however, advances in compression standards, network protocols, and transmission media will need to be made.

DISTANCE EDUCATION CLASSROOMS

Two-Way Video/Audio Classrooms

Video-based distance education requires a classroom or studio that is equipped with the technology needed for recording and displaying video and listening to sound. Initially, studios were used as distance education classrooms. Then as distance education became more widespread, regular classrooms were converted into distance education receive and send sites (Figure 4–13).

Video classrooms need recording, instruction, and display equipment. Recording equipment includes video cameras—usually three—one that shows the instructor, one for the students, and an overhead camera mounted above the instructor console to display printed graphics materials. A switching system is needed to permit the instructor to switch between cameras and instructional equipment, such as a computer, a videocassette recorder, and a video slide projector. Several companies offer devices that attach to video cameras and cause them to follow the action in the classroom. For example, when its activation button is pushed, the student camera automatically pans and zooms to the appropriate microphone location to show the student who is talking. Also, the instructor camera has sensing devices that, when activated, automatically direct the camera to follow the instructor's movements in the classroom.

Additionally, audio equipment is needed. Audio tends to cause more problems than video in distance education classrooms. Early classrooms used voice-activated microphones, but currently push-to-talk microphones are found most often.

Instructional media often found in distance education classrooms include a computer, a videocassette recorder, and a video slide projector. Laser disk players are

FIGURE 4–13 Distance learning classroom—teaching site view from rear.

Visual presenters permit the transmission of flat visuals such as book pages, pictures, and drawings.

Push-to-talk microphones are used most often in distance learning classrooms.

Distance education classrooms are configured in a variety of ways, depending on how they are used.

Electronic white boards permit the instructor to write and have the information transmitted to a computer screen at the distant site.

The CameraMan can be used with sensors that automatically follow the instructor as she or he moves about the classroom.

sometimes supplied. Student equipment includes desktop computers that are networked and that can be displayed for others to see both in the local classroom and at remote sites.

Display equipment includes large television monitors and audio speakers. Most often three display monitors are mounted in a classroom—two in the front of the room for students to view and one in the rear for the instructor. Audio speakers are connected to a volume control.

Sometimes classrooms are connected to a control room where technicians can monitor action and even control the recording and display equipment. Increasingly,

Touch panels and control systems make it easy for the classroom teacher to control a sophisticated distance education system.

however, classrooms are teacher- and student-controlled. In other words, the teacher is responsible for equipment operation and use, or students in the class are assigned these responsibilities.

Classroom Technologies for Online Instruction

The key to success in an online classroom is not which technologies are used, but how they are used and what information is communicated using the technologies.

Selecting Appropriate Technologies for Online Instruction

Step #1: Assess available instructional technologies

Instructional technologies can be organized into two categories: telecommunications technologies and instructional technologies. Since telecommunications means to communicate at a distance, telecommunications technologies are electronic methods used to connect the instructor, students, and resources. Obviously, this chapter discusses online technologies, which means a computer and network. However, embedded within computers and networks are capabilities permitting the delivery of instruction using a variety of media. Instructional media are ways that messages are stored, and for most online applications include verbal symbols (words spoken and written), visual symbols (line drawings and graphics), pictures, motion pictures, real-time video, and recorded/edited video.

    This list is similar to the one proposed by Edgar Dale discussed earlier in this chapter. The bottom levels of the cone listed realistic experiences, such as actually doing something in the real world, like going to Greece. Realistic experiences are the most difficult to make available to students. It takes a great deal of time and extensive resources to always provide totally authentic, real-world learning experiences.

Dale implied when discussing his cone that the tension between efficiency (abstract experiences) and effectiveness (realistic experiences) is at the core of instructional design. The professor should pick learning experiences that are no more realistic than necessary in order for outcomes to be achieved. Overly abstract learning experiences require the student to compensate or to learn less effectively. Overly realistic experiences waste resources. When the professor who is designing online instruction selects the correct media, it maximizes efficiency and makes available more resources for other learning experiences.

Assessing available technologies often requires that the instructor determine the level of lowest common technologies (LCT). This means that the sophistication of the computer and software of all learners and the instructor should be determined. Also, this means that the capabilities of the telecommunications technologies must be identified. Often, LCT is determined by having students complete a survey on which they clearly identify the technologies that are available to them.

Another strategy is to require a minimum computer and telecommunications capability before students are allowed to enroll in a course. For example, an 800 MHz, Pentium III computer with 128 Mg of RAM, a 30-GB hard drive, a sound card, video card, video camera, speakers, microphone, and 56-KB modem or DSL connection might be required of students. Either option has its advantages and disadvantages. Most likely, a minimum technology level needs to be required in order for online instruction to provide experiences equivalent to traditional instruction.

Step #2: Determine the learning outcomes

Learning outcomes are those observable, measurable behaviors that are a consequence of online instruction. When learning activities are designed it is important that some expectations for students be identified in order to guide the selection of appropriate technologies.

Since online environments should be media-rich and strive for authenticity, it is critical that many technologies be used. It is also important that students demonstrate learning outcomes by using a variety of technology-based activities. Students may be expected to take a test to demonstrate their competence, but more likely they will be expected to offer some kind of real-world project that gives an authentic assessment of what they learned. Rubrics, which simply are predetermined strategies for how assignments are to be graded, should be available for students to use to guide the development of the outcome materials they produce.

One strategy used by developers of online instruction is to collect student projects and use these materials as models for subsequent students. If this strategy is used, a thoughtful and comprehensive critique of the student projects should be included so mistakes are identified and not repeated. Some developers of instruction advocate that students should begin with existing materials produced previously and redesign them to eliminate weaknesses, build on strengths, and add new concepts. Specifically, text used in a lesson could be analyzed and replaced with graphics or word pictures, that are combinations of text and graphics that represent teaching concepts. Still pictures could be modified and upgraded to animations, and synchronous chats could be made more effective by including a threaded discussion strategy that involves asking questions, collecting answers, asking follow-up questions, and selecting most appropriate final responses. Traditionalists identify learning outcomes in terms of behavioral objectives with specific conditions under which learning will occur, a precise behavior to be demonstrated that indicates learning, and an exact standard to measure competence. Recently, learner-identified objectives have become popular: The student is expected at some point during the instructional event to identify what changes he or she feels are important indicators of learning. Whatever approach is used, it is critical that outcomes of instructional events be clearly identified at some point.

Step #3: Identify learning experiences and match each to the most appropriate available technology

Usually, the content of a course is divided into modules or units. Traditionally, a module requires about 3 hours of face-to-face instruction and 6 hours of student study or preparation, and a three-credit college course would have 12 to 15 modules. In an online course, the classical approach of organizing content around teaching and study time is no longer relevant. One approach would be to simply convert a classroom-centered course's content into online modules. For totally new courses, this approach will obviously not work.

An alternative approach is to organize a course around themes or ideas that directly relate to student activities or learning activities. For example, a course in history about the reconstruction period following the American Civil War might have 12 modules, each with 5 learning activities, for a total of 60. The learning activities would be content-centered experiences such as reading assignments, PowerPoint presentations, and audio recordings, or learner-centered experiences, such as threaded discussions on specific topics, research assignments utilizing web search engines, or self-tests.

One example for a module dealing a topic such as the economic redevelopment of the South in the first 5 years after the end of the Civil War might begin with a reading assignment from the textbook about the economic conditions in the South. This reading assignment would be prescribed by a web-based assignment. The reading would be followed by participation in an online discussion with a small group of classmates. This discussion would be to identify the five impediments to effective economic development. When the group agreed to the list, it would be posted to the course's bulletin board for grading by the instructor. The third learning experience in this module would be a review of a PowerPoint presentation with audio that was prepared by the instructor that discusses what actually happened economically in the South after the Civil War. Finally, the student would be expected to write a two-page critique of the period of economic development according to a rubric posted on the Web. This assignment would be submitted electronically to the course's instructor for grading.

Subsequent modules in this course would be designed similarly. At several points during the course, benchmark projects would be required of students, such as an individual online chat with the instructor, or the submission of a major project that synthesized work completed for module assignments.

Self-contained teleconferencing systems such as this one from VTEL Corporation are often used by businesses and in higher education settings.

A simple teleconferencing system.

Cameras for computer desktop systems are small, high quality, and relatively inexpensive.

Video cameras are normally included as part of video teleconferencing systems.

Once the course's content is organized into modules, the next design requirement is to match learning experiences to technology-delivery strategies. The reading assignments could be delivered using the textbook, or posted as files to be downloaded, or even read directly from the computer monitor. PowerPoint presentations could be handled the same way, and used directly from the computer, or downloaded and studied later. E-mail attachments could be used for assignment submission and chat rooms or e-mail could provide ways to hold threaded discussions.

In this example, the instructional media are relatively simple ones. What is sophisticated is the design and organization of the activities and content facilitated and delivered by the media.

Step #4: Preparing the learning experiences for online delivery

Basically, there are four strategies for organizing instruction for online delivery. They are linear-programmed instruction, branched-programmed instruction, hyper-programmed instruction, and student-programmed instruction.

In each case, the content of the course is subdivided into modules. The modules consist of topics that relate to one another or have some sense of unity or consistency, such as the economic condition of the South after the Civil War. The modules themselves, and the learning activities within the modules, are organized according to one of the four delivery strategies listed above.

Tandberg touch panel controller for compressed video system.

Linear-programmed instruction, a long-standing approach to individualized instruction, requires that all content be organized into concepts that are presented in blocks or chunks. Students review content, take a self-test, and if successful move to the next chunk/block of information. This happens sequentially until the content blocks are completed. Students move in the same order through the sequence of concepts. The teacher determines the order of the concepts/chunks.

Branched-programmed instruction is similar except the self-tests are more sophisticated so students can branch ahead if they are exceptionally proficient, or move to remediation if they are floundering. Similarly to linear-programmed instruction, the order and sequence of instruction, including branches, is instructor determined. Hyper-programmed instruction, widely advocated for web-based online instruction, also organizes content into modules and concepts, but permits the student to move through the learning activities at their own rate and pace, in a route they determine themselves. In other words, learning experiences are identified and mediated, and students use them until either an instructor or student determined outcome is met. Often, each module has a terminal, or final, activity that must be completed before the student moves to the next course module. Finally, the student-programmed approach uses an extremely loose structure where only the framework of the content is provided to on-line learners who are expected to provide the structure, outcomes, and sequence of learning activities. For example, students who enroll in a course on the *Period of Reconstruction* would be required to organize and sequence the modules and activities, and during the course to identify personal outcomes and activities to be accomplished.

When teachers attempt to make instruction equal for all students they will fail. Rather, the teacher of online instruction should provide a wide collection of activities that make possible equivalent learning experiences for students using an approach that recognizes the fundamental differences between learners, distant and local. Equivalency is more difficult but promises to be more effective.

SUMMARY

The technologies used for distance education fall into two categories: telecommunications technologies that connect instructors to distant learners, and classroom technologies that record, present, and display instructional information. Increasingly, video-and computer-based systems are being used.

Most often, teachers and students use classrooms that have been designed and installed by others. However, the effective utilization of distance education classrooms requires a new set of skills for most educators and learners. Teaching with technology to learners who are not physically located in the same site where instruction is taking place requires a different set of skills and competencies than traditional education. Technologies are tools that must be mastered to be effective.

SELF-TEST QUESTIONS

1. True/False. Abstract learning is possible because an individual can draw upon and relate to previously acquired realistic experiences. Discuss why abstract learning experiences are sometimes better than more realistic experiences.
2. According to Dale's cone of experience, which is most realistic, a video or a field trip? Why are both appropriate instructional strategies?
3. Define *noise*. Explain how the teacher overcomes noise.
4. Why must communication be based on the overlapping fields of experience between teacher and learner? Discuss what happens when the fields of experience of the teacher and learner do not share elements in common.
5. True/False. According to Dale, realistic instruction is almost always better. Discuss why some think realism is better for younger learners.
6. What is the most traditional and longest-used form of technology in distance education? Discuss why this approach is still important.
7. What does a CODEC do? Why is it important for educators to know about devices such as CODECs?
8. Describe the Iowa Communications Network. In your opinion, is this system a model for other states?
9. What is CU/SeeMe? Why is this technology important?
10. True/False. Increasingly, regular classrooms in schools are being equipped to be distance education classrooms. Discuss why you feel this trend will continue or not continue.

Answers to Self-Test Questions

1. True.
2. A field trip.
3. Noise is anything that interferes with communication.
4. Overlapping fields of experience are what the teacher and student have in common. Communication—teaching—must be based on what the two individuals who are attempting to communicate have as similar experiences, such as language or ability to understand meaning from visuals. If communication is not based on what is shared in common, then it is difficult, even impossible, for the receiver of the message to draw meaning from the transmitted message. As learners grow older, their level of experience increases, and it is possible for them to understand information, even construct meaning, from abstract messages.
5. False.
6. Printed materials made available by correspondence.
7. A CODEC is a device that codes and decodes information that is sent over telecommunications media such as fiber-optic cable. The CODEC codes the video and audio information generated in a distance education classroom for transmission to a receive classroom where another CODEC decodes the information for display.
8. The ICN is a 3,000-mile statewide, two-way, full-motion, interactive fiber-optic telecommunications network used for transmission of video, audio, and data in distance education. The ICN has over 700 classrooms connected to its fiber-optic backbone network.
9. A CU/SeeMe is a simple, inexpensive desktop video/audio system that permits the sending and receiving of video and audio information using a desktop computer and computer network, such as the Internet.
10. True.

For additional information and activities, visit the Prentice Hall Companion Website at http://www.prenhall.com/simonson

REFERENCES

Dale, E. (1946). *Audiovisual methods in teaching.* Hinsdale, IL: Dryden Press.
Mallory, J. (2001). Creating streamed instruction for the deaf and hard-of-hearing online learner. *DEOSNEWS, 11*(8), 1–6.

ADDITIONAL READINGS

Baumgarn, K. (1995). *Classrooms of the Iowa Communications Network.* Ames, IA: Research Institute for Studies in Education.

Cyrs, T. (1997). *Teaching at a distance with the merging technologies.* Las Cruces, NM: Center for Educational Development.

Kemp, J., & Smellie, D. (1994). *Planning, producing, and using instructional technologies* (7th ed.). New York: HarperCollins.

Moore, M., & Kearsley, G. (1996). *Distance education: A systems view.* Belmont, CA: Wadsworth.

Richardson, A. (1992). *Corporate and organizational video.* New York: McGraw-Hill.

Simonson, M., & Volker, R. (1984). *Media planning and production.* Columbus, OH: Merrill.

Zettl, H. (1995). *Video basics.* Belmont, CA: Wadsworth.

URL for Information About Distance Education Classrooms

http://www3.iptv.org/iowa_database/ICN/icnsites/prices/contents.html

PART

APPLICATIONS

Chapter 5
COPYRIGHT AND DISTANCE EDUCATION

Chapter 6
INSTRUCTIONAL DESIGN FOR DISTANCE EDUCATION

Chapter 7
THE DISTANCE EDUCATION STUDENT

Chapter 8
TEACHING AT A DISTANCE

Chapter 9
HANDOUTS, STUDY GUIDES, AND VISUALS

Chapter 10
DISTANCE EDUCATION, THE WORLD WIDE WEB,
AND THE INTERNET

Chapter 11
ASSESSMENT FOR DISTANCE EDUCATION

Chapter 12
EVALUATING TEACHING AND LEARNING AT A DISTANCE

chapter

COPYRIGHT AND DISTANCE EDUCATION

CHAPTER GOAL

The purpose of this chapter is to discuss the implications of U.S. copyright law for teaching in distance education environments.

CHAPTER OBJECTIVES

After reading and reviewing this chapter, you should be able to

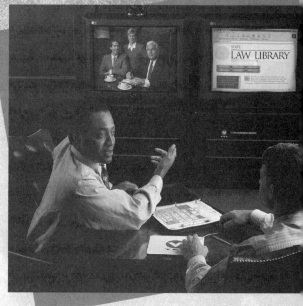

1. Differentiate between myth and fact related to copyright applications in distance education.
2. Recognize the exclusive rights granted to copyright holders by U.S. copyright law.
3. Determine when copyrighted material enters the public domain.
4. Apply the four essential fair use criteria and published guidelines to determine whether use of copyrighted materials requires permission from rights holders.
5. Identify and track the status of current copyright legislation in Congress, and be aware of the implications of new legislation.
6. Determine whether instructional media materials may be used in a video-based distance education course without permission or requires authorization from the rights holder.
7. Recognize what materials may be placed on the Internet without permission.
8. Recognize the circumstances under which Internet materials copyrighted by others may be forwarded, downloaded, and printed.
9. Follow appropriate procedures for obtaining permission from rights holders to use copyrighted materials in a distance education course.
10. Facilitate the development of an effective intellectual property rights policy.
11. Recognize the potential consequences of copyright infringement.

COPYRIGHT MYTHS

Not long ago, an instructional developer at a major state university was helping a faculty member create a web site for his course on Ancient Greece, that he was going to teach totally online the following semester. One day, the professor strolled into the instructional developer's office carrying a stack of books, each with dozens of tabs of paper marking pages of interest. He explained that in the face-to-face version of the course, he used a document camera and multimedia projector to display these photographs and illustrations to his students. "The Internet is great!" he exclaimed. "We can digitize these images and put them on the web site, and students can look at them and study them anytime they want!" He broke into a big grin, excited about how he could use this new technology to help his students learn. The instructional developer was stunned. "But what about copyright?" she asked. "Did you get permission from the publishers to digitize all these images for the Web?" The professor's grin broke into a sneer. "Get permission? Of course not. This is for educational purposes, and besides, we'll have password protection, so the publishers will never know. . . ."

This example represents the kind of mythology that has evolved as educators try to determine what is copyrighted and what is not, and what can be used in an online course and what cannot, at least without permission, and how it can be used. Misinterpretations of copyright are commonplace:

Myth 1. A work has to be published and registered with the U.S. Copyright Office to receive copyright protection.   Any work, published or unpublished, meeting the criteria specified in the copyright law receives protection as soon as it is fixed in a tangible medium of expression. For example, an original manuscript prepared on a word processor is protected as soon as the file is saved to disk or printed. Copyright covers a slide or digital image as soon as the image is recorded on the film or storage device. Registration with the Copyright Office is optional, not a requirement. However, a work must be registered before a plaintiff can collect statutory damages in the event of an infringement.

Myth 2. If it does not have a copyright notice, it is public domain.   As of March 1, 1989, when the United States adopted the Berne Convention international copyright treaty, a work is no longer required to include a copyright notice in order to receive protection. If a notice does appear, it may include either the familiar © symbol or the word *copyright*.

Myth 3. Anything on the Internet is public domain.   Nothing could be further from the truth. Original works of authorship placed on the Internet are entitled to protection just like any other works meeting the law's criteria. However, the Internet has made possible copyright infringements on a global scale.

Myth 4. A work copyrighted in another country is public domain in the United States.   This myth seems to arise when instructors want to use videotapes or publications from another nation in a U.S. distance education course. The Berne Convention treaty specifies that the copyright laws of any signatory country apply within that country to a work copyrighted in another signatory country. In other words, within the United States, any work copyrighted in any other Berne Convention nation (i.e., most nations) receives the same protection as a work copyrighted in the United States.

Myth 5. The doctrine of "fair use" means that copyrighted materials can be used in an educational setting without permission.   As a blanket statement, this is perhaps the biggest myth of all. Education is one of the purposes for which fair use *may* apply, but fair use can be determined only after careful consideration of four rather complex criteria. Many educational applications are completely beyond fair use and require permission—for example, the development of most coursepacks.

Myth 6. Any copyrighted materials can be digitized and placed on a course web site without permission, as long as the site is password protected.   Recent legislation has expanded the scope of materials that may be digitized and placed on a password-protected course web site, but fair use criteria still apply. In the example above, although a fair use case may be made for a limited number of images from each book to be incorporated into the course (depending upon whether each image was individually copyrighted, which often is the case), the sheer numbers involved likely extend well beyond fair use. (As a sidebar, the professor does not realize how easily a publisher can be made aware of a copyright infringement by a disgruntled student unhappy with a course grade.)

COPYRIGHT ESSENTIALS

Copyright is hardly a new concept. The first forms of legal copyright protection appeared in 15th-century Venice shortly after Gutenberg invented the printing press (Zobel, 1997). In 1557, Queen Mary chartered the Stationer's Company to "enlist the covetous self-interests of the very printers and booksellers," as a means of imposing censorship during a time of political and religious turmoil in England (Kaplan, cited in Miller, 1975). Registration of a book with the Stationer's Company provided the printer exclusive rights to print copies of the book and sell them.

The statute of Anne, passed by Parliament in 1714, contained features similar to some of those found in U.S. copyright law today. Existing books were entitled to 21 years of copyright protection. Books published subsequent to the statute were copyrighted for 14 years, with the copyright assigned to the author. If the author was still living at the end of this period, the copyright could be renewed for another 14 years. The law provided for the payment of fines for copyright infringements (one penny per page—a substantial amount in the early 18th century), with the penalties split evenly between the copyright holder and the Crown. Such protection was not extended to books that had not been registered with the Stationer's Company (Miller, 1975).

The first copyright legislation in the United States was enacted by Congress in 1790, a bill modeled after the statute of Anne. The law, Title 17 of the U.S. Code, has undergone several major revisions, the latest in 1976 as Public Law 94-553. Section 102 specifies that copyright protection subsists *in original works of authorship fixed in a tangible medium of expression, now known or later developed, from which they can be perceived, reproduced, or otherwise communicated, either directly or with the aid of a machine or device.*

Two critical conditions thus exist before a work is eligible for copyright protection. First, copyright applies to *works of authorship* representing the tangible expression of ideas, requiring originality and some degree of creativity. Copyrighted works of authorship in a distance education course may include the instructor's lecture notes, electronic-mail messages, graphic images in a course web page, videotapes and photographic slides, presentation graphics, literature that is read aloud, sound recordings, and printed materials reproduced for student study. Copyright protection does not extend to facts, titles, names, familiar symbols, standard forms, procedures, and works consisting of common property, although some items in these categories may be eligible for patent or trademark protection.

Second, the work *must be fixed in a tangible medium of expression.* The examples above are self-evident because they *can be perceived, reproduced, or otherwise communicated* (the actual terminology used in the law). Copyright would *not* apply to comments made in a live classroom discussion unless the interaction were recorded or otherwise transcribed. However, any comments made in an e-mail message or a text-based chat session meet the criteria for copyright protection. Courses themselves are eligible for copyright protection if they are videotaped or offered online via an Internet server. This would include courses that are delivered live via the Internet and archived on a streaming server.

EXCLUSIVE RIGHTS OF COPYRIGHT HOLDERS

The law grants to copyright owners exclusive rights to do, or to authorize others to do, any of the following:

- Reproduce the copyrighted work
- Prepare derivative works based on the copyrighted original
- Distribute copies of the copyrighted work
- Perform the copyrighted work
- Display the copyrighted work publicly

Fortunately, Congress recognized that *under certain circumstances* the use of protected materials could be acceptable without permission from the copyright holder. In fact, limitations on exclusive rights consume the majority of Chapter 1 of Title 17. Two sections are of particular importance to distance educators. Section 107 provides the criteria for "fair use," while Section 110 addresses public performance and display.

FAIR USE

According to Section 107, *the fair use of a copyrighted work . . . for purposes such as criticism, comment, news reporting, teaching (including multiple copies for classroom use), scholarship, or research, is not an infringement.* The legislative history of the law (House of Representatives Report No. 94-1476) noted that no adequate definition of the concept of fair use had emerged, and that no generally applicable definition was possible. Rather, the doctrine should be viewed as "an equitable rule of reason," with each case to be decided on its own merits against the criteria provided in the law.

The phrasing here is critically important. Section 107 does not grant educators wholesale permission to use copyrighted materials simply because they work in schools or colleges. Only a *fair use* is legal, and fair use cannot be determined until four essential criteria have been considered. Congress deliberately wrote the criteria in broad, general terms to provide a flexible structure that could be applied across a multitude of potential fair use scenarios without the need for constant revisions to the law. No single criterion is enough to deny fair use. Even if one criterion weighs against, the use may still be legal if the other three criteria weigh in favor. The criteria include the following:

- *The purpose and character of the use, including whether such use is of a commercial nature or is for nonprofit educational purposes . . .* Uses in a nonprofit, educational setting are more likely to be fair use than those in a corporate training or proprietary college setting. Reproduction for purposes of criticism or commentary may be considered more favorably, even if for commercial purposes.
- *The nature of the copyrighted work . . .* Nonfiction works are more likely to be considered fair use than fictional or artistic works containing a higher degree of creative expression. Published works are generally favored by courts more than unpublished materials, and printed works more than audiovisual materials. Publications designed to be consumable, such as workbook pages or standardized test forms, should never be reproduced without permission.
- *The amount and substantiality of the portion used in relation to the copyrighted work as a whole . . .* The law itself does not provide specific limits or percentages, although criteria have been set in negotiated guidelines that will be discussed below. In many cases with printed materials, the entire copyrighted work is desired, such as a journal article, illustration, or photograph. The case for fair use can be enhanced if no more of the published original is taken than is necessary to meet the user's needs. This criterion also has a qualitative component in that reproduction of even a small proportion of a work may exceed fair use if that portion contains the heart or essence of the original.
- *The effect of the use upon the potential market for or value of the copyrighted work . . .* In infringement suits, the courts consider whether it was reasonable to expect the ultimate recipient of a reproduction to have purchased that copy or paid a licensing fee. Courts also consider effect in the context of the potential financial harm to the copyright holder if the act in question were a widespread practice.

PUBLIC PERFORMANCE AND DISPLAY

Section 110 of the copyright law permits the performance or display of a work during the *face-to-face teaching activities* of a nonprofit educational institution, in a classroom or similar place devoted to instruction, with a lawfully made or acquired copy (if applicable). This has become known as the "face-to-face teaching exemption."

Section 110 covers activities such as the reading aloud of literature, performance of dramatic works by class members (but not by actors outside the class), performance of compositions in music classes, and display of videotapes and other audiovisual materials that take place *in the face-to-face classroom.*

The House of Representatives Report 94-1476 noted specifically that the face-to-face teaching exemption did not extend to the transmission of audiovisual materials into the classroom from a location outside the building. This restriction is quite problematic for libraries and media centers that transmit videotapes from centralized collections into classrooms via school networks, if transmission and reception occur in separate buildings. The distribution of materials in this manner required specific licensing agreements with the rights holders.

Of greater concern for distance educators has been the problem of incorporating videotapes and other audiovisual media (defined in the law as *works that consist of a series of related images which are intrinsically intended to be shown by the use of machines or devices such as projectors, viewers, or electronic equipment*) into courses transmitted to remote sites via distance education delivery systems, including both video- and Internet-based distribution. This issue has been relieved somewhat by recent legislation that will be described later in this chapter.

Section 110 cannot be applied to training events that take place in for-profit settings, for example in proprietary institutions and industry. Classroom display of materials such as videotapes in for-profit locations should be covered by licensing agreements when the materials are purchased.

DURATION OF COPYRIGHT

Several formulas have been devised to help determine when works pass into the public domain. Terms of protection vary according to the date of creation, whether the work was published, whether ownership resides with an individual or an employer or other legal entity, and whether the original copyright on an older work was renewed. Table 5–1 provides a general guide. In summary:

- A work published before 1923 is now in the public domain.
- A work created on or after January 1, 1978, is protected for the lifetime of the author plus 70 years, or if of corporate authorship, 95 years from publication. In other words, the earliest such a work could fall into the public domain is January 2048.
- A work published between 1964 and 1977 cannot fall into the public domain until at least 2059.
- A work created before January 1, 1978, but not published is protected for the lifetime of the author plus 70 years, or until December 31, 2002, whichever is later.

TABLE 5–1 ■ Duration of Copyright Under U.S. Law.

Status of Work	Term of Copyright	Earliest Public Domain Date
Published over 75 years ago	None	Now in public domain
Published between 1922 and 1963	28 years, renewable for 67 years	If not renewed, in public domain; if renewed, 95 years from publication date
Published between 1964 and 1977	95 years	2059
Created before 1978 but not published	Lifetime of author plus 70 years, or until 12/31/2002, whichever is later	2003, but only for author who became deceased before 1933
Created after 1/1/1978, personal authorship	Lifetime of author plus 70 years	2048
Created after 1/1/1978, corporate authorship	95 years from publication or 120 years from creation, whichever occurs first	2073

These dates reflect the term limits as revised in 1998 by the Sonny Bono Copyright Term Extension Act, named after the late entertainer and congressional representative who served as a member of the House Judiciary Committee until his untimely death in a skiing accident earlier that year.

The task of determining the actual term of copyright is compounded by the layers of protection that may exist for a given work. For example, Mozart's symphonies are long since in the public domain, but a 1994 recording of the Symphony no. 41 will receive protection until long after the playback device has become hopelessly obsolete. A textbook photo of an artwork may be copyrighted at several levels: by the publisher, the photographer, the owner of the original work, and perhaps even the owner of another intermediate stage, such as a digitized image taken from the photographer's slide.

PUBLIC DOMAIN

Any work in the public domain may be used freely in a distance education course. Works may enter the public domain several ways, most often simply through expiration of copyright protection. Most materials published by the U.S. government are specifically excluded from copyright protection by Section 105 and are in the public domain from the date of creation. However, audiovisual works produced for federal agencies by independent contractors *are* eligible for copyright protection and must be treated in distance education courses like any other audiovisual work. Also, restrictions on the federal government do not apply to states. Works developed by or for state agencies, including videotapes and other audiovisual materials, may be declared public domain according to the state's policies but are likely to be copyrighted.

The third means by which works enter the public domain is for owners to abandon their copyrights. For example, as Myth 3 previously illustrated, a popular and widespread misconception holds that materials posted to the Internet become public domain because the Internet is such a public and uncontrolled medium. Abandonment of copyright actually requires an explicit and overt statement from the copyright holder—and rarely occurs.

GUIDELINES

As the 1909 copyright law was undergoing revision in the mid-1970s, Congress recognized that the nonprofit educational community could benefit from guidelines that help define acceptable practices under fair use. The House report contained guidelines for classroom copying and educational uses of music that had been negotiated by educator and publisher groups. A third set of guidelines was approved in 1979 to cover off-air recording of broadcast programming for educational purposes.

Although the authors of the law tried to accommodate future technological developments with vague terminology such as "fixed in a tangible medium of expression, now known or later developed" and "with the aid of a machine or device," they had no way of anticipating the phenomenal growth of digital media authoring, storage, and distribution systems, or the incredible range of technology now easily available to both educators and consumers. As a result, application of a 1976 statute in the early 21st century is often the source of considerable frustration and confusion. The problem has long been evident. In September 1994, the U.S. Department of Commerce convened the Conference on Fair Use (CONFU), bringing together information proprietors and user groups in an attempt to develop fair use guidelines addressing new technologies. Over a 2.5-year period, representatives of more than 100 organizations met as a whole and in smaller work groups to draft guidelines for distance learning, image collections, multimedia, electronic reserves, and interlibrary loan. By May 1997, only the first three work groups had developed formal proposals, and none of the three garnered widespread support in the education community. Ultimately, CONFU elected neither to endorse nor to reject any of the proposals but to continue the negotiation processes. Table 5–2 summarizes the seven sets of fair use guidelines that have thus far been accepted by the U.S. Congress or have appeared in draft form under CONFU.

The draft Educational Fair Use Guidelines for Distance Learning and the other guidelines may be found on the World Wide Web. (See the list of web sites at the end of the chapter.) The Distance Learning work group agreed not to address online learning technologies in the proposal. At that time, the work group members felt the technologies were evolving too quickly and that the delivery of courses by educational institutions via the Internet was still in the experimental stage. The guidelines thus focused almost exclusively on video-based delivery systems. The greatest resistance to the guidelines came from K–12, higher education, and library groups, who felt the criteria were too restrictive. The lack of attention to online courses was also seen as a major shortcoming.

TABLE 5–2 ■ Status of Fair Use Guidelines of Interest to Distance Educators.

Guidelines	Applies to	Status
Guidelines for Classroom Copying in Not-for-Profit Educational Institutions	Text and other resources (e.g., photographs, illustrations) in printed publications	Accepted by Congress
Guidelines for Educational Uses of Music	Published music and sound recordings used in music classes	Accepted by Congress
Guidelines for Off-Air Recording of Broadcast Programming for Educational Purposes	Broadcast programming taped off-air (excludes cable channel programs)	Accepted by Congress
Fair Use Guidelines for Educational Multimedia	Copyrighted materials incorporated into multimedia works (includes use in distance education)	Accepted by Congress
Guidelines for the Educational Use of Digital Images	Digitized versions by visual images such as photographs, illustrations, and works of art	Conference on Fair Use (CONFU) draft; not widely endorsed
Educational Fair Use Guidelines for Distance Learning	Audiovisual works used in video-based distance education (excludes asynchronous delivery)	CONFU draft; not widely endorsed
Fair Use Guidelines for Electronic Reserve Systems	Digitized publications maintained online as counterpart to library reserve system for printed materials	Draft prepared as part of CONFU process but not submitted for consideration

RECENT COPYRIGHT-RELATED LEGISLATION

The copyright law itself is a document in a perpetual state of change. The law was amended by Congress a total of 46 times between its enactment in 1976 and the end of 2000. Typically, about two dozen copyright-related acts are introduced in each 2-year congressional session. (Educators can track the status of proposed legislation at the U.S. Copyright Office web site, http://www.loc.gov/copyright/legislation/.) Most of these never become law, and of those that have survived the process and been enacted, few have been significant for the education community. One of these was the aforementioned Sonny Bono Copyright Term Extension Act of 1998, which delayed the transition of many classic publications and audiovisual media, such as early Disney productions, into the public domain. Another was the Digital Millennium Copyright Act (DMCA), also of 1998, and the subsequent legislation it spawned.

Digital Millennium Copyright Act

The DMCA, 59 pages long in its PDF version, has been the most comprehensive revision of the 1976 copyright law to date, with far-reaching implications for distance educators. The Act was intended to bring the United States into compliance with two treaties agreed upon by the World Intellectual Property Organization (WIPO) in 1996. Three components of the DMCA are particularly relevant to this chapter.

Infringement Liability Protections.   The DMCA specifies that if a copyright infringement is found on a web site maintained by a service provider, the rights holder may request that the service provider "take down" or block access to the infringing material and escape institutional liability for the infringement. Many school districts and most higher education campuses provide Internet access for their faculty, staff, and students, and thus fall into the category of "service provider." (For the remainder of this section, "service provider" will refer to the school, district, or higher education institution providing Internet services for its internal constituencies. This responsibility is normally placed within an instructional or information technology department.)

If, for example, a faculty member has placed copyrighted material on a course web site without the appropriate clearance, the copyright owner can request that the service provider remove it, or at least block access to it. If the service provider does not, it may be liable for the infringement along with the teacher. The service provider must also provide notification of the takedown to the person who placed the infringing material on the web site. In order to be eligible for liability protection, the service provider must formerly be unaware of the infringing activity, meaning that course development staff employed by the service provider and working with the faculty member cannot have placed the infringing material on the web site, and the service provider cannot receive any financial gain from the infringement.

The DMCA lists several protective measures that schools and colleges must take to limit their liability as service providers. An "agent" must be registered with the Copyright Office to receive copyright infringement complaints and respond appropriately. Instructions for registration of an agent and a list of agents may be found at the Copyright Office web site, http://www.loc.gov/copyright/onlinesp/. Procedures for contacting the agent must be posted on the service provider's web site.

A current copyright policy for the service provider's Internet users must be in place and posted on the web site. The policy must contain provisions stating that access privileges will be terminated for repeat offenders.

The service provider must maintain an ongoing program for educating its Internet users about copyright and requirements for obtaining appropriate permissions before placing protected material on institutional web pages, including course web sites.

Education and library groups have pointed out that takedown of course materials that are the target of infringement complaints may have serious implications for fair use and academic freedom, not to mention a potentially deleterious impact on student learning. The DMCA permits the faculty member to serve a counternotification that she or he believes the initial complaint was filed erroneously, for example in a claim of fair use. Unless the copyright owner files legal action as the result of the counternotification, the service provider must restore access to the materials in question within 10–14 working days. However, filing the counternotification may place the faculty member at risk of litigation, and the period of time during which the materials are off-line may jeopardize the lesson plan.

Circumvention of Technological Protection Measures.   The DMCA addresses measures taken by copyright owners to control both access to and reproduction of their protected materials. For example, the Act contains a provision requiring the manufacturers of videocassette recorders (VCRs) to incorporate technology that prevents unauthorized copying of videotapes while permitting the recording of programs from off-air and basic and extended tier (excluding premium) cable television channels. Related to web sites, the DMCA not only prohibits the sale and use of devices that circumvent access restriction methods such as password protection, but it also makes illegal the simple act of informing others how to circumvent these measures and even linking to sites that provide this information. These provisions would protect the encryption schemes used in online banking and credit card transactions connected with Web-based commerce, which readers may find comforting.

However, as with the infringement liability issues described above, the education and library communities have vociferously protested the circumvention limitations of the DMCA as threats to fair use and academic freedom. Specifically, these organizations hoped for broader access to such materials as literary works and audio and video materials that exist online but require fee payment before access is granted. A ruling issued by the Library of Congress in October 2000 clarified that technological protections could be circumvented only for two categories of works: compilations consisting of lists of web sites blocked by filtering software applications, and literary works, including computer programs and databases, protected by access control mechanisms that fail to permit access because of malfunction, damage, or obsolescence.

Distance Education Study. Section 403 of the DMCA required the Copyright Office to collect information from all stakeholders and make recommendations to Congress on how to promote the use of digital technologies in distance education. The Office's *Report on Digital Distance Education* was released in May 1999. Most of its recommendations focused on amending Section 110 of the copyright law to extend the exemptions granted in face-to-face instructional situations to distance learning environments. Specifically, the report recommended the following:

- Update the exemption to permit digital transmissions over computer networks, expanding the rights covered to include those needed to accomplish such transmissions, to the extent technologically required.
- Eliminate the physical classroom requirement in section 110(2), permitting transmissions to students officially enrolled in the course, regardless of their physical location.
- Add language that focuses more clearly on the concept of mediated instruction, in order to ensure that the performance or display is analogous to the type of performance or display that would take place in a live classroom.
- Add safeguards to minimize the greater risks of uncontrolled copying and distribution posed by digital transmission, including limiting the retention of any transient copies, requiring the adoption of copyright policies and education, and requiring the use of technological measures that reasonably prevent unauthorized access and dissemination.
- Retain the current "nonprofit" requirement for educational institutions seeking to invoke the exemption.

- Add a new provision to the Copyright Act to allow distance education to take place asynchronously, by permitting a copyrighted work to be uploaded onto a server for subsequent transmission to students under the conditions set out in section 110(2).
- Expand the categories of works exempted from the performance right beyond the current coverage of nondramatic literary or musical works, adding other types of works but allowing performances of only reasonable and limited portions. (U.S. Copyright Office, 1999)

The *Report on Digital Distance Education* led to proposed legislation. Another major impetus leading to this legislation was the report of the Web-Based Education Commission compiled for the president and Congress, entitled *The Power of the Internet for Learning: Moving from Promise to Practice* (Web-Based Education Commission, 2000), which considered the challenge of providing 21st-century distance education with obsolete copyright laws as analogous to trying "to manage the interstate highway system with the rules of the horse and buggy era" (p. 97).

This is the legislation in response to the DMCA that addresses distance learning issues. The Senate has passed the Technology, Education and Copyright Harmonization (TEACH) Act. The Twenty-First Century Distance Learning Enhancement Act has been introduced into the House and approved by the Judiciary Committee. Action by the entire House is pending as this is written. The two acts are significantly different. "The TEACH act was passed and signed into law in November 2002."

Uniform Computer Information Transactions Act (UCITA)

UCITA is not a federal law but a proposed state law that promises to have significant implications for the education communities in those states in which it is enacted. It was drafted by the National Conference of Commissioners on Uniform State Laws (NCCUSL) to promote economic development by helping states appear friendly to the computer software industry. UCITA is intended to be a counterpart to the Uniform Commercial Code (UCC), to establish the rules for the distribution and use of software in the same way in which the UCC addresses the sale of goods and services.

Although the mission of NCCUSL, as its name implies, is to help states pass uniform, or at least compatible, laws to minimize interstate problems, UCITA is a large and complex piece of proposed legislation that can be changed in any number of ways by state lawmakers before passage. The essence of the basic UCITA draft will be described here, but readers should be aware that the text could vary in legislation being considered or passed by their own states.

Perhaps the most troublesome aspect of UCITA for educators is that it changes the relationship between software and its purchaser. With a book, for example, the customer buys it and owns it (the physical book, not the intellectual property the book contains, of course). When the owner is finished with the book, she or he can sell it, give it away, or otherwise dispose of it under the "first sale doctrine" associated with the copyright law. With software, the purchaser obtains a license to use the product but does not "own" the product. The license is a contract, with terms of the contract spelled out in the license agreement. This has always been the case, but UCITA takes the concept of licensing as a contract to new dimensions.

For example, UCITA legitimizes the "shrinkwrap license agreement," in which the purchaser agrees to the conditions of the license by destroying the shrinkwrap in which the product is packaged, even though the buyer cannot read the terms of the contract in most cases *until* the product has been opened, and has no opportunity for negotiation or reconsideration. The same would apply to "click on" buttons when software is purchased over the Internet. Educator and librarian groups fear that vendors could include conditions specifying use on one computer only, thus precluding use on a replacement desktop and negating the first sale doctrine. They are also concerned that contract terms could limit the vendor's liability for defective products, or at the least give purchasers a limited time period in which to discover product flaws. Rights now covered by fair use could be restricted by license agreements, although software manufacturers have been quick to assure educators that the criteria for fair use contained in the copyright law would still apply. UCITA could permit vendors to scan computers connected to the Internet and disable software without current, valid licenses, regardless of work in progress on those desktops utilizing those products. UCITA may even prohibit public criticism of software products.

UCITA has been vigorously opposed by the Federal Trade Commission, the majority of the state attorneys general, and education, library, and consumer organizations. As a result, although UCITA legislation had been considered by the legislatures of at least 26 states and the District of Columbia by mid-2001, it had been enacted into law only in Virginia and Maryland. Educators can track the status of UCITA legislation on a state-by-state basis at the web site of the Computer Professionals for Social Responsibility (CPSR), http://www.cpsr.org/program/UCITA/ucitastates.html.

COPYRIGHT APPLICATIONS IN DISTANCE EDUCATION

What then are the major implications of U.S. copyright law for distance education? For the purpose of this chapter, issues are grouped by video- and Internet-based delivery systems.

Printed Materials

Regardless of the delivery vehicle, teachers of distance education courses may want their students to have copyrighted articles and other printed materials in hand for study purposes. The Guidelines for Classroom Copying in Not-for-Profit Educational Institutions permit limited reproduction and distribution of copyrighted materials (no more than one copy per student in the course) *as long as the tests of brevity and spontaneity and the cumulative effects test are met.* A discussion of numerical limitations is beyond the scope of this chapter. Readers are referred to the guidelines for limits from a single author or publication. The test of spontaneity requires that the inspiration to use the work and the moment in time of actuai use in the course do not allow for a reasonable attempt to obtain permission. This test effectively prohibits use of the same materials in subsequent academic terms without the copyright holder's approval. The cumulative effects test caps the number of items copied for a single course at nine per academic term.

The criteria specified in the guidelines help determine what can be reproduced without the need to seek permission. The development of coursepacks, particularly those including the same materials term after term, normally requires licensing and the payment of fees. The licensing of printed materials is not an overwhelming task. The Copyright Clearance Center (CCC) (http://www.copyright.com/) has been established as the reproduction rights organization (RRO) for the United States and serves this clearinghouse function. The CCC can license the reproduction of any of over 1.75 million titles, including those of at least 9,600 publishers and hundreds of thousands of independent authors, already preauthorized by rights holders, and collects and distributes royalties. Many copy centers and bookstores serving academic institutions maintain accounts with the CCC, provide liaison on the instructor's behalf, and then duplicate and sell the coursepacks. Some 13 RROs exist worldwide, providing similar services to faculty in other countries.

The Electronic Course Content Service (ECCS) has been initiated by the Copyright Clearance Center to provide rapid clearances for electronic coursepacks and electronic reserves. This service may be of particular interest to distance educators who do not wish to distribute paper coursepacks to remote site students. The concept of the electronic coursepack is not exclusive to the CCC. The vendors of learning management systems such as WebCT and Blackboard normally can provide access to a wide range of copyright-cleared professional publications via the system portal, any of which can be incorporated into a course for no additional charge beyond the product license fee. Also, companies such as XanEdu (http://www.xanedu.com/) have emerged to help distance educators incorporate electronic coursepacks into their courses.

Audiovisual Materials

In conventional classroom settings, Section 110 permits the performance or display of a copyrighted work under what is termed the "face-to-face teaching exemption," provided that the activities take place in a classroom or similar place devoted to instruction, in a nonprofit educational institution, with a lawfully made copy (if applicable). For example, the law allows classroom activities to include the reading aloud of literature, performance of dramatic works and musical compositions by instructors and students enrolled in the course, and display of videotapes and other audiovisual materials. However, in the case of courses that are "transmitted" to remote sites, the law permits performance of musical and nondramatic literary works *but specifically excludes dramatic works and audiovisual materials.*

Section 101 defines "audiovisual materials" as "works that consist of a series of related images which are intrinsically intended to be shown by the use of machines or devices such as projectors, viewers, or electronic equipment. . . ." Allowable activities in a distance education course would thus include the display of photographs, illustrations, maps, and other printed materials, still images from videotapes, and 35-mm slides, as long as they are not shown in sequence from a copyrighted program. A course that is transmitted cannot include a videotape, videodisk, 16-mm film, or consecutive images from a photographic series without the copyright holder's permission. The same criteria would also apply to the display of digitized images downloaded from a server and then incorporated into a transmitted course, although the legality of digitizing third-party images and placing them on a server for faculty and student access represents a different copyright issue. The guidelines proposed to CONFU in 1997 by the digital images work group permitted the digitization and storage of images not already commercially available at a fair price, provided that the images were accessed through a secure network and available only to faculty and students associated with the course. Furthermore, the guidelines restricted use to a maximum of one academic term if the rights holder is known; thereafter, permission must be obtained. Educators should be aware that the digital images guidelines were not widely endorsed and may or may not be considered by the courts in deciding infringement suits.

The CONFU Fair Use Guidelines for Educational Multimedia provide numerical limits on the amount of copyrighted material that can be incorporated in a multimedia development project without permission and also permit the use of the completed products on a controlled access distance education network. Development of the multimedia guidelines was already well under way before CONFU was convened and took place largely outside the CONFU process. The completed draft was endorsed by more than 30 organizations, including the U.S. Copyright Office, and was recognized by Congress. As a result, the multimedia guidelines are likely to carry more weight in the courts than the other CONFU drafts. Resistance within CONFU came primarily from education and academic library organizations, which felt the guidelines were too restrictive.

The constraints on the use of audiovisual materials in a transmitted distance education course place an extraordinary burden on faculty accustomed to using instructional technology in their teaching. Whereas the Copyright Clearance Center provides licensing services for printed materials, no such clearinghouse yet exists for audiovisual works. Each copyright holder must be located and permission obtained. Often this is not an easy task. McKay (1995) described a litany of frustrations—including endless voice-mail messages, mail responses that did not address his request, operators in other countries who did not speak English, and terse rejections—during his attempts to gain permission to use videotapes in course lectures shown on a local cable television channel. As a result, students were required to drive to campus to view the tapes in the college library, hardly "distance education."

The CONFU guidelines for distance learning provide an indication of the degree to which some rights holders seem willing to bend. The guidelines require that the transmission be over a secure system with limited access and would not apply to courses broadcast via television stations or cable systems. Performance of an entire copyrighted work or large portion thereof would be permitted just one time for a distance learning course; permission would be required if the course is offered in a subsequent academic term. Receiving sites would be permitted to record the class sessions containing the copyrighted materials and make the tapes available for student viewing, but the tapes must be viewed only in a controlled-access environment and must be erased after 15 working days, and the playback system must prevent further reproduction of the portion of the class tape including the copyrighted material. As with the guidelines for digital images, it is unknown whether a court would consider these criteria the upper limits of fair use in a distance education course, because no case law yet exists on the topic. The safest alternatives are (1) seek permission and (2) use locally produced materials for which the copyright rests with the instructor's own institution. These would include not only videotapes but photographs, graphics, and digitized images as well.

Computer-Based Distance Education

The Internet is rapidly becoming the medium of choice for distance educators in a wide variety of academic, corporate, and government settings. The CONFU work group's reluctance to address online learning environments has left educators without fair use guidelines in this area, although the multimedia and digital images guidelines are equally applicable to video and computer networks.

Materials placed on the Internet, whether electronic-mail messages, postings to mailing lists (often inappropriately referred to as "listservs"), Usenet newsgroups, or files and images that make up World Wide Web pages, represent intellectual property fixed in a tangible medium of expression and are entitled to copyright protection just like any other work of authorship. From a legal perspective, placement of the material on the Internet is no different from any other form of distribution, except that access and the potential for abuse are both greatly expanded. Although some persons contend that such action implies an abandonment of copyright, clearly this is not the case without an explicit statement to that effect on the part of the copyright holder (which often is someone other than the individual who posted the material) (Templeton, 1997).

Many distance education courses are conducted via electronic mail and online discussion groups. The author of an e-mail message, whether sent to an individual or a list or newsgroup, retains ownership of the intellectual property that message contains. Under the concept of "implied license," a recipient can save the message, print it, and forward it to a limited number of individuals interested in the same topic without the originator's permission, but a person-to-person message should never be posted to a mailing list or newsgroup without permission. Forwarding a message from one list or newsgroup to another without permission may also extend beyond the boundaries of implied license, particularly if the forwarded message reaches an essentially different audience or is sent through a different distribution system. Courses offered via the World Wide Web provide excellent opportunities for copyright abuse. Course web page developers must be careful that all page components either are original or have the necessary clearances. For example, attractive buttons, bars, bullets, backgrounds, icons, clip art, and other graphics are available for downloading from dozens of web sites. Most of these locations specify their copyright policies within the site. Some offer their graphics freely with no restrictions, others require notification of use and/or reciprocal links, while others charge fees. Under no circumstances should a text document be copied and put on a course web site without permission.

The presence of Print and Save buttons on browser toolbars may imply that documents on the Web are fair game. On the contrary, unless they are specifically dedicated to the public domain or grant downloading privileges, Web documents are entitled to full copyright protection. A fair use handbook published by the Consortium for Educational Technology for University Systems (CETUS, 1995) suggests that copying a short Internet document for personal study or research likely falls within fair use but recommends that the four-factor fair use analysis be applied. Saving or printing from sites that have restricted access or contain documents that are commercially available may be more difficult to justify as fair use. Many web sites include copyright policies that provide the site sponsor's positions on downloading. Care must be taken to confirm that the site sponsor actually is the rights holder of the desired document.

Is it necessary to obtain permission before linking to someone else's web site? Although some purists insist that the answer is yes, most authorities feel that freely linking to the web sites of others not only is legal but is encouraged, and that those who object to setting up hyperlinks are essentially missing the point of the Web. Even if permission is not a legal requirement, "netiquette" dictates that the webmaster be notified that a link has been established and be given the opportunity to ask that it be removed. The waters become muddied when links are established to individual frames within the web sites of others. Some court cases have set the precedent that linking to frames without permission is not legal.

Many courses, particularly in higher education and corporate training settings, are now offered via some form of Internet conferencing, groupware, or learning management system such as WebCT or Blackboard. Some of the more advanced provide sophisticated communication tools, featuring one-to-one e-mail and threaded large- and small-group discussions, and content presentation via web pages. The copyright implications described above are equally applicable in these settings, even though most of these systems require special client software and/or passwords that restrict access to the participants.

OBTAINING PERMISSION

If guidelines are not applicable and fair use cannot be determined, distance educators should obtain permission from rights holders before using copyrighted materials in their courses, as challenging as that task may seem. Begin by contacting the publisher or distributor. If no address or telephone number is provided, check catalogs or ask a reference librarian for assistance. In the case of printed publications, the Copyright Clearance Center is a potential source. As a last resort, a plea for help sent to appropriate Internet mailing lists often delivers the desired information.

The first contact with the rights holder should be made by telephone to confirm precisely to whom the request should be addressed. A phone call also provides an opportunity to discuss the circumstances of the request and negotiate fees. Ultimately, the rights holder will likely ask for a written copy of the request, by either mail or fax, for record purposes and to minimize misunderstandings. See Figure 5–1 for a sample request letter. At a minimum, the rights holder will need the following information:

- Name, position, institution, mailing address, and phone and fax numbers for the person making the request.
- Identification of the item to be used, including title, author or producer, publication title and date in the case of periodicals, and amount desired.

July 16, 20XX

Mrs. Caroline B. Day
Manager of Permissions
American Heritage Productions
2877 Revere Highway
Boston, MA 02226

Dear Mrs. Day:

As a follow-up to our telephone conversation this morning, I am hereby requesting permission to show your excellent videotape, *The Life of Edgar Allen Poe,* in my distance education course this fall. Our department purchased this tape from your company in 1999 but did not obtain the transmission rights at that time.

The course is entitled "Early American Literature" and is expected to enroll around 25 students, including about 10 participating at off-campus locations. The course will be transmitted to four receive sites (in Sioux City, Clear Lake, Waterloo, and Ottumwa) via the Iowa Communications Network, a closed-access, statewide telecommunications system. The transmission will be received only in these four specially equipped ICN classrooms, and no local recordings will be permitted. A backup recording of the entire class period will be made at the origination site and made available to students who were not present. This tape will be provided for viewing only in a controlled access environment with no reproduction equipment accessible. The tape will be erased after two weeks.

The anticipated date of use is November 17, 20XX. I would appreciate your response by November 1 if possible so I can make alternative course plans if necessary. I do hope you will honor this request, however, because your tape is a highly informative reconstruction of Poe's life and is extremely valuable to my students.

Thank you very much for your consideration. Please contact me directly if I can provide further information.

Sincerely,

Michael T. James

Associate Professor English

Phone: (712) 555-2838
Fax: (712) 555-2840
E-Mail: mtjames@westiowa.edu

FIGURE 5–1 Sample permission letter.

- Complete description of the intended use, including purpose, course name, number of copies, means of distribution, intended dates of use, description of recipients, and precautions anticipated to prevent further reproductions (if applicable).
- Date by which permission is requested. (Allow at least 6 weeks.) Although approval can be granted over the telephone, for record purposes written permission is strongly recommended, preferably on the copyright holder's letterhead paper. This provides tangible evidence confirming exactly who provided permission for what, and when.

INTELLECTUAL PROPERTY RIGHTS

The matter of intellectual property rights is currently one of the hot buttons in distance education, particularly among faculty unions. Who owns an online course? The school/university? The faculty member providing the content? Should the ownership be shared between the two, and if so, under what conditions? Intellectual property rights related to multimedia and online course materials have long been an issue in higher education (Twigg, 2000; National Research Council, 2000) and are becoming an increasingly prominent concern at the K–12 level (Axelson, 2001; Guerard, 2001).

At the core of the issue is determining whether the development of the course and/or materials constituted a "work for hire." Under normal circumstances, the author of the work is the owner. However, under the concept of "work for hire," defined in Section 101 of the copyright statute as "a work prepared by an employee within the scope of his or her employment," the author's employer is the legal owner of the work. According to Burk (1997), "[f]actors that point to the creator being a regular employee include income tax withholding by the employer, . . . a working schedule set by the employer, the employer providing materials and equipment used to prepare the work, . . . and the right of the employer to assign projects to the worker" (p. 14).

Although these conditions would seem to indicate that the educational institution clearly owns online courses and materials that faculty are assigned to develop, particularly those that are part of an organized online curriculum, many individual institutions and systems have elected to negotiate intellectual property agreements with their respective faculties. These policies typically specify ownership (who owns what?), the royalty percentages paid to each party (which may include the faculty member, the institution, and the instructional technology or distance education unit involved in the course development), and the rights of the individuals involved. For example, a common model is for the institution to own the course and the faculty member to own the content. In this situation, if the faculty member accepts a position elsewhere, she or he can take the course content to the new campus and use it there. However, the course itself, including the content, also may be used by the former institution, with a new instructor assigned to teach the course. The intellectual property agreement would specify the royalty amount paid to the faculty member who created the course.

SUMMARY

Somewhere in the not too distant future, our homes, workplaces, and schools will be equipped with advanced telecommunications systems integrating what is known today as telephone services, Internet access, online financial and news services, and cable television, probably with many other features not yet conceived. Distance education will play a central role in that future, as multimedia-based curricula will be offered by educational institutions and private corporations on a global basis to anyone, anywhere, at any time. The current copyright law, even with all its revisions, will likely be unable to deal with the enormous complexity of protecting intellectual property rights while providing legal access in this international information marketplace and will require a major overhaul. The Web-Based Education Commission (2000) called for "a radical rethinking of the relevant body of regulation and law" (p. 97). Certainly, the basic concepts of copyright and fair use may need to be reconsidered. However, a more probable intermediate solution is the development of technologies that prevent reproduction of copyrighted materials from networked sources. The Digital Millennium Copyright Act took the first significant steps down that path.

Meanwhile, the present law may be inadequate, but educators must abide by its provisions or face the consequences. For the most part, the copyright statute is civil law, not criminal law. Unless violators have made a business out of infringements, they are likely to be sued, not sent to prison. The penalties can be severe—statutory damages of up to $100,000 per instance, plus payment of the plaintiff's legal fees, which can be substantial. Distance educators have not only a legal and ethical obligation to "practice safe copyright" but monetary incentives as well.

SELF-TEST QUESTIONS

1. True/False. If a printed document has not been published and does not include a copyright notice, it can legally be reproduced and distributed to distance education students without the author's permission.
2. What are the two critical conditions that determine whether a work is eligible for copyright protection?
3. What are the five exclusive rights granted to copyright holders by U.S. copyright law?
4. True/False. As long as the use of copyrighted materials is in a nonprofit, educational setting, and the first "fair use" criterion is satisfied, the other three criteria can be ignored.
5. One of your students has made an observation in a posting to the online discussion forum for your distance education course that you feel is of interest to others who subscribe to a mailing list (listserv) in your field. What must you do before you can forward the student's posting to the list?
6. True/False. In a distance education course offered via the World Wide Web, it is legal to link to a third-party web site as a course resource without the permission of that site's copyright holder.
7. What are the four key information elements that should be included in a letter requesting permission to use copyrighted materials in a distance education course?

Answers to Self-Test Questions

1. False. Unpublished materials are eligible for copyright protection. The copyright notice is recommended but not required. The presence of a copyright notice on a work prevents the defendant in a civil suit from claiming "innocent infringement."
2. The law applies to an *original work of authorship* that is *fixed in a tangible medium of expression.*
3. U.S. copyright laws grants the rights of reproduction, preparation of derivative works based on the copyrighted original, distribution, public performance, and public display.
4. False. All four criteria are equally important and must be considered for all uses, including those in education. No single criterion is sufficient to determine whether a use does or does not fall under fair use.
5. You must obtain the student's permission.
6. Generally true. Depending upon state or local laws that may apply, linking to other sites is not only legal but encouraged. Those site managers should be notified as a courtesy and given the opportunity to ask that the link be removed.
7. A permission request should include identification and contact information for the person making the request, complete identification of the item(s) to be used, complete description of the intended use, and date by which permission is requested.

For additional information and activities, visit the Prentice Hall Companion Website at http://www.prenhall.com/simonson

REFERENCES

Axelson, M. (2001). *Who owns the online content your teachers create?* [Online]. Available: http://www.electronic-school.com/2001/06/.

Burk, D. L. (1997). Ownership of electronic course materials in higher education. *CAUSE/EFFECT, 20*(3), 13–18 [Online]. Available: http://www.educause.edu/pub/ce/cem97/cem973table.html.

Consortium for Educational Technology for University Systems. (1995). *Fair use of copyrighted works.* Seal Beach, CA: California State University Chancellor's Office.

Guerard, E. B. (2001, January 29). AFT offers standards for online learning. *eSchool News* [Online]. Available: http://www.eschoolnews.org/news/showStory.cfm?ArticleID=2145.

McKay, G. (1995). *Copyright in the pipeline: An examination of distance learning issues and possible solutions.* Paper presented at the 1995 conference of the Council for Higher Education Computing Services, Roswell, NM, November 1995. (ERIC Document Reproduction Service No. ED398913)

Miller, J. K. (1975). A brief history of copyright. *Audiovisual Instruction, 20*(10), 44.

National Research Council. (2000). *The digital dilemma: Intellectual property in the information age.* Washington, DC: National Academy Press [Online]. Available: http://www.nap.edu/html/digital_dilemma/.

Templeton, B. (1997, May 19). *10 big myths about copyright explained* [Online]. Available: http://www.clari.net/brad/copymyths.html.

Twigg, C. A. (2000). *Who owns online courses and course materials: Intellectual property policies for a new learning environment.* Troy, NY: The Pew Learning and Technology Program, Rensselaer Polytechnic Institute [Online]. Available: http://www.center.rpi.edu/PewSym/Mono2.pdf.

U.S. Copyright Office. (1999). *Copyright and digital distance education* [Online]. Available: http://www.loc.gov/copyright/docs/de_rprt.pdf.

Web-Based Education Commission. (2000). *The power of the Internet for learning: Moving from promise to practice.* Washington, DC: Author. [Online]. Available: http://www.ed.gov/offices/AC/WBEC/FinalReport/WBECReport.pdf.

Zobel, S. M. (1997). Legal implications of intellectual property and the World Wide Web. In B. H. Khan (Ed.), *Web-based instruction* (pp. 337–340). Englewood Cliffs, NJ: Educational Technology Publications.

ADDITIONAL READINGS

O'Mahoney, B. (1997, May 1). *Newsgroups* [Online]. Available: http://www.benedict.com.

Oppedahl & Larson Law Offices. (1996, October 29). *Web law FAQ* [Online]. Available: http://www.patents.com/weblaw.sht.

SOURCES OF INFORMATION

Conference on Fair Use Home Page

http://www.uspto.gov/web/offices/dcom/olia/confu/
Activities and reports of the Conference on Fair Use (CONFU)

Copyright and Fair Use

http://fairuse.stanford.edu
Comprehensive fair use information site maintained by Stanford University Libraries

Copyright Clearance Center

http://www.copyright.com
Web site for the reproduction rights organization serving the United States

Copyright Law & Graduate Research

http://www.umi.com/hp/Support/DServices/copyrght/

Resources compiled by noted copyright authority Kenneth Crews and maintained on
   the University Microfilms Inc. web site

Copyright Law Materials

http://www.law.cornell.edu:80/topics/copyright.html

Site maintained by the Cornell University Law School, providing full text of the
   copyright law and copyright treaties, court decisions, and other resources

Copyright Resources on the Internet

http://www.groton.k12.ct.us/mts/pt2a.htm

A comprehensive guide to copyright resources maintained by the Groton (CT) Public
   Schools

Copyright Web Site

http://www.benedict.com

Comprehensive source of copyright information maintained by intellectual property
   attorney Benedict O'Mahoney

EDUCAUSE Archive of Copyright/Intellectual Property Policies

http://www.educause.edu/asp/doclib/subject_docs.asp?Term ID=112

Links to more than 35 institutional policies and other documents related to copyright
   and intellectual property policies in higher education

U.S. Copyright Office

http://lcweb.loc.gov/copyright/

Online source of Copyright Office publications, forms, and other information,
   including status of pending copyright legislation

UT System Crash Course on Copyright

http://www.utsystem.edu/ogc/intellectualproperty/cprtindx.htm

Georgia Harper's widely acclaimed guide to copyright, including applications in
   distance learning, maintained by the University of Texas System's Office of
   General Counsel

chapter

INSTRUCTIONAL DESIGN FOR DISTANCE EDUCATION

CHAPTER GOAL

The purpose of this chapter is to present a process for designing instruction at a distance.

CHAPTER OBJECTIVES

After reading and reviewing this chapter, you should be able to

1. Explain why it is important to plan ahead when teaching at a distance.
2. Describe a systematic design process for instructional design.
3. Describe the types of learner information to be collected for planning.
4. Explain the decisions about content that need to be made.
5. Explain why it is important to examine teaching strategies and media.
6. Discuss how technology and resources influence the distance learning environment.
7. Describe the process for planning to evaluate instruction.

"SIGNAL FIRES"?

In one of the greatest Greek tragedies, *Agamemmon,* Aeschylus begins his drama with word of beacon fires carrying news of the fall of Troy and the return of the king—news that set in motion Clytemnestra's plan to kill her husband in long-delayed revenge for his slaying of their daughter. These signal fires would have required a series of line-of-sight beacons stretching 500 miles around the Aegean Sea. Line-of-sight communication, as signal fires would require, have a long history. Most broadcast television applications require line of sight; even communications satellites orbiting in the Clarke Belt thousands of miles above the equator are "in sight" of the uplinks and downlinks on Earth.

Communication with someone you can see has a visceral element that is missing when that person or group of people is not "in sight." Certainly, considerable communication and distance education does not involve face-to-face instruction. The heart of distance education is the concept of separation of teacher and learner. Many say the meeting of students with teachers will soon be a relic of the past, like signal fires. This group touts the convenience of "anytime, anyplace" learning and the power of modern communications technologies to unite learners with instructional events no matter when they are needed and no matter where students may be located.

Others advocate the need for face-to-face instruction. This group stresses the importance of seeing and being seen, and the personal nature of the teaching-learning environment. Some even say that you cannot really learn some topics without being in a specific place with a select group of collaborators.

A third position is advocated by others who say that education should occur using a combination of instructional strategies. Schlosser and Burmeister (1999) even wrote about the "best of both worlds" where courses and programs would have varying percentages of face-to-face and distance-delivered learning experiences.

To date, however, no clear and verified process for determining whether face-to-face instruction, distance instruction, or a combination of the two is best. Most instructional designers and instructional technologists know that Richard Clark was correct when he said that media are "mere vehicles," but when courses are designed and instruction delivered, what are the templates, the processes, the approaches to be used to determine whether a module, course, or program should be delivered face to face or online? Or, what percentage of each is "best"? Where is the research? Certainly, decisions about how a course is to be delivered should not be based solely on the "beliefs" of the instructor, or the mandates of administrators. Signal fires told of the fall of Troy probably because that was the most appropriate technology available. Today, many technologies are available for instruction of the distant learner. Instructional design processes help the instructor make informed decisions about technology use.

WHY PLAN FOR TEACHING AT A DISTANCE?

Just like other kinds of teaching, teaching at a distance requires planning and organizing. However, teaching at a distance, whether synchronous or asynchronous, requires that greater emphasis be placed on the initial planning phase.

FIGURE 6-1   The Dick and Carey systems approach model for designing instruction.

Instructional design should consider all aspects of the instructional environment, following a well-organized procedure that provides guidance to even the novice distance instructor. (See, for example, Figure 6–1.) The instructional environment should be viewed as a system, a relationship among and between all the components of that system—the instructor, the learners, the material, and the technology. Especially when planning for distance education, the instructor must make decisions that will affect all aspects of the system (Moore & Kearsley, 1996).

This chapter presents an organized and systematic way to go about planning instruction. This design process allows the instructor to consider elements such as the content, the nature of the learner, the process by which the learning will take place (methodology), and the means for assessing the learning experience. By following through with this process, the instructor will find that teaching at a distance is an exciting and dynamic experience, one that will be welcomed by both the instructor and the learners.

PRINCIPLES OF INSTRUCTIONAL DESIGN SYSTEMS

Systematic Process

The process of systematic planning for instruction is the outcome of many years of research (Dick & Carey, 1996). An analysis of the application of this process indicates that when instruction is designed within a system, learning occurs. The process of instructional design is a field of study. Instructional design is considered the intellectual technique of the professional who is responsible for appropriate application of technology to the teaching and learning process. In other words, instructional design is to the instructional technologist as the rule of law is to the lawyer, the prescription of medicine is to the medical doctor, and the scientific method is to the chemist—a way of thinking and solving problems (Thompson, Hargrave, & Simonson, 1996).

A critical part of the process is to consider the components of a successful learning system (Dick & Carey, 1996). These components are the learners, the content, the method and materials, and the environment, including the technology. The interaction of these components creates the type of learning experience necessary for student learning.

The components must interact both efficiently and effectively to produce quality learning experiences. There should be a balance among the components—none can take on a higher position than the others. The attempt to keep the components equally balanced while maintaining their interaction effect is essential to planning quality instruction. Simply stated, a series of activities alone cannot lead to learning; it is only with the careful planning for their balance and interface that learning is the result.

Another critical part of the process is evaluation. For successful learning to take place, it is vital to determine what works and what needs to be improved. Evaluation leads to revision of instruction, and revision of instruction helps secure the final outcome of helping students learn (Heinich, Molenda, Russell, & Smaldino, 2002). Because of an emphasis on planning and revising, well-designed instruction is repeatable. This means that the instruction can be applied again in another class. For example, instruction designed for a televised, multisite class can be used again with a new group of students at different sites. Because it is "reusable," the considerable initial effort is well worth the time and energy.

Planning for Instruction at a Distance

The process of planning and organizing for a distance education course is multifaceted and must occur well in advance of the scheduled instruction. To eliminate trial-and-error preparation, distance learning faculty should:

- Keep in mind that courses previously taught in traditional classrooms may need to be retooled. The focus of the instruction shifts to visual presentations, engaged learners, and careful timing of presentations of information.
- In revising traditional classroom materials, consider ways to illustrate key concepts, or topics, using tables, figures, and other visual representations.
- Plan activities that encourage interactivity at all the sites. It is a common pitfall to focus on only one site during the process of managing the class and operating technology. Planning for interactivity reduces this problem and helps learners. Not only does the instructor have to plan for interaction, but students may require training to participate actively in these types of activities.
- Plan activities that allow for student group work. This helps construct a supportive social environment. For example, the instructor could present case studies related to theories and concepts covered in the course, and then groups of students, perhaps in different sites, could discuss case study questions and reach consensus on a solution to the problem.
- Be prepared in the event that technical problems occur. If the equipment fails, it is important for students to have projects and assignments independent of the instructor and alternative means of communication (e.g., fax, phone, e-mail).

Discussing with students ahead of time alternative plans in case there is a technological problem will eliminate confusion and loss of productive class time when a problem occurs (Herring & Smaldino, 1997).

In addition to considerations related to planning for instruction, there is also a need to examine issues associated with the separation of instructor and some or all of the students. Time constraints for class delivery, lack of eye contact, visualization of the materials, and planning for interaction require a reconsideration of classroom dynamics. Often instructors use visual cues, such as student facial expressions, within the traditional classroom and conversations with students after class to decide quickly to adjust the instructional approach for a course. These cues give instructors insights that help them personalize the instruction for the students and ensure a quality learning experience for all.

In an online course, it is more difficult to acquire visual clues about students. Even when using desktop conferencing technologies, the visual component provides limited information to the instructor. Students who incorporate emoticons into their writing do not help the instructor get a better view of the student within the nonvisual online environment.

Teaching at a distance eliminates many of these cues. Alternative approaches to ongoing evaluation of instruction must be incorporated. If instructors ignore this area of preparation, planning to teach as they always have, they will feel frustrated. Likewise, students may feel alienated and will begin to tune out the instructor. The instructional development process must be based on the unique characteristics and needs of students, meshed with the teaching style of the instructor and the course goals and content. Interaction must be maximized, the visual potential of the medium must be explored, and time constraints must be addressed.

ISSUES TO ADDRESS IN THE PLANNING PROCESS

Who Are the Learners?

There are several reasons for bringing students together in a distance learning setting. Students can be pooled into classes of sufficient size to create a critical mass (Dede, 1990). Students can aggregate for advanced courses in subjects that might not otherwise be available on-site. Distance education can be an important approach to responding to the growing pluralism of learners' backgrounds, characteristics, or unusual learning needs that may require or benefit from specialized instruction.

Taking the time to learn about the learners in the class yields a more productive learning environment. Knowledge of general learner characteristics can inform the instructor of the nature of the students at origination and distance sites. This knowledge can aid the distance education instructor in overcoming the separation of instructor and students.

Along with the general information about the learners, an instructor needs to know the number of students in the class. Knowing how many students there are at each site and the number of sites involved in a face-to-face class can influence the level of interactivity.

For example, in an Internet-based class (e.g., on the Web) with a large number of participants, it is likely that some students will fail to interact in discussions. Thus, an instructor needs to know how many students are enrolled, how many sites there are, and what technologies are available to them to plan effectively for interactive learning. Also, it is essential to know the nature of the audience. Are students from an urban area? A rural area? What is their age range, grade range, and educational background? All this can have a marked impact on the levels of interaction among students. The instructor may have to plan more carefully for the types and levels of interaction to ensure a quality learning experience for all members of the class. The cultural, social, and economic backgrounds of the students also constitute important information for the instructor (Willis, 1994). In addition, educational expectations of learners can also influence the quality of the learning experience. The attitudes and interests students bring to the class will impact the learning environment. Thus, an instructor who wants to create a quality learning experience for all members of the class, with the ultimate goal of learning as the outcome, will be certain to account for these variables in planning.

Analyze the General Abilities of the Class.   Analysis of the cognitive abilities of the class allows the instructor to observe how students relate to the content of the lesson. Such issues as clearly defining the prerequisite knowledge or skills for the specific learning experience are important to ensure a successful learning experience. The students' prior experience with similar types of cognitive tasks is important.

Further, learning styles have once again become an important area of consideration. With the introduction of Gardner's multiple intelligences has come the resurgence of an examination of learning styles (Gardner, 1993). How students approach learning is as important as how well they can function in the classroom. So knowing more about how students interact with information is important in creating a valuable learning environment.

An instructor can determine students' general knowledge and ability in a number of ways. Pretests and portfolio reviews can provide information about learners' abilities. Because students are coming to the class from a variety of backgrounds and learning experiences, they may be underprepared for the content intended for a particular course, and thus will be frustrated and even unsuccessful in the learning experience. Or, conversely, they may already be familiar with the content and will be bored and uninterested in participating in the class.

By knowing more about students, the instructor can develop supporting materials to individualize instruction. Varying the presentation of materials to match different learning styles (e.g., animation, text, verbal descriptions, visual messages) can also ensure the greatest potential for reaching all learners.

The instructor can present complex cognitive content in ways that give learners various tags for understanding the fundamental concepts, and thereby reach a wider range of individuals. People can remember complex material better if chunks of information are grouped into spatially related locations. Placing similar ideas in a logical sequence can aid retrieval of information at a later date.

Analyze Potential for Learner Interactivity.   Students who are less social may find the distance education environment more comfortable for them. Students may become more expressive because of the perception of privacy and the informative nature of mediated communication. They may perceive the increased and varied interactivity and immediate feedback as a positive input to their interface with the learning experience.

Additionally, students can benefit from a wider range of cognitive, linguistic, cultural, and affective styles they would not encounter in a self-contained classroom. The emphasis should not be on the inherent efficiency of the distance learning, but on the values and services offered to students through their exposure to others (Herring & Smaldino, 1997). Relationships can be fostered, values can be expanded, and shared purposes or goals can be developed. Distance learning experiences can serve as windows to the world by providing extended learning experiences.

When special efforts are made, distance education actually can enhance learning experiences, expand horizons, and facilitate group collaboration (Dede, 1990). Students can have more direct experiences with the information (e.g., close-up viewing of an experiment is possible). Time for reflection is possible before responding to the prompts presented, and the ability to work with peers or experts enhances the potential for learning.

Understand Learner Characteristics.   To be effective, it is necessary to understand the learners in the target audience. Willis (1994) suggested the following questions be asked prior to development of distance learning environments:

- What are students' ages, cultural backgrounds, interests, and educational levels?
- What is the level of familiarity of the students with the instructional methods and technological delivery systems under consideration?
- How will the students apply the knowledge gained in the course, and how is this course sequenced with other courses?
- Can the class be categorized into several broad subgroups, each with different characteristics?

These questions are not easy ones to answer. An instructor should attempt to find the answers prior to the first class meeting. Asking a few well-chosen questions of individual students will help the instructor understand their needs, backgrounds, and expectations. Additionally, students will feel they are important to the instructor. It may also be beneficial to discuss the learners with the remote-site facilitator. That person may be a valuable resource to the instructor by providing information about students prior to the instruction or by observing students at work. In an online environment, it is often more difficult for the instructor to get information about students, thus it is essential that the instructor plan a way of inviting students to share information about themselves. Be careful to respect their right to privacy, while trying to learn as much as you can about them.

Help Learners Understand the Context of the Learning Experience.   Morrison, Ross, and Kemp (2001) refer to three types of content: Orienting Context, Instructional Context, and Transfer Context. They suggest that the learners need to grasp the intent of the instructor when participating in various types of learning experiences. When the learners have an understanding of the reasons why they are participating in a particular type of instructional activity, they are better able to use that experience to expedite their own learning.

Each of these contexts serves a particular purpose for the learner. The Orienting Context refers to the students' reasons for being in a course. These reasons vary among the students. For example, a student may be participating in a course for credits toward a pay raise. Or, a student may wish to change positions within a company, which is dependent on completing the particular study area.

Instructional Context addresses the learning environment. Scheduling a course to meet at a certain time and location or specifying specific dates for completion of assignments also impact the manner in which the student interacts with the class. Knowing how convenient it is for students to access the resources or to rearrange their own personal and work schedules is important when planning instruction. The third context, Transfer Context, refers to the way in which the knowledge will be used by students. It is critical when planning that the instructor consider what information is important so the students will apply it to work or school applications. Students will value that information they perceive as useful. Knowing the students and their interests or needs will help the instructor plan useful learning experiences to ensure transfer of learning.

What Is the Essential Content?

The content of a course needs to reflect where this content relates to the rest of the curriculum. It is essential to examine the nature of the content, as well as the sequence of information. In any distance learning environment, one particular issue, that of time constraints, impacts other planning areas. Time constraints refer to the actual online time for delivery, which is often limited and inflexible. The issue of limited time makes it necessary to closely examine the essential elements of the course content. The instructor needs to balance content with the limited time for learning activities and possibly remove extraneous, nonessential information.

Generally speaking, the scope of the content for a course needs to be sufficient to ensure the entire learning experience will lead to the desired outcomes. Concepts, knowledge, and specific skills need to be identified (Dick & Carey, 1996). Supporting information or knowledge is important to the scope of content analysis. Follow-up and applications of the content should be considered.

The instructor's time is best spent on content analysis if the content is organized within a hierarchy. Starting with the general goals, followed by more specific goals and objectives, the nature of the structure of the content can be made to fall into place. The resulting framework of information about content helps the instructor decide the value and importance of specific information to the total instructional package. It is important to remember that no matter which technological formats are used in distance education, the trend is to reduce the "amount" of information delivered and to increase the "interactive value" of the learning experience (Herring & Smaldino, 1997). Thus, the instructor may need to throw out content that had been included in a traditional presentation of a course. Or, the instructor may need to consider delivering information through alternative means, such as additional readings or booklets designed specifically for the tasks.

The instructor also needs to examine the sequencing of information. A number of variables, for example, characteristics of the learners, their prior knowledge, content, time, and number of sites involved, are critical when deciding the order of presentation of information. Because the instructor and some or all of the members of the class are separated, the material must be sequenced in a logical fashion for the students.

Goals and Objectives for Instruction.   The challenge of education is to match the content of the subject to the needs of the learners. Broadly stated goals are a helpful starting place for the instructor. The instructor must decide what is appropriate for a group of students and for the individuals within that group. Each instructor constantly must face the challenge of adapting instruction to the student who is expected to learn it. Although content is important, instructors must remember their focus is on the students. This is critical when establishing goals for any course.

The traditional approach for writing objectives is also effective for distance education courses. Specifically, objectives should state the conditions under which learning should occur, the performance expected of the learner, and the standard to which the performance will be matched.

One way to write objectives is as follows:

Given: *the conditions under which learning occurs*

the learner will: *meet some predetermined level of performance*

according to: *a minimum standard*

The objectives of a particular lesson may not necessarily change simply because an instructor teaches at a distance. Good instructional goals should form the basis for instruction, regardless of the medium used. Instructional goals and objectives always should be shared with the students, helping both the origination and remote-site students to focus on the parameters of the instruction. This information may be included in course outlines, presentation handouts, or materials presented at the beginning of the course.

What Teaching Strategies and Media Should Be Used?

Students can provide insight into the design of the learning experience. They can give feedback in lesson design and instruction delivery. Using a simple feedback form, students can describe or indicate in some other way their expectations and perceptions of the class structure and the delivery mode. The instructor can examine the information from both origination and remote-site students to determine if the mode of presentation was effective for both types of locations. Evaluating these responses, the instructor can gain an understanding of how the learners perceived the class experience. An instructor's personal philosophy will influence the approach to teaching at a distance. An individual's philosophical belief will affect selection of goals and curricular emphases, and influence how that individual views himself or herself as a classroom instructor. The instructor who believes in the philosophical arena of realism, idealism, essentialism, or perennialism will see the instructor as the central figure in the classroom, delivering knowledge and modeling to the student, an instructor-centered approach. On the other hand, the instructor who believes in the philosophies of pragmatism, existentialism, progressivism, constructivism, or social reconstructionism believes that the student is the central figure in the classroom (Herring & Smaldino, 1997). The instructor is viewed as the facilitator of learning by guiding, rather than directing, the students, thus modeling a student-centered approach.

Although the dynamics of a philosophy will not predict an instructor's success in the distance education classroom, successful teaching at a distance places the recipients' needs before organizational convenience and at the center of planning and decision making. The individual needs of the learners are brought to the forefront in education that uses electronic technology, because separation of learners from the instructor requires students to take more responsibility for learning. Consequently, the learner's opinions and needs play a more important role in decision making than is usual in an instructor-centered environment (Macfarlane & Smaldino, 1997). It is oversimplified to suggest that there is one best way to teach at a distance. In any given content area, there are several potential ways of providing a quality learning experience for the students (Heinich et al., 2002). However, the one thing that has been repeatedly demonstrated through research is that lecture, or the "talking head" approach, is the least successful strategy to employ in distance education (Schlosser & Anderson, 1994). What is essential in deciding which strategy or strategies to employ is the issue of engaging the learner.

The instructor needs to focus on selecting instructional strategies that engage all the learners in active learning. To do this, the instructor may need to deemphasize the "informative" part of the instruction for more "discovery" of information. The emphasis on keeping the learners engaged in learning ensures that students will be in tune with the class.

Media Selection.   Several models are often used in selecting media (Dick & Carey, 1996). The common theme among these models is the learning context, which is the content, the intended outcome, and the nature of the students. Practical considerations such as available resources for creating media and the technologies for delivery of instruction also play a hand in the selection process. Mainly, though, the goals and objectives will influence the selection of media. McAlpine and Weston (1994) have come up with a set of criteria for selecting media, whether they are commercial media or media developed specifically for a particular course. The first criterion is to match the medium to the curriculum or content. Other criteria include the accuracy of information, motivational quality, engagement quality, technical quality, and unbiased nature of material. These should be considered in selecting media in order to match student needs to the strategies employed.

Media that are "off the shelf" are often considered sufficient for a quality learning experience in the traditional classroom (Heinich et al., 2002). However, in a distance learning environment, the "ready-made" materials may need to be adapted or modified to accommodate the technologies involved. Some materials may need to be enlarged or enhanced to be seen by students at a distance. With others, the format may need to be changed to allow access.

Because of the nature of distance learning and the separation of the instructor from the students, it is essential that the instructor begin to think visually. Too often, instructors do not place enough emphasis on designing and using quality visual materials. Taking the time to develop good visual media will enhance the quality of the learning experience (Heinich et al., 2002).

Visualizing Information.   Visuals provide a concrete reference point for students, especially when they are engaged in a nontelevised learning experience. Even if the visuals are just lists of concepts and ideas, they can help students. Visuals also help learners by simplifying information. Diagrams and charts often can make it easier to understand complex ideas. A visual that breaks down a complex idea into its components can show relationships that might be otherwise confusing to students. Also, visuals that serve as mnemonics can assist student understanding. Visuals help students in their study as well. They can use the visuals to prepare for tests and other means of assessing their learning.

When creating visuals, the instructor needs to keep certain things in mind (Herring & Smaldino, 1997). First is legibility. In a televised distance learning environment, even with the close-up capabilities of the cameras, the choice of font and size can influence how easily students can read the text. Several "rules of thumb" should be applied:

- Use a large font (e.g., 24 or 36 point).
- Use a sans serif font (e.g., Helvetica).
- Use just a few words per line of text (e.g., six words per line maximum).
- Use only a few lines of text per visual (e.g., six lines per visual).
- Use a combination of both uppercase and lowercase letters; all uppercase is difficult to read.
- Use plenty of "white space" to enhance the readability.

Color can also play an important role in designing visuals (Herring & Smaldino, 1997). Color can increase the readability of text or graphics. However, the key to good use of color is in the contrast. Use a dark background and light lettering, or vice versa. Make certain to select colors that will not be compromised by the technology used for transmission (e.g., red vibrates in a televised environment). Further, select colors that will not be a problem for students who might be color-blind. More will be discussed on the use of media in Chapter 8, "Teaching at a Distance."

There are two other very important issues to be raised. First is that of copyright. No matter what technologies are incorporated in the distance environment, the instructor needs to respect the copyright restrictions that might apply. For example, in a televised class, the instructor may not be able to use a video without first obtaining permission to display it to the class. In a Web-based class, the instructor may have to have permission to post a journal article. An instructor needs to be responsible in obtaining copyright permissions where appropriate.

The second issue is that of access. The instructor cannot assume that all students at a distance have equal access to resources. Students may not have the technologies available. Also, students may not have the facilities at hand. The instructor needs to be certain that all students have similar learning experiences, including access to the materials. For example, if the instructor wishes students to use certain books or journals for outside reading, it is important to check with local libraries to be sure these materials are available.

What Is the Learning Environment?

Educators are familiar with classroom settings. They are comfortable with using the space available to enable learning to take place. It is when the classroom shifts into a distance learning setting that the environment often becomes a challenge to the instructor. Several important elements must be addressed within the distance learning environment.

Technology.   The type of setting, be it place- or time-shifted, will influence planning decisions. Environments that are place-shifted are those that are synchronous but are not in the same location (e.g., a live video-based distance class). Those that are time-shifted are asynchronous, where students access the class at different times. Assessing the use of technology in a distant setting is essential. In any distance learning environment, the technology becomes the element of most concern for the instructor. The instructor must become familiar with the hardware and the nuances of the technology to use them effectively. The instructor needs to balance concern for the operation of the equipment with effective teaching. Once the technology becomes transparent in the educational setting, the instructor can reflect on the lesson quality, the outcomes, and the plans for subsequent lessons.

Several issues are associated with technology when teaching in a distance learning mode. First is the basic operation of the equipment. In a televised distance learning setting, switching between sites is usually a simple procedure, but it does require time to acquire the finesse to operate the switching buttons smoothly. Second, using additional cameras in the classroom can create some concern for the instructor. The overhead camera needs to be focused and materials lined up to ensure that learners in all sites can see the material. Third, the instructor should always consider what the student should be viewing during the lesson. Is it better to see the instructor, the visuals, or other students? When an instructor has had experience teaching with the equipment, these decisions become automatic, making learning the foundation for the decisions made (Herring & Smaldino, 1997).

In an Internet-based learning environment, the instructor needs to be concerned with the layout of the courseware and the types of resources available to the students at the distant sites. The instructor needs to be certain the material is designed in a way that is intuitive for the various types of learners who may be interacting with it. The instructor also needs to be concerned about student access to the appropriate hardware and software to be successful in connecting to the courseware. Further, the instructor needs to be concerned that the students can complete the tasks expected of them. Finally, the instructor needs to be certain that the students understand the terminology being used.

It is essential the instructor be prepared with alternatives for each lesson in case of system problems. What will the students do during the lesson time if the technology is not operating properly—or at all? Preplanned contingencies should continue the learning process even though the technology is malfunctioning. Alternative lessons must always be ready, but it is hoped, never needed. Students need to be prepared to know what to do with those materials. The materials must be designed to be used without instructor intervention.

Resources.   The second element to consider in the instructional environment is the resources available to students. What materials will they have at hand? What materials will be available in libraries and laboratories? Will students have access to resources for easy communication with the instructor?

Another consideration is the quality of the instructional setting. Is the room comfortable? Can students get to the room easily? Will the room accommodate the nature and type of learning activities planned? Can students move the tables and chairs about in ways to make learning easy?

These are the types of concerns that an instructor needs to address when thinking about the learning environment. It is difficult to plan for a particular type of learning activity if the room cannot be adapted or changed in any way. For example, if the instructor plans a group activity in which students will need to move chairs and tables, can they do it without causing technical problems?

Planning to Teach on the World Wide Web

Much of what has been suggested in the planning process is not specific to a particular type of distance technology or delivery mode. Rather, the instructional design process is relatively open to any instructional setting. But, when planning to teach on the Web, an instructor needs to address some essential considerations. One very important issue is that the instructor is "ready" for the course to begin. It is frustrating for students who begin an online course only to find that all the materials are not prepared or not accessible at the time they need them. It would be an advantage for the instructor planning an online course the first time to consider working 3–5 months in advance of the beginning date. This will ensure that the materials will be planned and prepared in a timely fashion. Another important issue when teaching online is that of establishing the communications framework. All too often, instructors of online courses "complain" that students expect them to be available all the time. If you do not intend to check your course materials daily, indicate that with the initial materials that are distributed. Tell students they can expect a response within a day or that you intend to be online checking the course specific days of the week. That way both students and faculty will not be frustrated by the interrupted communications process.

Instructors have found that to ensure quality and promptness with online coursework, it is necessary for the students to know exactly when assignments are due. A calendar or time line is very important. Providing students with rubrics or guides for how to complete assignments well is also very important. The more information students have about completing assignments, the fewer problems the students and instructor will experience during the course.

Finally, when planning to teach online, advise students (and this is a good piece of advice for the instructor as well) to set aside specific periods of time during the week to work on the course. It is so easy to "let it slide" that often the complaint is there is never enough time to get all the work done. This usually results from someone letting the work pile up before getting to it. With an online course, it is best to plan two shorter periods per week, rather than one longer one. This helps to check things out, do work off-line for a period of time, and then to finish up before the time period is up. Part of the initial materials presented to the students should provide guidelines for students to ensure a successful learning experience. When it is noted that a student is falling behind in the work or is not participating at an acceptable level, the instructor should contact that student privately, either by electronic mail or by phone, to check to see if there is a reason for nonparticipation. This takes time, but the instructor will find it beneficial for a successful distance learning experience.

How Do You Determine the Quality of the Instruction?

Assessment will be discussed in Chapter 11, and evaluation will be discussed at greater length in Chapter 12. However, there is a need to look at questions an instructor might consider as part of the planning process. These questions revolve around considerations related to the strategies selected, the learners' interaction with the learning experience, and the learning environment.

In the instructional design process, formative evaluation becomes an important aspect. Two questions need to be considered. The first relates to reflection on the action or activity: "Is this approach going to work?" (Schon, 1987). To be an effective educator, it is important to consider what can happen within an instructional event. All experiences, both positive and negative, have some element of surprise. Perhaps expectations were not achieved; perhaps a serendipitous event led to an altogether different, but pleasant, outcome. Whatever the nature of the event, it is essential to reflect upon what has happened.

Reflection may take the form of critical assessment of the events, satisfying curiosity about the nature of those events (Macfarlane & Smaldino, 1997). Reflection may focus on the success of the learning situation. It helps the instructor understand the learning event. Once the instructor has reflected upon what took place, it is time to move on to the second question of the formative evaluation process.

The second question is, "How can I make this better?" The instructor needs to examine the instructional event in terms of what worked and what appears to have been a problem. The second phase of the formative evaluation is concerned with helping the instructor ensure a more successful educational experience for students. The instructor needs to consider the learning task, the instructional materials, and the teaching strategies, and also the role that the technology may have played in the instruction.

The instructor needs to consider the elements of technologies and their effect on the students. Did the hardware components of the system cause the problem? If so, what was the nature of the problem? Was there a temporary interference with the transmission? Was weather or some other noncontrollable phenomenon causing problems with the transmission? Can the hardware be improved? Can changes be made in the interactive instructional classroom to aid instruction in the future? If the problem did not relate to the hardware, then what was the problem? Perhaps students needed to be better informed about how to use the equipment. It may be that students needed preparation for the lesson. Perhaps the instructor needed to prepare other types of handouts or manipulatives to ensure that the students could accomplish the tasks. Maybe the instructor needed to select an alternative teaching strategy to improve interactivity and student outcomes. Because so many different factors affect the interactive learning environment, reflective teaching practices play a vital role in developing effective teaching practices. The process of determining what has transpired and how to change it creates a dynamic educational experience for both the instructor and the learners. Formative evaluation is essential for successful interactive distance learning experiences.

OTHER ISSUES TO BE CONSIDERED

As with any planning, some of the aspects of the system that need to be considered are outside of the content, learners, and instructional setting. Three of these issues relate to student handouts, materials distribution, and the site facilitator.

Student Handouts

Even though the topic of student handouts is discussed at greater length in Chapter 9, it is also mentioned here because it is important for the instructor to think about handouts within the context of the planning process. The types of handouts will vary according to the age of the students and the content of the course. But whatever the type, it is important that the instructor realize that in a distance course, handouts are an essential communication link with students. Therefore, during the planning process, the instructor needs to invest time and energy in creating quality handouts for students.

Distribution of Materials

Even within a traditional class, the instructor is concerned with getting materials to the students. Often papers and books are distributed at the beginning of the class period. But when teaching at a distance, this task is rarely an easy one. Often the majority of the class is at a distance, and distribution of materials becomes a logistical nightmare.

An instructor needs to consider the following:

- getting the materials to the distant sites on time. A distribution network must be established for getting tests and other materials to those remote sites. The technology can be useful in transferring materials.
- communicating with the students. Geographic separation between instructor and students does affect this communication.
- dealing with time delays in material transfer. Students may have to wait a longer time than normally expected to receive written feedback. Instructors may elect to use other forms of telecommunications to facilitate this feedback.

Site Coordinators and Facilitators

The presence of a coordinator or facilitator at the distant sites is often an option. For many instructors and students, the presence of such a facilitator is important. Other instructors consider the extra person more work than necessary. The decision to have a coordinator or facilitator might be best made as it relates to the context of the course, the students, and the types of technology being used.

For example, if the students are on the young side or are unfamiliar with the distant learning environment, a facilitator might be valuable to get them started with the class. The facilitator can serve as an extension of the instructor. This person can help distribute materials, maintain organization and keep order, as well as proctor. This person can also help with the instruction.

Students need to understand the facilitator's role in the learning environment. They need to know what is expected of the facilitator. Further, the instructor needs to have input into the selection and evaluation of the on-site facilitator to ensure a quality experience for all.

MODELS FOR DESIGNING WORLD WIDE WEB COURSES

Generally, there are four approaches for the instructional design of courses that are to be delivered asynchronously using the World Wide Web. The four approaches are not entirely new. Two are based directly on the individualized instruction movement of the 1950s and 1960s. The four models are:

- Linear-designed instruction (Figure 6–2)
- Branched-designed instruction (Figure 6–3)
- Hypercontent-designed instruction (Figure 6–4)
- Learner-directed design (Figure 6–5)

These four designs are depicted graphically. Although they are different in approach and use, they have several similarities. First, instruction is divided into modules. Different instructional designers use terms such as *units* or *blocks* instead of *modules*, but all refer to a subdivision of a course's content. Generally, a three-credit college course would have about 12 modules, each taking about a week to complete. Designers further divide modules into topics that directly relate to the module. Topics then can be divided into concepts. An example of a unit of instruction—a course—that is divided into modules, topics, and concepts would be this book. This book has 12 chapters that identify the major subheadings of content. Each chapter is divided into topics, and topics are supported by concepts.

Linear-designed instruction is based on linear-programmed instruction. First, a content area such as distance education foundations is divided into about 12 important ideas. These ideas are called modules. Modules of instruction are divided into topics. Each topic has an instructional event, or learning experience, followed by some kind of an assessment. Before students are permitted to continue to the next topic within a module they must successfully complete the assessment. If the assessment is

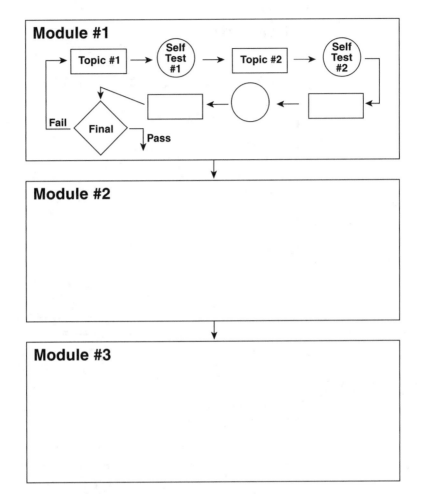

FIGURE 6–2   Linear design.

an objective test, they must pass the test. The sequence of topic-related instructional events followed by assessments continues until all topics in a module have been studied. Often, a module-ending assessment must be completed before the student moves to the next module. Similarly, there are often midcourse assessments, and end-of-course assessments that require the student to synthesize learning related to many modules.

Linear-designed instruction is sequential. Students move in the same path through the concepts, topics, and modules, and complete the same assessments and tests.

Branched-designed instruction is similar to linear with two major exceptions. First, assessments are more sophisticated in order to diagnose a student's progress and understanding of concepts and topics. If a student shows a propensity for topics in a module, it is possible to skip ahead, or branch forward. Similarly, if a student has difficulty,

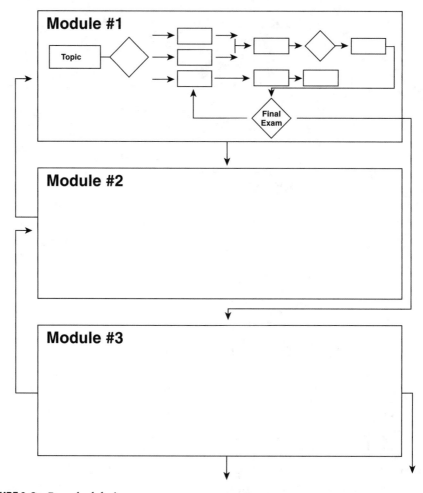

FIGURE 6–3   Branched design.

the assessment process will require that the student branch backward, or to remedial instruction before moving forward in the lesson.

The second distinguishing characteristic of branched-designed instruction is the use of alternative instructional events or learning experiences. In other words, students may interact with different instructional content depending on the results of assessments. Just as a human tutor might decide that an algebra student needs more practice with mathematics, a branched-designed lesson might require a student to complete a drill-and-practice lesson on long division. Branched-designed instruction is difficult and time-consuming to effectively produce.

Hypercontent-designed instruction also has modules, topics, and concepts. First, modules are identified. Next, topics related to the module are identified and learning

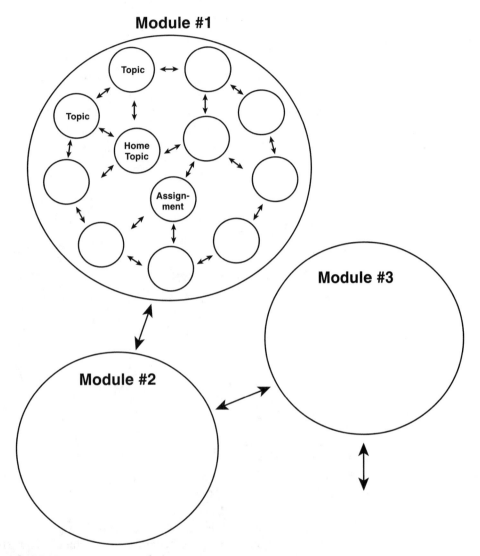

FIGURE 6–4 Hypercontent design.

experiences are designed and produced. These topics are presented using text, audio, graphics, pictures, and video. Finally, a module assessment activity is developed. This assessment is designed to determine if a student has successfully completed and understands the module satisfactorily. If so, the student moves to the next module in the sequence of modules.

Within the module, there is no instructor-determined sequencing of topics. Rather, the topics and corresponding learning experiences are studied in an order determined by the learner. In other words, the student has control and topics can be studied in a

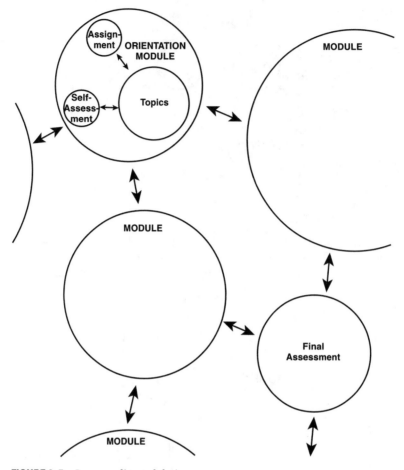

FIGURE 6–5   Learner-directed design.

random, nonsequential manner, or in a hypercontent order. Often a course-ending assessment, such as a major paper, presentation, or product is required.

The final design module is the *learner-directed design.* For this approach, the instructional designer identifies modules and topics, including learning experiences, but places no sequence or order on the topics within modules, or among the modules themselves. Learners decide what order of topics are studied, and sometimes even the topics themselves. Learners construct their own instructional strategies and even their own instructional design. Students move through modules in any order they choose. Few if any requirements are placed on the student by the instructional designer.

This approach requires considerable talent and effort on the part of the learner to be successful. Direction is given to students by module goals, and by outcome assessment activities. Some constructivists who advocate learner-directed design procedures ask students to construct their own outcome assessments.

Instructional design models for online instruction are evolving. These four approaches draw on the experience and research of the programmed instruction efforts of the past. Some teachers mix and match the four approaches into amalgams of design procedures.

SUMMARY

It is essential that the instructor take the time to plan and organize the learning experience when engaged in teaching at a distance. The instructional design process provides the framework for planning. Instruction must be at a standard that is acceptable in all venues. The students should be engaged, and the instructor should be satisfied. Planning makes the difference in a successful learning environment.

SELF-TEST QUESTIONS

1. Define *instructional design*. Explain its importance to distance education.
2. List the steps in the Dick and Carey model of instructional design.
3. Is it normally necessary for existing courses to be redesigned before offering them at a distance? Why?
4. Write an objective using the format presented in this chapter.
5. What purpose does evaluation play in instructional design for distance education?

Answers to Self-Test Questions

1. Instructional design is a systematic process for the development of learning materials.
2. See Figure 6–1.
3. Most often, existing courses do need to be redesigned before offering them at a distance.
4. Given: _____
   the learner will: _____
   according to: _____.
5. Evaluation permits the instructional designer to continuously improve the course and course components. Design is not a one-time activity. Rather, it is cyclical, and evaluation information permits continuous improvement.

For additional information and activities, visit the Prentice Hall Companion Website at http://www.prenhall.com/simonson

REFERENCES

Dede, C. (1990, Spring). The evolution of distance learning: Technology-mediated interactive learning. *Journal of Research on Computing in Education, 247–264.*

Dick, W., & Carey, L. (1996). *The systematic design of instruction.* New York: HarperCollins Publishers.

Gardner, H. (1993). *Multiple intelligences.* New York: Basic Books.

Heinich, R., Molenda, M., Russell, J., & Smaldino, S. (2002). *Educational media and technologies for learning* (7th ed.). Columbus, OH: Merrill/Prentice Hall.

Herring, M., & Smaldino, S. (1997). *Planning for interactive distance education: A handbook.* Washington, DC: AECT Publications.

Macfarlane, C., & Smaldino, S. (1997). The electronic classroom at a distance. In R. Rittenhouse & D. Spillers (Eds.), *Modernizing the curriculum: The electronic classroom.* Springfield, MO: Charles Thomas Publishers.

McAlpine, L., & Weston, C. (1994). The attributes of instructional materials. *Performance Improvement Quarterly, 7*(1), 19–30.

Moore, M., & Kearsley, G. (1996). *Distance education: A systems view.* Belmont, CA: Wadsworth Company.

Morrison, G., Ross, S., & Kemp, J. (2001). *Designing effective instruction* (3rd ed.). New York: John Wiley and Sons.

Schlosser, C., & Anderson, M. (1994). *Distance education: Review of the literature.* Ames, IA: Research Institute for Studies in Education.

Schlosser, C., & Burmeister, M. (1999). The best of both worlds. *Tech Trends, 43*(5), 45–48.

Schon, D. (1987). *Educating the reflective practitioner.* San Francisco: Jossey-Bass.

Thompson, A., Hargrave, C., & Simonson, M. (1996). *Educational technology: Review of the research* (2nd ed.). Washington, DC: Association for Educational Communications and Technology.

Willis, B. (1994). *Distance education: Strategies and tools.* Englewood Cliffs, NJ: Educational Technology Publications.

chapter 7

THE DISTANCE EDUCATION STUDENT

CHAPTER GOAL

The purpose of this chapter is to describe the characteristics and responsibilities of the distant learner.

CHAPTER OBJECTIVES

After reading and reviewing this chapter, you should be able to

1. Identify characteristics of the distance student.
2. Explain ways the student can be introduced at the beginning of class.
3. Describe the responsibilities of the student in a synchronous class.
4. Describe the responsibilities of the student in an asynchronous class.

AN EMPHASIS ON THE STUDENT

Often in a distance learning situation, much emphasis is placed on the technology, ensuring the operations end of the process. The audience, or the distant learner, is often considered after the planning and organizing of the hardware, the content, and the instructional plan. But it is the learner who is the crucial member of the distance learning system. It is the learner who needs to be considered early in the planning and implementation of a distance learning experience. The more an instructor understands the members of the audience, the better the distance learning experience will be for all involved (Moore & Kearsley, 1996).

The distance learner can be of any age, have attained any educational level, and have a variety of educational needs. One common characteristic of the distance learner is an increased commitment to learning. For the most part, these learners are self-starters and appear to be highly motivated. Frequently, distance learners live in rural areas, although a distant site may involve students who live in or near metropolitan areas located sufficiently away from where a class is traditionally offered. The educational areas of need are usually specific and may represent low-incidence needs (i.e., learning a foreign language or a technical content area). Further impetus for distance learning can result from limited statewide resources (e.g., a specialized area teacher training program) that must be shared across diverse geographical regions.

One can conclude, after examining the various tools and approaches for distance learning, that they have one purpose: to provide a valuable learning experience to students who might not otherwise have access to learning. Dede (1990) suggests that distance education can provide assistance for schools in an array of ways. Students can be pooled into classes of sufficient size to create a critical mass, thus ensuring that a course will be able to continue based on economic measures. Students can aggregate for advanced courses in subjects not otherwise offered, creating an opportunity for extended learning. Distance education can be seen as an important method of responding to the growing pluralism of learners' backgrounds, characteristics, or unusual learning needs that may require or benefit from specialized instruction. Simply stated, there are a number of reasons to bring learners together at a distance. It is equally important to understand the intent of those learners when planning the process for delivery. In any instructional situation, it is important for the instructor to know as much as possible about the students in the class. Knowing the students in a class provides the instructor with an understanding of how to best approach instruction to ensure an optimum learning experience for all. In a distance learning setting, the instructor must learn about students at both the origination and distance sites. Knowledge of students can assist the distance educator in overcoming separation of teacher and student and can ensure that the learning experience will be positive for all. And it will facilitate the design by the instructor to optimize the learning experience.

To begin with, the teacher must acquire some basic information about the class as a whole. In a synchronous-timed delivery course, knowing the number of sites and number of students at each site gives the teacher the "big picture." Equally important is information about subgroups such as urban or rural students as well as students from various cultural or social backgrounds represented within the class. Economics also plays a part in the nature of the class. Together, these factors provide the teacher with

Students of all ages can benefit from distance education.

an overview of the class, which can lead to learning about individuals in the class. Even in an asynchronous delivery mode, knowledge of the members of the class, even though they do not meet together, is crucial to design and delivery.

Each member of a class is an individual, although each individual may belong to one of the subgroups mentioned in the previous paragraph. Each individual has a cultural identity, as well as a socioeconomic "standing" in the community. However, each individual is unique and needs to be recognized for those unique characteristics. When the individual is considered, characteristics such as attitude or interest, prior experiences, cognitive abilities, and learning styles will all have an impact. Taking the time to learn about the individual will enhance the learning experience for that individual and for the class as a whole.

Attitude

The distance education literature from the past 20 years has suggested that one major difference between distance learners and traditional classroom learners is motivation (Office of Technology Assessment, 1989). In the majority of studies, distance learners were found to be highly motivated. Their reasons for participation in a distance learning setting varied from convenience for the nontraditional-aged student to accessibility to coursework. Most commonly, distance education learners chose to be in the distance education classroom. They indicated that they actively seek these classroom settings to ensure the continuation of their education. Bozik (1996) found that graduate students enjoyed the opportunity to meet others from across the state during their programs of study. This was considered one of the most positive aspects of learning at a distance.

Experience

A second indicator of preference by students is prior experience (Bozik, 1996; Smith & Dunn, 1991). Students reported that once they took a distance course, they were willing to enroll in additional classes. Students felt satisfied with the quality of their learning experience, and the convenience factors reinforced their participation. These same students also indicated they would, if necessary, drive to a centralized campus to attend classes; however, this was not their preference. They wanted to continue as distance students. Students who experience a distance learning situation for the first time may indicate to the teacher a discomfort with the learning situation. An effective educator who utilizes technological tools in a nonintrusive manner can allay these fears and encourage students to take advantage of a unique and dynamic learning experience. But this takes time and patience on the part of the educator. It also assumes much in the way of responsibility on the part of the student to grow and adapt personal learning characteristics to distance learning situations.

Cognition

The third indicator of success is cognitive abilities (Smith & Dunn, 1991). Students of average or high ability at distance sites have demonstrated achievement at levels similar to or better than those of students in origination sites. In fact, this is true of students in distance education classes as a whole compared with students in traditional classrooms. This is not to suggest that students in distance classes are smarter, but capable students tend to succeed in distance learning situations. Students at a distance seem to assume more responsibility for their own learning earlier in the process than do those students who are enrolled in traditional classes.

Learning Styles

Finally, the fourth indicator of successful learning at a distance is learning styles. For some students, the unique characteristics of distance learning tools facilitate better instruction than educational tools generally used in a traditional classroom. For example, in a distance classroom the teacher should place greater emphasis on providing visual cues, whether the technology is synchronous, such as audio only or two-way full-motion video (e.g., videotapes, overheads, concrete objects), or asynchronous, such as a complete Web-based course. When the instructor provides more visual cues, the visual learner may perform better in a distance education class. Auditory learners can focus on the instructor's words and generally listen better because there are fewer distractions, especially at sites with only one student. This situation does provide a challenge for the Web-based instructional situation. However, with the newer technologies, audio streaming is becoming less of a problem—as long as students have access to those new technologies. Students who display a reluctance to speak out or join discussions during class can find their "niche" by utilizing text-based communications through computer conferencing or completing written assignments. Even the needs of kinesthetic learners can be met with appropriate hands-on activities (Macfarlane & Stefanich, 1995).

All of this speaks to the need for the instructor to understand the characteristics of the members of the class. The more the distance education teacher knows about the individual student within the whole class, the more elegant the application of education tools to the learning situation. The instructor can learn about members of the class in a number of ways. Contacting instructors who have had students previously is one way of getting information. This works particularly well if a cohort group is moving through an extensive program of studies. As always, caution must be exercised when providing information about previous students in order not to pass on confidential information or to prejudice the teacher. Another way of getting information is simply to ask students directly about their own sense of what works for them.

A survey or similar type of information-gathering device could be distributed to the students before the start of the class. This provides the instructor with information that might not be available through school records or other teachers. An additional way to get to know students is to create class-time opportunities for getting to know them. Not only does this provide additional information to the teacher, but also it gives the students a chance to get to know the other members of the class. For example, Macfarlane (Macfarlane & Smaldino, 1997) had four or five students bring a "me bag" to the television-based class. Following her example, students shared photos, examples of hobbies, and objects portraying various interests (e.g., a recently read book). Each student spent approximately 5 minutes doing this activity. In addition to learning more about each other, the students utilized classroom technology (e.g., overhead camera) to share the contents of their "bags." The outcome of this activity resulted in the class as a whole developing a strong sense of support for one another in the learning process. Finally, if possible, an instructor can visit or teach from each distance site. If not possible, private phone conversations and electronic mail are alternatives to spending individual time with students.

In essence, what is crucial is to become familiar with the students in the class and to address their needs as they have identified them. Further, by putting time into this type of discovery of information, the instructor will find that the class will function more as a unit than it otherwise would have. This makes it easier to engage learners in the activities and in the learning outcomes designed into the class structure.

LEARNER RESPONSIBILITIES

Just as the instructor must take responsibility for learning about students, learners in the distance education classroom must assume ownership in their learning experiences (Macfarlane & Smaldino, 1997).

Microphones and Other Equipment

Students will need to respond in class or to post responses in the correct forum, ask questions, or make presentations as the result of assignments; therefore, it is imperative that distant students learn to use the tools available in the distant classroom.

Usually an electronic classroom allows for two-way audio transmission regardless of video transmission. Thus, the first tool any student will need to learn to use is the microphone to relay verbal responses to the teacher and other students in the class as a whole. Usually this involves pressing a microphone button (i.e., press-to-talk), although it is possible that the microphones might be voice-activated. A few comments about microphone protocol are essential to managing this tool. In general, whoever pushes the microphone button "controls the airwaves." That is, no one else can make a comment that will be heard by the entire class until the first microphone button is released. Thus, students need to limit remarks so that others may also contribute to the discussion. Furthermore, the first one to press the mike is the first to talk. Occasionally, a microphone is pushed "on" accidentally by the pressure of a book or other classroom materials or a stray arm or elbow, or is activated by a cough or a conversation between individuals at a site. Background noise from an open mike usually alerts the instructor to this situation, but he or she may not be able to identify the source or resolve the problem because of the temporary inability to transmit auditorily. A written message (e.g., "please check

The roles of students change significantly when they learn from distant instructors, but the advantages of being able to have classes in advanced topics such as chemistry outweigh any problems.

your microphone") transmitted visually (e.g., as an overhead) can sometimes remedy the situation; or if not, a telephone call to each site may be necessary.

Even though voices are distinct, students must learn to identify themselves by name and site (e.g., "This is Bob at Cedar Falls") when they push the microphone to ask a question or make a comment. Eventually, most students will learn to recognize individual voices; however, the initial courtesy is necessary and should continue in order to avoid confusion and enhance recognition. One unique difficulty often occurs with learners in the origination-site classroom. These learners can see and hear the instructor without the need for audio or visual transmission. Thus, when they need to ask a question or make a comment, they often forget to press the mike button so classmates at distance sites can also hear. In fairness to other students, learners in the origination classroom must remember to press the mike button and to identify themselves if that is the given protocol of the class. Reminders from the teacher or reinforcement (e.g., a small piece of candy) when done without a prompt can help to alleviate the problem of not identifying themselves when asking or answering a question.

Other equipment such as overhead cameras, video players, and fax machines may be used by students with less frequency. Despite the sophistication of some technology found in a distance classroom, most students can be talked through operating instructions by the teacher or a trained technician. Early exposure to these tools (e.g., during their personal introductions) and modeling by the teacher can reduce anxiety and alleviate problems later on when students must use the equipment to present information as part of an assignment.

Attendance and Class Participation

As in any instructional setting, class attendance is imperative. However, on occasion, learners may not be able to attend class because of conflicts, illness, or technical difficulties. In a video-based class, one solution is to record the class and send the tape (video or audio) to the learner(s) who missed class. Although no interaction is possible, at least learners do not lose out on content. It may be necessary to obtain the permission of all the class participants before making any recordings. It is best to obtain this permission in written form (Macfarlane & Smaldino, 1997). Class participation, be it in a traditional class or a distance class, always enhances learning for students. The nature of the environment in distance sites has a significant impact on class participation. As mentioned earlier, some students do not like to respond, either because of learning style or perhaps because of intimidation by the technology. Some students may ask fewer questions than in a traditional class. Instructional strategies that encourage all students to provide answers can increase class participation. Teachers have also experimented with alternative answering strategies. For example, Harmin (1994) suggests for students in a television-based class that each student write the answer on a large card or "slate." Students can hold up their answers on cue. Voting on possible answers can also encourage active participation. An open hand or "thumbs up" can signal agreement or a vote for choice A; a closed fist or "thumbs down" can signal disagreement or a vote for choice B. During discussions, some students need a brief period to prepare an adequate answer. Advance warning that a question is headed their way can ease discomfort and give the students time to think of an answer. Some learners feel intimidated by technology and are reluctant to respond to the teacher or initiate comments. The instructor needs to engage in strategies early in the course to alleviate this level of nonparticipation.

It is often the case that students at distance sites will talk with each other during class without sharing with the class. In a television-based environment, without a visual check the instructor may not know students are talking, a situation that would not happen in a traditional class or at the origination site. These "sidebar conversations" may occur as a result of a provocative piece of information presented during the class. That is, the content of the class can provoke an "in-house" discussion on the topic. Unfortunately, these comments are made to a few when the whole class could benefit. Students must be encouraged to share valid comments with the entire class. Occasionally, participants at distance sites engage in unrelated topics of conversation. Either way students not included or interested in the comments may be distracted by conversations at their site when two people talk with each other. Also, some may have difficulty hearing because of talking at their site. Out of respect for learners who are concentrating on the presentation or discussion, these conversations, whether task-related or not, must not occur. We refer to this as "netiquette," that is, showing courtesy for the learning needs of others with respect to the technology.

In an asynchronous, text, or graphical-based class, similar types of considerations are related to the students' responsibilities. Although they are not as specific, the directions will require some time. It is important that students' responsibilities be made clear.

Tone of Responses

Since the student in an asynchronous class must respond to prompts and activities in a text format, some ground rules about the nature of responses are essential. Humor is one aspect of text that can be "lost" when others are reading the text. If humor is intended, it might be wise to have a protocol among the members of the class to identify the "humorous" section by special markers or by stating it as such (e.g., "A NOTE OF HUMOR: . . .").

Also within the context of the tone of responses, it is important that members of the class refrain from using inappropriate or unacceptable language. This is general courtesy among students, but it is particularly important when these types of responses become archived, as might happen in a text-based setting.

Time for Class

In an asynchronous class, the class meeting time is a special issue. The fact that everyone does not have to be at the class at the same time is one of the advantages of this type of class for very busy people who are unable to rearrange their schedules. It is important that students understand the need to arrange a time within their weekly schedule to "attend" class on a regular basis, however. This might be on a Saturday night, or early on a weekday morning. The time selected is not important. What is important is that the student complete the class on a weekly basis.

There are a number of reasons to do this. First, if the course requires continual input from the students as part of participation, then the student must be online on a regular basis. If there are assignments, they must be completed in a timely fashion. It is imperative that the instructor make it clear what students are expected to do to complete a course, but it is the student's responsibility to adjust his or her schedule accordingly.

Equipment Requirements

A student who is planning to participate in an online class must be certain that the equipment requirements match what is available to use. If a student wishes to participate in a class that has very specific technical requirements, then those need to be clearly stated. But it is the student's responsibility to inquire if the requirements have not been identified.

Technical Know-How

For some online classes, students need to know how to use certain software packages, to use specific types of equipment (e.g., scanners), or to follow technical procedures (e.g., "ftp"-ing a file to a web site). The instructor may assume that students have this type of knowledge. Or, the student may be required to attend special workshops or classes just to prepare for this type of class. It is ultimately the student's responsibility to know how to do these things to ensure full participation in a class.

Technical Difficulties

In any situation where so much technology is involved, problems are bound to occur. When tools do not work, the learner has the responsibility to notify the instructor so that adjustments can be made. Sometimes, a technician can provide information to clear up the problem. At other times, the system manager must be notified to provide assistance. It is the student's responsibility to let the instructor know about problems. If the student does not assume this responsibility, the instructor might continue under the assumption that the student is not participating because of other reasons. Students should not let a technical problem delay their participation in a course. Nor should they let it alter their desire to participate.

Assignments

It is the responsibility of the learner to complete assignments in a timely manner and find an appropriate means to dispatch them to the instructor. Delay in sending them in will result in delays in grading and in receiving feedback.

SIXTY FREQUENTLY ASKED STUDENT QUESTIONS ABOUT DISTANCE EDUCATION

1. What is distance education?

   There are dozens of definitions of distance education, but one popular definition is: "Distance education is institutionally-based formal education where the learning group is separated and where telecommunications technologies are used to unite the learning group."

2. What are the differences between distance education and those correspondence schools seen in the infomercials?

Distance education means that a recognized educational organization offers instruction to learners separated by time and/or location. Correspondence schools require self-study, which means that there is no instructor and the student directs his or her own learning.

3. Do I have to fill out an application for distance degree programs?

As a matter of fact, this is one litmus test of legitimacy for distance education degree programs: If there is not a formal process of application and a review of qualifications, then the program offered could be suspect. If you're just interested in taking isolated courses for personal or professional enrichment, a formal application is most likely not necessary.

4. Are there any educational prerequisites for taking distance education classes?

Once again, the key here is the requirements for those taking courses offered at a distance similar to what traditional students must possess. If a class on statistics for on-site students requires two years of mathematics and one semester of algebra, then similar requirements and possibly more rigorous ones should be expected of the distance education student.

5. I keep hearing about "just-in-time learning." What is it?

Just-in-time learning is a catchphrase used most often by trainers in private businesses and corporations. In the workplace, required skills change constantly. Just-in-time learning most often provides modularized, online instruction so that it is continuously available. In this way, employees can access the training module when they need the information. Just-in-time learning makes work-related instruction available for refresher courses, new employees, or when a problem is encountered.

6. It's been awhile since I was in school. How can I assess my knowledge in particular subject areas before choosing a course?

This is a concern for many students. Potential students can take three distinct actions to determine if they are "ready" for a course. First, identify the prerequisites or requirements expected of students and match them to your background. Second, talk with current and former students in the course, and finally, talk with the course instructors. This is especially important for distance learners because both the course content and learning format will be new.

7. How do I choose a distance education program?

Programs are chosen the same way courses are chosen, with one additional step. Find out if the organization offering the program is recognized—this usually refers to accreditation. Most accreditation agencies review the curriculum, facilities, support services, and faculty and certify their quality. An accredited organization is one that has been reviewed and found to meet preestablished criteria for quality. Stay away from nonaccredited institutions.

8. I'd like to take online classes, but my computer skills aren't so great. What can I do?

Specific prerequisite skills, such as basic computer skills, are best acquired by self-study. Buy books, tapes, and manuals, and read, listen, and review them. Practice and explore. Many computer vendors will set up your computer for you, connect it to the Internet, and give basic training for little or no fee. After that, just practice.

9. What is a virtual classroom?

A virtual classroom is most often a computer environment that attempts to approximate a real classroom. There often is a lecture hall with seats that show computer-generated figures of the students who are participating in the class. There will be chat boards where messages can be typed, and even display capabilities so the teacher can post visuals such as PowerPoint slides.

10. How can I make sure I receive credit for distance training?

This is easy—only take distance training that meets the definition of distance education we stated previously. Any reputable institution offering distance education will have a system for registration, instruction, assessment, grading, and reporting. Check this before you enroll or start a formal distance education course.

11. How can I make sure I'm getting my money's worth?

As with any educational event, the best experience is one where you are actively involved. The more involved you are, the more likely it will be that you will learn. Ask questions, participate in discussions, and get to know the instructor and your fellow students. Remember, education is an activity not a product. You are not given education, you learn it.

12. Is there any way to convince my employer to pay for my distance training?

Many companies and organizations provide qualified employees with support for education. First, it is important to your own company's existing policies. If an employer is reluctant to accept distance education, try providing your employer with as much information about your proposed course of study as possible. With a little extra work, it is often possible to convince a skeptical employer that distance education not only provides quality learning that makes employees more qualified, but it also permits the employee to stay in the workplace and not have to take days, weeks, or even years away from the job. You might also point out to your employer that many distance education programs stress workplace-oriented applications of coursework.

13. What should I do if I am not satisfied with a distance education program?

As with any educational experience, if you are not learning what you expected, contact the instructor, talk with her or him, and ask for help. Don't just criticize, but offer suggestions—become an active learner by participating in the learning events of the course. Next, talk to the supervisor of the instructor. Dropping out should only be a last resort.

14. Can distance education courses be applied to a degree?

The answer to this question is yes. Decades ago, correspondence courses were not often accepted. Now, if the course is taught by an accredited institution it is almost a sure thing that a course will be considered for a degree. If the course fits the program, and is from an accredited institution, then it should count toward the degree. The requirements of the degree-granting institution determine the acceptability of transfer credits, including course credits received via distance education.

15. What should I do if I start a distance education class and realize it is too difficult/easy for me?

The answer to this is the same as for any traditional course. First, do your background work so you do not get into the wrong course. If you find yourself in this kind of a situation, then talk with the instructor. Perhaps there are remedial activities that you can take to get "up to speed." For an easy course, see if there is a way to test-out of your current course and into a higher level.

16. Do I interact with a professor in a class?

In the United States, there is almost always a designated instructor who teaches distance education classes. In Europe, Canada, and many South American countries, courses can be taught differently. Often, advisors are assigned to work and interact directly with students, rather than a professor. These counselors are like teaching assistants who help professors in traditional university courses. No matter the situation, get to know this person, interact with him or her regularly, and use his or her services to make the course effective for you.

17. What is a diploma mill?

This is a derisive term for schools that offer diplomas without much or even any instruction. The worst type of diploma mill just sells diplomas without any requirements of students at all—except that their check clears.

18. What does CBT mean?

This means Computer Based Training, or instruction offered using a computer to deliver content. Usually CBT is stand-alone instruction that does not require interacting with a teacher. CBT is individualized instruction delivered by a computer program. The original predecessors of CBT were programmed instruction and teaching machine modules, even programmed textbooks. CBT is most often used today for just-in-time learning, or as modules in a distance education course.

19. Is online training only for information technology courses? Can I take online courses in any subject?

Currently, almost any college course is offered online somewhere by some school. As a matter of fact, the most interesting applications of online education are in areas other than information or computer sciences. For example, you could take an online course in *Impressionist Art* that allows you to discuss with museum curators worldwide, see exhibits from major studios, and interact with students from widely varying cultural backgrounds.

20. In a virtual classroom, how can I make up a missed class?

Many courses don't have synchronous classes so there is nothing to miss. Instead, virtual learning usually offers asynchronous, or anytime classes, in which students can learn at the best and most appropriate time for them. Other online classrooms permit recording of the interactions and instructional events that may have already occurred. This is yet another advantage of online learning.

21. I took a couple of online technical training courses for work and now I'd like to apply them toward a technical certification. Is this possible?

Application of online technical courses to IT certification is becoming more common, but you'll need to take two steps. First, find out if the provider of the certification you're seeking accepts online instruction. Second, make sure that the certification organization accepts your particular online courses as credits toward the certification. Before enrolling in any online training, research the training provider, and then share that information with the IT certification organization. Most likely this process is what you would use for more traditional training, but in either case, check things out before you spend your time and your money.

22. Are there any recent advances in online learning that I should know about?

Many "futurists" in distance education and online instruction are excited about two recent technical developments. First, advances in media streaming—especially video—make it possible to send video clips over the Internet, or to store video clips on a CD/DVD for access during online instruction. This is considered a major improvement in online instruction because it adds the often-needed sounds and images needed to clarify instruction. Second, learning technology specialists are attempting to merge cell phone technology and handheld computers with online instruction. Many educators and Internet service providers are excited about these new wireless systems because they will make online learning even more accessible by expanding the range of environments in which wireless systems can function.

23. What does the expression "real-time lectures" mean?

Real-time almost always refers to distance education that is offered to learners in multiple locations, at the same time. A live instructor usually gives the lecture, although occasionally, the lessons are prerecorded or include broadcast programming that does not involve an instructor. Usually, when you see instruction advertised as real-time that means you must participate at a specific time, using a telecommunications technology such as audiobridge/telephone, interactive television/compressed video, or online computer-based chat rooms.

24. Who teaches an online course?

Domestically, online courses are usually taught by teachers, professors, or industry experts hired as trainers—the same people who teach traditionally. In other countries, instructors are often teams of educators who jointly offer a course or program; no *one* person is responsible for an entire course. These educators serve together as designers, content creators, technical support specialists, evaluators, and counselors.

25. I'd like to start taking online courses but I don't have my own PC. What can I do?

Those who want to enroll in online courses who do not have a PC, or more commonly, a sufficiently updated PC, have several options. Your best option is the public library. Increasingly, libraries are equipped with modern computers that are linked to the World Wide Web with high-speed connections, and these systems are available for free use. Local community colleges often have open computer laboratories that can be used, although sometimes for a small fee. Additionally, the local high school may open its lab after school hours. Finally, it is possible to lease or rent a computer and purchase a network connection for it. However, if you are considering a more long-term, degree- or certificate-oriented online education, then purchasing a computer system is advisable.

26. I've been thinking about taking online courses but in the TV ads that I've seen, it seems like they're geared more toward adult professionals (I'm 20 and not yet in a specific career track). Is distance learning just for a specific age level?

As a matter of fact, online/distance education is the largest growth area in education today. Community colleges, high schools, middle schools, and even elementary schools are offering programs, courses, and units to distant learners. Television advertisements may emphasize adult learners because they are typically out of the academic loop and may not be aware of courses and programs that are available. If you explore, you'll find hundreds of offerings that are not exclusively for the adult learner. The world lecture hall, for example, lists hundreds of college courses that are delivered either entirely or partially online (http://www.utexas.edu/world/lecture/ index.html).

27. At my previous job, I took a number of distance learning training courses, and now that I'm looking for a new job, I'd like to find a way to let interviewers know about my continuing education efforts. How can I do this?

Online courses can be highlighted on your resume. The person who has the initiative and self-discipline to seek, take, and complete online instruction—especially courses or units that add job-related skills and competencies—impresses many potential employers.

28. For distance learning classes, how is homework usually submitted?

Most often, assignments are sent as attachments to e-mails, or projects are posted on a web site where they can be retrieved by the instructor. Some organizations ask for copies of assignments—especially major or final projects—to be sent via the postal system, but most of the time e-mail attachments are the standard medium.

29. I'm in the process of upgrading my PC. What tools or software do most online courses typically use? Should I consider anything in particular?

A PC that is used for online education should be fairly fast (500 MHz), have adequate memory (64 MB of RAM), and a large hard drive (20 GB). A fast connection to the Internet is essential (56 KB modem, or DSL/cable modem connection). The computer should also have a fast CD player and probably a DVD/CD player as well as audio and video cards with sufficient memory to display DVDs. Many online courses use web sites and pages, so it's a good idea to have the current version of Internet Explorer.

30. Does a degree earned online garner the same respect from potential employers as a degree from a traditional college or university program?

Increasingly the answer to this question is yes. As a matter of fact, since so many colleges and universities are now offering—or planning to offer—online courses or programs, it is nearly impossible to know how instruction was delivered. The most important question to ask about any college or university degree program deals with accreditation. If the degree program is accredited by a recognized national or regional agency and is approved by the appropriate professional organizations, then the delivery strategies used for instruction should not matter.

31. What do I do if I need help with my homework or have a question about an assignment?

The most obvious place to seek assistance is from the course's instructor. Be sure to establish a personal relationship with the instructor: Contact him or her routinely, and be proactive in seeking advice about homework or assignments. Most quality distance education programs have help desks or counselors to assist students. Many online courses also require students to form study groups. I personally feel this is the best route to take, but be sure to first check with your instructor about the rules regarding student interaction on projects and homework.

32. Do instructors grant the same time to distance learning courses as they do to the courses they teach in a classroom setting?

Most instructors say that online course delivery requires more preparation time—up to 30% more—from them than similar courses delivered traditionally. This means they may be busy, and you will need to be proactive about seeking assistance. Make it a point to work as closely with your instructor as possible and to use all the other resources available to you, such as online tutors, help desks, other students, and printed resources.

33. How do I know how I'm doing in an online course?

A well-run online course should provide regular feedback to students. If you do not receive feedback, then you should contact your instructor and ask for information about your progress. If the instructor cannot or will not provide feedback, this is a bad sign, and you might want to consider enrolling in a different course.

34. How are distance learning courses created? What kind of structure do they typically use?

The development of online instruction is a branch within the field of education known as Instructional Design. Most often a high school, college, or corporation's course is divided into modules, usually 10–15. A module can have other names such as unit or topical area, but module seems to be the term used most often. Modules are sometimes compared to chapters of books and are further divided into concept areas. A concept area is a specific unit of information, sometimes also compared to sections within a textbook chapter. Finally, courses have homework and assignments. Most of the time each module has an assignment, so, for example, a three-semester college course might have about 12 assignments, one for each module in the course.

Assignments could be quizzes, reports, presentations, or papers. Homework usually relates to concepts within modules and often is not formally graded, but instead is commented on by the instructor. So, an online course might last 12–15 weeks, one week for each of the 12–15 modules. Students might have an assignment for each module, in addition to homework that would contribute to their course grade, and homework would be expected regularly.

Online instruction is not easy for the student or the teacher. Students are expected to be active, self-motivated learners who work hard to complete homework and regular assignments. Instructors spend a considerable amount of time and effort interacting with students, reviewing homework, and grading assignments.

35. Do distance learning courses have audio and video components, or are they strictly text?

Increasingly, instructors incorporate audio and video into online courses. Audio and video streaming (sending the audio and/or video information over the Internet) is growing in importance. This, in turn, requires the student to have a relatively fast Internet connection. Instructors can also save audio and video segments to DVDs, which are sent to students to use as part of online instruction. In these instances, the DVD is placed in the student's computer and accessed to retrieve segments at appropriate points during instruction.

36. Can I combine distance learning with a traditional degree program?

Some educators think that this particular approach to distance education will eventually become the more dominant form. The idea is that portions of traditional courses will be delivered using distance education technologies, or that isolated courses within larger programs of study will be offered at a distance. Learning experiences, courses, and programs will be developed using an amalgam of live instruction, online instruction, and real-time distance instruction. As more developments are made in the field of education, I'm also certain that almost every course or program will have some elements of distance instruction.

37. I learn better when I can interact with someone or actively participate in learning activities. Are there certain features that I should look for to get a good fit with my learning style?

For the person who learns best by interactively participating with other learners, the ideal distance education program is one that permits students to work collaboratively in teams or with partners. This enables the student to regularly interact with other students. In theory, most distance education courses should require considerable interaction, but if your course does not, then you should be proactive about filling that gap. Find another student with whom you can share ideas, either online via e-mail, over the telephone, or if possible, in person. Talk through the course, discuss ideas, and share insights. Actually, this is almost exactly what students do in traditional courses: meet for coffee after class, organize study groups at the library, etc. This is important and most effective distance education teachers encourage this type of interaction.

38. I'm a corporate manager. I'd like to set up a group of my employees with job-related training. Are there distance learning options I should consider?

Increasingly, corporate training is moving online. My recommendation is to begin by identifying components of traditional training that could be placed online. For example, agendas for training days could be online, resources and web sites that have important information about the training topic could be listed, and follow-up activities could be placed on an employee-accessible web page. The next step might be to shorten the training day by expanding the online aspect of the training topic. Ultimately, the face-to-face portion of training might be reduced to discussions of topics previously reviewed online and presentations of work completed.

Bear in mind that one additional advantage of online training is that it is available for review by current, new, and absent employees. Finally, exhaustive numbers of training programs are already available online. These can be easily—and often very inexpensively—incorporated into corporate training.

39. How long do online courses usually last?

This depends on whether you're taking job-specific training, personal development courses, or working toward some sort of degree or certification. For a three-credit college degree course, the normal "term" is 15 weeks. Certainly, courses may be shorter (6 weeks is about the minimum) or longer (no time limits are advertised by some organizations offering online instruction), but the 15-week period seems to be the dominant length for online college courses. High school courses are usually 10 weeks, and corporate training courses are often expected to be completed in a few weeks. These periods can vary greatly, but as online education has evolved, these time periods seem to be the most common.

40. If online courses are supposed to mean I can learn "anytime, anywhere," how does that work with "real-time" lectures?

This is precisely the reason why real-time instruction is frowned on by some distance education experts. Others feel that some real-time interaction is necessary. Most often, one of three approaches is used when offering real-time instructional events. First, they may not be required. In other words, a real-time chat between the instructor and students may not be a course requirement, but only attended by students if needed, desired, or convenient. In this instance, these real-time events act as "office hours." Second, real-time events are almost always offered at multiple times in order to accommodate students with different schedules. This places a burden on the teacher but permits greater learner flexibility. Finally, some instructors record real-time instructional events for those students who cannot attend or participate. Instructors preserve chat room conversations and post them for later review; audio conferences can be tape-recorded and mailed to students; real-time video sessions can be videotaped and sent out. Video and audio can also be recorded and stored on a server for downloading at a later date.

41. Are there any government grants that would help me pay for a distance learning program?

The first place to ask about financial assistance should be at the school, college, or university where you plan to enroll. A number of financial assistance programs are available, but most are only for accredited institutions. This is a great way to determine the legitimacy of the institution where you plan to enroll. If they do not have an office of financial aid, then you might be concerned about the institution.

42. If I get my associates degree online, will I be able to transfer to a traditional state university?

Most often, associates degrees from regionally accredited institutions (e.g., community colleges) are accepted by state universities. The key is that the institution granting the associates degree must be accredited, and most often accreditation should be by the appropriate regional accrediting agency. On page A27 of the June 8, 2001 issue of the *Chronicle of Higher Education* there is a discussion of transfer of credits. The theme of the report is that many universities will not accept transfer credits from institutions that are not regionally accredited. By the way, national accreditation does not seem to be as widely accepted as regional accreditation.

43. Are there any distance learning programs that allow students to pay on a monthly basis rather than the entire tuition up front?

Payment schedules vary by institution. There is no set rule for payment schedules, but many, if not most, institutions have a variety of tuition payment schedules.

44. What type of accreditation should I look for before I enroll in an online degree program?

Regional accreditation, such as from the North Central Association or the Southern Association of Colleges and Schools, is the most widely accepted and recognized type of accreditation. There are national accrediting agencies, and most states accredit institutions in their state, but the regional accrediting agencies seem to have the widest acceptance. You might want to look at the June 8, 2001 issue of the *Chronicle of Higher Education* (page A27) that discusses the issue of transfer of credits and accreditation.

45. Are distance learning programs ranked? If so, where can I find this information?

I am not aware of ranking of distance learning programs. However, many institutions that offer programs and degrees at a distance are ranked along with traditional institutions in the yearly rankings published in *U.S. News and World Report* and *Forbes Magazine,* for example.

46. I am a CIS major at a local university and am very interested in distance learning. What training would I need to be involved in providing distance learning to others?

A person interested in become involved in designing instruction to be delivered at a distance should have a number of courses related to technology, teaching, learning, and instructional design. A solid understanding of the field of instructional design is critical.

Nova Southeastern University, for example, offers a masters and doctorate in Instructional Technology and Distance Education. The categories of courses in this program include the following:

- Media and technology
- Distance education foundations and applications
- Leadership
- Research, evaluation and measurement
- Instructional design
- Instructional systems
- Management of technology programs
- Trends and issues in instructional technology and distance education

47. I am moving overseas and would like to continue my studies via distance learning. Is this possible?

Certainly, most institutions that offer courses and programs to distant learners do not limit enrollment to any one country or location. This is part of the attraction of distance education programs. It may be less convenient to take a course or program in a country different from the one where the institution is located, but it is certainly possible in most cases. Synchronous learning events may be offered at inconvenient times (e.g., the middle of the night), and some face-to-face sessions may require long airplane flights, but the beauty of distance education is in the ability to reach learners virtually any time and in any place.

48. Where can I find a list of available distance learning courses?

One of the best online sources is the World Lecture Hall, a clearinghouse of sorts maintained at the University of Texas. The URL for this site, which lists hundreds of courses, is: http://www.utexas.edu/world/lecture/index.html. There are also printed sources such as: *Peterson's Guide to Distance Learning Programs* and *Thorson's Guide to Campus Free College Degrees (Thorson's Guide to Accredited College Degrees Through Distance Learning)*. The printed guides tend to get out of date, but list sources that can be further explored.

49. Where can I find a list of online degree programs?

Probably the best printed sources are *Peterson's Guide to Distance Learning Programs* and *Thorson's Guide to Campus Free College Degrees (Thorson's Guide to Accredited College Degrees Through Distance Learning)*.

50. I'm in England and want to pursue online training in PC maintenance. Is there anything I should consider before taking an online course from another country? Or should I try to find online training from a British site?

Online courses in specific topics like PC maintenance are probably not from accredited colleges or universities, so you should be careful to check out the institution or organization that is offering the course. It might be best to stay with easily recognized companies such as Microsoft or one of the equipment companies, rather than a technical school. Many technical schools offer excellent courses, but if you enroll in one of their courses, be sure to check them out carefully first. One key is whether the school wants your money "up front." If they do, this is a concern.

51. I want to be able to read and spell better. Can distance learning help me?

Reading and spelling are skills best learned by intensive education and practice. I would think you would be better off looking for a course from your local community college, or an evening class offering by the local school system. Reading teachers can usually be found locally, and many classes are offered at times convenient for the working person.

52. Are institutions that offer college degrees through distance education only accredited by nontraditional bodies? Is this changing?

Accreditation is a major issue in distance learning. Many who study the field feel that regional accreditation should not be a problem for quality education programs offered at a distance. Most accrediting agencies have recognized that distance education is now a viable option that is widely accepted.

53. If a person achieves a bachelor's degree from a distance learning program, will that make it difficult to go on and get a master's degree at a local university?

As we have discussed several times in response to other questions, the key to any college degree is accreditation, and today, regional accreditation is the most widely accepted indicator of acceptability. Check to see if the institution offering the bachelor's degree is regionally accredited. If it is, then you are probably OK. If it is not, you should ask what organizations accredit the college, then you should ask what other institutions are also accredited by that organization. If only distance education institutions are accredited by the agency, this should be a concern. A final question to ask of the distance education institution offering the bachelor's degree is for a list of colleges and universities that have previously accepted credits and degrees from the college. Check out the list by calling or writing their admissions offices.

54. Are there any distance learning programs that will certify me in early childhood or elementary education?

I found three institutions that offer early childhood education degrees:

Atlantic Union College in Massachusetts
Elizabethtown College in Pennsylvania
Saint Mary-of-the-Woods College in Indiana

Also, the following three institutions offer elementary education degrees:

Johnson State College in Vermont
Grand Valley State University in Michigan
Southwestern Adventist College in Texas

55. Are there technical forums for people responsible for supporting the distance learning environment? Can you point me to them?

One of the best I have found is: "Educational Telematics" telematic@listbot.com.

56. My organization provides support services and training to participants located throughout New England. We're interested in pursuing distance learning, but many of the applications that we've looked into are real bandwidth hogs. Can you recommend a platform?

First, distance learning does not have to be Web/Internet-based, and as a matter of fact, many of the best programs integrate a number of different technologies in the delivery of instruction. For example, instead of streaming video and audio over the Internet, a program could use videotape or audiotape and the postal system to deliver motion and sound information to distant learners. The Web/Internet can be used for e-mail, chat rooms, and threaded discussions with very few connectivity problems. Audiobridges using the telephone are also cost-effective ways to have discussions for groups as large as 10–20.

Instructional design processes that look at the curriculum, identify goals and objectives, determine how learning experiences can be offered, and select available technologies efficiently are critical to selecting delivery approaches. It is wrong to merely take an existing course or program and convert everything to Web/Internet delivery. Rather, the course should be redesigned for distance delivery.

Two excellent platforms for Web/Internet-based activities are Embanet and WebCt.

57. What does the term "open university" mean?

Generally, these are characteristics of open universities, such as the British Open University:

- Any person can enroll, regardless of previous education
- Students can begin courses at any time
- Study is done at home or anywhere the student chooses
- Course materials are developed by a team
- Tutoring is provided
- The enterprise of the open university is national in scope
- The university enrolls large numbers and enjoys economies of scale

Traditionally, open universities are European in background and educational perspective.

58. Are there any subjects not well suited for distance learning? What are they?

"Well suited" is an interesting way to look at distance education. First, virtually any educational event, course, or program can be redesigned for distance delivery. There are dozens of success stories about chemistry, physics, music, art, and physical education courses that have been offered to distant learners. And, there are dozens of failure stories about distance-delivered courses in history, psychology, statistics, sociology, and education. The key to success and failure is not the course itself, but the design of the course. Appropriate instructional design is critical to the success of any course, especially one offered at a distance.

59. I'm a consultant, and I want to develop training to be delivered to corporate intranets. Where do I start?

A consultant needs a strong foundation in instructional design. A second skill is to understand the capabilities of the telecommunications systems. When I am asked, as I often am, I recommend to corporations that are thinking of hiring a consultant or a consulting company that the consultant or company have a strong background in instructional design and instructional systems design. These topics are areas of study and courses offered by universities (e.g., Florida State University is one of the best). Programs preparing instructional designers develop very specific and necessary skills in their graduates. These skills are critical to the success of any distance education venture.

60. Is it easier to cheat in distance learning courses? How do instructors prevent this?

Cheating has always been fairly easy for the determined person, and distance education is no different than regular education in this respect. Increasingly, we are seeing quality programs that offer education to distant learners moving away from objective testing (such as a multiple-choice exam) to more comprehensive methods of student assessment. Objective tests have always been the target of cheaters. A growing body of scientific literature indicates that objective tests measure only a portion of learning. Activities such as projects, portfolios, and reports measure learning also.

I like to use live synchronous audiobridges to question students about key ideas. These are a little like verbal quizzes, and although students can and often do have notes in front of them, their understanding of the idea or concept becomes apparent relatively quickly.

Student assessment in a distance learning environment needs to be redesigned just as the other components of a course should be redesigned for the distant learner. Some methods of assessment are easier to implement than others, but almost any strategy to determine student learning is possible in a well-designed and well-thought-out distance education environment.

When objective tests are given, they can be delivered online in either a timed or untimed environment. Some instructors ask on-site verifiers, such as school administrators, librarians, or work supervisors, to certify that the student took the test, according to the rules of the examination. Increasingly, objective tests are being used for self-testing purposes, and other assessment activities are being used for grading.

SUMMARY

The learning experiences of students are the core of equivalency theory discussed previously. Learning experiences of students not only depend on the efforts and preparation of the instructor, but also are largely determined by the efforts and preparation of the distant learner. This chapter attempted to identify the characteristics, duties, and expectations that students may have when learning at a distance. Remember, learning experiences for learners should be equivalent, not necessarily equal. Also, a learning experience is provided by an instructor and used by a student. Teaching and learning are two sides of the same coin, often referred to as a learning experience.

SELF-TEST QUESTIONS

1. Identify some characteristics of the distant learner. Discuss why these characteristics are important and how they differ from the characteristics of the effective traditional learner.
2. How might an instructor obtain information about distant students? Why is this important?
3. What are some responsibilities of the distant student in a synchronous distance education class? Why are these responsibilities important?
4. What are some responsibilities of the distant student in an asynchronous distance education class? Are these different from those in a synchronous distance class?

Answers to Self-Test Questions

1. Characteristics might include qualities such as is a self-starter, is highly motivated, has above-average ability, assumes responsibilities.
2. The instructor should consider the following: survey of students, require introductions, visits to distant sites.

3. The synchronous learner should learn to use the microphone, use proper microphone procedures, know how to gain attention while not interfering with others' questions, practice proper classroom etiquette.

4. The asynchronous learner should know how to use computers and computer communications software, be able to "understand" the intent of discussions that occur at different times, pay attention to deadlines and details, and be able to use resources provided to guide instruction.

For additional information and activities, visit the Prentice Hall Companion Website at http://www.prenhall.com/simonson

REFERENCES

Bozik, M. (1996). Student perceptions of a two-way interactive video class. *T.H.E. Journal, 24* (2), 99–100.

Dede, C. (1990). The evolution of distance learning: Technology-mediated interactive learning. *Journal of Research on Computing in Education, 22,* 247–264.

Harmin, M. (1994). *Inspiring active learning: A handbook for teachers.* Alexandria, VA: Association for Supervision and Curriculum Development.

Macfarlane, C., & Smaldino, S. (1997). The electronic classroom at a distance. In R. Rittenhouse & D. Spillers (Eds.), *Modernizing the curriculum: The electronic classroom* (pp. 171–195). Springfield, MO: Charles Thomas Publisher.

Macfarlane, C., & Stefanich, G. (1995). Teaching science to persons with disabilities. In M. Herring & S. Smaldino (Eds.), *Interactive television preservice teacher education innovative applications: A monograph.* Teacher Education Alliance Iowa Star Schools Project (Grant No. 95-035). Iowa State University, Ames.

Moore, M., & Kearsley, G. (1996). *Distance education: A systems view.* Boston: Wadsworth Publishing Company.

Office of Technology Assessment. (1989). *Linking for learning: A new course for education.* Washington, DC: U.S. Congress.

Smith, P., & Dunn, S. (1991). Human and quality considerations in high-tech education. *Telecommunications for Learning, 3,* 168–172.

chapter

TEACHING AT A DISTANCE

CHAPTER GOAL

The purpose of this chapter is to provide guidance for the instructor when teaching at a distance.

CHAPTER OBJECTIVES

After reading and reviewing this chapter, you should be able to

1. Describe the responsibilities of the instructor in distance education.
2. Explain the importance of introductions at the beginning of class.
3. Describe the responsibilities of the student in a distance class.
4. Identify items to enhance delivery of instruction.
5. Discuss the preparation of visuals.
6. Discuss policy issues related to distance education.

ASPECTS OF DISTANCE EDUCATION

Distance education provides opportunities for instructors to extend and expand their classrooms beyond the confines of a building. It is also an opportunity to revisit techniques for teaching since distance education incorporates both place and time shifting (Herring & Smaldino, 1997). A *place shift* suggests that all the participants in the class are not in a single location, whereas a *time shift* implies that the instruction is not "live." Both these aspects of distance learning present instructional challenges to even the most experienced educators. Distance education is an opportunity to revisit the role of the instructor and the student in the learning environment.

ROLE OF THE TEACHER

Lesson Organization

A primary role of the instructor in an educational setting is to provide guidance in the learning process (Herring & Smaldino, 1997). Student-centered learning is a direction that is taking a strong hold in education today. In particular, it is important in a distance education setting to center attention on the student and to focus the instruction away from the teacher and toward the learners.

After the initial planning and preparation for instruction is completed, it is time to concentrate on issues associated with the delivery of the instruction. One issue is the organization of content. Key elements of each lesson should be outlined. Cyrs and Smith (1990) recommend limiting the number of major concepts or points to be covered in a single lesson. They suggest incorporating no more than three or four major concepts or points in a 50-minute time period. Although it may be possible to cover more points through lecture, doing so appears to be less successful in an interactive television session. Cyrs and Smith (1990) recommend that "teacher talk" be limited to 10 to 15 minutes and be varied by incorporating visuals and student interactions. Attention also should be given to the number and choice of visuals used in the lesson.

Another issue is time allotment. Whereas the key elements of planning are essential regardless of the distance education format, the allotment of time for specific activities is crucial to ensure student success. Lessons should be planned to allow time for students to engage in the learning activities. In live interactive instruction, timing is critical because of an absolute time frame—transmission from the classroom is discontinued at the end of the scheduled period. Instructors cannot speak to the students as they head out the door! In a time-shifted Web-based learning environment, it is important to ensure the instructions are complete so that the learners are not struggling with how to use the technology or how to respond to tasks. It is important to focus on indepen-dent learning tasks, shifting the role of the instructor to that of manager of the prompts to encourage student learning. Planning the instructional sequence to allow students time to complete assignments is essential as well. The instructor needs to consider ways to balance the assignments and the expected time frame for completing them. Students need time to process information and to think about what they are learning. In an online course, the instructor needs to schedule due dates for work that are flexible enough to give students time to do the tasks at optimal levels of learning.

Instructional Methods

Teaching methods should be chosen based on the characteristics of the instructor, students, content, and delivery system (Herring & Smaldino, 1997). Because of the increased responsibility for learning placed on the students at a distance, methods that focus on the learners and incorporate interactivity have been shown to be most successful (Souder, 1993).

Besides determining the appropriate instructional methods to be used in delivering the content, the instructor should also determine ways to involve the class at all instructional sites. There is no ideal way to accomplish this. With some adaptations, the same methods and techniques that are successful in a traditional classroom setting usually work as well in distance instruction, especially if they encourage student interaction.

The instructor is responsible for the learning environment created in the traditional and distance classroom settings. The technology incorporated in distance learning should be considered as a tool to enhance instruction and not as an end unto itself. Thus, instruction should include the fundamental elements of planning, including the effects of the technology in design. Using the technologies of distance education should not limit the choice of strategies used by teachers, but should open new possibilities for those who wish to enrich their teaching (Greenwood & McDevitt, 1987).

It has been suggested that if a strategy works in a regular classroom, it probably will work in distance instruction with some adjustment (Herring & Smaldino, 1997). Considering a variety of techniques is important, but an instructor must remember to think of strategies that engage learners in active rather than passive learning experiences. Combining techniques is useful, and instructors should not be afraid to experiment, to explore, to be creative in their teaching.

Teaching at a Distance

Although few restrictions exist for the teacher in traditional classrooms of the early 21st century, there are some commonsense expectations for those preparing to teach in a distance learning environment. This section reviews some basics to help the instructor teach at a distance.

Beginning the Class.   Developing rapport with students is important at the beginning of any class. Such rapport is essential to ensure a successful distance learning environment. This is especially true when the environment is computer-based. Students who participate in distance educational experiences have been found to form lasting friendships, developing a strong cohort focused on supporting each other to ensure a quality learning experience for all.

Although a class composed of students who might know one another might not require introductory activities, groups of strangers, such as people across a span of distance within the class setting, can certainly profit from getting to know one another. Instructors, all too typically, merely warm up their groups of students with simple introductions. For example: "Let's go around the room and state our names, hometown, major, and why we're here." This type of introduction may have some value, but often it becomes meaningless. Students become bored by the repetitiveness of the activity,

The teacher's role often changes to that of facilitator rather than presenter in many distance education systems.

especially if the introductions are offered by more than 15 people in a group (Herring & Smaldino, 1997), and this is very difficult to initiate in a computer-based environment. Instructors need to employ more directive and creative ways of helping the participants learn about one another.

More dynamic, experiential activities for introductions allow students to become acquainted with one another in more meaningful ways. There is a benefit to learning about attitudes, values, aspects of personality, expectations, and so forth from the members of the class. Sometimes it is essential for the students to learn more than each other's names, hometown, and so on. When it is necessary for students to form learning groups, knowing about the other members of the class is crucial.

Using elaborate techniques for introductions also can reduce the lonely feeling that some students might be experiencing. Finding ways to involve shy people is important. By investing time at the beginning of class for introductions, students will become more at ease with the setting and potentially will become more spontaneous in class participation (Herring & Smaldino, 1997). By engaging in meaningful, often fun activities at the beginning of the class, students' anxieties and tensions are reduced, and students are more comfortable in participating in the class in the future. Strategies that engage learners at the beginning of the class focus the responsibility for learning on the learners.

Introduction strategies help the instructor demonstrate that the focus of the class is on the students, not on the instructor. Further, they give the instructor an opportunity to gather additional information about the members of the class. Are the members open to new experiences, fun-loving, and nondefensive? Or are they cautious, sedate, and inflexible? The level of energy that students exhibit in the initial phase of getting to know others helps the instructor decide on the instructional strategies to employ.

Several introduction strategies have been found to be highly effective (Herring & Smaldino, 1997). One is to have each participant meet someone new in the class, either within the same site or across sites, and then to provide an introduction of the person for the rest of the class. Another is to have each participant provide the information directly by way of "guided" or structured introductions. One very effective structured model is to identify specific topics that must be included in the introductions. For example, suggesting that each member of the class include "something personal," "something professional," and "something special" has been found beneficial to creating a learning community (Herring & Smaldino, 1997).

Structuring the Class.   In any instructional setting, students benefit when they have a clear view of such issues as class organization and student responsibilities. Class organization includes such items as class schedule, grouping for activities, and expectations for interaction. The instructor's responsibility is to ensure that students understand how the class is structured. In a television class, does the instructor begin with an activity that requires students to interact with each other? Or begin each class with a brief delivery of content? Or end each class with student reflections? In an online class, will the instructor post prompts or questions prior to the actual "beginning" time for discussion so students can preview them? Will there be responses to each student's postings, or will the instructor interject comments along the way without specifically responding to all the individual comments? These issues of format or structure are important to help students quickly and easily become involved in learning rather than focusing on trying to puzzle through the manner of delivery (Herring & Smaldino, 1997).

Instructors need to adhere to the predetermined schedules (Macfarlane & Smaldino, 1997). For synchronous settings, instructors need to maintain a class schedule that is congruous with the transmission schedule. For asynchronous distance learning settings, they need to post information and assignments in a timely fashion. They need to practice ways to use time wisely and to maintain the schedule of activities. Students need to know about the importance of presentation handouts if they are used and how to use them to benefit their learning.

Students need a clear understanding of their own responsibilities (Cyrs & Smith, 1990). They need to know what is expected of them in terms of preparation for class and participation in class activities. If students are expected to read assignments prior to class, then the instructor must plan to build on that material, not merely repeat it in class (Herring & Smaldino, 1997). Students will not read in advance if "the lecture is from the book." However, if the instructor has assigned a specific reading selection, then interactive activities related to that assignment would reinforce the need to read in advance.

Further, students need to know how their participation in class discussions is measured. Students who are reluctant to engage in discussion or are unprepared should be ready to accept the consequences of nonparticipation if a portion of assessment depends on a certain level of participation. Effort needs to be made to provide shy students with nonthreatening means for participating that serve to ease them into feeling confident about their abilities to participate in discussions. Instructors must assume responsibility to meet the needs of students who might be reluctant learners.

Students need training in communication protocols. In an audio setting, they need to be prepared to use microphones or other audio equipment. Further, they need to understand their responsibilities to be courteous and well-mannered, in both audio- and text-based communication formats. Respect for others is an important part of working in groups, especially at a distance (Herring & Smaldino, 1997).

Also, students need to assume responsibility for initiating communication with the instructor. Because of the venue, the instructor and students may not meet in person, but rather must meet via the technology. If students are having difficulty with the course or need additional information or assistance, it is their responsibility to contact the instructor. But the instructor must provide them with contact information. It is crucial that students have convenient and reliable means of connecting with the instructor. An e-mail address or a toll-free phone number is desirable, as it will not inflict much expense on the students. But if neither of these is available easily, then an office or home phone number needs to be shared.

It is also desirable to provide some framework for contacting the instructor. If the instructor wishes to receive phone calls, then it is necessary to indicate when and where to call. An instructor who shares a personal or home phone number needs to be aware that students may well use that number. So if the instructor has preferred times to communicate with students, the students need to know that information. Another related issue is what to do when there are technical difficulties. Provide students with alternatives; students need to know what is expected of them. If, in a televised class, there are transmission problems, students need to know what to do about the session and assignments. If there are problems with an Internet-based class, students need a way to follow through with the learning tasks without penalty. When teaching with technology, always assume the worst and be pleasantly surprised when everything goes well.

Preparing for Remote Resources.   When preparing to work with students at a distance, it is necessary to consider the resources available to students. Resources that should be assessed include:

1. Classroom equipment available for student use (e.g., computers, scanners, video equipment, cameras, projection devices)
2. Available computer software and resource people to assist students at a distance
3. Communication resources students can access (e.g., e-mail, toll-free phone numbers, fax machines)
4. Library and classroom resources for homework and outside-of-class work
5. Availability of means for distribution and collection of coursework materials

This information will provide an instructor with the data necessary for creating equal educational opportunities for all students in the distance education classroom. It is important for students to feel they all have equal status in the class regardless of where they are located. If this means creating new, different ways of achieving the same tasks, then the instructor must engage in creative endeavors. For example, one instructor liked to begin each class period with a quick quiz to assess student knowledge of basic facts that had been assigned. However, in her distance class quick quizzes were not practical because of the time needed to send and receive quiz papers. The instructor decided on a timed recitation exercise in which students worked in pairs to check their knowledge of the facts (Macfarlane & Smaldino, 1997). The instructor found this to be such a successful means for checking students that she began to incorporate this technique in other classes, even those offered in traditional settings.

Whereas many of the items previously identified deal with the mechanical side of the classroom resources, classroom resources also have a human side. The presence of a facilitator is often considered optional, but this person can be important for the success of the distant instruction (Herring & Smaldino, 1997). A facilitator is generally an adult who has been hired by an educational institution to be a local contact for students. Facilitators' roles vary depending on their capabilities. They may be on-site during instruction, they may be available prior to and following transmissions, or they may be responsible for hardware and software performance.

Several issues should be considered when deciding if a facilitator is appropriate. What role will the facilitator have in conducting the class? Can facilitators assist with the teaching and learning process, or are they responsible for noninstructional aspects of the class? Can facilitators team-teach with the instructor, or is their duty to monitor the classroom, pass out papers, proctor exams, or manage online discussions?

No matter what the role of the facilitator, it is important to set up a time for discussion about expectations of each member of the team prior to starting the course, to avoid misunderstandings once the course begins. Further, it is important to share this information about the facilitator's role with students.

Another issue to consider is who selects the facilitators for the distant sites? If the facilitators are to be actively involved in the teaching and learning process, the instructor may wish to have input in the hiring. A good working relationship is essential for a successful distance learning experience.

Finally, the instructor must consider the issue of facilitator evaluation. Should the instructor have a say in the end-of-instruction evaluation of the facilitator? If the facilitator is an integral part of the teaching and learning process, there should be an opportunity for the instructor to identify the contributions of the facilitator.

Using Visuals for Learning.   At a distance, visuals are an important aspect of a quality learning experience. Research has demonstrated that the use of visuals clearly influences the learning experience of students (Cohen, Ebeling, & Kulik, 1981). Visuals play a role in providing a concrete reference for concepts and ideas. Providing a visual, even if it is just a list of concepts or ideas, helps the students connect the spoken word with these ideas.

Also, visuals play a role in enhancing learning by simplifying information that is difficult to understand (Cohen et al., 1981). Students can focus on diagrams, graphics, and outlines while listening to the instructor or other students, to gain an understanding of complex topics. These types of visuals also help students by providing organization and structure to the topic. Finally, visuals serve to provide redundancy in the learning process (Cohen et al., 1981). Including some redundant information can be beneficial for students. When spoken or written information is supplemented with visual information, learners have a greater chance of comprehending the material.

Interpreting Visuals.   Learners need to be guided in learning to decode or interpret visual information (Heinich, Molenda, Russell, & Smaldino, 2002). They need to develop skills in understanding the meaning attached to the use of certain types of icons or graphics. Age and developmental ability affect the way students interpret visual information. Younger students are more likely to single out specific elements rather than looking at the whole picture.

Several other issues are related to interpreting visuals. Cultural background can affect the way in which students interpret visuals. Different cultural groups may perceive visual information in different ways. It is essential for the instructor to be sensitive to the different cultural backgrounds of the students in any class.

Students often have a preference for the types of visuals they view. However, research indicates students do not always learn best from the types of visuals they prefer (Cohen et al., 1981). Most learners state they prefer color, but black and white visuals are equally effective. Many say they prefer photographs over line drawings, but these are often too complex to facilitate interpretation of the message. It might be better to use drawings to simplify the information. Instructors need to experiment with different types of visuals to identify which seem to help students in the learning process. If a disproportionate amount of time is spent explaining the visual, it may indicate a need to simplify that particular visual. The more often students engage in learning experiences using visual information, the more likely they will successfully use visuals (Cohen et al., 1981). Providing students with frequent experiences with visuals, and guiding the students in their use, helps increase the possibility of successfully applying visuals in the learning process.

Distance education classrooms often are equipped with special equipment, such as this electronic white board, so instructors can easily visualize concepts to distance learners.

Creating Visuals for Televised Instruction. Instructors need to keep certain conventions in mind when creating visuals for televised instruction. Most educators are familiar with preparing transparencies for overhead projection in a traditional classroom. These follow standards in regard to font size and amount of information and are generally prepared in a vertical orientation. However, television uses a 3:4 ratio, horizontal orientation for its display. In addition to orientation, it is important to consider the design of the display (or visual). Good visual design tries to achieve at least four basic goals:

- Be legible.
- Be interpreted easily.
- Engage students.
- Focus attention.

In regard to legibility, it is important that all students can see the visual equally well. In the television arena, using the document camera or a prepared computer presentation can help ensure all can see the material.

When using prepared computer presentation programs, it is simple to prepare student handouts. Often these programs offer several options for student handouts, including an outline format or a set of reduced-size pictures of the actual screens. Providing the students, especially those at the distance sites, with a handout helps simplify note taking, and also ensures all can see the visuals clearly. Because some students have more difficulty taking notes in a distant class and focusing on the instruction, the pace of the class may be interrupted to accommodate these individuals. If everyone has copies of the visuals, it makes it easier for the teacher to keep the class moving along smoothly.

When designing visuals, three key design decisions must be considered:

1. Selecting the verbal and visual material
2. Choosing an underlying pattern for all displays
3. Arranging information within the pattern

The type of visual selected for the class depends on the learning task at hand. Visuals can be subdivided into three categories: realistic, analogic, and organizational (Heinich et al., 2002). Realistic visuals show the actual object under study. Analogic visuals convey a concept of topic by showing something else and implying a similarity. Organizational visuals include such things as flow diagrams, graphs, charts, and maps.

Designing Visuals. The style of lettering should be consistent and should follow some simple conventions (Cohen et al., 1981). For informational purposes, a plain lettering style is recommended. A sans serif style (such as Helvetica) or a simple serif style (such as Palatino) should be used. Using more elaborate styles often can create visuals that are difficult to read. If you must use a fancy font, then make certain the students have a good-quality copy of the materials at all sites.

In addition to style, instructors need to be cautious when using all capital letters (Cohen et al., 1981). Whenever using all capitals, make certain it is only for short lines of text, such as a title. Do not use all capital letters for through text, as this style is hard to read and gives the impression of someone shouting. Lettering size becomes somewhat less important when a distance education class has access to the document camera or when material can be forwarded using fax- or computer-based technologies. However, it is important to note that when a line of text is too long, you cannot show it in its entirety without moving the text across the document camera (Herring & Smaldino, 1997). Use plenty of white space around any visual, thus ensuring that all can see clearly the particular element or part you want them to see. If you put too much information into too small a space, you may find it is difficult for the students to focus on important elements. It is better to use a larger font size (e.g., 24 or 36 points) and fewer words per line (e.g., a limit of six words per line). Further, it is suggested that a visual should have no more than six lines per page.

Color can add interest and ensure that students find the important information. Good color contrasts are important, such as dark lettering on a light background or light lettering on a dark background (Cohen et al., 1981). Make certain to use colors that are appropriate for television (e.g., blue is excellent on television; red is not).

Pattern is also critical when designing good visuals. Selecting a pattern for visuals that is easy to "read" will enhance the learning experience. Using shapes that are familiar to students, for example, the shape of a circle to arrange the information, helps students focus on the material. Make certain the visuals are balanced, that is, with equal weight (Cohen et al., 1981).

The concept of best practices for instructors is an important one to many researchers (LaMonica, 2001). The three most important best practices identified by students and teachers are:

- Course content is structured so it is easy to follow
- Regular feedback to students is important
- Expectations of the instructor are clearly stated

Interestingly, both students and teachers indicated that promoting a collaborative relationship was the *least* important best practice.

POLICY ISSUES RELATED TO DISTANCE EDUCATION

Policy is defined as a written course of action, such as a statute, procedure, rule, or regulation, that is adopted to facilitate program development (King, Nugent, Eich, Mlinek, & Russell 2000). Distance education policy is the written course of action adopted by institutions to facilitate the development of distance education programs.

Importance of Policy

Policies provide a framework for the operation of distance education. They form a set of agreed-on rules that explain roles and responsibilities. Policies can be compared to laws of navigation, rules of the road, or language syntax. They provide a standard method of operation, such as "no-wake zone," "keep to the right," or "subject and verb must match." Policies give structure to unstructured events and are a natural step in the adoption of an innovation, such as distance education. The institutionalization of a new idea includes the development of rules and regulations (policies) for the use of the innovation (Rogers, 1995). One key indicator that distance education is moving into the mainstream is the increased emphasis on the need for policies to guide its effective growth.

Berge (1998), and Gellman-Danley and Fetzner (1998) have proposed models for distance education policy. These models have been reported and evaluated a number of times in the literature (King, Nugent, Eich, et al., 2000; King, Lacy, McMillian, Bartels, & Fredilino, 1998), and seem to provide a useful framework for an investigation of distance education policy.

Policy Categories

Policies for distance education will be divided into seven categories (King, Nugent, Russell, Eich, & Lacy 2000; Gellman-Danley & Fetzner, 1998).

Policy Area #1: Academic—The key issues in this area deal with academic calendars, accreditation of programs, course quality, course and program evaluation, Carnegie units, grading, admission, and curriculum review and approval processes.

Policy Area #2: Fiscal, Geographic, Governance—The key issues in this area deal with tuition rates, special fees, full-time equivalencies, state-mandated regulations related to funding, service area limitations, out-of-district versus in-district relationships, consortia agreements, contracts with collaborating organizations, board oversight, administration cost, and tuition disbursement.

Policy Area #3: Faculty—The key issues in this area deal with compensation and workloads, design and development incentives, staff development, faculty support, faculty evaluation, intellectual freedom, and union contracts.

Policy Area #4: Legal—The key issues in this area deal with intellectual property agreements, copyright, and faculty/student/institutional liability.

Policy Area #5: Student—The key issues in this area deal with student support, academic advising, counseling, library services, student training, financial aid, testing and assessment, access to resources, equipment requirements, and privacy.

Policy Area #6: Technical—The key issues in this area deal with system reliability, connectivity, technical support, hardware/software, and access.

Policy Area #7: Philosophical—The key issues in this area deal with the acceptance of distance education based on a clear understanding of the approach, organizational values and mission, and visions statements.

Academic Policies.   Academic issues are in many respects at the heart of why policies are critical. Academic issues deal with the overall integrity of a course. They deal with students, instruction, curriculum, and program. They probably have the longest and most widespread impact, as students take courses, earn diplomas, and move to other schools or on to higher education. Policies help ensure that institutional integrity is maintained.

A theme that increasingly is being applied to distance education policy development is referred to as an *integrated approach*. This approach advocates using the same procedures for distance education as for other academic issues. Instead of developing new structures and policies for distance education, the intent is to modify existing structures, regulations, rules, and policies to integrate a distance education approach. Flexibility is a necessary ingredient of an integrated approach. Teachers, administrators, and policymakers should recognize that changes do not reflect a weakening, or that modification is not a threat to integrity. Rather, policy changes necessitated by the development of a distance education program merely demonstrate a natural process and evolution of a school, district, or state to accommodate technology-based instruction. Watkins and Schlosser (2000) discuss Carnegie units and explain processes for demonstrating how distance education courses can be compared to traditional face-to-face classes where "seat time" is measured.

First, once an institutional commitment to distance education is made, academic policies should be reviewed and distance education requirements should be integrated into regulations. Specifically, the following academic issues are examples of those to be considered:

- Course schedules and academic calendars, especially for synchronous learning experiences
- Event, course, and program approval and evaluation
- Student admission
- Grading and assessment of students
- Grade record-keeping and reporting
- Accreditation

Fiscal, Geographic, and Governance Policies.   The central issue behind most fiscal, geographic, and governance (FGG) policies is one of ownership—ownership of the course, the student, and the curriculum. Ownership is defined in this context as the institution that has ultimate responsibility, and whose decisions are final.

Most of time, the school offering the unit, course, or program has ownership, but if a student is taking only one course as part of a locally offered diploma, then in most respects the diploma-granting school is the responsible institution. Most often several policy statements need to be in place that relate to various situations where courses are delivered or received.

With ownership comes the question of costs. Certainly the school offering a unit, course, or program has considerable expenses, but so does the receiving school and even the student. In sharing relationships, the hope is that costs will average out over a period of time. In other words, if three schools enter into a relationship to share courses, and do so uniformly, the costs of offering and receiving courses will be fairly equal for the three schools. Conversely, if one school does most of the offering of units, courses, or programs, then that school will have disproportionate expenses. Policies are needed to clarify how to deal with situations such as this.

Other fiscal policies for schools offering instruction include those related to tuition, network fees, room and equipment expenses, administration of student files and records, and troubleshooting. Schools receiving courses have costs for room maintenance, library and media support, reception equipment, and student support. Technology fees are often levied to support distance education costs. If fees are implemented, policies need to be in place to determine who collects and distributes this money, and how expenditures are monitored.

Finally, agreements to regularly review costs and to share revenues are important. Often it is difficult to anticipate costs, so if agreements can be made in good faith to yearly or quarterly review expenses and income it is easier to establish working consortia.

Geographic service areas are also difficult administrative issues. Traditionally, schools had clearly designated areas they served, such as districts, counties, or regions. With electronic distribution of instruction, these boundaries are invisible. Regulations that set particular geographic limits for schools may need to be clarified or altered when distance education programs are started.

Governance is closely related to finances and geography. What school board is responsible for courses delivered at a distance—the receiving or the sending board? Policies need to clarify this issue before problems emerge.

Faculty Issues.   Faculty, or labor-management, issues can easily be the most difficult for policy developers, especially if teachers are unionized. Increasingly, existing labor-management policies are being used to cover distance education. Clearly, faculty need to be recognized for their efforts and expertise in working with distant learners, and until distance education becomes mainstream and expected of all teachers, policies need to be in place that clarify distance teaching responsibilities.

Key issues include class size, compensation, design and development incentives, recognition of intellectual property of faculty, office hours, staff development for teachers, and other workload issues. Many recommend that labor-management issues be kept flexible since many are difficult to anticipate (Gellman-Danley & Fetzner, 1998). However, faculty issues should be resolved early on in order to avoid critical problems later. Once again, the concept of integration is important. Integrating distance education faculty policy with traditional labor-management policy seems most often to be the best strategy.

Legal Issues.   Many faculty and administrators are quite naïve about the legal issues involved in distance education. Policies about copyright and fair use, liability especially for inappropriate use of telecommunications networks, and intellectual property are important to resolve. When units, courses, and programs are offered at a distance, they are easily scrutinized and violations are very apparent. In addition to developing clear policies related to these issues, many institutions are developing comprehensive staff development/training experiences for faculty that deal with copyright and liability.

Ownership of intellectual property is an important issue for distance education. When courses or portions of courses are packaged for delivery to the distant learner, the question of who owns the "package" becomes an obvious issue, more obvious than when students entered a classroom in a traditional school. On one side of the issue are those that emphasize the *property* side of the intellectual property equation. This group argues that the school is the owner of any works produced during working hours, using school resources by faculty. At the other extreme are those that feel the contribution of knowledgeable faculty, the *intellectual* component of "intellectual property," is most important. This camp advocates course ownership by faculty. It is critical that schools, colleges, and universities establish clear policies related to ownership of curriculum materials prepared for the distant learner (Carlson, 2000).

Most would agree that both elements are necessary and that neither extreme best serves the school. Often, policies that share profits after expenses with faculty that develop instruction for distant learners are best. The exact split for this sharing should be negotiated and policies developed before courses are offered.

Student Policies.   Student services should be integrated. In other words, policies related to students learning at a distance should be reflected by general student policies. However, regular policies may need to be modified to accommodate the distant learner. Specifically, if asynchronous instruction is being offered, then support services will need to be available when students need them. For example, if a school offers courses such as AP Calculus to students in other schools, then distant students may need to be able to access support services outside of regular school hours. Homework "hotlines" may need to be established and be available to all students, not just distant learners. Library/media center resources should be available to everyone, and computer laboratories should be of equal quality. Policies related to students and their needs are often overlooked, but they become more critical in a distance education environment.

Student support policies should be clear, flexible, and widely understood, not only by students but also by faculty. Policies related to feedback from instructors should be monitored, and special requirements of distance learners, such as mailing of assignments, use of e-mail, access to web sites, and proctoring of exams should be clear and designed to assist the student to be a successful distant learner.

Technical Policies.   Usually, some organization owns the network used for distance education, or is responsible for its reliability. If a private-sector business is the provider, then clear expectations must be in place, and all members of a consortium should be part of the relationship. If a public agency such as a state education department or educational organization is the telecommunications service provider, then very clear chain of command responsibilities should be in place. Often, telecommunications policies are not the same as other policies related to the distance education enterprise since they are not related to the educational mission of the organizations involved and often the private or public provider of services mandates them. However, telecommunications procedures should be understood by all involved with managing distance education.

Policies related to student and faculty technical needs, such as the quality of personal computers needed by students who learn at home, should be established. Hardware, software, and connectivity minimum requirements should be clearly explained.

Philosophical Issues.   Often overlooked when policies are developed are those that relate to vision, mission, and understanding of distance education. Many advocate that when an educational organization decides to become involved in offering or receiving distance education, its vision and mission statements should reflect this commitment.

Of more direct importance to the success of distance education is the recognition that this approach is credible, high quality, and appropriate. Distance education is an innovation, new to most, and misunderstood by many (Rogers, 1995). Training, administrative support, publicity, and attention to quality are important components of a successful and accepted distance education program. Organizational policies related to these issues should include distance education.

Sample Policies.   Title 92—Nebraska Department of Education Chapter 10.

Academic

". . . to be an accredited high school in Nebraska, the school must provide access to 400 instructional units for each student each school year . . . schools provide required instructional units on site or through a combination of local and distance learning programs . . . up to 100 instructional units of the 400 unit instructional program requirements of the high school may be met through the use of courses presented primarily through one or more forms of distance learning technologies, such as satellite, regional course sharing, or other audio-video distance learning . . ."

"each course is shown on the high school class schedule . . . at least one student is enrolled and participating in each course to be counted . . . each student enrolled in a course is assigned to a local certificated teacher who monitors student progress and general appropriateness of the course . . ."

". . . off-site courses are made available to all students at the school's expense."

". . . at least one student enrolled in each course used towards compliance with the instructional program requirement."

". . . class is scheduled . . . each day that school is in session with a certificated teacher present (one teacher may supervise several courses within a single class period)."

". . . the distance education class must be shown on the high school class schedule."

". . . Carnegie class time equivalents will be the same for television courses as for any course."

Fiscal

"students pay the same fees for distance education classes as for classes delivered on-site."

Faculty

"Instructors must meet the standards and procedures used by the institutions for regular instructors."

"Instructors teaching on interactive distance education will be compensated at the rate of $500 per remote site."

"Instructor training, including system use and suggested teaching procedures, shall be a requisite prior to teaching a course via the distance learning system."

"The school will provide 12 clock hours of formal training, including at least 8 hours using the network."

Legal

". . . course materials will be reviewed by appropriate school officials to insure copyright regulations are strictly adhered to . . ."

". . . course materials developed locally will be the property of the originating school, unless special arrangements are made in writing."

Student

"students . . . must have the same services, the same options for continuing education, and the same choices of delivery methods as the traditional on-site students."

Technical

". . . students must remain in sight of the video camera."

". . . students must respect the equipment."

". . . three violations and students are dismissed from the distance education class."

". . . classes missed because of technical problems will be rescheduled and required . . ."

Philosophical

". . . is the mission of . . . [the] school district . . . using electronic or other technologies to provide high quality educational experiences?"

". . . courses delivered to distant learners are considered equivalent to those offered traditionally."

"Each student, prior to graduation, will enroll and complete at least one course delivered using distance education technologies."

Integrated policies for distance education are preferred (King et al., 1998). In other words, policies that provide guidance and direction to the educational systems should seamlessly include and incorporate the concept of distant delivery of instruction. Students should be defined by their enrollment in a course or program, not by whether they are distant or local learners (Simonson, Smaldino, Albright, & Zvacek, 2000). Initially, distance education policies will probably need to be infused with existing policies. Ultimately, they should be integrated to indicate that distance education is a routine and regularly occurring component of the educational enterprise (Figure 8–1). Policies are merely tools to facilitate program integrity.

SUMMARY

It is important to remember that distance education may be as new to the students as it is to the instructor. Preparing students for instruction is important in any teaching mode

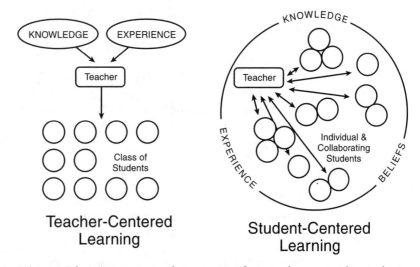

FIGURE 8–1   Distance Education promotes the movement from teacher-centered to student-centered learning

to maximize learning from class participation. But it is especially important to prepare students for settings where class participants are separated across distances. Students need to understand their responsibility to ensure a successful learning experience.

Teaching at a distance is a challenge. The instructor needs to be creative and imaginative in the design and structure of the course. One rule of thumb is that successful interactive learning experiences that work in a traditional classroom are adaptable to the distance learning environment. But they may require more than just some changes to the visuals or the handouts. They may require inventiveness and innovation.

Teaching at a distance can be a pleasurable experience for everyone involved, instructor and student alike. Keeping it interesting, and motivating the learners to remain active, can make it a valuable learning experience, as well as fun.

Many of these same guidelines apply to online learning settings. It is critical to select the font, size, color, and background that do not interfere with the message. When a student has to struggle to read the material or finds the web page too busy with animations and other irrelevant information, the learning outcomes can be lost. Do not clutter web pages with graphics or other visuals that do not relate to the message. It is wise to apply the KISS principle—Keep It Short and Simple.

SELF-TEST QUESTIONS

1. What are some of the organizational factors that a teacher must consider when preparing to teach?
2. What strategies might be used to formalize introductions among students?

3. What elements of class structure need to be included when preparing to teach at a distance?
4. Why is it necessary to determine resources available at distant sites when preparing to teach at a distance?
5. What factors need to be considered when deciding to use a facilitator at a distant site?
6. What issues are examined when preparing visuals for distance education classes?
7. Finally, discuss these questions and answers in small groups and determine how the teacher's role changes and stays the same in a distance education environment.

Answers to Self-Test Questions

1. A teacher must consider the organization of the content, time allotment, technology, and learning activities.
2. Responses might include student-to-student introductions among pairs of students, or whole-group introductions using PowerPoint slides that include something personal and professional about each person.
3. In structuring the class, it is important to ensure that students understand their responsibilities within the learning environment, understand the organization and structure of the learning activities, know the schedules and due dates, understand the process for responses in discussions, know the communication protocols, know how to contact the instructor and other students, and know what to do when there are technical difficulties.
4. It is necessary to know what hardware and software are available for students to use, what resources students will be able to access, what library and other related resources will be available outside of class time, and how coursework and related materials are distributed and collected.
5. The factors that need to be considered include what the role of the facilitator is, who selects the facilitator, and how the facilitator is evaluated.
6. Issues include the use of icons and graphics that may require explanation; developmentally appropriate graphics for a particular age group; the cultural background of the students; legibility, contrast, and simplicity; the need for visuals to engage the students in learning; and the use of visuals to focus attention.

For additional information and activities, visit the Prentice Hall Companion Website at http://www.prenhall.com/simonson

REFERENCES

Berge, Z. (1998). Barriers to online teaching in post-secondary institutions: Can policy changes fix it? *Online Journal of Distance Learning Administration, 1*(2), http://www.westga.edu/~distance/Berge12.html.

Carlson, S. (2000). When professors create software, do they own it, or do their colleges? *Chronicle of Higher Education,* July 21, A29–31.

Cohen, P., Ebeling, B., & Kulik, J. (1981, Spring). A meta-analysis of outcome studies of visual-based instruction. *Educational Communications and Technology Journal, 29*(1), 26–36.

Cyrs, T., & Smith, F. (1990). *Teleclass teaching.* Las Cruces, NM: Center for Education Development.

Gellman-Danley, B., & Fetzner, M. (1998). Asking the really tough questions: Policy issues for distance learning. *Online Journal of Distance Learning Administration, 1*(1), http://www.westga.edu/~distance/danley11.html.

Greenwood, A. N., & McDevitt, M. A. (1987). *Multiple teaching strategies for use with an instructional telecommunications network.* Paper presented at the meeting of the Society for Applied Learning, Orlando, FL.

Heinich, R., Molenda, M., Russell, J., & Smaldino, S. (2002). *Instructional media and the technologies for learning* (7th ed.). Upper Saddle River, NJ: Merrill/Prentice Hall.

Herring, M., & Smaldino, S. (1997). *Planning for interactive distance education: A handbook.* Washington, DC: AECT Publications.

King, J., Lacy, D., McMillian, J., Bartels, K., & Fredilino, M. (1998). *The policy perspective in distance education: A futures landscape/panorama.* Invited paper presented at the 1998 Nebraska Distance Education Conference, Lincoln, NE, http://www.unl.edu/NN21/jking.html.

King, J., Nugent, G., Eich, J., Mlinek, D., & Russell, E. (2000). A policy framework for distance education: A case study and model. *DEOSNEWS, 10*(10), http://ed.psu.edu/acsde/deos/deosnews.html.

King, J., Nugent, G., Russell, E., Eich, J., & Lacy, D. (2000). Policy frameworks for distance education: Implications for decision makers. *Online Journal of Distance Learning Administration 3*(2), http://www.westga.edu/~distance/king32.html.

LaMonica, L. (2001). The role of the instructor in web-based instruction: Are we practicing what we preach? *DEOSNEWS, 11*(6), 1–4, http://www.ed.psu.edu/acsde/deos/deosnews/deosarchives.asp.

Macfarlane, C., & Smaldino, S. (1997). The electronic classroom at a distance. In R. Rittenhouse & D. Spillers (Eds.), *Modernizing the curriculum: The electronic classroom* (pp. 171–195). Springfield, MO: Charles Thomas Publishers.

Rogers, E. (1995). *Diffusion of innovations* (4th ed.). New York: Free Press.

Simonson, M., Smaldino, S., Albright, M., & Zvacek, S. (2000). *Teaching and learning at a distance: Foundations of distance education.* Upper Saddle, NJ: Merrill/Prentice Hall.

Souder, W. E. (1993). The effectiveness of traditional vs. satellite delivery in three management of technology master's degree programs. *The American Journal of Distance Education, 4,* 37–53.

Watkins, R., & Schlosser, C. (2000). Capabilities-based educational equivalency units: Beginning a professional dialogue. *The American Journal of Distance Education, 14*(3), 34–47.

ADDITIONAL READINGS

Arizona Department of Education. (2000). *Policy on telecommunications.* Tucson, AZ: Author.

Bates, W. (2000). *Managing technological change.* San Francisco, CA: Jossey-Bass.

Epper, R. (1999). *State policies for distance education: A survey of the states.* Denver, CO: State Higher Education Executive Officers.

Kirby, E. (1998). Administrative issues for high school distance education. *Online Journal of Distance Learning Administration, 1*(2), http://www.westga.edu/~distance/.

Mackenzie, B., Chester, C., Kirby, E., Guarino, T., Davidson, T., & Ekhaml, L. (1999). *A policy and procedures survey of Georgia's statewide videoconferencing system (GSAMS).* Georgia Department of Administrative Services, http://coe.westga.edu/mit/gsamsreport/index.html.

North Carolina Board of Education. (2000). *The North Carolina education technology plan.* North Carolina Board of Education.

Rahm, D., & Reed, B. (1998). *Tangled webs in public administration: Organizational issues in distance learning,* http://www.pamij.com/rahm.html.

Simonson, M., & Schlosser, C. (2000). Beginning. *Quarterly Review of Distance Education, 1*(1), 1–2.

Simonson, M., Schlosser, C., & Hanson, D. (1999). Theory and distance education: A new discussion. *The American Journal of Distance Education, 13*(1), 60–75.

chapter 9

HANDOUTS, STUDY GUIDES, AND VISUALS

CHAPTER GOAL
The purpose of this chapter is to present information about the effective use of printed materials in distance education.

CHAPTER OBJECTIVES
After reading and reviewing this chapter, you should be able to

1. Develop a distance education course syllabus.
2. Use interactive study guides.
3. Apply graphic design principles.
4. Develop word pictures.
5. Use visual mnemonics.

PRINTED MEDIA

Distance education has its roots in print-based correspondence study. The printed lesson was used to convey content information as well as to assess learning in correspondence study. Today many people give little credit to the effectiveness of printed materials. Educators sometimes use technological media to replace printed media, even though there is no real need to do so.

Printed materials can enhance teaching, learning, and managing in distance education. In particular, two kinds of instructor-created print media can significantly improve the distance education environment—the course syllabus and the interactive study guide. Additionally, graphics design principles can be applied to develop study guides that use visual mnemonics and word pictures for the visualizations of key instructional ideas.

DISTANCE EDUCATION SYLLABUS

The typical distance education course syllabus is similar to the syllabus used in any other course. The primary difference is in the specificity and completeness of the distance education syllabus as compared with a more traditional one. Normally, the distance education syllabus contains the following:

Course Logistics

- Course title
- Course meeting dates, times, and locations
- Instructor information, including name, office address, telephone number, e-mail address, biographical information, and emergency contact information
- Office hours
- Textbook and course materials

Course Policies

- Attendance policies
- Homework policies
- Participation information

Instructional Activities

- Class schedule with topic list (if the course is a synchronous one with regularly scheduled class sessions)
- Topic list and topic organizational concept map (if the course is an asynchronous one with topics that can be studied at the learner's discretion)
- Course goals and objectives
- Reading assignments with links to topics
- Discussion questions for readings (if special discussion sessions are scheduled online, then the time line for discussing certain topics can be included)
- Assignments

- Test and examination information
- Interactive study guides

Assessment Information

- Grading scheme
- Project evaluation criteria
- Grading contracts, if used
- Student precourse assessment
- Student postcourse assessment

Additional Information

- Student biographical information
- Project/assignment examples

The distance education syllabus should be available to students no later than the beginning of the first class, and probably should be distributed much earlier to prospective class members. Often, the syllabus is a recruiting tool for the distance education course. If the syllabus is available online, then the distant learners can access it from wherever they are located. The syllabus is a guide for the student, and can serve as an organizing document for the entire course. Many designers of asynchronous distance education courses use the syllabus to provide the overall structure for the content, delivery, and evaluation of the course.

THE INTERACTIVE STUDY GUIDE

Tom Cyrs and Al Kent are often credited with proposing the interactive study guide (ISG) as an essential tool of the distance educator. Certainly they (especially Tom Cyrs, 1997) are staunch advocates of this technique. Basically, the interactive study guide is a structured note-taking system that leads the learner through a series of concepts, and that requires some active and interactive involvement by the student (Figure 9–1).

There are several reasons why the handout, generally, and the interactive study guide handout, specifically, are important to the distance educator. First, the use of handouts improves student note taking and makes it more efficient. Second, the ISG is a management tool that directs course activities before, during, and after instruction. Finally, the ISG handout can be used in any classroom, including all categories of distance education systems.

The interactive study guide is a handout designed to be used by students. It is a highly organized set of student notes, graphics, pictures, graphs, charts, clip art, photographs, geometric shapes, activities, problems, and exercises. It is planned before a teleclass to assist students with note taking and to guide students through a variety of instructional events so they understand the structure of the content of the lesson. ISGs are also meant to show the relationships among ideas and data presented during a class (Cyrs, 1997).

The ISG is different from other handouts because it is more organized and more systematically sequenced than other types. The ISG consists of two parts—the display

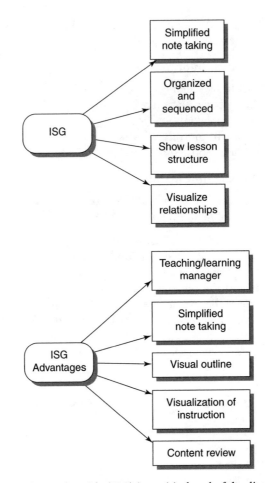

FIGURE 9–1   The interactive study guide (ISG) is a critical tool of the distance educator.

(with the word picture) and the notes section (Figure 9–2). A series of displays are sequenced (numbered) in the order that they will be discussed in class. Each display corresponds to one idea or one visual element of the lesson. Sometimes a display is equated to a concept, but most often, displays are less general and more specific than a concept.

Well-designed displays are made up of word pictures that are graphic representations of concepts, principles, and information derived from various patterns to organize a lesson. The best word pictures are visual mnemonics that relate to the key ideas of the lesson. Mnemonics are ways to remember things, so visual mnemonics are visual ways to remember things.

The ISG is a series of displays presented from the top to the bottom on the left side of the handout page. Normally three to five displays are presented on each page of the ISG. A display is sometimes referred to as a "chunk" of information that is numbered and then referenced by the student (Cyrs, 1997). A display is similar to a paragraph of

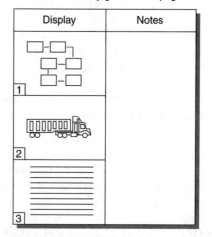

FIGURE 9–2   Interactive study guide components.

information in a written document, but the display attempts to present ideas visually rather than verbally, or at least with a combination of visual elements and words.

Displays can consist of the following:

- Word pictures with fill-ins completed by the student
- Activities or exercises
- A set of directions
- A quote, poem, definition, or other short written item
- Problems—either verbal or numerical
- Summaries of data
- Tables or figures
- Photographs
- Drawings
- Self-test questions
- Lists

An ISG display can contain directions for students to accomplish a task outside of class that is external to the ISG itself. An effective display is clear, easy to understand, and useful to the learner.

Normally, a 50-minute class session would require approximately 10 displays in an ISG. In other words, displays should be complex enough to require about 5 minutes to explain, or conversely, simple enough to cover in 5 minutes. This is an estimate. Some displays may take much longer to deal with, and others much less time, but the 5-minute estimate is good for planning purposes.

The steps necessary to produce an interactive study guide are as follows:

- Identify the behavioral objectives for the lesson.
- Create a detailed outline of topics that relate to each objective.
- For narrative sections, identify the key words.
- Use geometric shapes to show relationships or visuals to assist the learner in understanding each section.
- Create word pictures for the narrative sections by leaving blanks in the narrative where students will fill in the key words.
- Sequence the displays in the order that they will be presented or that they will be discussed.
- Develop subdisplays for topics that have more than one visual or word picture.
- Produce the ISG using proper graphic design principles.

The production of the ISG requires considerable planning. Once it is developed, the distance education course is considerably easier for the instructor to prepare for and to teach, and is more organized and easier for learners to follow, especially those in distance education courses where live, two-way interactive television is not available.

GRAPHIC DESIGN PRINCIPLES

Interactive study guides are often used as the basis for interactive television graphics in distance education courses. For this reason it is important to design ISGs to conform to appropriate graphic design principles. The size, font, color and contrast, alignment, and use of uppercase and lowercase in written graphics are critical to successful design.

- **Size.** Letter size is very closely related to legibility. Large, bold lettering is easier to see and read than is smaller lettering. Certainly lettering should not be smaller than 24 point (1/3 inch), and 32 to 36 point is preferable, especially if computer output is to be displayed on regular television monitors (Figure 9–3). Five words per line and five lines per page are a maximum for an ISG display or a screen of television information.
- **Font.** Sans serif fonts should be used instead of fonts with serifs, the thin extensions to letters often used in textbooks and printed documents. Serifs tend to be too fine for display on television. Bold fonts with thick stems display the best. Also, the same fonts should be used throughout a presentation, and no more than three different fonts should be used for any single display. Two font types work the best, when one is used for one category of information and the second is used for background or secondary information, for example. Fancy

Univers Bold Caps

Univers Bold Caps and Lowercase

9 point	**LEGIBILITY**	**Legibility**
12 point	**LEGIBILITY**	**Legibility**
14 point	**LEGIBILITY**	**Legibility**
18 point	**LEGIBILITY**	**Legibility**
24 point	**LEGIBILITY**	**Legibility**

36 point **LEGIBILITY** **Legibility**

48 point **LEGIBILITY**

Legibility

72 point **LEGIBILITY**

Legibility

FIGURE 9–3   The type has to be large enough to be easy to read.

typefaces and italics should be avoided unless there is an overriding reason for using them.

- **Color and Contrast.** Color is often misused in television. Colors should be bold and simple and should not be overdone. Some combinations, such as green and red, do not work well together. Avoid saturated colors like red. Use dark letters with a light background, or vice versa. Many television instructors like to use bright colors on a black background for displaying computer screens of information. This approach produces very readable displays.

■ **Alignment.** Centering text for television display is not as effective as aligning text to the left. Left-justified text seems to be most legible.

■ **Capitalization.** The literature on readability is quite clear that uppercase and lowercase lettering, rather than all uppercase or all lowercase, reads the best.

Elements of Design

Literate, effective visuals for display as part of ISGs or for instructor-led presentations can be developed by applying the elements and principles of design. The elements of design (Figure 9–4) are line, shape, space, texture, value, and color.

■ *Line* is generally considered to be one-dimensional. Line has length but not width. Line portrays direction, presents objects, and defines the outer shape of something.

Line

Texture

Shape

Value

Space

Finished product (lines in color)

FIGURE 9–4   Elements of design.

- *Shape* is used to symbolize objects or to show large or small spaces. Shapes have two dimensions, height and width.
- *Space* is either positive or negative. The outline of an object in a visual signifies its positive space. The most common negative shape of something is its background.
- *Texture* is the perceived or actual roughness or smoothness of a surface. Texture is used to help define shape or space.
- *Value* is the degree of lightness or darkness of a surface. Value is accomplished through shading. Value shows changes in space, and is often used to create the illusion of volume or solidity in a graphic object.
- *Color* is related to value and is used to visualize an object realistically or to differentiate an object from another object. Colors have hue, value, and intensity. *Hue* describes a specific color, such as red, green, or blue. *Value* is the lightness or darkness of a color. Yellow has the highest value. *Intensity* is the strength of a color, such as bright yellow or dull red. Intensity is determined by the purity of a color.

Principles of Design

The elements of design are combined according to the guidelines provided by the principles of design. There are six principles: balance, center of interest, emphasis, unity, contrast, and rhythm.

- *Balance* is the sense of equilibrium in a visual. The two kinds of balance are formal and informal (Figure 9–5). Generally, a visual should be balanced left to right and top to bottom. Formal balance means that objects of equal size and importance are placed at equivalent distances from the center of the visual (Figure 9–6). Informally balanced visuals are often more interesting to create and to view. Careful planning is important when informally balanced graphics are created. Several small images can be used to balance one large object, or words

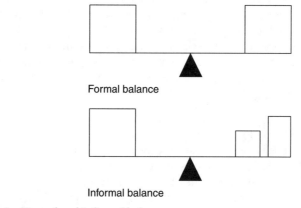

Formal balance

Informal balance

FIGURE 9–5   Formal and informal balance.

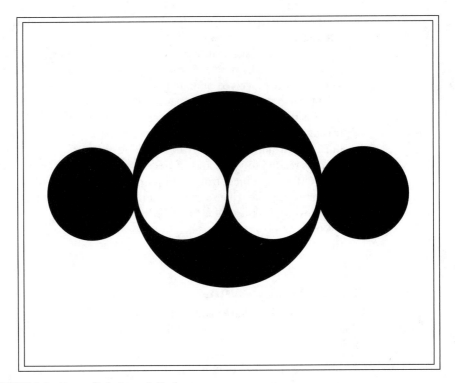

FIGURE 9–6 Formally balanced display.

can be used to balance pictures (Figure 9–7). Small, brightly colored objects will balance larger, duller items.

■ The *center of interest* is the visual focal point of the graphic and should relate to its purpose. Historically, well-designed visuals did not place the center of interest at the center of the picture. However, television places restrictions on the graphic designer. Since the area displayed on a television screen is relatively small and varies between television sets, it is probably safest to place the center of interest of a graphic at or near the center of the picture.

■ *Emphasis* is closely related to the center of interest. The key object should be emphasized so it is apparent to the viewer what is most important (Figure 9–8). There are several ways to emphasize the key element in a graphic, including the following:

1. Use pointers, such as arrows.
2. Use color to emphasize.
3. Use large objects at the center of interest.
4. Use different shapes for the center of interest.
5. Use more elements of design to create the center of interest for a graphic and fewer for less important elements.

FIGURE 9–7   Informally balanced display.

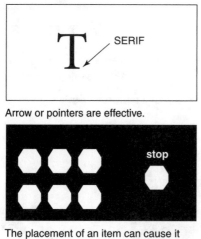

Arrow or pointers are effective.

The placement of an item can cause it to be emphasized.

A contrasting value can emphasize an area.

Size can be used.

FIGURE 9–8   Emphasis has to do with making the key item stand out.

- *Unity* means that a visual holds together to convey its purpose (Figure 9–9). If several graphics are used as part of a display, they should all convey or pertain to one meaning. Overlapping is a simple technique for promoting unity. Trees overlap buildings and each other. Houses overlap shrubs and people. A single background also promotes a feeling of unity. Another technique to promote the concept of unity is to place an outline or border around the elements of a display. Repetition of shapes, forms, and objects also can promote unity.
- *Contrast* refers to the characteristics of an object that cause it to stand out (Figure 9–10). Contrast is closely related to emphasis. Most often, contrast is achieved by the use of light- or dark-valued objects. Shapes, forms, and textures can be used to create contrasts and make one object stand out while others seem to recede.
- *Rhythm* comes from repetition through variety and is used to draw a viewer through the various objects in a visual (Figure 9–11). A row of houses in a display

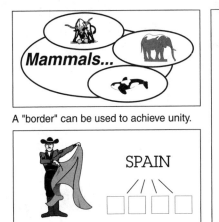

A "border" can be used to achieve unity.

Another technique is to use lines to unify.

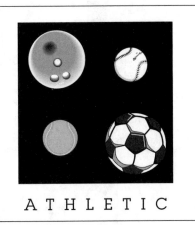

Perhaps the most effective method is to overlap a common shape.

FIGURE 9–9 Unity involves "oneness" or a tying together.

When light and dark values are used, contrast results.

Differences in size can create contrast.

FIGURE 9–10 The important parts of a display can be made to stand out (contrast) mainly through the use of color, size, value, and shape.

FIGURE 9–11   Rhythm results when an element is repeated in some systematic manner.

can present a sense of rhythm. The rhythm of a graphic helps tell the story of the picture by leading the viewer's eyes.

An effective graphic should provide visual information related to the topic being learned. The elements of design combined according to the principles of design can assist the distance educator in the development of effective interactive study guides and handouts that visually explain ideas and that facilitate understanding.

WORD PICTURES

A word picture is a graphic representation of concepts, principles, and information. Each concept, principle, or item of information usually contains key words that can be shown in nodes. A node is a symbol that contains words or stands alone to represent some idea. A node is the central point around which subnodes originate (Cyrs, 1997). The best word picture is a visual mnemonic that helps the learner remember the concept, principle, or item.

Word pictures do not need to be self-explanatory. Rather, they often require additional verbal information. Key words are usually shown in the nodes. Key words are the most significant words in a statement that provide clues to the idea the statement is communicating. Word pictures are graphic organizers that put elements of ideas together in a visual way so the learner can understand the relationship between the elements.

Cyrs does an excellent job of explaining how word pictures differ from other ways of organizing information. Cyrs (1997) says the following about effective word pictures:

1. Emphasis should be placed on the types of symbols used.
2. They should cover chunks of information rather than entire documents.

3. Student attention can be maintained through the use of fill-ins.
4. They emphasize the logical sequence of the class presentation.
5. They provide a complete review of the class content.
6. They can also be used for display by overhead video cameras.
7. They are inexpensive to produce and duplicate.
8. They condense ideas into a few key words.
9. They should be designed to fit the format of television.
10. They apply principles of graphic design.
11. They emphasize communication via the visual sense.
12. They require the instructor to think visually rather than verbally.

Cyrs discusses various graphic organizers that can be incorporated into word pictures. They are semantic maps, mind maps, cognitive maps, structured overviews, outlines, patterned note taking, webbing, pyramiding, and information mapping.

- *Semantic maps* are two-dimensional diagrams that use arrangements of nodes and links to communicate ideas and to show the relationships among ideas. Semantic maps use primarily two structures—top down and bottom up (Johnson & Peterson, 1984).
- *Mind maps* use key words or phrases organized in a design that is nonlinear. Mind maps are based on the idea that individuals mentally organize information in a variety of structures, not just top down or bottom up. Rather, mind maps usually start at the center of a page and branch out as individual ideas are presented. Mind maps (Buzan, 1982) have the following characteristics:
  1. The main ideas are clearly defined and placed in the center of the graphic.
  2. The relative importance of a subidea is indicated by its proximity to the main idea.
  3. Links between ideas are clearly indicated.
  4. New information is easily added to a mind map because of its nonlinear structure.
- *Cognitive maps* (Diekhoff & Diekhoff, 1982) are organized around the relationship between ideas, and they provide a graphic expression of the structure of a body of knowledge. Many confuse cognitive maps and mind maps. Cognitive maps are more structured and organized than mind maps and are usually developed by the instructor of a class.
- *Structured overviews* use graphics and hierarchical structures showing the relationship of key ideas, concepts, and other information (Figure 9–12). Structured overviews are commonly used for readings or lectures. Austin and Dean-Guilford (1981) define the structured overview as a conceptualized visual-hierarchical type of diagram used to show concept interrelationships within written material.
- *Outlines* are visual displays that are useful in presenting concurrent ideas. Outlines are largely verbal but use visual elements to present clusters of ideas in one display.
- *Patterned note taking* (Norton, 1981) is related to mind mapping. A key word or phrase is placed in the center of a space, and arrows and lines radiate out to subideas. Key words and phrases are used extensively. Lines are used to show relationships.

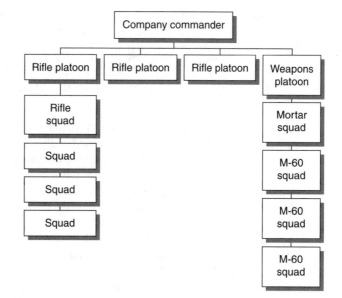

FIGURE 9–12   Word picture: Structural overview.

FIGURE 9–13   Word picture: Pyramiding Bloom's taxonomy of the cognitive domain.

- *Webbing* is a graphic representation similar to other techniques discussed above. The main idea is at the center, and subordinate ideas radiate out like the spokes of a wheel. Webbing resembles semantic maps.
- *Pyramiding* shows the levels of ideas in a graphic way using a bottom-to-top model (Figure 9–13). Information is grouped according to a hierarchy, such as details at the bottom, concepts in the middle, and principles at the top.
- *Information mapping* is a method of bringing together current research into a comprehensive materials development and presentation approach. Maps are

arranged hierarchically into blocks of information. Each block serves a separate purpose, but all relate to some central theme or idea.

Cyrs (1997) provides an excellent list of organizational patterns for distance education classes. The strategies listed by Cyrs are wonderful starting points for those beginning to develop a personal approach to distance teaching. Several of the most useful approaches are

1. **Problem solution.** In this situation, students are presented with a real or contrived problem with elements provided about the situation that caused or have impact on the problem. Students are then asked, often in collaborative groups, to make observations about the situation and then propose alternative solutions including the consequences of each alternative. One effective technique for dramatizing the problem is to use "trigger films/videos," which are short (2 to 4 minutes) scenarios dealing with the events that produced the problem. Students are then asked to respond to the problem. The film/video "triggers" a response. For example, a trigger film might dramatize a family in financial crisis with a stack of bills that are due at the end of the month. After watching the scenario unfold, financial counseling students would be required to work in small groups to develop a proposed solution to the situation depicted.

2. **Time sequence.** This presentation involves organizing information in a list or sequence of events that unfold chronologically. The sequence can be presented by the instructor, or the elements of the sequence can be presented visually and students can be asked to help order the elements and then explain the rationale for their decision. Examples of time sequences include developing film, completing a tax return, building a doghouse, and baking a cake.

3. **Definitions.** When a presentation is based on definitions, there is usually a statement of the concept to be defined, a listing of its attributes, and examples of how the term, phrase, or item is used. For example, terms in a chemistry laboratory exercise might first be defined by the instructor before students work together to complete the sequence of activities involved in the laboratory experience. Definitions lend themselves particularly well to sequential interactive study guides.

4. **Cause and effect.** In this approach an event and its causes or antecedents are presented (Figure 9–14). For example, the heavy rains in California would be discussed and would be followed by an exploration of why the rains occurred, such as the influence of El Niño water in the central Pacific Ocean. Actual or historic meteorological records could be used, as could weather reports in California newspapers.

VISUAL ANALOGIES

An analogy is a way to describe something that is unfamiliar by comparing it with something familiar. The two things that are being compared seem to be different but have some similarities. Analogies help improve thinking and help learners understand new ideas by giving insights and by allowing new relationships to be explained.

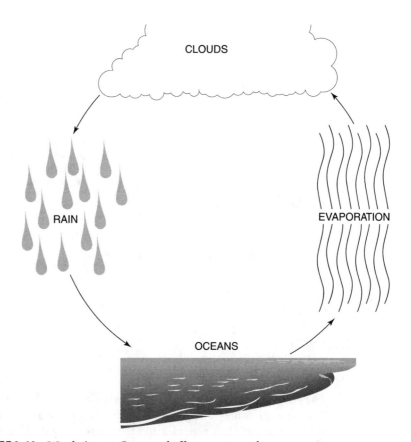

FIGURE 9–14   Word picture: Cause and effect—water cycle.

According to Cyrs, analogies have four parts (Figure 9–15): the new subject, the analog, the connector between the analog and the new subject, and the ground.

The *new subject* is the topic that is unfamiliar. The analogy is designed to help provide understanding of the new subject. Subjects normally are described by only a few words. The *analog* is familiar and is something that has been experienced by the learner. It is crucial that the learner knows the analog—the previously understood idea or concept. The *connector* shows the relationship between the two concepts: the new subject and the familiar idea, or analog. The connector is the critical element in the analogy and demonstrates the creativity of the author of the analogy. Connectors can be structural or functional.

- *Structural* relationships show the similarity in appearance and design of the two concepts. Examples of structural relationships include: (a) Sharon is as creative as Leonardo da Vinci. (b) Norman is as soft as a marshmallow. (c) Raindrops looked like balloons.
- *Functional* relationships describe what concepts do or how they work. Functional relationships show not only what the subject and the analog have in common but also what they do that is similar.

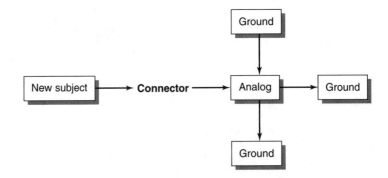

FIGURE 9-15   Components of an analogy.

Connectors that often are used include the following:

... tastes like ...
... resembles ...
... is comparable to ...
... feels like ...
... looks like ...
... is related to ...
... is like ...

The *ground* relates to the specific set of similarities and differences between the unfamiliar and the familiar. The ground can be verbal or visual, but the more concrete the ground, the more hints it provides and the more likely it will be that the analogy will work. Pictures are often used to help make real the analogy (Figure 9–16). Some examples of a ground include these:

Football is like war—it requires strategy, tactics, planning, and trained individuals.
Distance teaching is like singing and playing the piano at the same time. It requires
    simultaneous verbal skills and physical dexterity.
Media are like delivery trucks, since media carry ideas.

When constructing visual analogies one should follow five steps. First, identify clearly what the new subject is, the idea that is not clearly known. Second, identify the appropriate connector, such as "... is like ..." or "... is similar to ..." Third, identify the known analog—the familiar concept or thing that can be compared with the new idea. Fourth, provide a ground for the comparison of the new and familiar ideas. Describe the similarities and differences between the ideas. Finally, develop a visual way to demonstrate the analogy and to provide learners with a visual mnemonic to help them remember the relationship and to understand the new subject.

Analogies are difficult to develop. When a good analogy is identified, especially a visual one, it can be the center of an elegant discussion of instructional content. Naturally, the visual analogy should be incorporated as a word picture for an interactive study guide.

Media are like delivery trucks. They permit the delivery of ideas to learners.

FIGURE 9–16   Example: A visual analogy.

SUMMARY

Printed handouts and teaching and learning materials are critically important to the effective practice of distance education. First, the course syllabus is the "glue" that holds the course or the learning experience together. Sometimes the syllabus is expanded into the course study guide, which is a document that provides the student with a level of orientation to the distance education experience.

Second, the interactive study guide is a very important tool that provides the distant learner with a logical sequence for the distance education lesson. The interactive study guide is especially important when the student and instructor communicate asynchronously or when fully interactive two-way television is not used.

Interactive study guides are made up of two ingredients—the display and the notes section. The display is made up of a series of word pictures, which are visuals and words that involve student interaction and which attempt to provide the learner with ways to remember the key ideas that are to be learned. In essence, the word pictures are visual mnemonics to help learners remember things. Naturally, for visuals to be meaningful and instructional they need to be designed effectively. The guidelines for effective visual design should be followed.

Finally, printed materials are critical to the practice of distance education (Figure 9–17). Documents provide background information, amplify concepts, and give a sense of direction to instructional events. Printed materials are an important component of the distance education program.

SELF-TEST QUESTIONS

1. Define *visual analogy*. Why are analogies important?
2. Develop a visual mnemonic or word picture for these concepts:
   • Technology as productivity enhancer
   • Pythagorean theorem
   • Definition of distance education
3. Create a line drawing using the five elements of design.

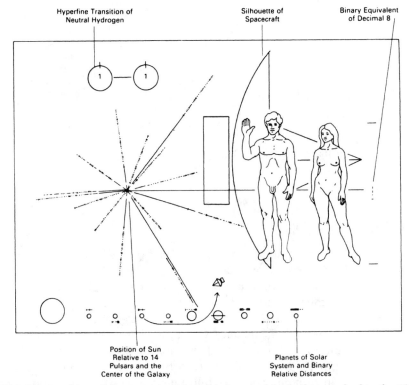

Hyperfine Transition of
Neutral Hydrogen

Silhouette of
Spacecraft

Binary Equivalent
of Decimal 8

Position of Sun
Relative to 14
Pulsars and the
Center of the Galaxy

Planets of Solar
System and Binary
Relative Distances

FIGURE 9–17   Speaking of distance education, this is a graphic display attached to the *Pioneer 10* spacecraft that is hurling into space. The designers of this display wanted to convey three ideas to whomever or whatever might find it thousands of years from now: (1) where the spacecraft came from: the earth; (2) who inhabited the earth: men and women; and (3) that men and women are friendly.

4. Write an analogy for these ideas:
   • Teaching
   • Golf
   • Learning
   • A pet dog
5. What is an interactive study guide, and what is it used for? Explain why study guides are important to the distance educator.

Answers to Self-Test Questions

1. Visual analogies are ways to describe something unfamiliar by comparing it with something that is familiar using four elements—the new subject, the analog, the connector, and the ground.

2.

Technology as productivity enhancer

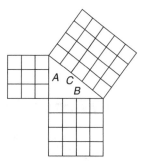

$$A^2 + B^2 = C^2$$
Pythagorean theorem

3.

Distance education

4. Sample answers:
- Teaching is like building a house. It involves materials and plans, and is successful if something useful results.
- Golf is like swimming—it is something you do individually, and in a special place.
- Learning is the same as living. We do it from birth to death, in a variety of locations and situations, and sometimes it is easy and sometimes it is difficult.
- A pet dog is like a friend. It is always glad to see us and we are glad to see it.

5. The interactive study guide is a handout designed to be used by students. It is a highly organized set of student notes, graphics, pictures, graphs, charts, clip art, photographs, geometric shapes, activities, problems, and exercises. It is planned before a teleclass to assist students with note taking and to guide students through a variety of instructional events so they understand the structure of the content of the lesson. The main advantage of the ISG is it keeps the students and the instructor moving together through the lesson.

For additional information and activities, visit the Prentice Hall Companion Website at http://www.prenhall.com/simonson

REFERENCES

Austin, R., & Dean-Guilford, M. (1981). Crashing content reading problems with reading strategies. Paper presented at the meeting of the Western College Reading Association, Dallas, TX. (ERIC Document Reproduction Service No. ED204703)

Buzan, T. (1982). *Use your head.* London: British Broadcasting Corporation.

Cyrs, T. (1997). *Teaching at a distance.* Las Cruces, NM: Center for Educational Development.

Diekhoff, G., & Diekhoff, K. (1982). Cognitive maps as a tool in communicating structural knowledge. *Educational Technology, 22,* 28–30.

Johnson, D., & Peterson, D. (1984). *Teaching reading vocabulary* (2nd ed.). New York: Holt.

Norton, L. (1981). Patterned note-taking: An evaluation. *Visible Language, 15,* 67–85.

ADDITIONAL READINGS

Carrier, C. (1983). Notetaking research: Implications for the classroom. *Journal of Instructional Development, 6,* 19–26.

Kiewra, K. (1987). Notetaking and review: The research and its implications. *Instructional Science, 16,* 233–249.

Smith, P., & Tompkins, G. (1988). Structured notetaking: A new strategy for content area teachers. *Journal of Reading, 32,* 46–53.

DISTANCE EDUCATION, THE WORLD WIDE WEB, AND THE INTERNET

CHAPTER GOAL

The purpose of this chapter is to discuss the structure and functions of the Internet and describe the many ways it can be used in a distance education environment.

CHAPTER OBJECTIVES

After reading and reviewing this chapter, you should be able to

1. Describe current trends in the use of the Internet for distance education in K–12, higher education, and corporate training.
2. Discuss the evolution of the Internet and its functions that most directly relate to distance education, such as electronic mail, mailing lists, and the World Wide Web.
3. Describe how the structure of the Internet makes its functions available to nearly anyone with a telephone line and a sufficiently powerful computer.
4. Discuss why the Internet relates well to transformations taking place in the general paradigms for teaching and learning.
5. Define and differentiate between asynchronous learning networks and computer-mediated communication.
6. Discuss the advantages and limitations of Internet-based courses.
7. Recognize the major components of an online course and account for them in course development and delivery.
8. Select course activities that maximize active learning opportunities for students in an Internet-based distance education course.
9. Assist students in thinking critically in assessing the credibility and worth of information found on the World Wide Web.
10. Plan and develop a course web site that enables students to achieve prescribed learning goals at a distance.

231

THE IMPLICATIONS OF THE INTERNET FOR EDUCATION AND TRAINING

Of all the delivery technologies described in Chapter 4, none has more explosive growth potential for distance education than the Internet. Indeed, the Internet or one of its descendants will likely become the dominant distribution system for education and training at a distance across much of the industrialized world.

At the heart of this trend is improved access to the Internet. Through the mid-1990s, access was quite limited, but now more than 10,000 Internet service providers (ISPs) in over 120 countries make the Internet available to almost anyone in those nations with a sufficiently powerful computer and a telephone line, for modest monthly fees. In July 1998, the Irish consulting firm Nua estimated the worldwide total of Internet users at about 130 million, including 72 million in the United States and Canada, 32 million in Europe, 19 million in Asia and the Pacific Island countries, and 7 million in South America (Nua Consultants and Developers, 1998). Nua noted that the Internet has become the fastest-growing communications medium of all time, reaching 50 million American users in just 4 years. By contrast, radio took 38 years and television 14 years to reach audiences of 50 million. As a result of the Internet's rapid growth, not only are more individuals given access to a remarkable array of education options, but students enrolled in those courses are only a few mouse clicks away from an information marketplace of unprecedented proportions. The implications for education and training are extraordinary.

The Internet and K–12 Education

By early 1998, three-fourths of all primary and secondary schools in the United States were connected to the Internet, but this figure was misleading in that most schools had limited internal distribution to classrooms, computer laboratories, and library-media centers. The Universal Service Program (USP), established by the Telecommunications Act of 1996 to provide affordable access to the Internet for schools and libraries, promises to have a major impact on connecting the remaining buildings and enhancing student access within schools, especially in rural areas and inner cities. The USP requires service providers to offer their lowest rates to elementary and secondary schools and allows additional 20–90% discounts on top of those rates (known as the *E-rate*) for telecommunications services, Internet access, and internal networking. Service providers are then reimbursed from a multibillion-dollar fund established as part of the program.

An increasing number of school districts are putting courses on the Web, either to supplement existing curricula, to promote course sharing among schools, or to reach students who cannot (for physical reasons) or do not (by choice) attend school in person. Some districts, among them the Eugene Public School District in Oregon and the Jefferson County Public School District in Colorado, planned to offer web courses not only to their own students but to others nationwide. As with satellites and terrestrial video networks, the Internet thus has significant potential for delivering courses that smaller, underfunded districts may not have the resources to offer on their own. Owston (1997) noted that alternative schools are beginning to make extensive use of web technology to gain greater access to quality learning materials, and that web-based courses also have high potential for adults attempting to complete their schooling through home study. In addition, some colleges and universities are now offering freshman-level courses online to allow students to get a head start on their postsecondary work while still enrolled in high school.

Home-schooled students, in particular, stand to benefit from courses and curricula offered online. The Web can help overcome two of the main limitations of home schooling—the lack of interaction with other students and, as with many alternative schools, limited access to high-quality learning materials (Owston, 1997). A new genre of educational institution, the "cyberschool," has arisen to provide 9–12 or K–12 curricula, with an emphasis on college preparation, completely via the Internet to home-schooled students nationwide. Private online schools such as Cyber High School in California and the Christa McAuliffe Academy in the state of Washington either are fully accredited or promise to seek appropriate accreditation as soon as they have graduated their first four-year classes. (As with any other product or service purchased through the Internet, a caveat emptor warning applies. Parents should fully investigate these schools before enrolling their children and paying tuition.)

Higher Education

Although colleges and universities have been offering online instruction since the early 1980s, the World Wide Web has provided them with new means of reaching out not only to their traditional service areas but well beyond, as the Internet knows no state, province, or national borders. More than 800 U.S. colleges and universities now offer online courses for academic credit, and the majority of these programs are open to any student, anywhere, as long as entrance requirements are met and tuition is paid. Conventional brick-and-mortar institutions hardly hold the exclusive franchise on online degree and certificate programs. Proprietary (for-profit) institutions such as the University of Phoenix and Magellan University are enrolling large numbers of students via the Internet. Another important trend is the emergence of consortia of traditional colleges and universities to develop and deliver academic programs by a variety of nontraditional means. The Western Governors University, with affiliated public universities from Guam to Indiana, is the highest profile "campus without walls" institution yet established. Consortia such as the California Virtual University and the Southern Regional Electronic Campus have been set up to broker courses and degree programs developed by their member institutions.

Why does Internet-based distance education have such strong potential for academe? For one thing, the population of typical college-age students is expected to increase much faster over the next 20 years than campuses can find space to accommodate them, particularly in the Western states. Collectively, college students also are getting older. More than 40% of today's college students are "nontraditional," over 25 years of age, and these are the most likely to have Internet access either at home or at the workplace. Twenty-nine percent of the respondents to a 1997 national survey of Internet users conducted by the Emerging Technologies Research Group (ETRG) said they probably would engage in educational activities via the Internet, second only to banking (30%) among anticipated future online functions (Miller & Clemente, 1997).

The growing expense of traditional higher education is another important, related factor keeping some students home. Adjusted for inflation, the cost of attending a traditional residential college or university has doubled in the past 15 years. A recent survey by InterEd, a higher education research organization, found that over 1 million students in the United States were taking courses by distance education, many via the Internet, and that number was expected to triple by the turn of the century (Gubernick & Ebeling, 1997). With online courses, students can live at home and save on travel and the costs of maintaining two residences, and many can maintain their normal full-time jobs while completing their studies at their own pace and convenience.

Training and Development

The need for learning does not cease when graduates enter the workforce. Oblinger and Rush (1997) predicted that in the next 5 years, 95% of all workers will use some form of information technology in their jobs. They estimated that each employee will need to accumulate learning equivalent to 30 credit hours of instruction every 7 years just to stay current.

Executives of American Management Association member companies expected use of the Internet for training and development purposes to increase more than 270 percent in the next few years (American Management Association, 1997). Bassi, Benson, and Cheney (1996) identified revolutionary advances in delivery technologies as one of the top-10 trends in corporate training. They noted the "almost unlimited" potential of the Internet for reaching multiple sites with training events, and that the Internet has "tremendous advantages over current CBT [computer-based training] technology in both cost and convenience."

Simonson (2000) offered the following about the movement in corporate training from stand up, instructor centered training, to sit down, online instruction:

Stand Up or Sit Down: Training for the Next Decade

Starbucks coffee—regular and decaffeinated—and two stacks of cups and saucers fill a table in the back of the room. An InFocus projector and IBM ThinkPad laptop are in the front. At 8:00 A.M. promptly, twenty-four sales reps from ten branch offices file into the Dallas Hilton conference room. Their badges clearly give their nicknames and in smaller print their branch offices and city locations are printed. It takes them about 10 minutes to get coffee and to find their seats behind the name tents strategically placed around the three tables set up in a U-shaped pattern.

At 8:15 their *stand up trainer* begins by saying, "I hope you all had a pleasant trip. I realize most of you know one another, but let's go around the room and say our names, our branch office, and something about ourselves that we would like to share with the group," and another corporate training session, a stand up corporate training session, begins.

The question is, will "stand up" training be replaced by "sit down" computer-based, online distance delivered sessions? What will be the training scene for the next decade in corporate America? Stand up training is so familiar it needs no explanation other than the scenario presented above. Sit down training is instruction delivered at a distance—in either time or location—most often to students who are sitting behind a computer connected to the World Wide Web. Often other technologies are used, such as audiobridges, compressed video sessions, and satellite downlinks, but in all cases there is not an instructor in the front of a classroom of students.

Obviously, predicting the future is not simple. Sometimes research provides understanding. These understandings make forecasting the future more accurate. So, by looking at the research is it possible to determine if stand up training is going to be replaced by sit down, online instruction.

First (as was discussed earlier in this book), if the research on learner preferences is examined two conflicting results are obvious. Learners are increasingly demanding to be permitted to learn at a distance. They appreciate the convenience of instruction delivered to locations near where they live or work, and if training is available anytime they want it, or need it, then learners are even more pleased. The more learners find out about distance education, the more they are demanding the opportunity to learn at a distance, at least some of the time.

On the other hand, when asked, almost 90% of any group of learners say that if they have complete freedom to choose—freedom from time constraints, travel problems, and financial obligations—they prefer to learn face-to-face, in the classroom, laboratory, seminar room, even lecture hall. The problem is that many, even most learners, especially adult learners, do not have freedom to choose because of time constraints, travel problems, and financial obligations.

The tension between learner demands and preferences is at the root of the training dilemma. How do training organizations balance learner preferences with their student demands? How do trainers plan for the future that increasingly makes technology available to nearly every adult learner.

Many are now advocating this theme—effective education and training should include both face-to-face and online instruction, and the decision for the corporate trainer is what is the correct percentage of each. In other words, there is a continuum with face-to-face instruction on one extreme and online instruction on the opposite end. Instructional delivery for a unit, course, or program can be planned and delivered anywhere between and including the two extremes.

Actually, an obvious compromise is a best of both worlds strategy that has training divided into a two-thirds versus one-third split, with two-thirds of any major instructional event such as a course, being delivered at a distance, and one-third delivered face-to-face. This split is a good starting point for instructional design, especially for adult learners.

As researchers explore the relationship between face-to-face instruction and distance instruction it is possible that a formula, model, or recipe can be developed that will help the trainer determine the appropriate mix for a given course with specific objectives, and learners with a certain set of characteristics. Just as instructional design models permit the development of instructional events with predictable outcomes, a distance education model should predict delivery strategies that will optimize learning while achieving the best cost effectiveness.

Stand up and sit down instruction will exist together in the training environment of the next decade, of this there is considerable agreement. It is also becoming clear that some organizations will gravitate toward one extreme or the other, but that most trainers and training departments will use both strategies as part of a comprehensive training scheme.

Access in the workplace is generally not an issue, and training is a vital and continuing aspect of the modern workplace. White-collar employees in most U.S. corporations either have direct access to the Internet or enjoy Internet-like functions through restricted-access company networks called *intranets,* and over half of all small businesses in the United States have Internet connections. An increasing number of partnerships are being established between corporate training units and higher education institutions, with universities providing customized training programs delivered via the Internet and videoconferencing. It is apparent, however, that online instruction will increase in importance in training environments.

WHAT IS THE INTERNET?

A basic understanding of what the Internet is and how it works can be helpful to distance educators in their quest to use it effectively. The Internet is not a single, clearly defined entity, but a meganetwork of interconnected networks that share a common language, TCP-IP (transmission control protocol/Internet protocol). (A *protocol* is an electronic language that computers use to communicate with one another and exchange data. Protocols are roughly analogous to the languages humans use to communicate and exchange information.) These networks are in a perpetual state of evolution. Jack Rickard (1997), editor of *Boardwatch Magazine*'s Directory of Internet Service Providers, described the Internet as "a complicated matrix of connections in a constant state of upgrade with some 3,600 vendors making changes on a daily basis" (p. 1).

Internet Management

The Internet has no international headquarters or mailing address, no chief executive officer or board of directors, no stockholders to whom it must be accountable, and no toll-free number to call for information. This is not to say that the Internet is an anarchy, although some cynical observers may disagree. Much of the planning and coordination responsibility is assumed by the Internet Society, an international, nonprofit organization established for the purposes of "global cooperation and coordination for the Internet and its internetworking technologies and applications." Founded in 1991, the society facilitates the development and implementation of Internet standards and

One advantage of web-based courses is the availability of excellent graphics to explain key concepts.

policies and holds oversight responsibilities over several important boards and task forces that address Internet issues.

Among these are the Internet Engineering Task Force (IETF), the protocol engineering and development arm of the Internet, and the Internet Architecture Board (IAB), responsible for the overall structure of the network. Addressing responsibilities are assumed by the Internet Assigned Numbers Authority (IANA) for Internet Protocol (IP) numbers (the four-element 123.456.78.90 addresses) and the Internet Network Information Center (InterNIC) for domain name system (DNS) addresses (somebody@somewhere.edu) and registration processes. Although some national governments restrict access and practice censorship, in general the existing oversight bodies are concerned with technical and network management matters rather than what information is placed on the Internet, who puts it there, and who has access to it. This is an important issue for students and teachers using the Internet for educational purposes, because no quality-control mechanism exists to ensure that information found on the Internet is accurate and unbiased, and that it may be freely viewed by the fainthearted.

Evolution of the Internet and Its Services

The Internet has its roots in the ARPANET, a network created in 1969 to link the computing systems of military and other government agencies to those of their research partners around the United States, including universities and corporate contractors. As the ARPANET grew, important technologies such as the TCP-IP, electronic mail, and Ethernet were developed to enhance its capabilities. In 1985, the National Science Foundation (NSF) established the NSFNET, a high-speed data transmission network that interconnected a series of NSF-funded supercomputers across the United States, and invited other networks running the TCP-IP to connect to it, including the ARPANET participants. This NSFNET national backbone and its affiliated networks became known as the Internet, and 1985 is generally regarded as the Internet's birth year. The ARPANET was absorbed into the Internet and ceased to exist in 1989.

A simultaneous but separate development was the evolution of the Because It's Time Network (BITNET), founded as a general-purpose academic network in 1981 by the City University of New York and Yale University. BITNET ultimately grew to include about 600 educational institutions in the United States and was affiliated with networks in Canada, Europe, and other parts of the world. BITNET used a different protocol (RSCS/NJE) and therefore technically was not part of the Internet, but it interconnected with the Internet through "gateways" that functioned as translators between the two protocols. Mention of BITNET in this chapter is important for two reasons. First, BITNET was the first computer network available for widespread academic use. Hundreds of thousands of college faculty members and students became acquainted with international computing networks and their capabilities through BITNET. Second, BITNET mainframes hosted the LISTSERV mailing list management software that enabled both BITNET and Internet users to participate in online, asynchronous group discussions on thousands of topics. BITNET finally ceased operations in late 1996, as its functions also became absorbed into the Internet.

The Internet itself continued to expand through the 1980s, but for educators its primary functions remained electronic mail and online discussion groups, file transfers (using file transfer protocol, or ftp software), and remote access to computers ("remote login," commonly through telnet software). Use of the Internet at the K–12 level was minimal during this period, primarily because of access issues, although some schools were engaged in innovative e-mail exchange programs with other schools all over the globe.

In the early 1990s, two types of menu-driven server systems emerged that demonstrated the compelling nature of an online information database presented in a user-friendly environment—Wide-Area Information Server (WAIS) and Gopher. Thousands of Gopher sites were established worldwide, and for a time Gopher accounted for a substantial portion of all Internet traffic. WAIS and Gopher laid the groundwork for what was to become the "killer" application of the 1990s, the World Wide Web (WWW, or the Web).

The Web was conceived by Tim Berners-Lee of the European Center for Particle Research (CERN) as a means of sharing data among scientists and was first used in 1989. It did not become a standard desktop icon until four years later, when the National Center for Supercomputing Applications (NCSA) at the University of Illinois unveiled Mosaic as an all-purpose World Wide Web "browser." Within a year, more than 2 million persons around the world had downloaded Mosaic, and when Netscape appeared as the next-generation web browser in late 1994, interest in the Web spread even more dramatically. As access grew, the number of web sites online increased exponentially—from just 130 in June 1993 to 50,000 by November 1995 and over 3 million by mid-1998.

The World Wide Web brought the "point and click" technology of the desktop computer to the Internet. Although such features as graphics, photographs, audio, and video were possible with Gopher, the Web was the first Internet application to integrate them into a single screen along with text. The use of multifont text also became possible. Perhaps the most dynamic feature of the Web was hypertext, the ability to link words, phrases, or graphics with other files, located on the same server or on someone else's server on the other side of the world. As a result, web page developers could easily organize information from multiple sources and make any of it accessible to users with the single click of a mouse. The addressing system developed by Berners-Lee for the Web, ultimately called the uniform resource locator (URL), included three elements: [protocol]://[host computer]/[file location].

The WWW protocol, hypertext transfer protocol (http), became the most popular by far, but the URL structure also permitted use of the Gopher, ftp, telnet, and WAIS protocols. The two elements following the double slash identified the name of the computer on the Internet upon which the desired information rested and the location of the information within the file structure of that computer. Browser vendors quickly added electronic mail capability and access to the popular Usenet newsgroups, making web browsers all-purpose tools that revolutionized the way people used the Internet.

Before Mosaic and Netscape turned the Internet into a playground for the masses, interest had been limited primarily to the education and research communities. The rapid growth and powerful capabilities of the Internet quickly caught the attention of the commercial sector. A survey by the International Data Corporation (IDC) found that by the end of 1996, about 80% of all Fortune 500 companies had set up web sites, up from 34% in 1995, and over half of all U.S. companies, regardless of size, had a web presence (IDC, 1997). According to the IDC, commerce on the Web expanded from a negligible amount in 1995 to $1.1 billion in 1996 and to an estimated $5.5 billion in 1997. Some estimates placed the value of web commerce at over $300 billion by the year 2002.

Structure of the Internet

The potential for commercialization of the Internet led to a radical change in the network's architecture, as the National Science Foundation decided it should not continue to fund the backbone infrastructure in competition with private telecommunications carriers. A new structure was put in place by April 1995, and the NSFNET was retired. The transition to commercial backbone operators was seamless and unnoticed by most Internet users. Rickard (1997) described the current Internet structure in the United States as having five levels.

Level 1: Interconnect level network access points (NAPs)

Four NAPs have been established—in San Francisco, Chicago, Washington, DC, and New York—where the national backbones interconnect and exchange data traffic. Four metropolitan area Ethernet (MAE) systems also serve as de facto NAPs, and the U.S. government operates three additional access points for its own traffic.

Level 2: National backbones

Rickard described a national Internet backbone provider as "a company that has physically located a high-speed TCP-IP router in a number of cities, and then leased high-speed data lines from long distance exchange carriers to link the routers—thus forming a national 'backbone@c> connecting those cities' " (p. 7). The winter 1998 Boardwatch Directory of Internet Service Providers listed 41 companies providing national backbone services in the United States alone, including CompuServe, IBM, MCI, and Sprint.

Level 3: Regional networks

Regional networks operate backbones on a smaller scale, typically within a state or among adjacent states, connecting to one or more national backbones. Rickard noted that many of the existing regional networks have been around since the NSFNET days.

Level 4: Internet service providers

This is perhaps the most important component for distance educators. The individual Internet service providers (ISPs) are connected to regional networks and provide dial-up or hard-wired access to the Internet at the local level. These are the companies that provide direct Internet access to schools, businesses, private homes, and other community entities such as libraries, churches, and government offices if not available through other networks. ISPs have been largely responsible for the worldwide Internet boom.

Level 5: Consumer and business market

Rickard included this level to illustrate that "each time a small office leases a line to an Internet Service Provider's point-of-presence, it has in fact extended the Internet by that number of linear feet" (p. 9). Dial-up ports maintained by companies and educational institutions so that employees and students can connect from home or on the road extend the Internet.

Further Internet Discussion

Further discussion of the Internet is beyond the scope of this chapter. A list of web sites that offer additional information about the Internet can be found at the end of this chapter. Unfortunately, as the World Wide Web continues to evolve, web sites tend to come and go, or at least change their online locations. The URLs provided in the list were verified shortly before this book went to press, but readers are cautioned that long-term accuracy cannot be ensured.

OVERVIEW OF WEB/INTERNET-BASED DISTANCE EDUCATION

The emergence of the Internet as a delivery tool for distance learning comes at a time when education itself is undergoing a significant transformation. The teacher-centered "sage on the stage" model that has dominated education for centuries, or the "sage in a box" model (Bourne, McMaster, Rieger, & Campbell, 1997) as it often applies in video-based distance education, is slowly giving way to a learner-centered paradigm, with the teacher in the role of "guide on the side." Diana Oblinger (1999), Manager of Academic Programs and Strategy for IBM, observed the following transitions:

- From lecturing to coaching
- From taking attendance to logging on
- From distribution requirements to connected learning
- From credit hours to performance standards
- From competing to collaborating
- From library collections to network connections
- From passive learning to active learning
- From textbooks to customized materials

Barr and Tagg (1995) drew similar conclusions. They noted that the focus in the learner-centered paradigm shifts from the delivery of instruction and courses, passive learning, and competition to the creation of learning environments, active learning, and cooperation. Learning comes under the control of the student, the time at which learning takes place becomes variable, and a "live" teacher is no longer required. These are the very foundations upon which the concept of asynchronous learning networks (ALNs) is built. An emerging model for online distance education, ALNs attempt to move beyond the simple transfer of the conventional face-to-face classroom to the Internet. A well-conceived ALN-type course creates an online environment that includes all modes of learning appropriate for the specific educational goals being addressed. The idea that learning can take place at any time, anywhere, as in Coldeway's "different-time, different-place" context described in Chapter 1, is central to the ALN concept.

Not all use of the Internet has to be as sophisticated as a high-end ALN course. Courses offered through text-based applications have been around since the early days of BITNET and are still being offered. The Internet may also be used as a supplement to courses delivered primarily by video, audio, and even print. For example, courses offered through video networks often include online discussion groups as well as learning materials and assignments on the Web.

Clarification of Terminology

Two terms frequently used to describe online learning systems are *asynchronous learning networks* and *computer-mediated communication*. The terms apply to similar concepts but have subtle differences.

Asynchronous Learning Networks.   An ALN is defined as a people network for learning that is largely asynchronous. It combines self-study with substantial, rapid, asynchronous interactivity with others. In ALN, learners use computer and communications technologies to work with remote learning resources, including coaches and other learners, but without the requirement to be online at the same time. The collaborative component is further emphasized by Odin (1997), who describes ALN as "any technology enabled collaborative learning environment using remote resources that

When web-based systems are used, learners can study anytime and anyplace they choose.

can be accessed from anywhere at anytime and yet create a community of learners who are actively interacting, sharing ideas, learning, and helping each other learn."

ALNs represent the broader application of instructional technology described in this section. An ALN may include not only computer-based activities but also audio, video, print, and any other available tools for learning. Moreover, although asynchronous learning networks are frequently associated with distance education, an ALN may be employed as a component of a face-to-face course or as a nontraditional means of instruction with students or trainees within a single campus or company. This chapter is written primarily from the perspective of an ALN-type distance education delivery system.

Computer-Mediated Communication.   According to G. M. Santoro (1995), "Computer-Mediated Communication (CMC) is the name given to a large set of functions in which computers are used to support human communication. CMC can be defined narrowly or broadly, depending on how one defines human communication. At its narrowest, CMC refers to computer applications for direct human-to-human communication. . . . At its broadest, CMC can encompass virtually all computer uses" (p. 11). CMC thus is similar in many ways to asynchronous learning networks but is a more narrowly defined term. ALNs use CMC as conversation, collaboration, and general learning tools but also employ noncomputer media such as fax machines and audio and video technologies (Sener, 1997). Like ALNs, CMC may also be used as a supplement to conventional face-to-face courses or video-based distance education.

Santoro (1995) described three broad categories of CMC functions. *Conferencing* provides direct communication among learners and with the instructor, using such tools as electronic mail, Internet mailing lists, newsgroups, and bulletin boards. *Informatics* is the term used by Santoro to refer to organized information resources maintained online to support learning, such as library catalogs, electronic reserves, online indexes and databases, and now the World Wide Web. *Computer-assisted instruction* (CAI) consists of the interactive learning and management tools that facilitate student achievement of course objectives. These may be accessed online or made available for use on the students' own computers.

Advantages of Internet-Based Courses

The advantages of Internet delivery of courses and training sessions, compared with conventional face-to-face teaching, are numerous.

- Unless access is deliberately restricted, courses could be available to any qualified individual in the world with a properly equipped computer and an Internet connection. Students can participate from school, home, office, or community locations.
- Asynchronous course components are available 24 hours a day, at the learner's convenience, and are time-zone independent.
- Students can work at their own pace.
- Course materials on the Web and most group communications software are distributable across multiple computer platforms; it makes no difference if users are on PC/Windows or Macintosh computers.
- The technology is relatively easy for students to use.
- Learning resources are available across the entire Internet.
- Online course materials, particularly those on course web sites, are easy to update or modify, providing student access to current information.
- The Internet can provide a student-centered learning environment, if the materials and methods are designed to take advantage of the interactivity the Internet provides.
- The Internet promotes active learning and facilitates students' intellectual involvement with the course content.
- A well-conceived ALN course provides a variety of learning experiences and accommodates different learning styles.
- Students become skilled at using Internet resources, a factor that may improve employment options upon graduation.
- When personal identities remain concealed, all students, regardless of gender, ethnicity, appearance, or handicapping condition, are on equal ground.
- Corporate training programs conducted via the Internet can yield significant savings in employee time and travel costs, and training can be conducted on a "just in time" basis.

Limitations of Internet-Based Courses

The limitations of Internet course delivery may also be substantial.

- Access may still be a problem, especially in rural and lower socioeconomic areas, contributing to a technology "haves and have-nots" situation (Berge & Collins, 1995). Even if the Internet is available, many potential students do not have ready access to computers.
- Traffic congestion on the Internet can be a major problem, particularly at peak times during the day and among students dialing in via slow modems. The World Wide Web is rapidly becoming known as the "World Wide Wait."
- Courses may focus on the technology rather than the content.
- Well-designed Internet-based courses may be labor-intensive to develop, requiring time and personnel resources not available to most instructors.
- The instructor may have to accept a new teaching paradigm, that of facilitator and manager of learning rather than as a dispenser of information.
- Although today's students as a whole are more technologically literate than ever before, many are technophobes who find the Internet confusing and intimidating.
- The active learning emphasis of Internet-based courses may be difficult for students conditioned by previous courses to be passive.
- Unless access restrictions are put in place, course materials and discussion groups on the Internet may attract undesired nonstudent participants. This is a problem in some web courses that are not password-protected.
- Copyright violations on course web pages sit in plain sight for viewing by the rights holders and their attorneys.
- Some topics may not adapt well to delivery by computer.
- Bandwidth limitations make it difficult to present advanced technologies, such as video, multimedia, and memory-intensive graphics, over the Internet.
- Online courses require students to take more responsibility for their own learning. To be successful, students must be motivated, be self-directed, and have the self-discipline to participate (Hiltz, 1994). This is difficult for some students.
- Although responses to questions may be instantaneous in the conventional classroom, feedback may be delayed by hours or even days in an asynchronous, online learning situation (Hiltz, 1994).
- The support infrastructure, providing training and technical assistance to both students and instructor, is often minimal or nonexistent. Instructional design support during the conceptualization and development of a course is also frequently unavailable.

Components of Web/Internet-Based Courses

Delivery of instruction via the Internet, particularly complete courses for which academic credit is given, should be viewed within the broader context of an effective distance education system. Anthony Kaye (1981) identified four subsystems that compose such an endeavor.

The *regulatory subsystem* consists of the management, decision-making, planning, funding, and evaluating processes, normally the responsibility of the administrators of the program and of the institution. The *course subsystem* includes course design and the production, distribution, and reception of the learning materials, along with management of the communications system maintained for course interaction. The *student subsystem* is responsible for admitting students and then managing and controlling their progress through the course. The *logistical subsystem* includes the purchasing and maintenance of equipment and software and the employment and training of personnel. As in any system, each of these subsystems must function effectively, both independently and in synchronization with the other subsystems, for the system as a whole to operate as it should.

This model provides insights into the factors that make an Internet course successful. Effective management is essential and depends heavily upon administrative support for funding, staffing, and resolution of issues that arise when an alternative instructional delivery system is introduced. For example, conventional colleges and universities are heavily bound by tradition. The credit hours awarded for a course are typically determined by the number of face-to-face contact hours. How are credit hours determined in an asynchronous, self-paced, online course with no face-to-face meetings? Can the campus curriculum committee be convinced that a proposed course designated for the Internet carries the same academic rigor as an on-campus course? If the admissions office requires that new students present evidence of measles shots, is this policy enforced for online students participating from Hong Kong and South Africa (suggesting perhaps that measles is contagious through cyberspace)? Conservative institutions can easily find any number of barriers to discourage innovative faculty from proposing courses in nontraditional structures.

Kaye's model identifies other issues that contribute to the success or failure of an online academic program, especially at the college level. If online courses are part of organized degree curricula, remote-site students who pay full tuition (and probably a distance education surcharge as well) should be entitled to the same level of support services as residential students, including advising and counseling. For example, a student who has been away from college for a few years may have rusty study skills. Assistance should be available online. Off-campus students should have access to financial aid, career exploration and placement services, and peer support groups. The logistical subsystem should provide technical support and training to students as well as faculty.

The course subsystem is particularly important. Any successful distance education program, whether delivered via the Internet, a video network, or any other technology, begins with well-conceived and well-organized courses. It is impossible to take weak teaching from the conventional classroom and improve it simply by moving it online. Placement of course materials on the Internet, such as the syllabus, lecture outlines, announcements, sample exams, assignment information, and study tips, does little more than change the distribution method for those resources. The Internet is at its best when its powerful capabilities are used to enhance learning, and these are the features that differentiate between mediocre teaching and highly effective teaching in an online environment. The course subsystem must account for the following.

Delivery of Course Content.   The traditional textbook may be equally appropriate in an online course. Course content may also be distributed via electronic mail or placed on a course web page. Copyright-cleared videotapes or audiotapes, CD-ROMs, and computer disks may be part of the course materials purchased by students. During the course planning stage, the instructor needs to consider what behaviors are expected of the students at the end of the course (the learning objectives), what information is required for the students to meet those objectives, and what is the most effective, efficient means of getting that information to the students.

Active Learning Experiences.   Learning theorists today recognize that active learning is required before students can fully comprehend the course content and be able to apply it to life situations. As Chickering and Gamson (1987) explained, "Students do not learn much just by sitting in class listening to teachers, memorizing prepackaged assignments, and spitting out answers. They must talk about what they are learning, write about it, relate it to past experiences, apply it to their daily lives. They must make what they learn part of themselves" (p. 5). Students participate in active learning through interaction, either with the instructor and other students on a person-to-person basis via online discussions or with the subject matter of the course itself.

Numerous tools are available to facilitate online discussion and will be described below. Interactivity with the course content is best enabled on the World Wide Web through assignments that require students to make use of web resources or custom-designed learning experiences requiring student intellectual activity. For example, animation tools that work with web browsers can provide simulations to which students respond. Some wonderfully creative learning activities have been developed using "plug-ins," third-party software applications that extend the capabilities of a web browser and allow instructors to include more complex learning materials in their course web pages. Indeed, the Web offers extraordinary opportunities for simultaneous interaction with people and subject matter, such as student participation in ongoing dialog with astronauts or explorers during scientific expeditions, in conjunction with content-rich web sites.

Access to Learning Resources.   Santoro (1995) listed *informatics*, organized online information resources, as one of the three primary components of a course offered by computer-mediated communication. An online course should provide remote students with a means of accessing all the resources necessary to complete course assignments. This is not as difficult a task as it might seem. Copyright-cleared materials can be placed directly on course web pages. The Web itself provides a wealth of resources, including sites that provide search tools to help students identify books, periodical articles, and other print sources for potential use in course written assignments. More than 4,000 journals and newsletters are available online, most of which provide article abstracts if not full text. Those materials not on the Web can be obtained from local or regional public libraries, by interlibrary loan if necessary. If quick turnaround time is desired, online sources such as UnCover enable students to identify journal articles and order them through the Web for receipt via express package delivery services. The accessibility of these resources should be made known to students early in the course.

Submission of Course Assignments.   Means can be provided for the submission of course assignments. The postal service may be one option, depending upon the geographic distribution of the students. Many assignments can be submitted in electronic form, either as attachments to electronic mail messages or via input tools such as forms on course web pages. Electronic submission results in the quickest feedback to students, particularly if the system provides for immediate evaluation.

Student Evaluation.   Every method of student assessment used by faculty in conventional face-to-face teaching should be available to a web course instructor as well. The traditional objective test can be administered using the forms capability of a web page, although this type of examination rarely reflects the actual application of course material in real-world situations, and exam security becomes a serious issue unless the course web site permits the random selection of test items from a fairly large pool. (Nothing prevents the first students taking an online exam from sharing the questions with others.)

Other means of student evaluation, including essay and take-home exams, homework assignments, term papers and projects, class presentations (which may be delivered by e-mail or web pages), and class participation, are equally appropriate for an online course. Self-evaluation may be an assessment component in the case of nontraditional students. A common criticism of online courses is that the instructor has no way of knowing if the student actually did the work, but the same question may be asked of many assignments in a conventional class as well.

Online Help.   As noted above, an effective support system for students is an essential component of an online course. Support begins with the instructor, who may conduct "virtual" office hours via electronic mail. Many faculty who teach Internet courses check their e-mail several times a day. Online tutoring should be available from a course teaching assistant or central tutoring service on the campus. Advising, counseling, and other support services should also be provided, commensurate with those available to on-campus students.

Course Evaluation.   Course evaluation is particularly important in courses delivered by nontraditional means. Evaluation may be *formative* or *summative.* Formative evaluation is conducted for the purpose of identifying weaknesses and making improvements. If the course is to be offered again via the Internet, formative evaluation may be conducted at the end of the course. Under any circumstances, students should be surveyed during the course, preferably before midterm, to determine if changes can be made or additional assistance provided. Questions should be made specific to the course but should include the following general ideas.

- Are you having problems with the course delivery system? If yes, what are they?
- Are the course materials clear and helpful? If not, what suggestions can you make for improvement?
- Are the course communication tools working OK for you? If not, what problems have you encountered and how can they be fixed?

- Do you feel you are receiving feedback on a timely basis?
- Are you having problems communicating with the instructor?

Summative evaluation is normally conducted at the end of the course for the purpose of determining worth or merit. Administrators may use this information in decision making regarding subsequent iterations of the course and even institutional plans and policies related to future use of the Internet for distance education. Factors examined often include the level of student achievement, student satisfaction with the course, response to the course among potential students (did it reach the students expected to enroll?), performance of the Internet as a delivery system, and whether the course made or lost money.

INTERNET COMMUNICATION TOOLS

Numerous tools are available to facilitate online learning, ranging from the use of electronic mail and Internet mailing lists to fully integrated web course software providing content presentation, communication systems, testing, and course management, all in the same package. To help illustrate the big picture of the types of tools available, this section is divided into web and non-web applications, with non-web, computer conferencing tools further divided into synchronous and asynchronous systems, but these distinctions are not pure. A single course may use a variety of these tools, and applications such as World Wide Web browsers cross over these artificial boundaries.

Computer Conferencing (Non-Web)

Computer conferencing as a delivery system for distance education courses dates from 1981 and achieved fairly widespread use by the middle of that decade. It is still fairly common, although much activity now has shifted to the Web. Collins and Berge (1997) noted many advantages to computer conferencing as a tool for online learning, including convenience for both faculty and students, independence of time and distance, and the ability to create virtual communities of learners regardless of location. Among the disadvantages are the nature of computer conferencing as a text-based medium that tends to favor the well-educated and articulate, the potential for both students and teachers to go into information overload, and the need for technical support.

Synchronous Systems. Synchronous activities are those in which the participants are online at the same time. Brainstorming and role-play are two functions particularly well-suited for synchronous course tools, although it is most commonly used for simple discussion of course content. Since synchronous activities must be scheduled in advance, they cancel the advantage of time independence. If students are separated by several time zones, finding convenient times for online meetings may be difficult.

Text-Based Systems. The most common synchronous, text-based application is *chat*, available in a variety of forms. In a chat system, participants carry on a conversation

Modern desktop systems permit connecting multiple sites for conferences involving the instructor, content specialists, and students.

in real time by keystroking their contributions. Some software posts the message after it has been typed, whereas others post it on a stroke-by-stroke basis, placing participants at the mercy of the slowest typist. Chat has been criticized because the messages often are not carefully considered and organized, and it is difficult to maintain the thread of a conversation.

A variation on chat is the MOO. MOO stands for MUD, object-oriented, with MUD an acronym for multiuser dimension or multiuser dungeon. MUDs originated with the Dungeons and Dragons game, in which the participants take roles in the game activities. Transferred to the Internet, MOOs are online, real-time, text-based, virtual-reality environments in which each participant plays a role. MOOs have been devised for numerous scenarios and are accessed via telnet. Several variations on the MOO structure have evolved, including a WOO (Web, object-oriented).

Other Systems.   A wide variety of other systems have been developed for online conferencing via the Internet. Many of the more sophisticated were intended for use in the business community for meetings and corporate training. For example, Microsoft NetMeeting is based on Internet videoconferencing technology, permits use of presentation graphics (Microsoft's own PowerPoint), and has a markerboard feature that allows participants to make on-screen pen strokes using the mouse. Online videoconferencing is possible with a limited number of sites using products such as CU/SeeMe, developed by Cornell University and now marketed in an enhanced version by White Pine Software. CU/SeeMe requires that each participating site have a video camera mounted on or near the computer. Although functional cameras are available in the $300–400 range, this cost may be excessive for an individual student.

Another type of computer conferencing system is groupware, software that enables participants not only to converse but to share documents and collaborate on projects. Lotus Notes was the original groupware application, and numerous others are now on the market. Groupware is most commonly found in corporate settings rather than schools and colleges, although groupware features are incorporated into some of the integrated web course tools to be discussed below.

Asynchronous Systems.   Asynchronous activities are those that do not take place in real time. Although most asynchronous, online courses maintain general schedules and set deadlines, within that framework students are able to participate at times convenient to them. This type of structure is particularly appropriate when students are spread across multiple time zones. Self-pacing and time for reflection before contributing to class discussions are important advantages of asynchronous course activities. The disadvantages include the lack of immediate feedback, the length of time required to carry on a discussion (often several days or longer), and the problem of information overload with an entire class posting messages on multiple discussion threads (Collins & Berge, 1997).

Electronic Mail and Mailing Lists.   By far, the most common asynchronous tool is electronic mail. E-mail on a one-to-one basis enables students to communicate directly with the instructor as well as with other students to discuss course questions and collaborate on projects. Group discussions can be maintained via Internet mailing lists (often inappropriately identified as "listservs"). A mailing list is exactly that—a computer file containing the e-mail addresses of subscribers interested in a specific topic, in this case the members of a class. Messages sent to the list mailing address are distributed by the listserver software to all subscribers on the list. Recipients can then reply back through the list to continue the discussion, with the response also distributed to all subscribers. Separate mailing lists may be established for individual work groups within the class.

The web site Liszt (http://www.liszt.com/) maintains information about more than 80,000 publicly accessible Internet mailing lists. Lists are available on every conceivable topic from brine shrimp to tuba playing. Participation in one or more mailing lists on topics related to the course can provide excellent learning opportunities. Students can discuss current issues with professionals throughout the field and make important personal contacts.

Usenet Newsgroups.   Course discussions may also be maintained via Usenet newsgroups. Usenet (User's Network) is an independent network, not part of but accessible via the Internet, dedicated to online conversations on tens of thousands of topics. A newsgroup can be established for a specific course. Students then access the newsgroup via a web browser or newsgroup reader software.

Internet mailing lists and newsgroups have several important distinctions. Access to a mailing list can be controlled. Only subscribers receive the postings, which are distributed in the form of e-mail messages. Each list may be set so that subscriptions are closed (e.g., must be approved by the "list owner," which essentially keeps out non-class members) and only subscribers can post (send messages) to the list. Mailing lists can be quite private. Newsgroups, on the other hand, are very public. Anyone who finds a newsgroup on Usenet can read the messages and contribute a posting, regardless of affiliation with or interest in the course. This may be a significant barrier if the course content includes sensitive or controversial material. Moreover, whereas mailing list messages come to the student via e-mail, students must remember to go to Usenet to read the course messages. The major advantage of Usenet over a mailing list is that a newsgroup normally requires less maintenance on the part of the teacher. Also, since newsgroups are open to public scrutiny, students may put more thought into their postings.

Computer Conferencing (Web)

Many of the computer conferencing systems that appeared during the past decade have been adapted for use with web browsers. Software such as WebCaucus, CommonSpace, and Allaire Forums permits both large- and small-group communications to take place in online courses. These applications are especially beneficial when classes are broken into groups for discussions or collaborative projects. Woolley (1996) and LaLiberte and Woolley (1997) have written helpful summaries of web conferencing tools and their functions. In addition, more than two dozen software products have come on the market since 1995 that provide fully integrated web course development, delivery, and management systems. (These will be discussed below.) One-to-one electronic mail and group discussion tools, both synchronous (chat) and nonsynchronous, are common features of these products.

TEACHING WITH THE WORLD WIDE WEB

With its broad capabilities and wealth of online resources, the Web has rapidly overtaken computer conferencing as the primary vehicle for online distance education. The Web may be a resource in an ALN-type course involving multiple technologies, or it could be a stand-alone delivery system.

The Web as a Learning Resource

During its most explosive growth period in 1996–1997, the Web was doubling in size about every 50 days, and a 1998 study by the NEC Research Institute counted more than 320 million web pages (Kolata, 1998). Although many of the new sites were student shrines to their favorite rock stars and others of dubious worth to young scholars, a wealth of extraordinarily valuable resources has been placed on the Web in virtually every subject area. For example, the Internet was a prominent source of citations for this chapter. Internet technologies are changing so rapidly that most print publications on the topic (regretfully, including this one) have outdated material before they reach the bookstores. The most current source of information *about* the Internet *is* the Internet. The same is true with many other areas of study. But given the enormous quantity

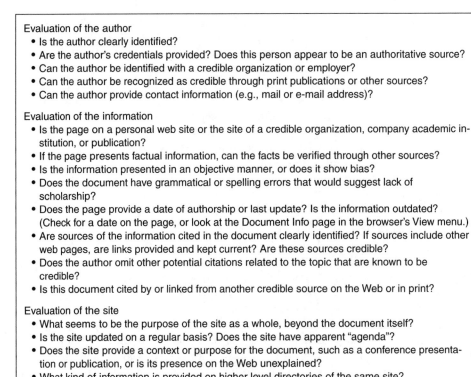

Evaluation of the author
- Is the author clearly identified?
- Are the author's credentials provided? Does this person appear to be an authoritative source?
- Can the author be identified with a credible organization or employer?
- Can the author be recognized as credible through print publications or other sources?
- Can the author provide contact information (e.g., mail or e-mail address)?

Evaluation of the information
- Is the page on a personal web site or the site of a credible organization, company academic institution, or publication?
- If the page presents factual information, can the facts be verified through other sources?
- Is the information presented in an objective manner, or does it show bias?
- Does the document have grammatical or spelling errors that would suggest lack of scholarship?
- Does the page provide a date of authorship or last update? Is the information outdated? (Check for a date on the page, or look at the Document Info page in the browser's View menu.)
- Are sources of the information cited in the document clearly identified? If sources include other web pages, are links provided and kept current? Are these sources credible?
- Does the author omit other potential citations related to the topic that are known to be credible?
- Is this document cited by or linked from another credible source on the Web or in print?

Evaluation of the site
- What seems to be the purpose of the site as a whole, beyond the document itself?
- Is the site updated on a regular basis? Does the site have apparent "agenda"?
- Does the site provide a context or purpose for the document, such as a conference presentation or publication, or is its presence on the Web unexplained?
- What kind of information is provided on higher level directories of the same site?
- Does the site look professional, or amateurish?

FIGURE 10–1   Guidelines for screening information sources on web sites.

of unscreened and potentially erroneous or biased material on the Web, how can students sort out the wheat from the chaff? Assisting students in thinking critically when evaluating web resources has become a major challenge for teachers. Figure 10–1 provides some guidelines to help with this process.

Dozens of search tools are available to assist students in locating desired information. Search tools may be classified into three general categories. A *directory* provides listings of sites organized in the form of a subject index, with many of the listed sites voluntarily submitted to the directory. A search vehicle is generally provided but only searches the directory's own database rather than the entire Web. Yahoo, LookSmart, and G.R.A.D.E.S. are examples of directory-type search tools. The second category, *search engines*, uses "robots" or "spiders" to search the Web for keywords specified by users. Even the most powerful of the search engines (HotBot) searches only about a third of the entire Web. Other search engines include AltaVista, Excite, InfoSeek, and Lycos. *Meta search engines*, the third category, search other search engines. Since search engines use different mechanisms for searching the Web and often provide different results, meta search engines can provide the most comprehensive list of hits. Examples of meta search engines include MetaCrawler, Highway61, Dogpile, Internet Sleuth, and All4One.

"Push" technology (also called channel-casting or web-casting) also has some promise for distance educators, although the initial high expectations for push technology have been largely unfulfilled. With the World Wide Web, users must seek out the information they desire, using search tools that typically turn up many more misses than hits. With push technology software such as PointCast and MyWay, service providers do the searching. They scan numerous news (such as Cable News Network, the *Wall Street Journal,* and the *New York Times*) and industry sources and "push" relevant articles to the user's client software via the Internet. The users specify the topics and industries to be scanned and set other parameters such as download times. Push technology allows class discussions and student projects to be based on the very latest information available, literally up to the minute.

The Web as a Course Delivery Vehicle

In a distance education setting, a course that is completely online with no face-to-face meetings is often called a "virtual" course. Virtual courses without real-time chat components epitomize the concept of different time, different place, because students work largely independently, according to their own schedules. Communities of learners may be created via the communication tools, normally asynchronous, and group assignments involving students at various locations but communicating via small-group forums, e-mail, and even telephone, and sharing drafts through e-mail attachments, fax, or the postal service. Many faculty report that communities of learners are easier to form in virtual courses than in conventional face-to-face classes because of the necessity for students to become involved and communicate with one another.

Most virtual courses are now built around course web sites. Every good web course begins with a plan. In fact, the most critical steps in the development of a course for Internet delivery take place before the first page is authored. In Chapter 4, four models for the design of online courses were presented. These models represent general approaches for web-based courses. In practice, most courses are an amalgamation of the four models presented in Chapter 4.

The teacher must think through not only how information (both administrative information and course content) is to be presented to students but, particularly, what learning activities will help students master the course material. In a sense, this is no different from a conventional course, but the delivery medium and the fact that students may be scattered over a broad geographic area change the teaching paradigm rather significantly. The importance of advance planning cannot be overemphasized.

Polyson, Saltzberg, and Godwin-Jones (1996) identified eight common components of quality course web sites:

- An *online syllabus* enables the instructor to make changes as necessary and provides students with a complete and convenient means of obtaining current course information.

- *Personal home pages* can help to create communities of learners by enabling students to learn about each other, make contact, and share mutual interests.
- *Interactivity* can take the form of asynchronous chat sessions or asynchronous electronic mail, discussion groups, and/or bulletin boards.
- *Assignments* can be submitted via course web sites and can be linked from content pages and the class schedule.
- An *announcements* section can provide course updates and other current information that students need to know.
- *Testing* modules can be provided in a variety of forms from simple self-help questions over content pages to complete unit mastery examinations.
- *Course management* features might include online grade books, test item analysis, course evaluation, and maintenance of student data such as user IDs and passwords, remote locations, and group assignments.
- *Course content* sections constitute the heart of the course and emphasize student intellectual involvement with the course material via active learning activities.

Content pages may contain not only text materials but also graphic illustrations, photographs, tables, audio, video, presentation graphics files (e.g., PowerPoint), animations, and virtual reality, as well as links to other web sites relevant to the course topics.

Essential Site Design. A course web site must be designed so that students can easily navigate their way around it and move from any page or function to any other with no more than three or four mouse clicks. An easy-to-understand site organization is imperative, preferably with an index or table of contents accessible from every page. Navigation tools such as a list of internal links or Forward, Back, and Home buttons can be extremely helpful to students. Consistency in page design throughout the site also is important.

In addition to navigation tools and a clear title, each page could contain any of the following, depending upon the page function:

- Date of creation and revision
- Owner information (name and e-mail address)
- Page URL
- Copyright statement

The course "home page," the first page that students access, should contain links to the content presentation and communication components of the course, as well as to an index and/or table of contents. Assignment and quiz pages can be accessed from individual content pages or from the home page. The home page might also link to other pages of information that can be very helpful to students, such as the following:

- Course syllabus and schedule
- Technical requirements for the course, including computer specifications and a list of browser "plug-ins" or other software required for the course, and how to obtain these technical resources

- Instructions to students, including how to use the site and obtain assistance
- Biographical pages for each student enrolled in the course, to help students get acquainted with each other
- Course rules and policies
- Study guides
- Sample test bank
- Examples of assignments completed by past students in the course, to demonstrate expectations
- Course resources, such as archives of visual material found on content presentation pages
- Links to related web sites

Authoring Course Web Pages.   All web pages must be authored using hypertext markup language (HTML), the system of "tags" or codes that web browsers read and interpret to display the appropriate information on our computer screens. Although basic HTML is not difficult to master—correct use of 15 or 20 HTML tags is sufficient to create web sites that are attractive and fully functional—most site creators now use web page authoring tools such as PageMill, FrontPage, or HomePage. This software is relatively inexpensive and enables users to create fairly sophisticated web sites with little training.

Integrated Web Course Systems.   Recognition of the World Wide Web's high potential for the delivery of instruction has led to an explosion of fully integrated web course tools on the market. These products have, in essence, shifted many of the course design and page creation functions described above from the teacher to the software developer. These tools provide complete content presentation, communication, assignment submission, testing, and management functions in a secure environment, easily accessible to both instructor and students via a web browser. They also provide standard page templates with convenient navigation tools that facilitate student movement around the site. Examples of these systems include Learning-Space, IntraKal, CourseInfo, TopClass, Web Course in a Box, and World Wide Web Course Tools (WebCT).

Using such a package, a typical student logs in, reads or downloads the current assignment, looks at the visuals, reads and responds to a thread of e-mail messages discussing the present topic, performs and submits the lab assignment for that material, takes a quiz or unit exam, sends a message to the instructor about the unfairness of question 8, and then logs off to surf elsewhere on the Web. The instructor logs in, modifies some upcoming course material to keep it updated, reads the student's complaint and runs an item analysis of the quiz to find out if that question has been a problem for other students, then clarifies the wording of the question and adjusts the grades accordingly, reads the e-mail messages posted to the course discussion group and sends a new message redirecting the train of thought, monitors how each student is doing in the course, and posts an announcement regarding the special guest participant next week. All this can be accomplished with a single piece of software.

Issues in Teaching Web Courses.   Teaching a course via the Web presents a number of issues that are nonexistent or of lesser concern in the conventional classroom.

Time Commitment.   For example, the time commitment can be hefty in any Internet component of a course but can be extraordinary in web-based teaching. Students must make a commitment to learn how to use the course delivery tools and adjust to a teaching and learning environment that is likely unfamiliar to them. They must take much more responsibility for their learning. In addition, they must develop the discipline to access the course communication tools on a regular basis (most likely daily) to read announcements and to keep from falling behind in discussions. For the faculty member, much more time is required for course planning and development. The teacher must also access the course site or communication tools daily to follow and orchestrate the discussions, receive assignments, solve problems, and serve other course management functions. Ongoing site maintenance and updating of links and student resources constitute another important teacher responsibility.

Security.   Course security is a significant issue. Faculty and administrators must decide whether, and how much of, a course should be open to the public and how much should be retained behind a password protection screen. Open access may be desirable for general information about the course and some content pages, as a means of attracting interest and possible fee-paying registrations. In some cases, all of the course content may be intended for the public—for example, university extension courses designed for outreach purposes but with participant assessment and fee-payment requirements for credentialing or receipt of continuing education credits. On the other hand, some components of web-based courses should always be password-protected, including the grade book, quizzes, and other student assessment measures, course communications (particularly chat room logs if controversial or sensitive information is discussed), and student biographies, photos, and other personal information.

Intellectual Property Rights.   As more and more schools and colleges engage in online course delivery, the intellectual property rights involved have become a major issue. At one level, as pointed out in Chapter 5, course developers must be sure that proper clearances are in hand for all copyrighted material posted on the web site, including the work of former students. At a higher level is the basic matter of ownership of the intellectual property contained in the course. It has long been assumed at most locations that teachers/professors own the intellectual property expressed in conventional face-to-face courses. As these courses are developed for Web delivery and become in a sense "packaged," some institutions have taken the viewpoint that the courses are "works for hire," and therefore are the property of the school or college. This is not a popular stance among faculty unions. The ownership of online course materials and division of any royalties accrued should be negotiated between faculty and administration before any institution puts its courses on the Web.

Accessibility.   For many students with disabilities, "[T]he Web threatens to become the equivalent of a classroom building without an access ramp" (Young, 1998, p. A31). According to Young, many persons with disabilites have found the Web so frustrating that they have stopped using it. Although legal implications of the Americans with Disabilities Act (ADA) for educational institutions regarding course web pages are unclear, course sites should be authored to maximize access opportunities for persons with disabilites. For example, web pages should be kept relatively simple. A page should contain no more text than necessary, especially preceding information of relative importance. The HTML coding for all images (including graphics and photographs) should contain "ALT" tags that provide brief text descriptions of the material. Audio and video files should be accompanied by optional links to pages containing transcripts for persons with hearing impairments. Burgstahler (1998) has provided additional suggestions for making web pages universally accessible.

SUMMARY: THOUGHTS ON THE FUTURE OF ONLINE LEARNING

As education itself is in a period of transition, so is distance learning. Although distance education's roots are in the asynchronous form of correspondence study, the predominant electronic delivery systems of the 20th century have been synchronous—radio, telephone, broadcast television, audio networks, instructional television fixed service (ITFS), microwave networks, communications satellites, local cable systems, and compressed video and fiber-optic networks. The Internet can provide either form—asynchronous or synchronous—but for the most part, it is used in an asynchronous mode. As such, the Internet has by far the greatest potential among all of today's delivery options for involving students intellectually with the course material in personal and productive ways.

The conclusion of Chapter 5 noted that the recent deregulation of the telecommunications industry will likely result in the blending of telephone, television cable, Internet access, and other electronic consumer services via a single connection to our homes, schools, and workplaces. Online educational opportunities, whether for corporate executives, third graders, or nontraditional college students, will proliferate in this environment. We have only begun to explore the possibilities, but it is safe to say that the delivery of instruction by some form of networking, at all levels of education, will become more and more common as the 21st century progresses.

SELF-TEST QUESTIONS

1. Identify the major areas of potential growth for online distance education at the K–12 and higher education levels.
2. What international organization is responsible for planning and coordination of the Internet?
3. Why is BITNET significant in the history of online distance education?
4. What two software applications revolutionized the way people use the Internet?
5. In Rickard's description of the current Internet structure, which level promises to have the greatest impact on distance education, and why?

6. Differentiate between asynchronous learning networks and computer-mediated communication as delivery tools for distance education.

7. What are the four subsystems described by Anthony Kaye that must be accounted for in an Internet-based distance education course?

8. How can active learning experiences be built into an online course?

9. What are the primary advantages and disadvantages of synchronous activities in an online course with students spread over several time zones?

10. Under what circumstances would an instructor likely select a newsgroup over a mailing list as a tool for asynchronous course discussion?

11. What are two main advantages of the World Wide Web as a source of information for course assignments?

12. What three aspects of a web document should be scrutinized in determining its credibility as a source of information?

13. What is the most imperative first step in developing a course web site?

14. What is the advantage of using software such as WebCT or Web Course in a Box compared with developing a course web site from scratch?

15. Name three important current issues in web-based teaching.

Answers to Self-Test Questions

1. K–12: Promote course sharing among schools; provide curricula to home-schooled and alternative school children; enable adults to complete schooling through home study. Higher education: Provide courses and degree programs to students who are unable to attend college in residence; partner with industry in providing customized training programs via the Internet.

2. Internet Society.

3. BITNET introduced hundreds of thousands of college faculty members and students to international computing networks, hosted the LISTSERV mailing list management software, and enabled the first online courses in 1981.

4. Mosaic and Netscape.

5. Level 4, Internet service providers, promises to impact distance education most significantly because the ISPs provide direct access to the Internet from homes, schools, local businesses, and other community locations.

6. ALNs incorporate CMC as conversation, collaboration, and general learning tools but may also employ noncomputer technologies; thus, asynchronous learning networks is a slightly broader term.

7. The four subsystems are regulatory, course, student, and logistical.

8. Active learning experiences may include technology-based interactive components integrated into course web pages, assignments involving exploration and study of web resources, synchronous and asynchronous online discussion groups, one-to-one online communication, conventional course assignments (e.g., research reports) incorporating web sources, and a virtually infinite array of other activities.

9. Advantages: Provides live discussion opportunities similar to conventional classroom; creates virtual community of learners; effective for brainstorming and role playing. Disadvantages: Negates time independence and self-pacing features

of online instruction; may be difficult to find online meeting time convenient for all students; participants may be at the mercy of the slowest typist; text-based systems favor the well-educated and articulate.

10. A newsgroup might be a better choice if the instructor has minimal time for list management and the course content does not include sensitive or controversial material.

11. The World Wide Web contains a wealth of valuable information that may not be easily accessible elsewhere; the Web may often be the most current source of information.

12. The author of the page, the information itself, and the overall site upon which the information rests should all be considered.

13. Begin by planning the entire site, with special attention given to conceptualizing active learning activities.

14. Software provides content presentation, communication, assignment submission, testing, and course management functions in a secure environment, with standard page templates and navigation tools provided.

15. Any three of the following are important issues in web-based teaching: time commitment required for students and instructor, course security, intellectual property rights, and accessibility of course materials to persons with disabilites.

For additional information and activities, visit the Prentice Hall Companion Website at http://www.prenhall.com/simonson

REFERENCES

American Management Association. (1997). *Business use of the Internet* [Online]. New York: Author. Available: http://www.amanet.org/research/archives.htm.

Barr, R. B., & Tagg, J. (1995). From teaching to learning: A new paradigm for undergraduate education. *Change, 27*(6), 13–25.

Bassi, L. J., Benson, G., & Cheney, S. (1996). Position yourself for the future: The top ten trends. *Training & Development, 50*(11), 28–42.

Berge, Z. L., & M. P. Collins. (1995). Overview and perspectives. In Z. L. Berge & M. P. Collins (Eds.), *Computer-mediated communication and the online classroom* (Vol. 1, pp. 1–10). Creskill, NJ: Hampton Press.

Bourne, J. F., McMaster, E., Rieger, J., & Campbell, J. O. (1997). Paradigms for online learning: A case study in the design and implementation of an asynchronous learning networks (ALN) course. *Journal of Asynchronous Learning Networks* [Online] *1*(2). Available: http://www.aln.org/alnweb/journal/issue2/assee.htm.

Burgstahler, S. (1998, January). Making web pages universally accessible. *CMC Magazine* [Online]. Available: http://www.december.com/cmc/mag/1998/jan/burg.html.

Chickering, A. W., & Gamson, Z. F. (1987). Seven principles for good practice in undergraduate education. *American Association for Higher Education Bulletin, 39*(7), 4–6.

Collins, M., & Berge, Z. (1997). *Facilitating discussion in online environments.* Workshop presented at the 13th Annual Conference on Distance Teaching and Learning, Madison, WI, August 1997.

Gubernick, L., & Ebeling, A. (1997, June 16). I got my degree through e-mail. *Forbes* [Online], pp. 84–92. Available: http://www.forbes.com/forbes/97/0616/5912084a.htm.

Hiltz, S. R. (1994). *The virtual classroom: Learning without limits via computer networks.* Norwood, NJ: Ablex Publishing Corporation.

International Data Corporation. (1997). *Information industry and technology update, 1997–98.* Framington, MA: Author.

Kaye, A. (1981). Origins and structures. In A. Kaye & G. Rumble (Eds.), *Distance teaching for higher and adult education* (pp. 15–31). London: Croom Helm.

Kolata, G. (1998, April 9). It's confirmed: Web's size bogs down searches. *The New York Times,* p. G3.

LaLiberte, D., & Woolley, D. (1997, May). Presentation features of text-based conferencing systems on the WWW. *CMC Magazine* [Online]. Available: http://www.december.com/cmc/mag/1997/may/lalib.html.

Miller, T. E., & Clemente, P. C. (1997). *The 1997 American Internet users survey: Realities beyond the hype.* New York: Emerging Technologies Research Group.

Nua Consultants and Developers. (1998). *How many online?* [Online]. Dublin: Nua Consultants and Developers. Available: http://www.nua.ie/surveys/how_many_online/index.html.

Oblinger, D. G., & Rush, S. C. (1997). *The learning revolution: The challenge of information technology in the academy.* Bolton, MA: Anker Publishing Company.

Oblinger, D. G. (1999, October). Hype, hyperarchy, and higher education. *Business Officer, 33*(4); 22–24, 27–31.

Odin, J. K. (1997). *ALN: Pedagogical assumptions, instructional strategies, and software solutions* [Online]. Available: http://www2.hawaii.edu/aln/aln_tex.htm.

Owston, R. D. (1997). The World Wide Web: A technology to enhance teaching and learning? *Educational Researcher, 26*(2), 27–33.

Polyson, S., Saltzberg, S., & Godwin-Jones, R. (1996). A practical guide to teaching with the World Wide Web. *Syllabus, 10*(2), 12–16.

Rickard, J. (1997, May). *Internet architecture* [Online]. Originally available: http://boardwatch.internet.com/isp/internetarch.html.

Santoro, G. M. (1995). What is computer-mediated communication? In Z. L. Berge and M. P. Collins (Eds.), *Computer-mediated communication and the online classroom* (Vol. 1, pp. 11–27). Creskill, NJ: Hampton Press.

Sener, J. (1997). Summary of the discussion on affordable ALNs: An online discussion. *ALN Magazine* [Online], *1*(2). Available: http://www.aln.org/alnweb/magazine/issue2/sener_alntalk.htm.

Simonson, M. (2000). Stand up or sit down: Training for the next decade. *Quarterly Review of Distance Education, 1*(3), 187–188.

Woolley, D. R. (1996, November). *Choosing web conferencing software* [Online]. Available: http://thinkofit.com/webconf/wcchoice.htm.

Young, J. R. (1998, March 13). For students with disabilities, the web can be like a classroom without a ramp. *Chronicle of Higher Education,* p. A31.

SOURCES OF INFORMATION ABOUT THE INTERNET

An Atlas of Cyberspaces

http://www.geog.ucl.ac.uk/casa/martin/atlas/atlas.html

Atlas of maps and other graphic representations of the Internet, compiled by Martin Dodge of University College London.

Internet Learner's Page

http://www.mnsfld.edu/depts/lib/learn.html

Comprehensive source of Internet-related information, maintained by Larry Schankman of Mansfield University.

Internet Mailing Lists Guides and Resources

http://www.nlc-bnc.ca

An extremely comprehensive source of information about Internet mailing lists, maintained by the International Federation of Library Associations and Institutions.

Internet Service Providers

http://boardwatch.com/

The online version of *Boardwatch Magazine's Directory of Internet Service Providers.*

Internet Society Home Page

http://www.isoc.org/

Information about the Internet itself and the society's mission and functions.

NetLearn: Internet Learning Resources

http://www.rgu.ac.uk/~sim/research/netlearn/callist.htm

Another comprehensive source of information about the Internet, from the School of Information & Media, Robert Gordon University, Scotland.

Nua Internet Surveys: Latest Surveys

http://www.nua.ie/surveys/

chapter 11

Assessment for Distance Education

CHAPTER GOAL

The purpose of this chapter is to present approaches for assessment of student learning.

CHAPTER OBJECTIVES

After reading and reviewing this chapter, you should be able to

1. Discuss the role of assessment in the instructional design process, especially for distance education.
2. Describe the characteristics of several types of traditional assessment activities and the appropriate uses of each.
3. Describe the characteristics of several types of alternative assessment activities and the appropriate uses of each.
4. Explain how the elements of assessment may be influenced by and integrated into a distance education environment.

ASSESSING LEARNING GAINS

Mike is studying French via satellite and is preparing for his weekly conversation group during which he and other international marketing professionals talk with native speakers of the French language via audioconference. At 5:00 in the morning, Lakeisha logs on to a web site that presents a series of geology simulations that allow her to practice working with GIS data, followed by a self-test of those skills. Carlos opens his e-mail and finds his midterm essay test waiting, sent out this morning by his Renaissance literature professor, with instructions to complete the test and return it via e-mail within the next 24 hours. What do these students have in common? They're all involved in some form of learning assessment. Through their respective efforts, they are demonstrating their level of understanding of the subject matter. The above activities reflect the learning gains the individual students have made, and let their instructors know how well they're progressing.

Although this chapter focuses on assessment in distance education, much of the discussion is not exclusive to distance education. Just as exemplary "distance" teaching closely resembles our best models of face-to-face teaching, assessing student achievement has a core of good practice that remains constant across a multitude of teaching-learning configurations. In addition, many of the examples provided will refer to institutionally based (formal) education, but most of the issues related to assessment could also be applied in a workplace training program, technical certification course, or professional development workshop.

WHAT IS ASSESSMENT?

If assessment is a way to measure learning gains, what can we do with that measurement? Are there uses for the information? The answer is a definite yes. In fact, there are at least five ways that this knowledge can be used to facilitate learning, and there are many other uses that may indirectly influence the learning environment or help to formulate related policies. Some of the more "administrative" uses of assessment include program evaluation and improvement, facilitation of student placement in programs, justification for funding priorities, and reporting of long-term trends to state, federal, or corporate entities. In a distance education environment, the results of assessment may sometimes be used to compare the academic performance of remote-site students with the performance of those at the origination site. Although this is not a particularly helpful comparison (we know that even if we could control the confounding variables, the results would very likely show "no significant difference"), it is often a necessary exercise to ease the worries of program administrators who must be able to "prove" that students at a distance are actually learning the material.

Probably the first use that comes to mind for learner assessment is to enable the instructor to assign grades or sign off on certification/licensure at the end of a course, unit, or lesson. Although this is important (and, typically, required of teachers) and often helpful in determining how to improve the instruction for future students, there are other, more direct ways of applying assessment techniques for enhancing teaching and learning.

Students gain a sense of control and can take on greater responsibility for their own learning if they know how well they're doing, compared with an established set of criteria. Feedback from frequent assessments, informal or otherwise, provides this scale. When the instructor has this information, he or she can provide remediation or correction where necessary, or determine if a student needs additional assistance. At the same time, this feedback helps the instructor to monitor the effectiveness of the instruction. If many students have difficulty with the same concept or skill, this could signal a lesson design problem. By using assessments carefully, the teacher can identify and address weaknesses or gaps in the instruction. When students encounter an assessment activity, they not only recall the needed concepts or skills, they also reinforce them through application. This is especially important to remember if course content is highly sequential or hierarchical in nature. Frequent assessments help to emphasize the correct concepts and skills (necessary to advance through later material), and also pinpoint learner misconceptions that would eventually present obstacles to further progress.

Assessing a learner's readiness to begin an instructional unit can be particularly important in a skills-training environment. Time, effort, and money can be wasted if students do not have important entry-level abilities or if, conversely, they already have achieved many of the class's final objectives. By designing effective entry-level tests (to determine readiness) and pretests (to determine placement), workforce training becomes more efficient and reduces time spent by employees in activities that are either too advanced or an unnecessary review of previously mastered concepts.

Finally, assessments are often a motivational activity. Most learners want to do well, and knowing that they'll be held accountable for a body of knowledge or set of skills can be the nudge that keeps them on track. Many a teacher has adopted group discussions, pop quizzes, or in-class exercises to ensure that required readings or out-of-class assignments are completed on time. Additionally, in countries such as the United States, where competitive activities (in school and out) constitute a large part of the culture, testing is often seen as an opportunity to pit one's abilities against those of others, while hoping to excel (or at least measure up). Competitive games are a frequently used assessment technique that can motivate, provide opportunities for teamwork, and reinforce important concepts or skills.

Assessment and Evaluation

How does assessment differ from evaluation? These terms often are used synonymously, but in an instructional context they have different meanings and applications. Assessment, as explained above, denotes the measurement of progress toward a learning goal—for example, student performance compared with a desired level of proficiency at a task. In this chapter, the word *assessment* will be used specifically to refer to this process. Evaluation, on the other hand, suggests the attribution of significance or quality of the current status of a particular object or condition. As its root word, *value*, suggests, *evaluation* implies that a judgment will occur regarding the information that assessment activities provide. Summative evaluation of an instructional unit is a way of assigning value to a learning package; formative evaluation determines the level of quality of an unfinished product for purposes of revision and improvement. The techniques of assessment and evaluation may sometimes overlap, but their purposes make them distinct.

Assessment and Instructional Design

The role of assessment in the instructional design process is as a corollary to the development of learning objectives, and a precedent to the development and implementation of instructional strategies (Dick & Carey, 1995; Gagne, Briggs, & Wager, 1987). In this way, the assessment activities are matched to expectations, and instruction is then based on assessment plans. A less formal way of expressing this is: Figure out what learners should get out of the instruction, determine how you'll know whether or not they were successful, and then decide what they should do to reach that point. In this manner, "teaching to the test" becomes a desirable basis for instruction because the test (in whatever form it takes) is a measure of what is considered important.

Unfortunately, this ideal is realized only occasionally, and assessments typically are created after the instruction is planned and often after it has been implemented. This doesn't preclude the use of objectives as a basis for determining progress, but care must be taken to ensure that the instruction has also been based on the same expectations and has not wandered from the original goals. If students prepare for an examination thinking, "What's going to be on this test?" or face an out-of-class project wondering what is expected of them, that may indicate that the objectives have been forgotten along the way. Those desired outcomes must act as a continuous thread that binds the instructional process together from beginning to end.

Characteristics of Good Assessments

As described in the previous section, assessment is one element of the teaching and learning process that grows from the determination of desired performance outcomes. It follows, therefore, that one of the characteristics of a good assessment tool is that it matches the objectives; learners know what to expect because they have already been made aware of what is important and how they will be expected to demonstrate their mastery of this knowledge or skill. The objectives, ideally, specify what the students will do to demonstrate their mastery of the content, how well they will be expected to perform this task, and under what special circumstances, if any, they should perform it.

Occasionally, instructors will find that a test item or exercise that they have created does not match the objectives, although they believe it to be an important skill or concept for learners to grasp. In this case, it makes sense to return to the list of objectives and consider the possibility that there are gaps or missing items. Herein is an excellent reason for creating assessment measures before implementing instruction. If there are gaps in the objectives list that become apparent only when developing an assessment activity, it is likely that the missing material will not have been included in the planned learning activities. Instructional design should be conducted in an iterative, dynamic manner that allows enough flexibility for changes to be made throughout the development process, but revisions during implementation (i.e., while the training is in progress) are often more difficult to put into practice and can confuse learners.

An assessment may, on the surface, match the objectives but still not reflect the student's progress. This characteristic, the degree to which an assessment provides an accurate estimate of learning gains, is known as *validity*. If a learner who has mastered the specified body of knowledge does poorly on the test, exercise, or project intended to measure this mastery (or, conversely, if learners who have not mastered the material perform well), that particular assessment would be said to have low *content validity*. For example, test items intended to measure analogical reasoning may, instead, reflect the learner's reading ability if vocabulary level is not considered in test design. Or if a project is supposed to demonstrate the learner's ability to design process controls in a laboratory environment, but an unrealistic time limit for completion is imposed, this assessment may indicate that some learners have not mastered the concepts when in fact they simply were not given adequate time to demonstrate their expertise.

Criterion-referenced validity, also called predictive validity, is a form of validity with significant implications for workforce training. If an employee successfully completes a series of training units on using a new software package but then can't apply those skills on the job, the instrument that assessed his or her performance had low predictive validity. This is also important if the content being taught is part of a hierarchically organized series of learning modules in which foundational concepts or basic skills must be mastered before the learner moves on to more advanced tasks.

A concept related to validity, and an important characteristic of good assessments, is *reliability*. Reliability refers to the stability of an instrument or activity; this could be thought of as how consistently the assessment measures learning gains. If students perform poorly, as a group, on one occasion and then do much better later, the predictability of this assessment is called into question. Or if learner mastery is measured by observation and scored by several different raters, the scores must be highly correlated to ensure consistency (also known as *interrater* reliability). Low reliability signals that the results are not dependable and could vary significantly from day to day.

A characteristic of good assessments that is especially important in distance education settings is *clarity* of expectations. This refers to how easy the assessment is for the learner to understand, whether the instructions are clearly written, and whether any special conditions are to be met. For many distant students, examinations will be proctored by someone other than the instructor ("I *think* this is supposed to be an 'open-book' test"), projects may be completed based only on the directions initially provided ("Well, she never told us that using our own software package would not be allowed!"), and papers may be written according to instructions given in the course syllabus ("Was that 10 to 12 pages double-spaced or single-spaced?"). If the directions are not comprehensive, specific, and clearly worded, the assessment may ultimately prove useless.

Finally, although there are other criteria for judging the merits of a particular assessment, they all are designed to help answer the question "Does this assessment measure learning gains and allow an accurate generalization of results beyond the immediate situation?" In other words, a useful assessment reflects the learner's progress and understanding, as well as the transferability of skills and knowledge. The obvious purpose of an assessment is to document the direct results of instruction, but if the student performs a task in a learning environment but cannot do so elsewhere, the instruction has been futile.

Norm-Referenced and Criterion-Referenced Scoring

Once a student completes an assessment and it is scored or rated, there are two systems that are used to report this score. *Criterion-referenced scoring* is used when the rater compares the learner's performance with that of a predetermined set of standards, drawn from the learning objectives. The rater asks, "Did the learner master the content?" The score that is reported reflects this level of mastery, in terms of how closely the student's performance matched the ideal. *Norm-referenced scoring,* however, reports these same ratings by comparing each student with the others who have completed the same assessment (and, theoretically, the same instruction). The term *grading on a curve* reflects this type of scoring, and in this case the rater asks, "How well did the learner do compared with the others?" There are appropriate uses for each type of scoring. If our concern, as teachers, trainers, or instructional designers, is that each student master the course content, then their performance compared with one another is irrelevant; we need to ensure that they have performed well compared with our expectations by using criterion-referenced scoring. Norm-referenced scoring is used, appropriately, to report long-term trends and comparisons of extremely large groups of learners (e.g., nation-wide or worldwide, in the case of some university preadmission examinations), but should never be used to determine grades, award certification, or licensure, or determine mastery of content. Grading on a curve tells the teacher and learner how well students did relative to one another, but does not give a clue about whether any of them mastered part or all of the content.

TRADITIONAL ASSESSMENT TOOLS

When considering how to determine if a student has achieved the desired level of content mastery, one of the first thoughts that might come to mind (especially in a formal instructional environment) is to administer some kind of paper-and-pencil test. In this section, four of the more frequently used test styles—multiple-choice, true/false, short-answer or free-response, and essay—will be described and their particular strengths and applications discussed.

Multiple-choice tests can be an efficient way to measure learning, especially if the objectives are written at a low level of cognitive effort, such as knowledge or comprehension, where students are expected merely to recall previously memorized information (e.g., state capitals, vocabulary words, or bones of the human skeleton). As objectives move up the cognitive processing scale toward analyzing and synthesizing (inferring relationships or creating models), multiple-choice test items get more difficult and time-consuming to create. Unfortunately, in many cases, instructors expect students to gain higher order thinking skills but then test them using items that only reflect comprehension, or maybe application, of the content area. Writing multiple-choice test items that require higher order thinking skills demands creativity and careful attention to the course or unit objectives. For example, a question at the analysis, synthesis, or evaluation levels might present learners with a written paragraph and then expect them to identify gaps in logical reasoning, recognize data elements relevant to the solution of a problem, or judge which statement presented fits a set of given criteria. The students would apply their comprehension of the course content to demonstrate these skills, but would not be able simply to pick out a correct answer from rote memory.

When writing multiple-choice items, the "stem" (usually written as a question or an incomplete statement) is presented along with one correct answer and several "distractors" (incorrect responses) in a list from which learners choose. Distractors should appear to be plausible answers and should include choices that are often confused with the correct answer, to ensure that students are discriminating among possible responses. When testing for higher order thinking, it may be necessary to direct students to select the "best answer" from those presented, rather than assume that there is only one correct answer to any given question. "All of the above" and "none of the above" responses should be avoided; these items and others that are unclear or obscure can be confusing and result in a score that does not reflect actual learning.

Multiple-choice questions can also be written with one stem and a list of responses from which students choose all that are correct. Or one set of responses can be used for several stems, with students selecting the correct response for each stem. In this case, there may be a mix of correct responses and distractors, and some of the responses might be appropriate answers for more than one stem. One of the greatest advantages of multiple-choice testing is the ease of scoring and item analysis. These types of items (along with true/false) are considered "objective," because human judgment is unnecessary in scoring; an answer is either right or wrong and a subjective interpretation is not needed to determine the accuracy of each response. Where once nearly all multiple-choice tests were scored from optical scan forms ("bubble sheets") that were marked with the requisite No. 2 pencil, now inexpensive and easy-to-use testing packages that allow students to take the test electronically make even this obsolete. With appropriate password protection and student verification (to ensure that the person taking the test is, in fact, the one who is getting credit for it), these packages are a major leap forward for distant learners and their teachers. No more of the formerly inevitable turnaround wait time and massive stacks of papers to score and mark. However, as mentioned previously, multiple-choice tests are difficult and time-consuming to create unless the subject matter is at a very low level of cognitive difficulty. Other weaknesses include the possibility of students guessing correctly or responding to verbal associations that do not require an understanding of the content.

Another type of objective test item is the *true/false* (sometimes called *alternative response*) question. True/false items typically are used when objectives call for students to determine which of two possible responses is appropriate—whether a statement is true or false, fact or opinion, or some modification of this. One should use these items when there can be only two possible responses (yes or no, agree or disagree, valid or invalid, etc.), one of which is correct. If you find it difficult to create an unambiguous stem that clearly will have only two possible answers, consider using another type of test item. Like multiple-choice items, true/false questions can be clustered by providing a stem that asks students to identify specific responses from a list of several possible answers. For example, the stem might ask, "Which of the following are synonyms for the word *synchronous?* Responses, to be marked as "yes" or "no," could include "concomitant, sequential, coincident, simultaneous, consecutive." Some obvious advantages exist for true/false items: They provide for simple, easy-to-automate scoring; test administration can be handled more quickly (many items can be answered in a short amount of time); and results usually do not depend heavily on the reading ability of the student. Unfortunately, guessing offers the learner a 50% chance of success, and when the stem statement is false, it can be difficult to determine if learners actually know the right answer or if they just knew that the statement given was incorrect. (One way to mitigate this effect is to require test takers to rewrite a false stem so that it becomes a true statement. This, in turn, reduces the ease of scoring, however.) True/false items, to be effective, must be precisely written and free of irrelevant information or verbal clues to the correct response. And, finally, avoid designing the test so that students may miss items simply because they think they are being tricked in some way (the use of all "true" statements on a test, for example). Although this might test the strength of the learners' convictions in their responses, it may not provide a realistic measurement of learning.

Short-answer test items (sometimes called *free-response items* or *supply items*) straddle the fence between objective and subjective assessments. These items are written either as direct questions requiring the learner fill in a word or phrase or as statements in which a space has been left blank for a brief written answer. Because students can fill in any answer, care must be taken to create items that are precise and not open to a wide variety of interpretations. In some distance education environments, this is crucial; test proctors at remote sites cannot be expected to answer questions about particular test items and what the instructor meant to say. Like multiple-choice tests, short-answer items are mostly useful when learners are expected to recall information from memory, rather than analyze or synthesize complex concepts.

An advantage of short-answer items is that learners must actually know the correct answer, as opposed to recognizing it among choices in a list. Also, tests can be scored by teaching assistants or those who know little or nothing of the content area. Like multiple-choice tests, electronic versions of a short-answer test are easily created and delivered via e-mail or web site, but scoring is more difficult to accomplish electronically. The scoring system must include the desired correct answer, answers that are synonyms for the correct answer, and the likely misspellings that could appear. In a large class, however, it might still be more efficient to use automatic scoring and deal with the resulting problems as they arise.

Essay questions, or *extended response items,* provide the instructor with the greatest degree of flexibility and can be used to assess higher order learning, such as analyzing concepts or designing plans. Students also have greater freedom in providing an answer that shows their level of understanding and ability to present an organized response. Questions must, however, be written with a clearly stated "assignment" for students to complete. Vaguely worded essay questions not only make scoring responses difficult, they may not provide a valid assessment of whether the student has achieved the desired learning goals. Once the question has been written, a scoring rubric should be created to assist in grading answers so that, even though the rating is subjective in nature, it remains criterion-referenced, and answers are judged according to their accuracy and completeness, rather than whether they are better or worse than another student's answer. For many students, it may be helpful to suggest how much time should be spent on each item or approximately how long the answer should be, to help them organize their time and use it wisely. Students in a distance learning environment can easily take advantage of electronic delivery of questions (either directly through electronic mail or from a static web site) and then submit their responses via e-mail.

The two main advantages of essay questions are flexibility and the option of testing for high levels of learning outcomes, but there are several disadvantages that should be considered. The most readily apparent of these is that scoring of essay responses is extremely difficult and time-consuming. Students who are "test savvy" may be skilled bluffers (for example, the student who writes extensively about what he or she knows and then attempts to fit it to the question, relevant or not), and good writers tend to score well on essays, regardless of actual content. Conversely, poor handwriting or bad spelling can also pull scores down unfairly, although having students write their essays using word processing software can eliminate (or at least reduce) this problem. Also, because of the time required to write the essay, only a limited amount of material can be covered. For this reason, many test design experts (e.g., Gronlund, 1998) suggest mixing objective items, such as multiple-choice, with some short-answer and essay items to increase the amount of material that can be covered on a single test.

Using Traditional Assessments in Nontraditional Environments

The traditional types of paper-and-pencil tests—multiple-choice, true/false, short-answer, and essay—can be used successfully in a distance education setting when they are designed and administered appropriately. Electronic versions of these instruments help with the problems of scoring and turnaround that have been the bane of many a program's existence, although logistical concerns regarding test security and proctoring must be addressed.

Whereas traditional assessment instruments typically are administered in a classroom with accompanying time limits, there are valid reasons to consider using take-home tests, especially if testing for higher order thinking. If an objective for the course or unit specifies that learners will apply concepts in tasks requiring analysis, for example, one option is to provide essay questions that meet this criterion. The pressure to memorize facts, names, or dates is relieved, and students will have a chance to revise their responses to more accurately reflect their knowledge of the content. Also, this more closely mimics our use of these cognitive skills in real life—rarely is there a brief, strict time limit for this type of task, and the use of available resources is encouraged, not forbidden. The wise instructor, however, will suggest a page limit or word limit for responses, thus avoiding the volumes of prose that some overeager learners would happily supply.

Online tools have brought new opportunities to the distance education environment, including enhanced features in web-based assessment. Online testing software, whether included in a course management package (e.g., Blackboard or WebCT) or as a stand-alone component of a course (e.g., QuestionMark or Respondus), offers anytime, anyplace access to quizzes, tests, and practice exercises. In addition, many textbook publishers now include a value-added component in their standard array of materials by offering test banks of items that correspond to individual book chapters or units. These pools of questions typically are designed to "plug in" to a course management package or can be downloaded for use in a traditional paper-and-pencil format. Also, online testing can be accomplished by contracting with an assessment service provider (e.g., Prometric) that will handle test creation, administration, and response analysis.

Online assessment usually resembles its traditional counterpart in test design and use, and the advantages it offers are primarily logistical in nature. For example, online testing packages can easily randomize the order in which test items appear or the order in which possible choices in a multiple-choice question are presented. Test items can be categorized by learning objectives and a predetermined number of items from each category selected at random each time the test is administered. Test security features may include a "browser lock-down" in which test takers are prevented from printing, saving, or accessing other computer resources until the test has been submitted. Finally, automated scoring reduces the labor-intensity of frequent assessment and student scores can be immediately entered into an online gradebook for easy record-keeping.

Other features that offer meaningful instructional advantages might include the option of branching within an assessment activity, based on the test-taker's responses. Learners could be presented with additional questions on a particular topic, or routed to remedial instruction. In addition, immediate feedback tailored to the student's response can be presented, and item analysis may provide useful guidance for fine-tuning the questions themselves. Online assessments can also easily accommodate graphics, audio, and video clips as part of the activity, allowing a wide variety of question types and options.

The most significant disadvantage of online assessment remains the time that it takes to create the initial test pool of items. Although existing document files can often be imported into a testing package, the questions must be coded in some way to indicate, for example, which response in a multiple-choice item is the correct one. Also, although test security has improved significantly, proctoring is still required to ensure that the test taker is who he or she claims to be and that additional resources (such as textbooks or notes) aren't being used if the assessment has been designed as a "closed book" examination. Finally, although the Web seems ubiquitous, every student may not have easy access to the online materials or may be limited to a slow, dial-in connection that limits their ability to download media-rich course components.

ALTERNATIVE ASSESSMENT

The types of assessment measures described above are considered traditional tests. *Alternative assessment*, as its name implies, is a method of gauging student progress in ways unlike those just described. In academic circles, this term has taken on an even more specific meaning, in which assessments are considered "alternative" not simply because they are dissimilar to traditional ideas, but because they represent a constructivist or cognitive processing learning philosophy. Three approaches—authentic assessment, performance-based assessment, and constructivist assessment—have come to the forefront of this movement, with areas overlapping in each category.

Authentic assessment refers to tasks that simulate real-world challenges. Ideally, the student is presented with the full array of expectations for a task and is expected to engage in activities that reflect a meaningful response. Wiggins (1990) described an effective authentic task as one that includes "ill-structured challenges and roles that help students rehearse for the complex ambiguities of . . . adult and professional life." These types of assessments emphasize the transfer of skills to unfamiliar situations beyond the classroom. *Performance-based assessment* is, in fact, what it sounds like—expecting the learner to perform a skill. In addition, it may include determining what the learner knows *about* the skill itself. Some also include the criterion that assessments focus on higher order thinking and critical reasoning. Simply requiring that the student perform a science experiment, for example, does not guarantee that critical thinking will occur. Exploring how learners arrive at their answers or why they performed the task in the manner they did will provide evidence of the desired cognitive activity. Some performance assessments will reflect a process (giving a speech, for example) or have no tangible outcome (speaking a foreign language).

Assessment activities that reflect a *constructivist approach* encourage students to choose their own mode of expression, to work collaboratively with others, to think about their learning, and to rethink and revise their ideas as they build their cognitive structures (Herman, Aschbacher, & Winters, 1992). The emphasis is on the creation of personal meaning and divergent thinking, which poses some interesting challenges for the instructor who has experience only with more traditional forms of testing or projects. This need not mean that assessment activities lack scholarly rigor, however, and allowing for variance in learning style, memory, and developmental pace may, in fact, require that learners actually take on greater responsibility for their progress toward the instructional goal.

Assessments may incorporate characteristics of these approaches singly or in varying combinations, but, for the sake of clarity, the term *alternative assessment* will be understood to encompass these ideals. Some examples of alternative assessments include portfolios, projects, and problem-solving activities.

Portfolio assessment, a means of collecting and judging examples of student work, has received considerable attention in educational circles in the recent past. A portfolio can consist of a wide variety of materials (papers, videotapes, computer files, etc.) reflecting generalized learning across disciplines, or it can be a more specific gathering of content-based materials, such as tests, worksheets, or art projects. One of the key elements of portfolio creation is that the student decides (typically with an instructor's guidance) what materials to include in the portfolio. Self-reflection, leading to the development of standards and the determination of criteria to use in selecting these materials, are integral components of this process. Identifying what constitutes the student's "best" work represents a level of self-assessment that requires thoughtful consideration of learning goals and progress toward significant milestones.

The increasing attention given to portfolio development can be attributed to a shift away from learning as the accumulation of knowledge to a perspective that emphasizes the application of cognitive skills such as evaluating, problem solving, and analyzing. When education was considered—by learners and their prospective employers—a discrete event encountered in school and then left behind after the conferring of a diploma or degree, the school transcript with its notations of courses taken and grades awarded was sufficient evidence of learning. Now, however, employers demand workers who not only can apply these important cognitive skills but who will continue to learn on their own as the world's information base expands. The portfolio offers tangible evidence of what individuals can do as a result of learning and how well they apply this learning to a variety of challenges.

The assessment of the portfolio by a teacher or advisor can be a highly subjective process, but is often accomplished with the use of a standard rubric developed for that purpose. A rubric is simply a set of criteria against which products may be judged. It may include various performance levels ranging from a baseline of adequacy to higher levels that indicate excellence and work that demonstrates understanding beyond that required. For example, one criterion included in the scoring rubric may be that a wide variety of student projects be present or that the work be organized according to a thematic idea. In this way, systematic scoring of the portfolio helps to reduce the subjectivity of the final rating.

Projects constitute a large category of alternative assessment activities. These could include individual assignments as well as group activities, but they typically involve the creation of a product as the final result. Projects may be designed to simulate real-world challenges or be connected to the personal experiences of the learners, and can result in the development of plans, works of art, research proposals, multimedia presentations, or almost any other method of demonstrating mastery of a specific body of knowledge. Proponents of cognitive learning theory argue that when students are given the opportunity to design their own projects, individually or as a group, the potential benefits include improved performance, better management of their own learning, increased motivation, and improved self-esteem (Herman et al., 1992).

One of the main advantages of group projects is that students learn to collaborate and work with others toward a common goal. Today's work world depends on teamwork; the social and interpersonal skills necessary for successful collaboration can be developed and honed through the use of activities that unite students with those of differing viewpoints, cultural backgrounds, and value systems. Projects also facilitate informal peer review of work. This can be a highly motivating force, and the benchmarking that it provides assists learners in self-evaluation and the definition of learning goals. (One important caveat applies here: Using peer review to determine student grading can be problematic and the instructor must ensure that his or her academic judgment of the learner's progress toward the objectives remains the basis for assigning a grade.) Also, as the nature of classroom teaching and learning shifts from teacher-as-information-provider to teacher-as-facilitator, group work becomes a much more natural event. No one individual is seen as the center of attention, and the teacher can move to a more collaborative role, with students depending on each other to move the group toward its goals.

Another type of alternative assessment, *problem-based learning,* is actually an entire instructional strategy in which students are presented with a situation that they must then investigate to determine how to respond. For example, learners may be given a scenario or case study for analysis and then be required to recommend one or more strategies or solutions. (This approach has been used successfully in medical education for many years and is now being explored by other content areas.) Problem-based learning truly represents how challenges appear in real life; few of us are faced with dilemmas or untoward circumstances that we—coincidentally—have just spent several weeks researching. Instead, as in real life, students must learn about the problem itself, analyze its components, gather resources, and then synthesize this information to prepare a plan of action or recommended strategy. Individuals or groups may be assigned to a particular problem (or "case"), and the final result—the deliverable—may take the form of a presentation, written report, multimedia demonstration, or other tangible product.

Advantages and Disadvantages of Alternative Assessment

Alternative assessment, however it is applied, has advantages and disadvantages that may render it more or less appealing to the instructional designer or teacher. The advantages include the ability to simulate real-world settings, in which learners participate in activities that mimic those found in the workplace, home, or social environment. Transferability of skills to other environments may be strengthened by such challenges, and the relevance of course content may be heightened; thus the classroom (in whatever configuration it takes) becomes just one link in the chain that connects learning and doing, theory and practice, goals and outcomes.

Workplace skills, such as teamwork, can be reinforced through instruction that emphasizes collaboration and assessment activities that reflect this perspective. Critical thinking, selection and evaluation of resources, effective interpersonal communication, and project planning are abilities characteristic of today's ideal citizen, worker, and learner. Instruction and assessment that require the acquisition, development, and use of such skills reflect a philosophy of education that includes lifelong learning as an essential goal.

Proponents of alternative assessment suggest that the content validity of "authentic" tasks is ensured because there is a direct link between the expected behavior and the ultimate goal of skill/learning transfer. Multiple-choice tests (or other "proxy" assessments) measure learning that we must infer can be applied to an unfamiliar or novel challenge. The claims of improved validity make sense for some categories of learning; consider the assessment of psychomotor tasks such as handwriting or objectives related to literary composition without observing the direct performance of their accomplishment. Determining the mastery of some learning outcomes may be dependent, also, on a specific set of circumstances or environmental constraints that simulate the transferability of skill; completing a federal income tax form within a predetermined time limit, or teaching someone else how to do so, can demonstrate abilities beyond basic skill levels that could not be judged without being observed under these circumstances.

One of the major disadvantages of alternative assessments is how difficult it can be to assign a score or rating to learner performance. Portfolios, for example, can be extremely time-consuming to evaluate. Each element in the collection of papers, videotapes, computer programs, or other pieces of "learning evidence" must be examined and scored to make a reliable judgment of completeness, quality, organization, or other desired criteria. Before this can be done, however, a comprehensive set of scoring guidelines must be developed. Herman and colleagues (1992) suggested a nine-step process for the creation of a portfolio rubric that included such procedures as "Gather samples of students' and experts' work that portray a range of quality" after which you would "discuss characteristics of work that separate the excellent from the poor" and then "write descriptors for the important qualities." The amount of work represented by these steps includes only one-third of the total process, and the actual assessment itself has not yet begun. Unfortunately, without a finely detailed and clearly illustrated set of standards that would result from this sequence of steps, the subjectivity of the scoring process can result in unintentional bias or low interrater reliability. Finally, assuming that a reliable scoring procedure is created and implemented, how does a college or university compare a student's portfolio with the standardized tests traditionally required of applicants? And what institution has the personnel available to do so if it could?

Recently, however, generic "rubric generators" have begun to appear on the Web for teachers to use as templates that can then be customized to their instructional needs. For example, RubiStar is a template that guides the instructor through the rubric creation process and provides example criteria for use in developing a scoring matrix for assignments ranging from oral presentations to science fair experiments. (RubiStar is provided freely for educational use through the High Plains Regional Technology in Education Consortium, one of 10 federally funded R-TEC centers nationwide. See RubiStar at http://rubistar.4teachers.org.)

Another disadvantage to the use of alternative assessments is their general unfamiliarity within traditional educational institutions. The little training that teachers get in the design of assessments cannot begin to prepare them adequately for the demands of such tasks. This "little training," however, is more than most college professors ever get, and their design of assessments is most likely to be guided by their experiences as students—under the tutelage of college professors who taught as those before them had. If the lack of awareness or understanding were the only reason for college faculty to turn away from alternative assessments, this could be remedied relatively easily; but accreditation concerns may also stand in the way of adopting such innovative practices. The standards by which postsecondary programs are judged are not casually or frequently revised, however, and traditional assessments that are understood and somewhat standardized across a profession or discipline may hinder any improvident "creativity" on the part of faculty.

One caveat regarding the use of alternative assessments must be offered. Educators should be cautious about abandoning tests that measure knowledge in favor of those that focus on thinking skills; this one-or-the-other approach creates a false dichotomy between content and its application that is counterproductive to creating a well-rounded learner. Pomperaug Regional School District 15 (1996) coined the term *process creep* to describe the insidious, and sometimes nearly unnoticed, orientation to process at the expense of connecting assessments with course content.

Finally, the terminology associated with alternative assessment has antagonized some educators and created an image problem for such practices. The use of the term *alternative* does not explain what these assessments are, but rather what they are not. Unfortunately, the use of this alienating jargon has given impetus to those who would relegate these procedures to a substandard or fringe element status. Terwilliger (1996) takes exception to the use of the term *authentic* to describe some assessment approaches as being "superior to others because they measure outcomes that are more 'genuine' or 'real.' " The assumption that a specific type of assessment is unequivocally more effective than another ignores the role of the instructional design process in developing measures to match the desired outcomes. This perspective is just as limiting as those that would shun alternative assessment out of hand and deserves no recognition.

ASSESSMENT AND DISTANCE EDUCATION

Much of the information and content in this chapter could be applied to any instructional setting, regardless of where the participants are. As mentioned previously, explaining good assessment, like defining good teaching, requires an understanding and explication of a core of methodology that remains constant. There are, however, some elements of assessment that apply especially to the distance education environment. Although many K–12 schools have adopted distance education, adult learners make up the majority of students involved in such programs, whether affiliated with an educational institution, as part of a privately administered training sequence for certification or licensure, or professional development activities offered through their employer's human resources department. These students may have been away from the traditional classroom for several years, they may be working full time, and they may have families to care for, as well as social or community obligations. In most instances, however, they are extremely motivated and eager to learn. For these students, alternative assessments may be especially appropriate.

Distance education students who are returning to formal education, in particular, derive great benefit from the use of *ongoing assessment.* Ongoing (sometimes called *embedded*) assessment activities are woven into the fabric of the instructional process so that determining student progress does not necessarily represent to students a threat, a disciplinary function, or a necessary evil, but simply occurs as another thread within the seamless pattern of day-to-day classroom or training events. One advantage of this approach is that any misconceptions held by learners that might interfere with later progress are identified and addressed before they become obstacles to further learning. The American Association for Higher Education encourages this in its "9 Principles of Good Practice for Assessing Student Learning" (2000) and goes on to state, "The point is to monitor progress toward intended goals in a spirit of continuous improvement." A natural advantage for the instructor is that the dreaded "crunch" of grading that presents itself when assessments occur in large blocks is avoided; ongoing assessment provides

Assessment is possible at a distance, especially when live, two-way interactive systems are used. Students can complete their assignments and present them to classmates and the teacher.

information on student progress in smaller increments over the course of a unit, training module, or academic year (Hart, 1994; Wiley & Haertel, 1996).

One easy-to-use technique for ongoing assessment is known as the "Minute Paper" and was described by Angelo and Cross (1993) as a way to gather "manageable amounts of timely and useful feedback for a minimal investment of time and energy." Students simply write a brief paragraph (hence the name) about what they learned as a result of the instructional activities they have just completed. This method helps identify misconceptions, as well as provides an overall view of what students consider to be the important concepts presented.

Many distance delivery configurations do not provide the conditions for the creation of the informal learning group that develops almost automatically in traditional, face-to-face instruction. One characteristic of the learning group is that an unofficial benchmarking system, by which students compare their progress with that of the group, is created to provide feedback to individuals and enhance student motivation to keep pace with their peers. Ongoing assessment can provide this information and a motivational nudge through frequent feedback and reinforcement. For returning students who may be unsure of their competence in the classroom, these ongoing activities help them achieve small successes early on without the stress of a major examination or assignment. Examples of ongoing assessments include creating and implementing in-class exercises, holding students responsible for collaborative work, or expecting students to participate in online, asynchronous discussion groups. For many distance education teachers, large class sizes make formal assessment activities a daunting prospect. (Many distance education programs begin with a mission of making formal educational opportunities available to previously unserved markets, and find that these groups take advantage of the chance for learning in quantity.) Using *nongraded assessment measures* for part of the course, however, alleviates much of the strain of grading massive amounts of student work while still providing several of the benefits of traditional assessments. Spontaneous question-and-answer activities (either verbal or written, similar to pop quizzes) can be integrated easily into synchronous classroom "instruction where they act to reinforce content, supply feedback on student progress to students and teacher, and provide motivational support. Students can check their own work and participate in the discussion of correct answers; the instructor may or may not choose to collect the anonymous "quizzes" to get a sense of the strengths and weaknesses of a particular lesson, but the pressure of grading and turnaround is relieved.

Self-paced assessment activities also offer benefits to distant learners. Without the pressure of time constraints, adult learners, who may have less-than-flexible schedules, have the opportunity to prepare papers, projects, or other tangible "deliverables" that demonstrate learning while not tying them to a rigid (and potentially unworkable) timetable. Unless learning goals require the student to create products within a specific time frame, it makes little sense to demand adherence to an inflexible program. Different learners require varying levels of external structure, but this may be considered a negotiable item based on performance and learning style. An example of this might be the assignment of a research paper with a series of milestone deadlines (topic and rough outline, first rough draft, second edited draft, etc.) jointly determined by the student and teacher. Duffy, Duffy, and Jones (1997) suggest asking students to generate not only their assignments and the evaluative criteria, but also a set of guidelines for how the class will "work" and function as a group. Standards for online "netiquette" and acceptable behaviors are created and approved at the start of the course, leading to a sense of buy-in and establishing known parameters.

Another issue of importance when assessing distant learners is the *fairness* of the assessment activity. Care must be taken to avoid penalizing remote-site students by requiring the use of resources not readily available to them or expecting them to adhere to a different set of time lines than students who are taking the course at the origination site. (In one regrettable instance, an instructor expected distant students to submit papers by mail earlier than on-site students turned theirs in at the origination site so that he would receive them all on the same day.) Distant students do not deserve special treatment on the basis of their location, nor should they be punished. Here again, adult students who have been absent from the classroom for some time may not have the same mental "set" that traditional students do, and terminology, procedures, and expectations should be defined as clearly as possible.

Students enrolled in their first distance education course may need practice utilizing the technological resources for a class, or they may be unfamiliar with alternative forms of assessment. Instructors would be wise to require students to practice using such tools as their online "dropbox" for assignments, asynchronous discussion platforms, or web-based quizzes, well before their use as a point-generating event. In addition, in-class or real-time simulations of performance-based assessments can provide students more familiar with rote learning with experience in these activities.

Also of concern is the issue of *diversity*. Many distance education programs, by mission and design, enroll a highly diverse group of learners. These differences (e.g., age, race, socioeconomic status) provide a richness to the learning group that might otherwise not occur and can offer many opportunities for cross-cultural interactions. Such differences may, however, pose a problem if the assessment of learning is biased in favor of "traditional" students—those who fit a preconceived notion of the type of person the instructor expects to have in the course. An example of this might be the instructor who uses examples or scenarios in course assignments that make sense only to young adults, a particular religious group, or native speakers of English. Unfortunately, the students affected might not speak up about the problem and will either perform unsatisfactorily (regardless of how well they know the content) or simply give up in frustration and drop the course. Obviously, the validity of any assessment that required such noncontent-related knowledge would be threatened and the results no longer meaningful. As discussed earlier, one of the purposes of assessment is to provide *feedback* to learners. In some distance education environments, the turnaround time for tests, papers, or projects is long enough to interfere with the usefulness of the feedback, returning to the student's hands only after so much time has elapsed that the comments or corrections are nearly meaningless. Also, because the opportunities for personal communication between the teacher and learner may be limited, feedback must be clear, detailed, and constructive. Unlike the student who can linger after class to ask "What did you mean by this squiggly line?" the distant learner is left to ponder the underlines, circles, arrows, and sometimes cryptic notes provided as guidance for further assignments or revisions.

CHEATING AND PLAGIARISM

Although cheating and plagiarism are not problems exclusive to the distance education domain, the use of advanced communications technologies, coupled with the perceived absence (at least geographically) of an authority figure, has led to what many teachers and trainers consider a growing problem on campuses and in training programs. Cheating and plagiarism have never been easier, thanks to the increased computer literacy of our students and the wide availability of term papers (among other things) for sale online. Typically, cheating takes the form of stolen pencil-and-paper tests that are circulated among students, the use of restricted materials (such as notes or reference books), or tests taken by someone other than the enrolled student. Plagiarism (i.e., submitting the work of others) may be more often a result of ignorance, when students don't realize how to credit their sources or what constitutes plagiarism to begin with. Distance education programs walk a fine line between creating a climate of suspicion and mistrust and promoting a completely laissez-faire attitude toward these transgressions. Some of the ways in which education and training programs have dealt with these issues is to focus on strategies for the prevention of cheating and helping students to resist the temptation to do something they might regret. Building awareness of what plagiarism is and how to avoid it is a first step toward this, and a preventive strategy might include requiring students to turn in rough drafts of their work prior to submitting the final product. Other techniques include the use of ongoing assessment (to reduce the pressure of one-shot tests or assignments), the use of an institutional honor code, and involving students in the design of assessments (to reduce the us-versus-them feeling).

Of the technologies that have influenced cheating and plagiarism, the most frequently cited as troublesome are the online entrepreneurs who sell papers already formatted for easy submission. Kerlin (2000) found that "term paper mills" are considered both a cause and by-product of the perceived growth of student cheating in recent years, and that this has, in turn, fueled interest in "plagiarism detection" software products. Unfortunately, students who are determined to misrepresent themselves in this way are finding routes around these electronic dragnets, leading some institutions to consider increasing the penalties for such infractions.

Utilizing tools such as browser lock-downs during online tests or secure logins can help, but the real issues related to cheating and plagiarism may be cultural. Many teachers are now questioning the increased emphasis on cheating because of the adversarial feeling it can generate, and are advocating a more moderate approach that promotes trust and balances the seriousness of the offense with only as much attention as it deserves. In the end, it really is the student who loses out by avoiding accountability and opportunities for scholarly growth.

SUMMARY

Assessment is the means of measuring learning gains and can be used to improve the teaching-learning process. Determining content mastery and transferability of skills helps teachers and students identify gaps in learning; it gives feedback to the teacher about the instruction and feedback to the student on strengths and weaknesses in performance. It also can reinforce content and identify misconceptions, as well as act as a motivating force that prods learners toward content mastery. Traditional assessments, those that are most often identified as "paper-and-pencil tests," can be used to gauge a student's learning of a large body of content and can focus on the comprehension and application of information when declarative knowledge is the objective. Or a narrower slice of content can be explored in greater depth with assessment instruments that require higher order thinking skills, such as analysis, synthesis, or evaluation. Each type of activity has its appropriate uses and should be selected according to desired outcomes, amount of time available for assessment, and level of the students' intellectual and developmental maturity.

Alternative assessments are those activities that are not identified as traditional and that are guided by the philosophies of constructivism, performance assessment, and authentic assessment. These include, but are not limited to, portfolio development, individual or group projects, and problem-based learning. Alternative assessment is not yet well-accepted in many educational institutions and will only catch on as the movement grows and becomes more stable. Although most of what this chapter has included could apply to any instructional environment, there are elements of assessment that are of special concern for instructional designers, teachers, and learners (many of whom are adults returning to formal education) involved in distance education. These considerations include the use of ongoing, nongraded, or self-paced assessments; the fairness of the assessment activity; awareness of the diversity of the student group; and the provision of detailed, timely, and abundant feedback to learners. Some final conclusions and recommendations remain. First, assessment must be an integrated and transparent component of the instructional process. If extensive effort and resources go into designing activities that measure higher order thinking but the instruction does not guide learners in achieving this level of cognition, the assessment and the learners will fail (Baker & O'Neil, 1996). Everyone involved must be aware of what the expectations are and how learners will achieve them. If our testing is to reflect what is important and "make concrete what is valued by the educational system" (Bank Street College of Education, 1990), testing cannot be a secret.

Distance education can serve as a catalyst for change and growth in the education arena. By rethinking our ideas about what a classroom is, what teaching and learning are, where learning can occur, and how to measure it most effectively, we can use the best of what we know that works and discover new ways to facilitate this change. Distance education can be more than doing the same old things in many places instead of just one, and we need not feel bound to emulate worn-out models. Assessment, as a component of the instructional design process, can explore new ideas and refine the old as we reflect on our best practices for teaching and learning in whatever environmental configurations may confront us in the future.

SELF-TEST QUESTIONS

1. Although instructional design models prescribe the development of assessment instruments or activities prior to instruction, in reality, many (if not most) teachers wait until after instruction. What are some reasons for this, and how might this affect the assessment results?

2. Traditional assessments are often based on the student's ability to recall or comprehend information. How might these be designed, instead, to reflect higher order skills such as synthesizing? What are some examples of knowledge or comprehension-level tasks that could be converted to a higher level of assessment to better reflect student learning and transfer of skills to a real-world situation?

3. Proponents of alternative assessments suggest that, to obtain an accurate picture of student progress, sampling student performance over time is necessary. What implications does this present for one-time, standardized testing programs (e.g., the SAT examination) used for university admission? What potential policy implications might this present at the university level if the decision is made to accept portfolios as a substitute for high school transcripts when making admission decisions?

4. Norm-referenced testing is a widely accepted method of assigning grades and determining certification or licensing qualifications. What might be the arguments for and against this type of scoring? (*Food for thought:* Would you want to take an airplane ride with a pilot whose skill level was assessed based on how well she performed compared with her classmates or compared with a set standard of excellence?)

Answers to Self-Test Questions

1. Classic instructional design approaches require a clear statement of what is to be learned and the minimum level of competence that is expected. In many situations this approach is very effective. However, often during instruction and learning, new ideas are developed and new competencies are identified. Additionally, sometimes content areas are not adequately covered or are determined to be of minimal importance. For these reasons and others, many educators feel that assessment items and criteria should be developed after instruction has occurred.

2. Traditional assessments often concentrate on lower levels of cognitive learning because it is easier to measure knowledge and comprehension. Increasingly, educators realize that application, syntheses, and evaluation competencies are important. Assessment strategies that require a demonstration of the ability to apply what has been learned, such as by participating in teams that develop solution strategies to real-world problems, are ways to assess high levels of learning. Instead of asking students to define terms, it might be better to ask students to use new terms in a verbal presentation that discusses how the terms apply to a certain job situation.

3. Alternative assessments determine students' progress by providing a way for them to actually show that they can use the new knowledge they have learned. Actually, many feel that one-time testing determines very little about what a person knows, and others look at a person's entire collection of school grades, activities, and test scores as a kind of traditional portfolio. Concerns for fairness and completeness of assessment are balanced against efficiency and timeliness.

4. Norm-referenced testing basically pits learners against one another instead of against some standard. Advocates of norm-referenced assessment state that this is how the real world assesses people, so that is how schools should assess them also. Others state that a level of competence should be met in order to be considered competent (certainly the airline pilot would need to be able to demonstrate competence to some level, not just as compared with other would-be pilots). From a practical standpoint, both norm- and criterion-referenced assessments will probably be used most often in most courses.

 For additional information and activities, visit the Prentice Hall Companion Website at http://www.prenhall.com/simonson

REFERENCES

American Association for Higher Education. (2000). *9 Principles of good practice for assessing student learning.* Available: http://www.aahe.org/assessment/principl.htm.

Angelo, T. A., & Cross, K. P. (1993). *Classroom assessment techniques: A handbook for college teachers* (2nd ed.). San Francisco, CA: Jossey-Bass.

Baker, E., & O'Neil, H. (1996). Performance assessment and equity. In M. Kane & R. Mitchell (Eds.), *Implementing performance assessment: Promises, problems, and challenges* (pp. 193–194). Mahwah, NJ: Lawrence Erlbaum.

Bank Street College of Education. (1990). *Applications in educational assessment: Future technologies.* Washington, DC: Office of Technology Assessment. (ERIC Document Reproduction Service No. ED340773)

Dick, W., & Carey, L. (1995). *The systematic design of instruction.* Glenview, IL: Scott Foresman.

Duffy, D. K., Duffy, J. J., & Jones, J. W. (1997). "Tuning up your class: Using assessment for optimal student performance." *Journal on Excellence in College Teaching, 8*(2), 3–20.

Gagne, R., Briggs, L., & Wager, W. (1987). *Principles of instructional design.* New York: Holt, Rinehart & Winston.

Gronlund, N. (1998). *Assessment of student achievement* (6th ed.). Boston: Allyn & Bacon.

Hart, D. (1994). *Authentic assessment: A handbook for educators.* Menlo Park, CA: Addison-Wesley.

Herman, J., Aschbacher, P., & Winters, L. (1992). *A practical guide to alternative assessment.* Alexandria, VA: Association for Supervision and Curriculum Development.

Kerlin, S. (2000). *Query on student plagiarism: Problems and remedies.* Contribution to discussion list TL@LISTSERV.EDUCAUSE.EDU. Posted 12-6-00.

Pomperaug Regional School District 15 (1996). *A teacher's guide to performance-based learning and assessment.* Alexandria, VA: Association for Supervision and Curriculum Development.

Terwilliger, J. (1996). *Semantics, psychometrics, and assessment reform: A close look at "authentic" tests.* Paper presented at the Annual Meeting of the National Council on Measurement in Education, New York. (ERIC Document Reproduction Service No. ED397123)

Wiggins, G. (1990). *The case for authentic assessment.* Washington, DC: ERIC Clearinghouse on Tests, Measurement, and Evaluation. (ERIC Document Reproduction Service No. ED328611)

Wiley, D., & Haertel, E. (1996). Extended assessment tasks: Purposes, definitions, scoring, and accuracy. In M. Kane & R. Mitchell (Eds.), *Implementing performance assessment: Promises, problems, and challenges* (pp. 61–89). Mahwah, NJ: Lawrence Erlbaum.

chapter 12

EVALUATING TEACHING AND LEARNING AT A DISTANCE

CHAPTER GOAL

The purpose of this chapter is to present two approaches for evaluation of distance education programs and systems.

CHAPTER OBJECTIVES

After reading and reviewing this chapter, you should be able to

1. Differentiate between research and evaluation.
2. Define *evaluation*.
3. Explain the six categories of evaluation information including measures of activity, efficiency, outcomes, program aims, policy, and organizations.
4. Describe the AEIOU approach to evaluation and its five levels—accountability, effectiveness, impact, organizational context, and unanticipated consequences.

RESEARCH AND EVALUATION

> The best way to find things out is not to ask questions at all. If you fire off a question, it is like firing off a gun—bang it goes, and everything takes flight and runs for shelter. But if you sit quite still and pretend not to be looking, all the little facts will come and peck around your feet, situations will venture forth from thickets, and intentions will creep out and sun themselves on a stone; and if you are very patient, you will see and understand a great deal more than a person with a gun does. (Huxley, 1982, p. 20)

This marvelous quote from Huxley's *The Flame Trees of Thika* illustrates a metaphorical rationale for a major refocusing of procedures for evaluation of distance education systems. Traditional evaluation models have concentrated on the empirical and quantitative procedures that have been practiced for decades (Stufflebeam & Shinkfield, 1985; Worthen & Sanders, 1987). More recently, evaluators of distance education programs have begun to propose more qualitative models that include the collection of many nonnumerical types of information.

Because it is easy to think of them as being the same thing, it is important to differentiate between theory-based research and evaluation. Hanson and Maushak (1996) have provided an excellent review of distance education literature including research on and about distance education. Hanson summarized distance education research as follows:

- Distance education is just as effective as traditional education in regards to learner outcomes.
- Distance education learners generally have more favorable attitudes toward distance education than traditional learners, and distance learners feel they learn as well as nondistant students.

The research clearly shows that distance education is an effective method for teaching and learning (Hanson & Maushak, 1996).

Evaluation, as contrasted to research, is the systematic investigation of the worth or merit of an object. Program evaluation is the systematic investigation of the worth of an ongoing or continuing distance education activity (Joint Committee on Standards for Educational Evaluation, 1994). This chapter focuses on approaches to evaluation for the purpose of improving distance education and determining the worth of distance education activities. Rose (2000) identified a number of databases related to evaluation of distance education courses that are available on the World Wide Web. These online databases provide a repository of up-to-date information about online courses. Additional information related to evaluation and distance education is available in Cyrs and Smith (1990), Willis (1994), Fitz-Gibbon and Morris (1987), Worthen and Sanders (1987), and Rossi and Freeman (1993).

EVALUATION AND THE OPEN UNIVERSITY

Program evaluation at the Open University of Great Britain is the systematic investigation of the merit of a particular distance education program, curriculum, or teaching method, and how it might be improved compared with alternatives. As part of evaluation procedures for distance education by the Open University (Woodley & Kirkwood, 1986), two alternative strategies have been merged. The first is the traditional, positivist-empiricist approach to evaluation. This represents an attempt to apply the rules and procedures of the physical sciences to evaluation. The second is a more eclectic view of evaluation that incorporates qualitative and naturalistic techniques for the evaluation of distance education.

The traditional strategy normally includes an experiment that determines the effectiveness of a distance education strategy. The distance education project is structured from its beginning with the requirements of the evaluator in mind. Carefully matched samples are picked, controls are established, and variables are selected for which comparison data will be collected. Next, objective tests of variables are selected or constructed. Data are collected before, during, and always after the instructional event or procedures. Then the evaluator takes the data and prepares the evaluation report, which is submitted weeks or months later.

The primary outcome of this type of evaluation is the comparison of the data collected from the two or more categories of learners. For example, the distant learners are compared with those taught locally, and conclusions about the effectiveness of the distance education activity are made.

This approach represents the traditional process for the evaluation of distance education. Recently at the Open University and elsewhere, a countermovement has emerged (House, 1986). Advocates of this counterapproach are united in one primary way: they are opposed to the traditional, quantitative procedures for evaluation.

Increasingly, evaluation activities are incorporating more naturalistic methodologies with holistic perspectives. This second perspective for evaluation uses focus groups, interviews, observations, and journals to collect evaluation information in order to obtain a rich and colorful understanding of events related to the distance education activity.

From a practical standpoint, most evaluators now use a combination of quantitative and qualitative measures. Certainly, there is a need to quantify and count. Just as certainly, there is a need to understand opinions and hear perspectives.

According to Woodley and Kirkwood (1986), six categories of evaluation information can be collected about distance education activities:

1. **Measures of activity.** These measures are counts of the numbers of events, people, and objects. Administrative records often provide data for activity questions. Activity questions are ones such as
   - How many courses were produced?
   - How many students were served?
   - How many potential students were turned away?
2. **Measures of efficiency.** Measures of efficiency are closely related to measures of activity, and often administrative records can be the source of efficiency information. Efficiency questions often asked are ones such as
   - How many students successfully completed the course?
   - What was the average student's workload?
   - How many students enrolled in additional courses?

- How much did the course cost?
- How much tuition was generated?

3. **Measures of outcomes.** Measures of adequate learning are usually considered the most important measures of outcomes of distance education activities. Often interviews with learners are used to supplement course grades in order to find students' perceptions about a distance education activity. Mail surveys are also efficient ways to collect outcome information from distant learners. Other outcome measures include documenting the borrowing and use of courses and course materials by other institutions as an indicator of effectiveness, and the enrollment by students in additional, similar courses as indicators of a preliminary course's success.

4. **Measures of program aims.** Some distance teaching programs specify their aims in terms of what and whom they intend to teach, and evaluation information is collected to establish the extent to which these aims were met. One common aim of distance education programs is to reach learners who otherwise would not be students. Surveys of learners can be used to collect this type of information.

5. **Measures of policy.** Evaluation in the policy area often takes the form of market research. Surveys of prospective students and employers can be used to determine the demand for distance education activities.

   Policy evaluation can also include monitoring. Students can be surveyed to determine if tuition is too high, if appropriate courses are being offered, and if there are impediments to course success, such as the lack of access to computers or the library.

   Sometimes policy evaluation can be used to determine the success of experimental programs, such as those for low achievers or for students who normally are not qualified for a program. The purpose of policy evaluation is to identify procedures that are needed or that need to be changed, and to develop new policies.

6. **Measures of organizations.** Sometimes it is important to evaluate a distance education institution in terms of its internal organization and procedures. Evaluators sometimes are asked to monitor the process of course development or program delivery to help an organization be more efficient. This category of evaluation requires on-site visits, interviews, and sometimes the use of journals by key organization leaders.

These six categories of evaluation are not used for every distance education activity. Certainly, some modest evaluation activity is almost always necessary. It is important that the activities of evaluators be matched to programmatic needs. Woodley and Kirkwood (1986) have summarized evaluation in distance education as being a fairly eclectic process that utilizes procedures that should match program needs to evaluation activities.

THE AEIOU APPROACH

Recently, Fortune and Keith (1992) proposed the AEIOU approach for program evaluation, especially the evaluation of distance education projects. The effectiveness of this approach has been demonstrated in evaluating the activities of the Iowa Distance Education Alliance Star Schools Project (Simonson & Schlosser, 1995a; Sorensen, 1996, 1997; Sweeney, 1995), a multiyear, statewide distance education activity. Additionally, the model has been used to evaluate a number of other innovative projects such as the Iowa Chemistry Education Alliance in 1995, the Iowa General Chemistry Network in 1994, and the DaVinci Project: Interactive Multimedia for Art and Chemistry (Simonson & Schlosser, 1995b).

The AEIOU approach is similar to Woodley and Kirkwood's in that it is an eclectic one that uses quantitative and qualitative methodologies. It has two primary purposes as an evaluation strategy. First, the model provides formative information to the staff about the implementation of their project. Second, it provides summative information about the value of the project and its activities.

The AEIOU evaluation process provides a framework for identifying key questions necessary for effective evaluation. Some evaluation plans use only parts of the framework, whereas other, more comprehensive plans use all components. Some examples of evaluation questions asked in comprehensive distance education projects include the following:

COMPONENT 1 *Accountability*

Did the project planners do what they said they were going to do?

This is the first step in determining the effectiveness of the project or course and is targeted at determining if the project's objectives and activities were completed. Evaluation questions typically center on the completion of a specific activity and often are answered "yes" or "no." Additionally, counts of numbers of people, things, and activities are often collected.

Questions such as the following are often asked to determine project accountability:

- Were the appropriate number of class sessions held?
- How many students were enrolled?
- How many copies of program materials were produced, and how many were distributed?

Methods Used: Accountability information is often collected from project administrative records. Project leaders are often asked to provide documentation of the level of completion of each of the project's goals, objectives, and activities. Sometimes evaluators interview project staff to collect accountability data.

COMPONENT 2 *Effectiveness*

How well done was the project?

This component of the evaluation process attempts to place some value on the project's activities. Effectiveness questions often focus on participant attitudes and knowledge. Obviously, grades, achievement tests, and attitude inventories are measures of effectiveness.

Less obvious are other ways to determine quality. Often, raters are asked to review course materials and course presentations to determine their effectiveness, and student course evaluations can be used to collect reactions from distance education participants.

Examples of questions to determine effectiveness include

- Were the in-service participants satisfied with their distance education instruction?
- Did the students learn what they were supposed to learn?
- Did the teachers feel adequately prepared to teach distant learners?

Methods Used: Standardized measures of achievement and attitude are traditionally used to determine program effectiveness. Surveys of students and faculty can be used to ask questions related to perceptions about the appropriateness of a project or program. Focus groups (Morgan, 1988) also provide valuable information. Participants are systematically asked to respond to questions about the program. Finally, journals are sometimes kept by project participants and then analyzed to determine the day-to-day effectiveness of an ongoing program.

COMPONENT 3 *Impact*

Did the project, course, or program make a difference?

During this phase of the evaluation, questions focus on identifying the changes that resulted from the project's activities, and are tied to the stated outcomes of the project or course. In other words, if the project had not happened, what of importance would not have occurred? A key element of measurement of impact is the collection of longitudinal data. The impact of distance education courses is often determined by following learners' progress in subsequent courses or in the workplace to determine if what was learned in the distance education course was useful.

Determinants of impact are difficult to identify. Often evaluators use follow-up studies to determine the impressions made on project participants; and sometimes in distance education programs learners are followed and questioned by evaluators in subsequent courses and activities.

Questions might include

- Did students register for additional distance education courses? *does not prove how much they liked the course*
- Has the use of the distance education system increased?
- Have policies and procedures related to the use of the distance education system been developed or changed?

Methods Used: Qualitative measures provide the most information to the evaluator interested in program impact. Standardized tests, record data, and surveys are sometimes used. Also, interviews, focus groups, and direct observations are used to identify a program's impact.

COMPONENT 4   *Organizational Context*

What structures, policies, or events in the organization or environment helped or hindered the project in accomplishing its goals?

This component of evaluation has traditionally not been important even though evaluators have often hinted in their reports about organizational policies that either hindered or helped a program. Recently, however, distance educators have become very interested in organizational policy analysis in order to determine barriers to the successful implementation of distance education systems, especially when those systems are new activities of traditional educational organizations, such as large public universities.

The focus of this component of the evaluation is on identifying those contextual or environmental factors that contributed to, or detracted from, the project or course's ability to conduct activities. Usually these factors are beyond the control of the project's participants. Effective evaluation of organizational context requires the evaluator to be intimately involved with the project or course in order to have a good understanding of the environment in which the project or course operates.

Questions typically addressed in evaluating organizational context include

- What factors made it difficult to implement the project or to successfully complete the course?
- What contributed most to the success or failure of the project or the students in the course?
- What should be done differently to improve things and make the course more effective?

Methods Used: Organizational context evaluation uses interviews of key personnel such as faculty or students, focus groups made up of those impacted by a program, and document analysis that identifies policies and procedures that influence a program or course. Direct participation in program activities by the evaluator is also important. Sometimes evaluators enroll in distance education courses. More often, a student is asked to complete a journal while enrolled in a course. By participating, the evaluator is confronted directly with the organizational context in which a program exists, and can comment on this context firsthand.

COMPONENT 5   *Unanticipated Consequences*

What changes or consequences of importance happened as a result of the project that were not expected?

This component of the AEIOU approach is to identify unexpected changes of either a positive or negative nature that occurred as a direct or indirect result of the project or course. Effective evaluators have long been interested in reporting anecdotal information about the project or program that they were evaluating. It is only recently that this category of information has become recognized as important, largely because of the positive influence on evaluation of qualitative procedures. Often evaluators, especially internal evaluators who are actively involved in the project or course's implementation, have many opportunities to observe successes and failures during the trial-and-error process of beginning a new program. Unanticipated consequences of developing new or modified programs, especially in the dynamic field of distance education, are a rich source of information about why some projects are successful and others are not. Central to the measurement of unanticipated outcomes is the collection of ex post facto data.

Examples of questions asked include

- Have relationships between collaborators or students changed in ways not expected?
- Have related, complementary projects been developed?
- Were unexpected linkages developed between groups or participants?
- Was the distance education system used in unanticipated ways?
- Did the distance education system have impact on student learning other than that expected?

Methods Used: Interviews, focus groups, journals, and surveys that ask for narrative information can be used to identify interesting and potentially important consequences of implementing a new program. Often, evaluators must interact with project participants or course students on a regular basis to learn about the little successes and failures that less sensitive procedures overlook. Active and continuous involvement by evaluators permits them to learn about the project as it occurs.

Sweeney (1995) advocates an eclectic approach to evaluation, an approach also supported by Worthen and Sanders (1987). The AEIOU model is a dynamic one that permits the evaluator to tailor the process of program evaluation to the specific situation being studied.

PROGRAM EVALUATION: EXAMPLES

South Dakota

South Dakota has a network for distance education that connects every school in the state. Currently, over 200 classrooms make up the Digital Dakota Network (DDN). The DDN was paid for with state funds and grants from telecommunications providers, such as QUEST. Implementation of the DDN was called the Connecting the Schools project. As the network came online and began to be used, it was decided that a comprehensive evaluation effort was needed. Evaluators used the AEIOU approach and collected both quantitative and qualitative information.

Quantitative information was collected using a locally developed survey called the Connecting the Schools Questionnaire (CSQ). The CSQ asked respondents to provide four categories of information: demographics, information about personal innovativeness, questions about organizational innovativeness, and questions about distance education.

Demographic information was collected in order to obtain a profile of the teachers in the state and included questions about age, years of experience, gender, academic background, and professional involvement. The second part of the CSQ was a modified version of Hurt, Joseph, and Cook's (1977) innovativeness scale (IS). The IS is a standardized measure of how innovative a person thinks they are. Part three of the CSQ was a modified version of Hurt and Tiegen's (1977) Perceived Organizational Innovativeness Scale (PORGI). The PORGI is a standardized measure of a person's perception of their employer's organizational innovativeness. The final section of the CSQ asked questions about distance education. These questions were to find out how much South Dakota teachers knew about distance education and to determine their general feelings about the impact of distance education on teaching and learning.

The qualitative portion of the CTS evaluation in South Dakota used focus groups, participant observations, interviews, and site visits. Three questions were at the heart of the quantitative evaluation. First, evaluators tried to determine what educators thought would be the greatest benefits provided by implementing distance education. Second, attempts were made to determine what was preventing individuals from becoming involved in distance education. Finally, questions were asked about the impediments to distance education. When quantitative data were combined with qualitative information, a rich understanding was provided to education leaders about South Dakota's ability to adopt distance education (Learning At A Distance: South Dakota, http://www.tresystems.com/projects/). The results of the evaluation were reported in Simonson and Sparks (2001).

Iowa

Several years ago, it was decided that a three-phase plan should be implemented to establish distance education classrooms throughout the state of Iowa. For the first phase, 15 area community colleges, 3 public universities, and Iowa Public Television had classrooms built and connected with fiber-optic cables capable of carrying 48 full-motion video signals in addition to virtually unlimited voice and data information. The second phase of the plan connected a classroom site in any of Iowa's 99 counties that was not already served by a community college site. These classrooms were connected with 12 fiber-optic cables. A total of 103 sites were built and connected as part of phases one and two. During phase three, additional sites were connected throughout the state. Recently, over 750 sites were connected to this distance education infrastructure, which was named the Iowa Communications Network (ICN).

As part of the implementation plan for the ICN, a comprehensive evaluation program was put into action. This program utilized the AEIOU approach and collected data from thousands of sources and individuals. The evaluation approach went through several stages during the 5 years it was used. First, evaluators concentrated on evaluating the construction, connection, and implementation of the ICN's physical infrastructure. Records related to classroom design, construction schedules, and dollars spent were collected and reviewed, and summary results were reported. This related to the accountability component of the AEIOU approach.

Next, those involved in the decision-making process for establishing the network were interviewed and completed surveys. Evaluators used the results to develop reports on the effectiveness of the processes used to construct the ICN. To determine impact, evaluators conducted follow-up investigations of classroom utilization and examined records of how the system was used.

The program evaluators examined many interesting organizational issues, such as who made decisions about where classrooms were located, how funds were obtained and spent, and who controlled access to the system. Finally, program evaluators identified unanticipated outcomes. One of the most significant was the infusion of several millions of dollars from federal, state, and local sources to support the development of the network. How these funds were obtained and used added to the importance of the evaluation report.

Once the network was built and a plan for its continued growth was put into place, evaluators shifted their primary focus to the human side of the growth of distance education in the state. Staff development, technical training, curriculum revisions, and school restructuring became the focus of network planners and funding agencies, so program evaluators used the AEIOU model to obtain information about these activities. The approach was used to provide formative information about the development of programs and their impact on teachers and learners, and also to provide information on outcomes, or summative information, to document the successes and failures of various program activities.

A true understanding of activities of evaluators of this statewide, multiyear project can only be gained by reviewing the yearly reports they submitted. However, it is important to note that the evaluation plan provided the following information:

Accountability.   Evaluators checked records, interviewed staff, and visited classrooms to determine the status of the development of the ICN, both as a physical system and as a tool used by teachers to deliver courses to distant learners. The accountability focus shifted during the project as its activities shifted from construction to implementation and finally to maintenance.

Effectiveness.   Evaluators conducted interviews and focus groups to determine what impact the availability of the ICN had on classroom education. Surveys were sent and reports were generated that helped education leaders to better understand what role distance education was playing.

Impact.   As the network became widely available and the number of courses and activities increased, it became possible to determine the impact of the ICN and distance education events on education in the state. Students were tested and grades reported. Most of the achievement data showed that learning occurred and good grades were obtained. More important, the availability of new learning experiences grew considerably.

Organizational Context.   From the beginning of the ICN project, the role of the state as compared with local educational organizations was a focus of evaluation activities. One outcome was to identify where cooperation between agencies was necessary, such as in scheduling, and where local control, such as in course selection, should be maintained. Project evaluators identified and reported on what the data seemed to indicate were the barriers and the contributors to the effective growth and utilization of the ICN.

Unanticipated Outcomes.   During the project, scores of unanticipated outcomes were identified and reported. Among the most interesting were

- The movement of the ICN into the role of Internet service provider
- The role of the ICN in attracting external grants
- The role of distance education and the ICN in the movement to restructure schools
- The impact of the ICN on positive attitudes toward technology in education
- The emerging role of the public television station in Iowa education

There were also many other unanticipated outcomes. The AEIOU approach was useful in helping the state's educators in evaluating the role of distance education as an approach and the ICN as an infrastructure. Evaluation played a significant part in the positive implementation and use of this new technology in the state of Iowa.

SUMMARY

As distance education in the United States increases in importance, evaluation will continue to be a critical component of the process of improvement. Certainly, the literature is clear. Eclectic models of evaluation such as the ones advocated by Woodley and Kirkwood (1986) and Sweeney (1995) are most applicable to distance education program evaluation. Evaluators should use quantitative and qualitative procedures. Distance education programs and even single courses should be accountable to their goals, should be at least as effective as alternative approaches, and should have a positive impact. Evaluators should attempt when possible to identify what organizational contexts support effective distance education systems, and unanticipated events both should be shared with interested readers and should be used to improve courses.

If you are very patient, you will see and understand. (Huxley, 1982, p. 20)

SELF-TEST QUESTIONS

1. What term means "the systematic investigation of the worth or merit of an object"?
2. The systematic investigation of the merit of a particular distance education program, curriculum, or teaching method is a purpose of which of the following:
   a. Research about distance education
   b. Program evaluation, especially at the Open University
   c. Curriculum building in the AEIOU approach
   d. Activity planning and evaluation
   e. Organizational context research
3. What are measures of activity?
4. When costs are identified and compared with tuition, the evaluator is determining which type of measure?
5. Give the five levels of the AEIOU approach.
6. True/False. Eclectic models of evaluation are increasingly the preferable ones.

Answers to Self-Test Questions

1. Evaluation.
2. b.
3. Counts of numbers of events, people, and objects.
4. Measures of efficiency.
5. The five levels are accountability, effectiveness, impact, organizational context, and unanticipated outcomes.
6. True.

 For additional information and activities, visit the Prentice Hall Companion Website at http://www.prenhall.com/simonson

REFERENCES

Cyrs, T., & Smith, F. (1990). *Teleclass teaching: A resource guide* (2nd ed.). Las Cruces, NM: Center for Educational Development.

Fitz-Gibbon, C., & Morris, L. (1987). *How to design a program evaluation.* Newbury Park, CA: Sage.

Fortune, J., & Keith, P. (1992). *Program evaluation for Buchanan County Even Start.* Blacksburg, VA: College of Education, Virginia Polytechnic Institute and State University.

Hanson, D., & Maushak, N. (1996). *Distance education: Review of the literature* (2nd ed.). Ames, IA: Research Institute for Studies in Education.

House, E. (Ed.). (1986). *New directions in educational evaluation.* Lewes, England: Falmer Press.

Hurt, H., Joseph, K., & Cook, C. (1977). Scales for the measurement of innovativeness. *Human Communications Research, 4*(1), 58–65.

Hurt, H., & Teigen, C. (1977). The development of a measure of perceived organizational innovativeness. *Communication Yearbook I* (pp. 377–385). New Brunswick, NJ: International Communications Association.

Huxley, E. (1982). *The flame trees of Thika: Memories of an African childhood.* London: Chatto and Windus.

Joint Committee on Standards for Educational Evaluation. (1994). *The program evaluation standards* (2nd ed.). Thousand Oaks, CA: Sage.

Morgan, D. (1988). *Focus groups as qualitative research.* Newbury Park, CA: Sage.

Rose, E. (2000). An evaluation of online distance education course databases. *DEOSNEWS, 10*(11), 1–6. (Available: http://www.ed.psu.edu/acsde/deos/deosnews. deosarchives.asp.)

Rossi, P., & Freeman, H. (1993). *Evaluation: A systematic approach.* Newbury Park, CA: Sage.

Simonson, M., & Schlosser, C. (1995a). More than fiber: Distance education in Iowa. *Tech Trends, 40*(3), 13–15.

Simonson, M., & Schlosser, C. (1995b). *The DaVinci Project.* Iowa Computer Using Educators Conference, Des Moines.

Simonson, M., & Sparks, K. (2001). Learning at a distance in South Dakota: Evaluation of the process. *Tech Trends, 45*(3), 38–43.

Sorensen, C. (1996). *Final evaluation report: Iowa distance education alliance.* Ames, IA: Research Institute for Studies in Education.

Sorensen, C. K. (1997). Localizing national standards for evaluation of distance education: An example from a multistate project. In C. L. Dillon & R. Cintron (Eds.), *Building a working policy for distance education.* New Directions for Community Colleges, #9, pp. 53–82.

Stufflebeam, D., & Shinkfield, A. (1985). *Systematic evaluation.* Boston: Kluwer-Nijhoff.

Sweeney, J. (1995). *Vision 2020: Evaluation report.* Ames, IA: Research Institute for Studies in Education.

Willis, B. (Ed.). (1994). *Distance education: Strategies and tools.* Englewood Cliffs, NJ: Educational Technology Publications.

Woodley, A., & Kirkwood, A. (1986). *Evaluation in distance learning.* Paper 10. Resources in Education. (ERIC Document Reproduction Service No. ED304122)

Worthen, B., & Sanders, J. (1987). *Educational evaluation.* London: Longman.

ADDITIONAL READINGS

Cronbach, L. (1982). *Designing evaluations of educational and social programs.* San Francisco: Jossey-Bass.

INDEX

Accreditation, 16, 182
Adult learners. *See* Learners
Adult learning, 44
AEIOU approach. *See* Evaluation of
  distance education
Andragony, 44–45
Apple QuickTime, 103
Assembly line, 40
Assessment
  advantages of alternative types,
    275–277
  alternative forms, 272–275
  authentic, 273
  characteristics of good, 266–268
  cheating prevention, 280, 281
  constructivist approach, 273
  criterion-referenced scoring, 268
  definition, 264, 265
  distance education, relationship
    between, 277–280
  in instructional design, 266
  norm-referenced scoring, 268
  performance-based, 273
  portfolio type, 273, 274
  purpose, 264, 265
  self-paced, 279
  traditional tools, 268–271
  traditional tools, used in nontraditional
    settings, 271–272
  vs. evaluation, 265–266
Associates degrees, online, 181–182
Asynchronous distance learning, 8
Asynchronous learning networks,
  241–242
Audio-tutorial approach, 92
Audiovisual materials, copyright for,
  132–133. *See also* Copyright
Auditory learners, 168–169

Barriers to learning, 69
  analysis of, 74, 75
  reasons students give as to why, 75
Branched-designed instruction, 158,
  159–160
Branched program instruction, 112

CD usage, 103
Centralization, 42
Chautauqua College of Liberal Arts, 32
Cheating, 185–186, 280–281. *See also*
  Plagiarism
China, use of distance education in, 12
Clark, Richard, 9, 10, 11
Clarke, Arthur C., 9
Classrooms, distance education
  technologies, choosing appropriate,
    107–109, 111–113
  two-way video/audio classrooms, 104,
    105–106
CODEC, 98
Cognitive maps, 222
Coldeway, Dan, 8
Communication
  channels of, 88
  effective, 87
  model, 86–88
  types of, 144
Completers, *vs.* noncompleters, 67, 68
Compressed video, 96, 98
Computer-based distance education,
  copyright issues. *See* Copyright
Computer Based Training, 176
Computer conferencing
  alternative systems, 249, 250
  asynchronous systems, 250
  electronic mail, 250
  mailing lists, 250
  non-Web, 248
  synchronous systems, 248
  text-based systems, 248–249
  Usenet groups, 250–251
  Web-based, 51
Computer networks, 35
Concentration, 42
Cone of experience, 88–90
Conference on Fair Use, 126, 133
CONFU. *See* Conference on Fair Use
Connections 2000 Star School Project of
  Los Angeles County Office of
  Education, 14
Constructivism, 51, 151

Copyright
  applications, in distance learning,
    131–135
  audiovisual materials, 132–133
  computer-based distance education
    issues, 134–135
  Digital Millennium Copyright Act,
    127–130
  duration, 124–125
  fair use, 123, 126
  first sale doctrine, 130
  guidelines, 126
  historical overview, 121–122
  holders, rights of, 122
  legislation, recent, 127–131
  myths, 120–121
  overview of basics, 121–122
  permissions, obtaining. *See* Permissions
  public domain. *See* Public domain
  public performance and display laws, 124
  Sonny Bono Copyright Extension Act
    of 1998. *See* Sonny Bono Copyright
    Extension Act of 1998
  Uniform Computer Information Trans-
    actions Act, 130–131
  U.S. legislation, 122
Copyright Clearance Center, 132
Corporate intranets, 185
Corporate training online, 180–181, 185
Correspondence study
  approaches used, 90, 91
  effectiveness, 92
  historical overview, 32–33, 92
  inexpensiveness, 91
  Turner's program, 8
Credits for distance learning, 175
Criterion-referenced scoring, 268
CU/SeeMe technology, 101

Dale, Edgar, 88, 90, 107, 108
Degree credits, 175
Delling, Rudolf Manfred, 29
Design principles
  alignment, 216
  balance, 217–218

capitalization, 216
center of interest, 218
color use, 153, 215–216, 217
contrast, 215–216, 220
elements of, 216–217
emphasis, 218, 219*f*
fonts, 153, 214–215
rhythm, 220–221
size of lettering, 214
space, 217
texture, 217
unity, 220
Disabled students, accessibility for, 256–257
Didactic conversation, 42
Digital Dakota Network, 98
Digital Millennium Copyright Act, 127–130
Display equipment, 106
Distance education
  applications, 174
  assessment in. *See* Assessment
  asynchronous distance learning. *See* Asynchronous distance learning
  autonomous *vs.* nonautonomous programs, 39
  cheating in. *See* Cheating
  choosing programs, 174
  classrooms. *See* Classrooms, distance education
  computer-based. *See* Computer-based distance education
  computer requirements, 178
  computer skills, 174–175
  correspondence study. *See* Correspondence study
  cost-effectiveness, 6
  definition, 7–8, 28–31, 173
  educational prerequisites for, 174
  effectiveness, 9
  frequently asked questions, 173–186
  innovations, 5
  institutions offering, number of, 8
  lists of available courses, 183
  mainstream use, 5
  pioneering, comparison to, 10
  policy issues. *See* Policy issues, distance education
  pressure on educators, 6
  professor interaction, 176, 179
  ranking, 182
  research. *See* Distance education research
  respect for programs, 178
  as "room with a view," 20–21
  students. *See* Distance education students; *See* Learners
  synchronous distance learning. *See* Synchronous distance learning
  technology. *See* Technology, distance education
  theoretical framework, 47, 48

theory. *See* Theory, distance education
time/place combinations in, 8
universities. *See* Distance teaching universities
U.S. usage, 13–19
video components, 180
virtual schools. *See* Virtual schools
  vs. correspondence studies, 173–174
  vs. face-to-face learning, 37
  worldwide examples, 11–13, 33, 182–183
Distance education research
  focus, 62
  myths pertaining to, 77–79
  structure, 62
Distance education students. *See also* Learners
  anxiety levels, 65
  attributes, 67–71
  bonding between, 72
  criticisms of remote-site learning, 66
  high-risk students, 68
  motivation. *See* Motivation
  perceptions, 64–67
  persistance, 69
  personality characteristics, 70
Distance teaching, 30
Distance teaching universities, 35–36
Division of labor, 40
DMCA. *See* Digital Millennium Copyright Act
DVD isage, 103

ECCS. *See* Electronic Course Content Service
Educational Fair Use Guidelines for Distance Learning, 126
Education degrees, through distance learning, 184
Electronic communications, 34
Electronic Course Content Service, 132
Electronic mail. *See* E-mail
E-mail, 250, 254
Equivalency theory, 46–47
Europe, use of distance education in, 12–13
Evaluation of distance education
  AEIOU approach, 288–289, 290, 291, 292, 293, 294, 295
  categories of, 287, 288
  Iowa example, 293–294, 295
  at Open University. *See* Open University
  overview, 286
  South Dakota example, 292–293
  traditional *vs.* nontraditional, 287
  vs. assessment, 264–265
Existentialism, 151

Facilitators. *See* Site coordinators and facilitators
Fair use, 123, 126
Feedback, 87–88

Fern Universitat, 35
Fiber-optic networks, 4
  capabilities, 100, 101
  flexibility, 100
  Iowa program, 9, 34, 99, 100, 101
  origins, 34
  usage, 34, 98–99
Finn, Jim, 10
Ford, Henry, 49
Fordism, 49, 50, 51, 52
Foster, Thomas J., 32

Globalization, 15, 31
Government grants, for distance learning, 181
Guidelines for Classroom Copying in Not-for-Profit Educational Institutions, 131

Handouts, 157, 197
Harper, William Rainey, 32
Hermod's, 33
High-speed videoconferencing, 102
Holmberg, Börje, 30, 36, 37, 42, 43, 44, 62
Home pages, 254
Hong Kong, use of distance education in, 12
H.310 protocol, 102
H.323 protocol, 102, 103
Hypercontent-designed instruction, 158, 160–162

Independent study theory
  Moore, Michael, 39
  Wedemeyer, Charles, 38–39
Industrialization of teaching theory, 40–42
Information mapping, 223–224
Instructional Context, 149
Instructional design
  access, 153
  assessment, role of, 266
  color use, 153
  content, essential, 150–151
  creation of course, 179
  distribution of materials, 157
  fonts, 153
  goals for instruction, 151
  handouts, 157
  importance, 144–145
  learners, assessing, 147, 148–149, 150
  learning environment, 154–155
  media selection, 152–153
  objectives for instruction, 151
  planning, for distance learning, 146, 147
  quality issues, 156–157
  site coordinators and facilitators, 158
  systematic process, 145, 146
  teaching strategies, 151–152
  visualizing information, 153
  white space use, 153
  for World Wide Web, 155–156, 158–163
Intellectual property rights, 137, 256

Interaction, 71–74, 88
Interaction and communication theory,
    42–44
Interactive study guide, 211–214
    design principles. *See* Design principles
Interactive telecommunications
    systems, 47
Internet. *See also* Online courses; World
    Wide Web
    access, 238–239
    active learning experience, 246
    advantages of courses taught via, 243
    asynchronous learning networks,
        241–242
    based learning environment, 154
    computer conferencing. *See* Computer
        conferencing
    computer-mediated communication,
        242–243
    course assignment submission, 247
    course-content delivery, 246
    course evaluation, 247–248
    course subsystem, 245
    as delivery tool for distance learning,
        240–241
    expansion, 238–239
    high education, 233–234
    K-12 education, 232–233
    learning resources, access to, 246
    limitations of courses taught via, 244
    logistical subsystem, 245
    management, 236–237
    online help, 247
    origins, 237–238
    overview of education, 240–243
    point and click technology, 239
    regulatory subsystem, 245
    structure, 239–240
    student evaluation, 247
    student subsystem, 245
    training and development, 234–236
    usage, 34–35
IntraKal, 255
Intranets, 185
Iowa Communcations Network, 9, 14, 99,
    100, 101

JPEGs, 102
Just-in-time learning, 174

Keegan, Desmond, 30, 36, 37, 46, 47, 48
Knowles, Malcolm, 44, 45

Learner-directed design, 158, 162–163
Learners
    adult, 44
    assessing, 147–148
    attitude, 167–168
    attributes, 67–71
    auditory, 168–169

centered instruction, 21
    characteristics, 149
    cognition, 168
    emphasis on, 166–167
    experience, 168
    experiences, 149–150
    general abilities, 148
    interactivity, 148–149
    learning styles. *See* Learning styles
    motivation, 167
    perceptions, 64–67
    responsibilities. *See* Responsbilities of
        learners
    satisfaction, 65
Learning
    barriers to. *See* Barriers to learning
    outcomes, 62–64, 108–109
Learning-Space, 255
Learning styles, 168–169
Linear-designed instruction, 158–159
Linear programmed instruction, 112
Locus of control, 67
Low-speed desktop video, 102–103

Mass production, 40
Mechanization, 40
Media and learning debate
    research, 9
    unrealistic claims, 9
    usage, 10
Mind maps, 222
Minute Paper, 278
Moody Bible Institute, 33
Moore, Michael, 30, 36, 39, 52
Motivation, 71
MPEGs, 102
MyWay, 253

Neo-Fordism, 49, 50, 51, 52
Noise, 88
Noncompleters *vs.* completers, 67, 68
Nonverbal behaviors, 73
Norm-referenced scoring, 268

Objectification, 41
Online courses. *See also* Internet; World
    Wide Web
    associates degrees, 181–182
    of corporate training, 180–181
    degree programs, 183
    delivery, 111
    future predictions, 257
    help available, 247
    length of courses, 181
    real-time lectures, 181
    syllabus, 254
Online syllabus, 254
Open learning, 51
Open University, 35, 185
    program evaluation, 286–287

Organization, 41
Orienting Context, 149
Outlines, 222

Participatory learning, 44
Patterned note taking, 222
Payment schedules, for distance
    learning, 182
Permissions
    obtaining, 135, 137
    sample letter, 136f
Perraton, Hilary, 29, 45, 46
Peters, Otto, 30, 40–42
Philosophy of instruction, 151–152
Phonographic Correspondence Society, 32
Plagiarism, 280, 281. *See also* Cheating
Planning, 41
Point and click technology, 103, 239
PointCast, 253
Policy issues, distance education
    categories of policy, 199–200
    faculty, 201
    fiscal, 200
    geographical, 201
    governance, 201
    importance of policy, 198–199
    legal, 201–202
    philosophical, 203
    sample policies, 203–204
    student, 202
    technical, 202
Portfolios, 273, 274
Post-Fordism, 49, 50, 51, 52
Pragmatism, 151
Preparatory work, 40
Printed media, 210
Problem-based learning, 275
Progressivism, 151
Public domain, 120, 125–126
Push technology (Internet), 253
Pyramiding, 223

Ranking, of distance education
    programs, 182
Rationalization, 40
RealNetworks RealPlayer, 103
Real-time lectures, 177, 181
Reintegrating teaching, 48
Responsibilities of learners, 169
    assignments, 173
    attendance, 171
    class participation, 171–172
    equipment requirements, 173
    microphones/equipment, 170–171
    technical difficulties, 173
    technical know-how, 173
    time for class, 172–173
    tone of responses, 172
Royalties, 137
Rumble, Grenville, 29

Satellites, used in distance education, 9, 34
Scientific control methods, 41
Search engines, 252–253
Semantic maps, 222
Sir Isaac Pitman's Correspondence Colleges, 32
Site coordinators and facilitators, 158
Skerry's College, 32
Social reconstructionism, 151
Society to Encourage Studies at Home, The, 32
Sonny Bono Copyright Extension Act of 1998, 127
South Dakota distance education use, 15
    evaluation, 292–293
Standardization, 41
Star Schools, 9, 14
Stationer's Company, 121
Student achievement, 62, 63
Student evaluation, 247
Student-programmed instruction, 112
Students. *See* Learners
Study guide, interactive. *See* Interactive study guide
Sub-Saharan Africa, use of distance education in, 12
Syllabus, distance education, 210–211, 254
Synchronous distance learning, 8

Teacher, role of in distance education
    beginning class, 191–193
    instructional methods, 191
    introduction strategies, 192–193
    lesson organization, 190
    remote resource, preparing for, 194–195
    shy students, helping, 193–194
    structure of class, 193–194
    visuals, interpreting, 196
    visuals, preparing, 195–196, 197
Teaching behaviors, 73
Teaching/learning contract, 30
Teaching strategies, 151–152
Technical certification, 176–177
Technical forums for distance education support, 184

Technology, distance education
    computer requirements, 178
    correspondence study, 90–92
    CU/SeeMe technology. *See* CU/SeeMe technology
    desktop two-way audio/video, 101–104
    efficacy of various types, 75–77
    forums for support, 184
    one-way live audio, 94
    prerecorded media, 92
    two-way audio, 92–93
    two-way audio, one-way video, 95–96
    two-way audio/video, 96, 98–99
    two-way audio with graphics, 93
Telecommunications technology, 4
Telemedicine, 9, 16–17
    applications, 17
    impediments to, 18
    payment policy issues, 18
    remote consultation, 17
    remote monitoring, 17
    telementoring, 17
Theories, existing, synthesis of, 45–46
Theory, distance education
    classifications, 37
    of independent study. *See* Theory of independent study
    need for, 36, 37
Theory of independent study
    Moore, Michael, 39
    Wedemeyer, Charles, 38–39
Theory of industrialization of teaching, 40–42
Theory of interaction and communication, 42–44
Third Distance Education Research Symposium-Conference, 62
Ticknor, Anna Eliot, 32
TI-IN Network, 96
Transfer Context, 149
Turkey, use of distance education in, 11
Turner, Frederick Jackson, 8

UCITA. *See* Uniform Computer Information Transactions Act

Uniform Computer Information Transactions Act, 130–131
United States Distance Learning Association, 9
University Correspondence College, 32
Usenet groups, 250–251

Virtual classroom, 175, 176
Virtual schools, 7
Visual analogies
    overview, 224
    parts of, 225–226
    steps, 226
Visuals
    design, 197–198
    interpreting, 196
    preparing, 195–196, 197

Webbing, 223
Web Course in a Box, 255
WebCT. *See* World Wide Web Course Tools (WebCT)
Web site design, for courses, 254–255
Windows Media Player, 103
Word pictures, 221–224
World Wide Web
    as course delivery system, 253–257
    course web pages, 255
    integrated web course systems, 255
    as learning resource, 251–253
    models for, 158–163
    planning instruction, 155–156
    point and click technology, 239
    real-world example of use, 4
    site design for courses, 254–255
World Wide Web Course Tools (WebCT), 255

Zimbabwe, distance education experience of, 86